tear here

40 Ways to Save $10 a Week

Little savings turn into big savings when they're invested over a period of time. Here are 40 nearly painless ways to save money. Some are worth $10 on their own, and others need to be combined to make a $10 savings

1. Buy regular gas instead of premium grade. Most experts agree that the benefits of premium gas aren't worth the extra 30-or-so cents per gallon.

2. If you use an ATM, take out the money you need for a week all at once to avoid paying fees each time you make a withdrawal.

3. Carry your lunch to work a couple of times a week instead of dropping $5.95 for a sandwich at the corner deli.

4. Go to a good stylist for every third or fourth haircut, but look for a less-expensive place for maintenance cuts. Better yet, have a friend trim your hair to minimize expensive hair appointments.

5. Give up your daily soda from the machine at work or the cappuccino from the downstairs coffee bar. Buy cases of soda at the grocery store and bring one to work.

6. Be on the lookout for gifts all the time and buy them when they're on sale. There's nothing that says you can't buy your mother-in-law's birthday gift a month after her last birthday.

7. Hand-wash your sweaters instead of sending them to the dry cleaner. Most items can be safely hand-washed in cold water, even if the tag says dry clean only.

8. Think twice before buying that new blouse. Remember that no one is nearly as concerned about what you wear as you are. Will your boss really notice that you've worn the same blouse to two meetings in a row?

9. Buy foods that are in season, and shop at farm stands and markets if possible. Buying tomatoes from a farm stand in August makes far more financial sense than buying tomatoes-on-the-vine from Mexico in February.

10. Shop around for the phone plan that's right for you, and look for special deals. Some services offer a flat fee for all calls within a certain area code, for instance.

11. If you have young kids, check out consignment shops for their clothing, especially dress-up stuff. These stores are full of fancy clothes that kids wore once and grew out of.

12. Dress cooler and keep your air conditioner at 78 degrees instead of 75.

13. Dress warmer and keep your heater at 68 degrees instead of 72. Turn it way down at night and use an extra quilt.

14. Wash your car yourself instead of going to a full-service car wash. If you have access to a hose, you can do this at home. If not, use a self-service car wash.

15. Get friends together for a pot-luck dinner at your apartment instead of going out to eat.

16. Buy spring water by the gallon and refill smaller bottles. You can buy a gallon of spring water at the grocery store for the price of a small bottle of Evian at the convenience store.

17. Quit your gym and buy a pair of running shoes.

18. Cut your grocery bills. Buy store brands instead of national brands, and cut down on prepared foods such as Lean Cuisine or Hot Pockets. Use less meat and look for specials.

19. Get what you need in the grocery store and get out. Studies show that you spend an average of $1.70 every minute you're there.

20. Use manufacturers' coupons for items that you'd buy anyway. But don't buy things you wouldn't ordinarily buy just because you have coupons for them.

alpha
books

W9-AAC-535

21. Know what you want before you get to a store, and don't let a salesperson talk you into buying something you don't need.

22. Buy season passes or books of tickets for activities you do frequently. These often are less expensive than buying tickets each time.

23. Get a library card. Buying books is great, but it can be an expensive habit. Get your novels from the library, and buy only reference books or others that you'll want to keep.

24. Use your debit card at the gas pump. Paying for your gas with a debit card at the pump keeps you out of the mini-mart and eliminates the temptation to get a quick cup of coffee and a donut.

25. Save on cosmetics and drug items by using store brands or "no-frills" brands instead of national brands. Many of the no-name brands contain the same ingredients as the more expensive national brands.

26. Rent videos instead going to the movies. Just one movie plus popcorn a week can cost more than the $10 you're trying to save.

27. Cut your cable service bills by getting rid of HBO or another premium channel. You'll save money and have more time to do other things besides watch TV.

28. Drive by, not through, that fast-food restaurant on your way home from work and make yourself dinner at home instead. We tend to think of fast food as cheap food, but it adds up. Most of it's not healthy for you, either.

29. Buy in quantity when it makes sense. Buy soda and beer by the case and large containers of laundry soap. Think carefully, though, before you buy that 12-pack of artichokes that seems like such a good deal. It's not economical if you end up throwing them away.

30. Use the postal service's priority mail instead of other services. For $3, you can send a package anywhere in the United States in about three days.

31. Buy a plant instead of fresh flowers. A plant will last for years, with care, and save you the cost of replacing cut flowers.

32. Look for cheap parking or share a ride and split the costs. A lot or garage that's a little farther away from your destination might be less expensive.

33. Skip one-hour photo developing and other premium services unless there are extraordinary circumstances.

34. Think twice about buying tickets to sporting events or concerts. These tickets can go for big bucks, and you often can see the same thing on TV. If you go, limit the number of events.

35. Keep your credit card in your wallet for most purchases. Many people buy more when using a credit card than with cash.

36. Look for restaurants that offer fairly inexpensive dishes. Check out ethnic or health food restaurants that have meatless dishes. They're often less expensive than other restaurants.

37. Shop around for an Internet service provider, and find one that will require you to pay only for features you need and use, not unnecessary extras.

38. Go easy on the spending during holidays. Avoid excessive buying of gifts, decorations, food, and the like. Many people get carried away during holiday seasons and spend far more than they should.

39. Have money automatically deducted from your paycheck and deposited directly into a savings or other account. Direct deposit is a great way to save money because it takes it out of your hands.

40. Re-evaluate your spending philosophy and think twice before buying anything. Take a look at all that you have, and ask yourself whether you really need more.

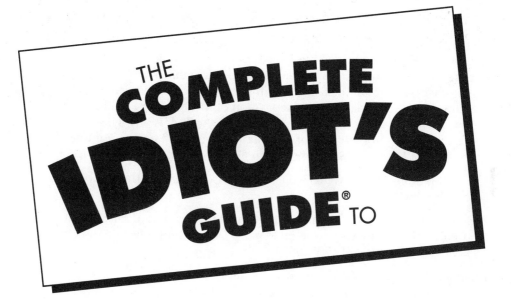

THE

COMPLETE
IDIOT'S
GUIDE® TO

Personal Finance in
Your 20s and 30s

by Sarah Young Fisher and Susan Shelly

alpha
books

A Division of Macmillan General Reference
A Pearson Education Macmillan Company
1633 Broadway, New York, NY 10019-6785

International Standard Book Number: 0-02-862415-7
Library of Congress Catalog Card Number: 99-61364

01 00   8 7 6 5

Interpretation of the printing code: the rightmost number of the first series of numbers is the year of the book's printing; the rightmost number of the second series of numbers is the number of the book's printing. For example, a printing code of 99-1 shows that the first printing occurred in 1999.

Printed in the United States of America

Contents at a Glance

Contents

Foreword

Organizing your financial affairs and making the most of your money can be a tough challenge—especially when you're a young adult busy building a career and, perhaps, a family.

It's particularly tough because, most likely, no one ever taught you much about managing your money. We've learned to talk openly about sex in recent years, but money seems to be the last taboo subject. Chances are your parents were fairly secretive about their own financial affairs. And it's dollars to doughnuts that you went through 12 or 16 or more years of education without a sensible course in money management.

So this is the time to get started. For one thing, the principles learned here will stand you in good stead throughout life. The fine points may change as you grow older and move through various stages of life, but the underlying principles are the same.

And, as Benjamin Franklin so wisely said back in the eighteenth century, compound interest is the eighth wonder of the world. In his words, "Money makes money and the money that money makes makes more money."

In other words, if you get started saving now, while you're young, you'll have far more money later in life than you ever dreamed possible. Put away $2,000 a year in a tax-sheltered retirement account—that's just $166 a month—and, as Sarah Fisher and Susan Shelly point out, you'll have $439,000 by the time you reach age 65. And that's if you put the $2,000 away each year for just 10 years and then stop. If you can keep going—and it should get easier to save as you get older and earn more—just think how much you'll have!

Sarah Fisher and Susan Shelly make personal finance come alive for Generation Xers and Baby Boomers, the men and women in their 20s and 30s who are just beginning to grapple with issues of spending and saving, credit, housing, insurance, and taxes. As the authors sensibly note, it may seem overwhelming, but if you can memorize baseball scores—or cope with Windows 98—you can learn to manage your money.

Just take it small bites at a time and you, too, can learn the secrets of budgeting, the intricacies of investing, and the strategies for managing credit wisely. If you *don't* pay attention, as the authors note, you'll survive. If you *do* start to pay attention to managing your money, you'll do far more than survive—you'll thrive and prosper for decades to come.

The Complete Idiot's Guide to Personal Finance in Your 20s and 30s is an essential road map to personal finance for every Gen Xer and Baby Boomer. Whether you have a lot of money or just a little, you'll be miles ahead on the road to riches by reading this book.

—Grace Weinstein

Grace W. Weinstein is the editor-in-chief of the monthly newsletter *Money Matters with Grace W. Weinstein: A Woman's Guide to Financial Well-Being*. She also writes a regular column on personal finance for *Investor's Business Daily* and is the author of 10 books, including *The Lifetime Book of Money Management, Financial Savvy For the Self-Employed,* and *Men, Women & Money: New Roles, New Rules.* Ms. Weinstein recently served a three-year term on the Consumer Advisory Council of the Federal Reserve Board.

Introduction

If personal finance is so important, how come so many people pay so little attention to it? The biggest reason, we think, is because they're intimidated. Why? Because they're not taking their finances personally enough.

Your personal finances are all about you, not the guy you work with, not your mom and dad, and not that nosy neighbor on the third floor of your apartment building. They're not about the stock market, capital gains, or compounding interest either. Although those things all factor into your personal finances, they are not the essence.

Personal finance is attitude and mindset. It's being able to look down the road and sacrifice a bit now for big returns later. It's knowing when to go for the new car and when to buy a used one. It's a matter of knowing how to make the right choices and doing just that.

To know how to make those choices, you need some financial education, and that's what you'll find in this book. You'll also need to examine your financial attitudes and mindsets and be prepared to make some adjustments to them, when necessary. Your personal finances affect the way you live now and how you'll live in the future. How much more personal can you get?

What You'll Find in This Book

The Complete Idiot's Guide to Personal Finance in Your 20s and 30s is written in five sections. Each section covers a different time of your life.

Part 1, "The Real World," deals with personal financial issues that come up when you're just starting out. You've just hung the old college diploma on your wall or finished the technical school program. You're ready to set the world on fire, but there are a few details you need to attend to first.

You need a place to live, a car to drive, the right bank accounts and credit cards—help! Relax. This section gives you all the info you need to make your way through these thorny issues without a scratch. We also take a look at the deplorable lack of financial education in American schools (that's fancy talk for why the heck you haven't learned this stuff before now!).

Things are a little more laid back in Part 2, "On Your Own and Loving It." This part covers some pretty exciting life events. You get your first real job with a salary, benefits, and everything. No more flipping burgers for you!

Now that you're making some money, we want you to think about how you're using it. That's where the "b word" (budgets) comes in. We'll help you to examine your attitudes concerning spending, saving, and using credit. We'll explain how credit works, and tell you how many people know all about your spending habits. You'll see that your finances might be personal, but they're not all that private! We'll also give you lots of good tips for saving money on just about everything.

By now, you have a pretty good feel for this financial stuff, and you're ready for Part 3, "Coasting Along." Here, we broach some subjects that are important to consider once you're doing okay with the day-to-day expenses and managing to save some money: investments, taxes, and insurance.

There are better places for your money than your piggy bank or a savings account, and we'll tell you what to consider when you start looking at where to put it. We'll also talk about some fun stuff, like vacations, your own apartment, and that cool new modem you've been looking at.

Things get moving pretty fast in Part 4, "To Everything There Is a Season." Don't worry. We're not going to have you doing estate planning—you're way too young for that. We will, however, talk about things such as buying an engagement ring, paying for a wedding, and pumping up your retirement account. If all that makes you too nervous, try to calm down and persevere. These are important issues to consider during this time of your life. This is also the section in which we'll introduce you to Wall Street and tell you how to find a financial advisor, if you need one.

In Part 5, "So You're Thinking of Buying a Home," we talk about the financial, practical, and psychological aspects of buying and owning a home. We'll tell you what to look for when you're choosing a real estate agent, how to come up with more money for a down payment, and how to find that house of your dreams. We also cover mortgage talk, tell you how owning a home affects your taxes, and explain what insurance you'll need to protect your investment.

When you finish the last part, you'll have a basic, sound understanding of how your personal finances work in various stages of your life. You won't be an expert, but you'll have a lot more confidence about handling your money and building a financially secure future.

More Bang for Your Buck

You'll find four types of sidebars in this book. These little snippets of information are geared toward keeping you out of trouble, providing tips, telling you what something means, or just giving you something to talk about with your friends.

Dollars and Sense

These tips or bits of upbeat information keep you on top of and up-to-date with your personal finances.

Pocket Change

Wow everybody at the next party with these snippets of little-known information. You'll impress your friends and sound oh-so smart.

Show Me the Money

There's a lot of financial mumbo-jumbo out there, and these sidebars will help you through it. We give you clear definitions for some of the financial jargon you'll encounter.

Money Pit

Be sure to read these gems of wisdom because they could keep you from making some common mistakes regarding your personal finances.

Acknowledgments

The authors would like to thank the many people who provided time, information, and resources for this book. Especially, we thank our editors at Macmillan Publishing, Gary M. Krebs, Michele Morcey, Michael Thomas and Heather Stith, for their thoughtful suggestions, able guidance, and a good joke every now and then. Thanks also go to our technical reviewer, Lawrence F. Hinnecamp, MBA, CPA, Esquire for his expertise and patience.

Many thanks and apologies for those weekend and holiday phone calls to Bert Holtje of James Peter Associates. Your calm patience, insights, and wonderful humor help make these endeavors fun.

A very special thank-you goes to our families and friends, especially to Dallas (Chuck) Fisher, who went above and beyond the call of duty as chart maker and data processing expert. You were always there in a pinch, usually with patience and perseverance. Thanks also go to Lois Young, who, as always, took precious time to review material and share her knowledge and insights.

The most special thanks, again, go to Michael, Sara, and Ryan McGovern.

Part 1
The Real World

Nobody told me it was gonna be like this! If you've uttered that, or a similar phrase recently, take comfort in knowing that you're not the only one. This can be a rough period in your life. You're out of college and anxious to get started on your own. You just didn't think there would be so much to think about or so many responsibilities.

You thought all those term papers were bad, but now you've got to think about different kinds of bank accounts and getting the best deal on (not to mention paying off) your credit cards. And you need to find a place to live and a car to drive! You can't imagine how you'll pay for everything.

Relax. Chapters 1 through 6 will give you all the information you need on these and other mind-boggling financial topics. You'll feel a lot better when you're finished with this section, so settle in and start reading.

Chapter 1

Personal Finance: The *Stuff* They Didn't Teach You in College

> ## In This Chapter
>
> ➤ The meaning of personal finance
>
> ➤ Finding out how much (or little) you know about personal finance
>
> ➤ Money attitudes
>
> ➤ Starting to save and plan now
>
> ➤ Navigating the misleading, confusing world of personal finance information

If the phrase *personal finance* makes you think of long and serious (and oftentimes boring) discussions about stocks, bonds, annuities, and interest rates, well, your impression is partially correct—all those subjects do have their place in the vast world of money and finance. In most ways, however, the emphasis in personal finance is on the first word, *personal*, which means it's all about what *you* do with *your* money. And what could be more interesting than that?

Exactly What Is Personal Finance?

Simply put, *personal finance* is every aspect of your life that deals with money—everything from buying a ticket to the movies, to finding an affordable apartment, to leasing that new Beetle you've had your eye on, to putting money into a retirement plan. Your personal finances affect your relationships, your lifestyle, and, very possibly, your perception of yourself.

Show Me the Money

Personal finance includes every aspect of your life that deals with money. The emphasis of the phrase is definitely on the word "personal."

Let's face it, money is extremely important in our society. We place a lot of emphasis on owning big homes in the right neighborhoods (*Vanity Fair's* August 1998 issue includes an eight-page story on industrialist Ira Rennert's proposed 66,000-square-foot house in Sagaponack on Long Island), cars that send a message of status in addition to getting us to work, labels on our clothing, and vacations to the right places. Even kids as young as six and seven are affected. Look at a group of kids sometime and see how many are wearing hats or shirts bearing trademark logos.

It's difficult to say whether, as a society, we admire sports heroes more because of their athletic abilities or because of the wealth they amass as a result of those abilities. With Michael Jordan pulling down $36 million a year along with his rebounds, he's not only a great athlete, he's also a very rich guy. That $36 million, by the way, doesn't count what he gets for hawking shoes, underwear, and sports drinks—it's just for playing hoops. The money, along with his athletic ability, is part of the aura of Michael Jordan.

Money is a big deal. It buys us what we need, what we think we need, and what we want. In many ways, it defines who we are, just as Jordan's wealth helps to define him.

Our country's fascination with money is anything but new. Way back in 1835, Alexis de Tocqueville observed in his work *Democracy in America*, "I know of no country, indeed, where the love of money has taken stronger hold on the affections of men…"

No doubt about it, money is a big motivator in America. People work for money, gamble for money, marry for money, fight for money, and even kill for money. We look up to people who have a lot of money, pretty much regardless of where or how they got it. Money commands respect, even when the person who has the money doesn't.

Show Me the Money

Generation Xers (also called Gen Xers) and **baby boomers** are mentioned frequently in this book. *Generation X* refers to the 46 million Americans in their 20s and early 30s. *Baby boomers* are defined as those 78 million Americans who are in the 34 to 52 range.

However, it's important to keep money in perspective, and polls show that people in their 20s and 30s are tending to do so. Studies show that family, spirituality, and personal satisfaction will become increasingly important to *Generation Xers* as we move into the next century. Sociologists explain these priorities as a generation's backlash to the high divorce rate, obvious consumption, and get-ahead mentality of their *baby boomer* parents. Who knows? But if money is of any importance to you, then personal finance must be important to you, too. You can't separate the two things.

Personal finance is planning and implementing financial goals. It's putting away some money each week for that Jeep you've been looking at. It's whether you shop at Sam's Club or the gourmet specialty shop, and it's whether your vacation is one week or two. How well you accomplish your personal financial determines whether you buy a house or keep renting the condo, and eventually it will influence where your kids will go to school and the quality of your retirement.

Why Don't I Already Know This Stuff?

In many ways, we live in a strange society. At an early age, we learn the capitals of every state and can recite the nightly television schedule without consulting *TV Guide*. We debate the merits of upgrading Windows 95 to Windows 98 and spout Red Sox batting averages from 1992. When it comes to our personal finances, however, many of us are lost. We've never learned the basics of managing our money.

On the surface, personal finance sounds complicated. It sounds scary. It sounds like something we'd rather not have to deal with. So we let our hard-earned money lie in a bank account, making little or no interest, while we go about tackling the finer aspects of parasailing.

Money Pit

More than one million American households, roughly one out of every 100, filed for personal bankruptcy protection in 1997, and the number is expected to continue rising.

It's not that we *can't* learn about personal finance and managing our money. We *don't* learn about them because

➤ No one tells us how important they are.

➤ We think personal finance is only for people who have a lot of money.

➤ It seems like a lot of work to maybe save a little bit of money.

➤ They seem overly complicated and intimidating.

➤ We think that the money will take care of itself.

If these reasons sound familiar, it's time to rethink your attitudes about personal finance and managing money. These topics are extremely important because your future depends on how you handle them. Left unattended, your financial situation may survive, but it surely won't prosper.

Once you decide to start learning about personal finance and how it affects you, you're halfway there. Personal finance and money management are not all that complicated once you understand the basics.

Whatever Happened to Personal Finance 101?

When you're in school, learning the state capitals, the multiplication tables, and the periodic table is important business. I can still see my third-grade teacher with those flash cards, running through the six tables. You just had to know those tables, remember? Had you not learned them and all that other must-have information you probably would have ended up repeating a grade.

Show Me the Money

Financial planning is the process of evaluating your present financial situation, identifying financial goals, preparing a plan (often written) to achieve those goals, and carrying out the plan.

Money Pit

There's no shortage of companies willing to take advantage of a person's lack of personal finance knowledge. Bank card companies and retail stores make it very easy for young, financially uneducated people to start racking up debt at an early age. Often, the first real financial lesson occurs when somebody realizes he's got too much credit card debt and little or no means to pay it off.

Things weren't too much different in college, either. You couldn't move to the next college history level until you were able to speak with authority about the political situation of early 20th century Russia or advance in the English program without being able to analyze at least three Shakespearean sonnets. But I bet money, personal finance, and *financial planning* weren't even part of the curriculum.

A recent survey of high school seniors showed that more than half of them thought U.S. Savings Bonds had a better potential for returns over time than the stock market. More than a quarter of the seniors said you'd get the most back on your money by putting it in a savings account. Almost one-third of those surveyed thought that social security is what you get from your former employer when you retire, and half of them thought that income from interest on a savings account wouldn't be taxed.

This lack of knowledge, experts say, should not be a surprise. Kids can't know what they've never been taught. If no one tells you that personal finance is important, how are you supposed to know it? Granted, the subject of money will arise if you happen to take an economics class, but it's more likely to be in relation to China or the Great Depression than to your bank account or retirement fund. The theories of simple and compound interests are taught in some schools, but they are rarely applied to the students' savings accounts. These concepts are taught in the abstract, so kids have little incentive to remember them once the class ends.

But America's schools can't bear the blame for financial ignorance all by themselves. Experts say that kids aren't learning responsible personal finance from their parents either. Kids often pick up bad money habits at home and continue in those habits when they're on their own.

Before you get too depressed about the sad state of financial education, though, it looks as though things might be starting to change. Although it will take some time to know for sure, there is encouraging news concerning attitudes toward teaching and learning about finance.

The Jump Start Coalition for Personal Financial Literacy, a group advocating that financial education be taught in schools, was founded in 1997. Based in Washington, D.C., it's made up of 25 organizations, including non-profit groups and universities. Its goal is to fight financial illiteracy, which it calls one of our country's worst enemies. It hopes that by 2000 every student coming out of high school will have been taught the skills necessary for financial competency. The group is lobbying individual states to make financial education required in public schools from kindergarten through high school.

Still, too many people just don't understand that personal finance is important. They have no idea that their financial future is at risk. Those who do realize the importance of financial planning, like you (after all, you bought this book), are to be congratulated. By taking time to learn how to make the most of your money, you're giving yourself a huge advantage over those who aren't paying attention.

But I Don't Think I'll Be Able to Understand It

The subject of personal finance can seem intimidating. It includes topics such as taxes, insurance, investments, and interest. But when you begin learning about each of these topics, you'll find that personal finance is not all that complicated. A lot of personal finance and money management is just good common sense. Sure, mastering all the nuances of Wall Street would be a major challenge, but you don't need to do that to manage your own finances and ensure your future financial health.

As you move through different stages and situations in your life, you'll need to know different things concerning personal finances. Say, for instance, that you're in your early 20s and just out of college. You've just landed your first job, and the salary isn't as much as you had hoped. In fact, you're trying to figure out how you'll get enough money together for a security deposit on that apartment you've been looking at.

At this point of your life, you don't need to learn about dividend reinvestment plans or dollar-cost averaging. You do, however, need to worry about budgeting your income to meet all your expenses, finding some transportation to and from work, and paying off college debt.

Pocket Change

Dividend reinvestment plans, by the way, are plans that allow shareholders to reinvest the dividends they receive as stock earnings into more shares of stock without paying any brokerage commissions. Dollar-cost averaging is a method of investing money by dividing the total into equal chunks and investing it at regular intervals.

Those things don't sound quite as complicated as dividend reinvestment or dollar-cost averaging, but they're extremely important to you at this moment. As you get older, stock earnings and dollar-cost averaging might become relevant and important. But right now you've got more pressing matters to think about.

Somebody's Got to Mind the Store

You can take shortcuts when it comes to your personal finances or pretty much just ignore them altogether, and things will be okay, for a while. After you've rounded up the security deposit, you probably can get by with your personal finances just by paying what you owe and stashing any leftovers in a savings account.

In 20 years, though, you're likely to be sorry. Investing some time and effort (and money!) now will pay big dividends down the road and help you avoid some potentially major pitfalls. Most bankruptcies aren't caused by any great misfortune or catastrophe within a family, just by a lack of attention and mismanagement of its finances.

You might not remember all those state capitals when you're 50 years old, but you'll know that you've made the most of your money and helped to ensure financial security for yourself and your family.

Money's Not a Dirty Word

Before the 1960s, sex wasn't an acceptable topic of conversation. Young women who "got into trouble" disappeared for six or seven months under the pretense of visiting long-lost relatives in Peoria. And many weddings were quickly planned and executed before the bride's dress got too tight across the middle.

Forty years later, sex talk is as commonplace as mosquitoes in a swamp. No longer a taboo topic, sex is everywhere. Even the president is not immune; details of his sex life have become fodder for reporters, special prosecutors, and comedians. Sex scenes fill daytime soaps and prime-time series. If it weren't for sex, Howard Stern would have long ago faded into oblivion.

Although sex has become an acceptable conversation topic, talk about money is still somewhat taboo. Studies have shown that parents are more likely to talk with their kids about sex than money (and you know how reluctant most parents are to talk about sex).

Couples fight more about money than any other issue, mostly because they don't talk about it unless it gets to be a problem in their marriage. Money problems are blamed for much of the marital strife

Pocket Change

In a survey of married couples, more than half of them said that sooner or later, money is the most important concern in a marriage. Yet most couples don't talk about it until it becomes an issue.

that leads one out of every two married couples in this country down the road to divorce court.

Money matters aren't traditionally taught in school, and friends usually don't discuss them. Money is a "private" matter, best left to intimate (or angry) discussions between partners, spouses, or financial consultants and clients.

Okay, it's reasonable to think you don't want the guy living two doors down the hall to know the amount of your weekly paycheck or the balance of your savings account. But what could be wrong with a little 401(k) discussion among friends? Or an intelligent talk about the merits of buying store brands instead of name brands in order to save a couple dollars at the cash register?

Isn't it interesting that we don't think twice about talking about money as it relates to Donald Trump, the balance of the Powerball lottery, or the price of a gallon of gas? But when it comes to investments, budgets, or our savings accounts (our personal finances), we're decidedly close-mouthed. If we continue to avoid talking about our money or to talk about it only in hushed voices when nobody is around, it will remain taboo.

So next time you get together for a drink with some friends, test the waters. Mention that you're thinking about leasing your next vehicle instead of buying it. Or that you think you'll be increasing your contribution to your 401(k). If they all move away from you or pointedly change the topic of conversation, you'll know they're not yet ready for money talk. But who knows? You may start a lively and interesting conversation and add a new dimension to bar talk.

Dollars and Sense

There are indications that 20- and 30-somethings are becoming increasingly interested in personal finance. One reason cited is the growing number of 401(k) plans, in which many Gen Xers participate. There is a personal finance newsletter just for Gen Xers called *Green*. You can get more information about it by calling 1–800–477–2968.

Personal Finance Is for My Parents

Who needs to think about personal finance? Anyone with any money at all should be concerned about where it's going and whether it's being managed to its best advantage. Sure, that includes your parents, but it also includes you. If your parents are nearing retirement age or perhaps still have a child in college, they're probably painfully aware of their personal finances. Hopefully, they've been smart about managing their money and will have financial security in the future.

This book, however, is for 20- and 30-somethings who traditionally are notorious for not paying much attention to their personal finances. Polls do show that Generation Xers are saving more money than baby boomers did in their 20s and 30s, but that's

Pocket Change

Studies show that 25 percent of adults between the ages of 35 and 54 haven't even started to save for retirement.

not exactly great news. Baby boomers are notorious spenders, and many of them are still not saving any money. Still, there are many Gen Xers who aren't saving anything either. The decision to not save or the lack of a decision to save occurs for various reasons, including the following:

➤ You're too busy having a great time spending the first real money you've ever made to worry about saving any of it.

➤ You figure you'll have plenty of time to worry about saving later (like after you get married).

➤ You've got an apartment, a car, and plenty of spending money; what else could anyone want?

These carpe diem attitudes offer no security or comfort for later in your life. Time does fly, however, and the older you get, the faster it seems to pass.

Baby boomers listened to rock-and-roll while they spent their money, borrowed some more, and spent that too. They talked of peace and love and spent some more money. Then they discovered (or created) the self-help movement, and spent some more money there. Twenty and thirty years later, many boomers are still wondering where the flowers and their money have gone, while they ponder whether they'll be able to retire before they're 70.

Pocket Change

Don't shoot the messenger, but here's some not-so-great financial news for 20-somethings. An article in *USA Today* stated that the median income (half make more, half less) of workers in their 20s is less than what baby boomers were making in 1980. After adjustments for inflation, the median salaries were $23,000 for 20-somethings versus $25,000 for boomers. That's all the more reason to learn and practice good personal finance!

Keep the mistakes of your elders in mind as you cruise on through your 20s, spending just about every dollar you make from that job you landed. You're finally living on your own in a pretty nice apartment. You're eating out or ordering in most nights because, well, who wants to cook? You're dating, and you're buying those Abercrombie & Fitch shirts you always liked, but couldn't afford, in college. Your car is just so-so, but hey, you can dream about that little BMW you pass on your way to work every morning, right?

In the back of your mind, you probably know you should be saving some money, and many people your age are. But too often, saving just doesn't seem to happen. There's always something else to buy. But you're not too worried about it. You figure you'll probably be married in 5 or 10 years, and then you'll have to get serious about many things, money included.

Your 20s are a perfect time to check out all the things life has to offer. You're likely to have financial resources (income) without too many responsibilities. That combination adds up to a great time. You're being shortsighted, however, if you don't save something from those years. What happens if you're waiting to start saving money until you're married, but Mr. or Ms. Right doesn't show up for another 8 or 10 years? You will have lost a lot of savings time and interest in those years.

Even if you can't save a lot, you should be saving something in your 20s and 30s. No one's saying you have to save half of each paycheck. Small savings don't add up as quickly as big savings, but they do add up. Remember, saving money is a big aspect (but not the only aspect) of personal finance.

Dollars and Sense

If you start saving $2,000 a year in an IRA when you're 25, and you save that much for 10 consecutive years, earning about 9 percent interest per year, you'll have $440,000 when you turn 65. That should be some pretty good incentive to put some money away!

How Hard Is This Gonna Be?

There's no denying that there's a lot to learn about personal finance. All you have to do is walk into your local Barnes & Noble and head for the money section. The vast number of titles on display should give you a good indication of the huge amounts of information out there dealing with money management.

With so much material available, it's very easy to get confused. And some of the material out there is more than confusing; it's unreliable. It might even be downright wrong. Even popular, respected financial magazines occasionally miss the boat.

One of those magazines published a piece in the 1980s that recommended buying oil and gas limited partnerships as an investment that would result in "safe, high yields." Limited partnerships, an investment option that typically carries high costs for the buyer and huge commissions for the salesperson, are long-term investments, generally considered unsuitable for all but a few investors. Still, many people followed the advice of the magazine, and many of them lost very large amounts of money.

Although some of the popular financial books available are comprehensive, many of them deal only with one area of personal finance, such as investing for retirement, or reducing your taxes, or paying for a college education. Learning about taxes or college funds is useful, but it's only one piece of the pie. Personal finance is a lot more than any one of those areas, and to understand the big picture, you've got to have information about all of it. You want the whole pie, not just a piece.

This book will give you a lot of information about nearly every aspect of your personal finances. It won't, however, be difficult to understand. We're not going to give you page after page of impossible-to-read charts and formulas, designed to drive you crazy and leave you more confused than you were before. We will provide you with basic forms and easy-to-use worksheets that you can fill out using your own numbers. We'll tell you exactly what those things that you might not understand mean, and we'll discuss various aspects of personal finances that will apply to different stages of your life.

Reading and understanding this book won't be difficult, but it will require your attention. Think about how the information you're reading applies to your particular situation and your personal finances.

Let's Get Started

There's no time like right now to start learning about and improving your personal financial situation. Managing your personal finances will become a natural part of your life, once you understand the basic ideas and concepts. After you've practiced managing your personal finances for a while, it becomes second nature, like brushing your teeth or checking the oil level in your car. If you've decided to save a certain amount a week, and you're diligent about it, you'll very quickly get used to saving that amount.

If you haven't got much money at this point of your life, you'll feel better knowing that you're using what you have to its greatest advantage. If you're comfortable financially, you'll learn how to use your money to assure that you'll remain comfortable, even if your circumstances change. If you're just starting in the workplace, but anticipating a bright financial future, you'll learn how to stash away extra money as you start making it, while maintaining or improving your standard of living.

The fine points of personal finance will change as you move from your 20s to your 30s to your 40s, 50s, and beyond, but the general principles remain the same. Learning effective personal finance will help you throughout your life.

Personal finance is an exciting and interesting topic and is one you'll easily be able to understand and master. When you do, you'll thank whoever recommended this book to you for putting you on the road to good financial health.

Let's get started by taking a look at the real world. It will be decidedly different from the MTV version and, at times, much less attractive. But it's your world now, and you're going to do just fine in it. In Chapter 2, you'll take a Personal Finance Assessment Quiz (don't worry, it's just our version) to see how informed you already are on the topic of personal finance. After you've taken the test, you'll know what areas you're fairly well-versed in and the ones to which you'll have to pay close attention.

The Least You Need to Know

➤ Personal finance is every aspect of your life that deals with money.

➤ Personal finance is an often-overlooked or ignored topic by people of all ages.

➤ Talking about money is sometimes still considered impolite or even taboo, but it shouldn't be.

➤ The younger you are when you learn about personal finance and managing money, the better off you'll be later in your life.

➤ There's a glut of information about personal finance, much of which is confusing and inaccurate.

Chapter 2

You're Out Here—
Now What Are You
Gonna Do?

In This Chapter

➤ The financial challenges of living on your own

➤ Being on your own versus living with Mom and Dad

➤ Striking a balance between lifestyle and finances

➤ The low salary and high debt pitfalls

➤ Your financial situation will improve, really

➤ Testing your financial knowledge

You now have a good understanding of why learning about personal finances is important and how the way you handle your personal finances has a major effect on the way you live. Personal finance will become increasingly important to you as you get established on your own. You'll probably have more money during the next few years than you did in high school or college, and you'll need to know the best way to handle it.

Along with more money, you'll have additional responsibilities. You might already have college loans to repay, or maybe you're still paying for a master's or doctorate program. In addition, you've got to pay for a place to live, transportation, food, clothes—the list goes on and on.

Living on your own can be great, but nobody said it would be a walk through the financial park. There will be, shall we say, challenges. That's why you need a thorough understanding of what your personal finances entail and how to manage them to your best advantage.

Hey! Nobody Told Me It Was Gonna Be Like This!

Remember when you were in school? Sure, there was a lot to do, but looking back, it probably seems that life was a breeze. Tests and term papers pale in comparison with that important project due Friday at work, the one that your boss can't wait to see.

Getting to the cafeteria before it closed seemed like a big deal sometimes during college, but compared with shopping, cooking, and cleaning up afterwards, it was nothing. Remember when you thought buying those textbooks every semester was a hassle? It wasn't so bad when you compare it with all the stuff you have to buy now, huh?

It's easy to get overwhelmed as your responsibilities mount, but try to relax and enjoy yourself. Getting started careerwise, socially, and financially might be unsettling, but once you've lived on your own for a while you'll become savvy and streetwise—and do just fine.

The next time you get discouraged because work isn't going as well as you'd hoped, or you don't have the right apartment, the right girlfriend, or enough money, think back to your first day of college. Remember how you felt when your parents dropped you off, leaving you on your own? First-time college students describe that feeling as lonely, sad, or even desolate. But soon you had made friends, gotten used to the class schedules, and were having a great time. Although starting a career and a life on your own is more demanding than college, it too will become easier as you get used to it.

Dollars and Sense

Finishing school and moving out on your own is a major life transition and, therefore, a time of high stress. If you feel overly anxious or unable to handle the situation, it's important to find some help. Your employer may offer counseling as a benefit, or you can talk to someone at your church or synagogue or confide in a trusted friend. Remember, there's no shame in asking for help.

Mom and Dad, Where Are You?

Finishing college is a milestone. The cap, the gown, flowers, gifts, hugs, and handshakes are all symbols of the ending to an important part of your life and the start of something even more challenging and exciting. For many new graduates, figuring out what to do after college is the biggest initial challenge. Our society has this expectation that when somebody graduates from college, she'll find a job, move out on her own, and begin advancing her career. But it doesn't always work like that.

Studies show that most college graduates do not make a seamless transition from student to employed person living on their own. If their degree is not in a field where employment is readily available, it can take a while to find a job. If there's no job, there's no money. Having no money delays the process of getting out into the world on your own.

As a result, more young people are moving home with Mom and Dad after graduating from college or having been away for another reason. It's estimated that nearly one third of those who had moved out to go to college or for other reasons come home within five years. Some others don't move out at all, but live at home while attending college or working. Even many graduates who find jobs right after college aren't in a hurry to get out and live on their own, preferring the security and ease of living at home.

U.S. Census figures show that in 1994, 65 million people between the ages of 18 and 34 were living at home with a parent or parents. There's a name for this group: *ILYA* (incompletely launched young adults). The great majority of these people have never been married, and more men than women stay home with Mom and Dad.

Not having to pay rent, or paying just minimal rent to parents, gives recent grads a lot more money to save—or to spend. Many of these stay-at-home grads are the ones with the fancy electronic equipment or sport utility vehicles. Others, though, use the money they save on living expenses to pay back college loans or to put into a fund for a down payment on a house.

If you have a job, but are living rent-free, or nearly rent free, at your parent's house, realize that you're in a great position to save money. We'll get into saving and spending in more detail in Part 2 of this book, but realize that if you are living in this situation, you may never have another such opportunity to save.

Still, if one-third of all 20-somethings are living at home, that means that two-thirds are not. They're busy getting started on their own.

Show Me the Money

A professor at Northwestern University in Evanston, Illinois has come up with an acronym for the group of 65 million people between 18 and 34 who still live at home. He calls them **ILYA**, which stands for incompletely launched young adults.

It's a Big, Cold World Out Here

You didn't expect life on your own to be perfect. Still, you didn't realize it would be so much hassle. If living independently isn't turning out to be what you had expected, try to relax.

No two people want to live exactly the same way. Some prefer living with a group of roommates; others just want to be by themselves. Some practice orderly, strict schedules; others eat and sleep when the mood strikes. There are as many lifestyles as there are people. We vary greatly in ethnicity, health, geographical location, sexual preference, relationships,

Pocket Change

An increase in the average age that people are marrying is partially attributed to young people living at home longer than their parents did. During the Vietnam era, the average marriage age was 20.8 for women and 23.2 for men. In 1994, the median age for first marriages was 24.5 for women and 26.7 for men.

religion, and many other areas. The trick is to find out how you want to live and how it's most financially feasible for you to live in that way.

Money Pit

If you're considering a lifestyle change, be sure you take time to figure out how it will affect your wallet. If you make a decision based strictly on emotion, you could compound your troubles by ending up in financial trouble.

If you live by yourself and are lonely or worried about your safety or your financial situation, maybe you should think about getting a roommate. Even if you have to move to a bigger place and don't end up saving much money, you may be more comfortable and happier living with someone.

If, on the other hand, you live with someone or with a group and are unhappy because of that, it's time to start looking for your own place. You'll probably have to move to a smaller, less expensive apartment, but you'll probably think it's worthwhile to be able to live by yourself. Only you can know what's best for you both personally and financially. You must reach a balance between the two in order to achieve maximum happiness.

A Look at Where You Are

There's good news and bad news for those starting out on their own and trying to get established in today's marketplace and in society. The good news is the economy. The unemployment rate hasn't been so low in decades, and jobs, especially in certain areas such as engineering and computers, are there for the taking.

The bad news is that many of you are starting out with significant debt. About half of the college grads in this country have borrowed money to pay for their educations, and the average college debt is between $12,000 and $15,000. If you've opted for graduate work, your debt can be much, much more. Even if you don't have to start paying on that debt for several months, it's there, looming over your head like dark clouds before a thunderstorm or sex scandals around Bill Clinton.

Money Pit

A recent survey by the Consumer Federation of America showed the average credit card debt among U.S. graduate students is $5,800. Experts are calling credit card debt a national epidemic.

And your college loans might not be the only money you owe. Because credit cards are so accessible to students these days, and because marketers are so good at making us think we have to have so many things, credit card debt among recent college grads is at an all-time high. The situation has gotten so bad that some students are leaving college to get full-time jobs in order to pay off their credit cards.

In addition to worrying about paying off debt, you're looking at a lot of expenses at this point of your life. If you're just renting an apartment, you need a couple of months' rent, plus a security deposit. A little furniture would be nice, too. We're talking significant money.

Maybe you need to buy a car to get to and from work or at least round up enough money to pay for the bus every day. Also, you'll probably have to replace some of your jeans and sweaters with career clothes. Speaking of careers, you probably won't be pulling in $60,000 or $70,000 to start. Your salary doesn't seem to stretch very far when you think about all the things it has to pay for.

Mom and Dad might be pretty interested in your new job and where you're living and with whom, but they probably aren't being much help financially these days. Better face it, your time of being fully financially supported is over. Lest we paint too glum an economic picture, you should know that many 20-somethings are on their own and doing just fine. Let's take a look at the flip side.

A Look at Where You're Going

If you're a bit financially strapped at the moment, consider it a temporary situation and focus on the future. If you have a job and are making enough money to support yourself, you're off to a great start. Sure, there'll be things you'd like to have that you can't afford—but that's okay. Keep telling yourself that you'll be in better financial shape next year and enjoy the experience of being out on your own.

To stay on the right financial track, remember these two things:

1. Resist the temptation to use credit cards to buy what you want, but can't afford. You'll get yourself in a huge rut if you do this and end up with less in the future. Be patient and know that eventually, you'll have more buying power.

2. Be aware of financial opportunities, and take advantage of them when they're available.

Many people miss chances to improve their financial positions because they don't know what's available to help them do so. By reading this book, you've shown that you're interested in your personal finances and are willing to take the initiative to learn how to get, and keep, your finances healthy.

We'll look closer at these areas of financial opportunity later in the book, but it's important that you know what opportunities to look for. The sooner you start making the most of your money, the more money you'll have later.

➤ **401(k)plans.** We'll get into more detail about these little goldmines in Chapter 13, but suffice it to say that 401(k)s are a great way to save money. If you're eligible to participate at work, make sure you do. IRAs and the new Roth IRAs and other retirement plans also are good vehicles for saving.

➤ **Compounding interest.** Starting to save even a little bit of money when you're young will pay off big time because of time. The longer money is invested, the faster it grows. That's called compounding, and it's a great way to see your money grow. More about this in Chapter 10.

➤ **Lower interest rates.** If you're paying 18 or 20 percent interest on your credit card, you might be able to get a significantly lower rate just by shopping around and asking. A couple of points can make a big difference. Check out Chapter 4 for more on credit cards.

➤ **The best possible bank accounts.** If you're paying big bucks in bank fees, you're not making the most of your money. It takes some work, but it's worth it to look around and compare what's available. We'll get into this in more detail in Chapter 3.

➤ **A budget.** Most people wouldn't consider a budget a financial opportunity, but it definitely is. Preparing and using a budget gives you a chance to see where your money goes and an opportunity to cut back and save. More about budgets in Chapter 9.

➤ **Learning opportunities.** There is a wealth of financial information around for anyone willing to take the time to find and study it. Books, magazines, pamphlets, seminars, and the Internet are full of financial advice and learning opportunities. Many of the most informative resources will be mentioned throughout this book, and the "Additional Sources" appendix lists additional resources.

Money Pit

We have a tendency to believe that what we read is true, simply because it's been printed. Don't fall into the trap of thinking all printed financial information and advice is correct. Some of it is not, and you could be at risk, financially, if you don't distinguish between true and untrue. The more you learn and understand about personal finance, the better you'll be able to sort out information and misinformation. Be sure to get your information from reliable sources, and remember! If it sounds too good to be true—it probably is.

These two steps, resisting credit card debt and taking advantage of financial opportunities, will go a long way in moving you toward your financial goals. Ask for help if you're confused about a financial matter. Many issues concerning money, investments, and so on can be confusing, even to people who study them on a daily basis, so don't be discouraged if some financial issues seem confusing at first. They'll become clearer as you learn more.

But be sure you take all the financial advice you'll get with a large grain of salt. If you follow the advice of every financial guru who comes along, promising on one talk show or another to quadruple your investment in six months or less, you're likely to end up losing some serious money along the way.

Remember that if you seek advice from a friend or family member, you're likely to hear what's worked best for him. What worked best for him, however, just might not be what will work best for you. Nobody wants to sound like a dummy (or a complete idiot), so you're likely to hear about the good financial move your brother made back in '96, while he completely skips over the bonehead deal he struck in '97.

Once you start looking, you'll see financial advice all over the place. Check out the number of financial magazines sometime; you'll be surprised at how many there are. Financial columns run daily in many newspapers, and there are newspapers that deal solely with business and finance. Take a look at the financial section the next time you hit Barnes & Noble, or tune into a financial show on TV or radio such as *Wall Street Week* or *Moneyline*, both popular TV shows aired nationally. Personal finance is a hot topic among Americans these days.

A Personal Finance Test

It's quiz time! To assess what you already
know about personal finance and what you need to learn, we've prepared a question-naire dealing with basic and not-so-basic issues. The questions pertain to areas such as checking and savings accounts, credit cards, investments, health insurance, car insur-ance, and other issues.

Take the quiz and then check your answers to see how you've done. But don't be too concerned if you don't finish in the financial wizard category. If you did, you wouldn't need this book in the first place!

Your Personal Finance Knowledge Assessment Quiz

Circle either True or False for each of the following statements:

Checking and Savings Accounts

1. If you deposit $200 in your checking account Monday morning, you can be sure that a withdrawal for that amount will be available Monday afternoon.
   True False

2. All banks calculate the balance of your checking account the same way.
   True False

3. If you write a check and it bounces, your bank will usually charge both you and the person to whom the check was written.
   True False

4. If you have $1,000 in your savings account, you'll earn the most money if your interest is compounded quarterly.
   True False

5. If you open a savings account that compounds your interest daily and credits you quarterly, you'll have to leave your money in the account for three months before earning any interest.
   True False

Credit Cards

6. If you pay off your credit card bill each month, it doesn't matter whether your interest rate is 7 percent, 11 percent, or 20 percent.
   True False

7. If you have a card that you use to purchase items, but you're required to pay the balance each month, that card is called a debit card.
   True False

8. The annual fee on your credit card is the amount of interest you'll pay on the card for one year.
   True False

9. It's smart to take a cash advance on your credit card because you can get it interest-free, and you'll save money by doing so.
   True False

10. If a credit card advertises an extremely low interest rate, use caution when applying for it, because the rate will probably increase in a short period of time, or you may not be qualified to receive the low rate.
    True False

Investments

11. The best way to get started with investments is to find a good stockbroker who will tell you what to buy.
    True False

12. It's not a good idea to put your money in stocks or real estate because they're considered to be fairly risky investments.
    True False

13. Although it can be nerve-wracking, usually the best thing a stockholder can do when the stock market takes a dive is to sit tight and wait it out.
    True False

14. Mutual funds are tricky investments and should only be purchased by people who have a lot of money to risk.
    True False

15. Qualified retirement plans are considered good investment vehicles because the money in them is "growing" tax-free until withdrawal.
    True False

Insurance

16. If you have collision insurance on your car, you can still end up in big financial trouble if somebody sues you following an accident.
    True False

17. Everybody who owns and drives a car is assessed the same amount for auto insurance.
    True False

18. If you're young and in good shape, you don't have to worry about health insurance. If your employer offers it, you should see if you can get cash instead of a health plan.
    True False

19. If you're not covered through work, and you have to buy your own health insurance, a healthy, single person can expect to pay upward of $120 a month.
    True False

20. Everyone should have life insurance, even kids.
   True False

Miscellaneous

21. People who don't earn a lot of money, don't own property, and don't have high expenses from medical bills, charitable contributions, or other out-of-the-ordinary situations are generally better off filing for a standard tax deduction rather than an itemized deduction.
   True False

22. If you have more than $10,000 to invest, you'll need a financial advisor.
   True False

23. The best time to make a will is when you start working, and the best time to update it is when you retire.
   True False

24. When you rent an apartment, your landlord most likely will require that you pay a security deposit. This money is to cover any damage to the property that might occur while you're living there.
   True False

25. When you're ready to buy a home, you should put the very least amount down as possible, never more than 10 percent.
   True False

Answers

Checking and Savings Accounts

1. **False.** It depends on how long it takes your deposit to clear and what regulations your bank has concerning withdrawals. It can take up to five days for a check you deposit into your account to clear, depending on what type it is (for example government check, local check, or out-of-town check).

2. **False.** Your bank will use either the low minimum balance method, which penalizes you if your balance falls beneath a certain level at any time during the month or an average daily balance method, which considers the monthly average of your account.

3. **True.** Most banks charge both the person who wrote the check and the party to whom the check was written. The charge the bank imposes on the person or business to whom the check was written is known as a returned deposit fee. That's why a business will charge you a fee if your check is returned—it's recouping the cost of the bank fee.

4. **False.** You'll earn the most money if your interest is compounded daily, rather than quarterly, semi-annually, or annually.

5. **True.** If your interest is credited quarterly, you'd have to have your money in the account on the last day of the quarter in order to receive it.

Credit Cards

6. **True**. If you pay the balance of your account within the specified time period each month, no interest will accumulate, making the interest rate not applicable. Just be prepared to pay the high rate if there's a month that you don't pay your balance in full!

7. **False**. A card that requires you to pay off the balance each month, such as an American Express card, is called a charge card. A debit card is a card that takes money immediately out of your checking account to pay for a purchase.

8. **False**. The annual fee is the amount you pay just for the privilege of having the card for a year. Sometimes a bank will waive the annual fee if you ask. Many credit card providers don't charge an annual fee, so shop around.

9. **False**. Just the opposite! If you take a cash advance on your credit card, look out! The interest rate on a cash advance is likely to be higher than the card's normal interest rate, and you'll probably have to start paying interest immediately. Usually, there's even an extra fee for a cash advance.

10. **True**. Many banks will offer a very low interest rate to lure customers to their credit cards, but will raise the interest rate after three or six months. Some will include a phrase such as "guaranteed low rate to those who qualify," but they make it very difficult for you to qualify.

Investments

11. **False**. Nearly all investments can be purchased without a broker, who may, or may not, have your best interests (or his commission) in mind. This isn't to say you'll never need advice or help with investments, but you don't necessarily need a salesperson to make the investments for you. Always be aware of who's giving advice and how that person is getting paid for the advice.

12. **False**. Stocks and real estate do carry more risk than some other types of investments, such as bonds or a savings account, but they also have the potential for higher returns. When purchased carefully, these types of investments should have a place in your portfolio. Your *portfolio* is a group of investments, planned to meet a specific investment goal.

13. **True**. The stock market fluctuates, but during the past 65 years, it has produced an annual average rate of return of about 10 percent. That's not to say there haven't been setbacks, but bad periods generally last less than two years. If you can wait it out, it's best to do just that. The worst time to sell is after the market has had a big drop. Selling should be based on your investment objectives, not fear.

Show Me the Money

An **investment portfolio** is a group of investments, carefully planned to meet specific financial goals.

14. **False**. Managed by investment companies, mutual funds are as safe as the underlying securities (investment). Mutual funds provide diversification and accessibility to many people because they don't require a lot of money to get started.

15. **True**. Only the money you withdraw from a retirement account before a specified time is taxed and frequently penalized. Funds invested in a retirement account are generally pretax dollars. That means income taxes are not paid until the money is withdrawn. This gives you more money to invest and more money for growth.

Insurance

16. **True**. Collision insurance protects you in the event of property damage. To be protected from lawsuits for personal injury and so on, you need to carry liability insurance.

17. **False**. Insurance companies consider numerous factors when deciding how much to charge an individual or family for car insurance. Past driving performance, where you live, and the kind of car you drive all affect your rates.

18. **False**. Anyone who thinks they don't need health insurance is pushing fate. Accidents can happen to anyone, and even a cut finger that requires some stitches in the emergency room can cost between $300 and $400. A serious accident with no insurance could be financially catastrophic.

19. **True**. You'll pay a hefty fee if you have to buy your own health insurance. Be sure to shop around. The rates vary greatly.

20. **False**. Life insurance usually is considered necessary only for persons upon whom others are dependent. If a child (God forbid) dies, there is no loss of income, and life insurance is not necessary.

Miscellaneous

21. **True**. Unless your financial situation is more complicated than the one described, you're generally better off with the standard deduction.

22. **False**. This is sort of a trick question. Some people feel they need a financial advisor to help them make any kind of financially related decision; other people make their own decisions involving hundreds of thousands of dollars. Hiring a financial advisor is a personal decision, but the process requires some homework to make sure you get a good one.

23. **False**. You should make a will early (when you start a first job is fine) and update it regularly, whenever there is a major change in your life. Having children, changing jobs, buying property, getting married or divorced, and retiring are all good reasons to update your will.

24. **True**. The intention of a security deposit is to assure that there will be money available to pay for any damages. If there are no damages when you leave, the money should be refunded.

25. **False.** A 20 percent down payment on a house is ideal, because it pretty much assures you'll qualify for favorable mortgage terms. It also means you probably can avoid having to buy private mortgage insurance, which can cost hundreds of dollars a year.

These questions and answers and many other topics will be discussed in detail later in this book. Take a minute to add up your score and see how you did. Score one point for each correct answer.

➤ **22 to 25 points.** You're a financial wizard, but even wizards could learn a thing or two from this book.

➤ **18 to 22 points.** You've got the basic knowledge and a sound foundation on which to build.

➤ **14 to 18 points.** Your financial knowledge could use some fine tuning. It's a good thing you found this book.

➤ **Fewer than 14 points.** You have to start somewhere. Keep reading.

If you did well on this quiz, congratulations! But don't stop reading. There's lots of stuff in the book that wasn't mentioned in the quiz. If you didn't do well, don't be discouraged. To learn new stuff is why you have the book in the first place. Keep reading, and you'll know all the answers when you finish.

The Least You Need to Know

➤ If you're finding that managing your own finances and living on your own is challenging, remember that the longer you do these things, the easier they'll be.

➤ Many young people are postponing living on their own and are staying at their parents' home longer.

➤ It's important to balance your lifestyle with your finances.

➤ Your early financial picture might not be exactly what you had hoped, but hang in there. It will get better.

➤ You need to keep believing that you're headed for success, both financially and personally.

➤ Taking a quiz on personal finance will help you assess your knowledge and what you need to learn.

Chapter 3

Taking a Look at Your Bank Accounts

In This Chapter

➤ Shopping around for the best bank bargains

➤ The big three: banks, credit unions, and savings and loans

➤ Balancing interest rates with bank fees

➤ Cutting costs when using the ATM

It's tough to keep up with banks these days, even your own. You just get used to dealing with the First Bank of Smithsville, when it merges with a bigger bank and changes its name to the First National Smithsville Bank. Just when you adjust to *that,* it merges again and changes its name to the National Smithsville Bank of Jonesburg. It's a full-time job just keeping up with all the changes.

It wasn't always like that, though. Not too many years ago, people banked at small institutions where they were known and called by name. They could get an appointment with the bank president if they had something to talk to him about, and tellers gave lollipops to their kids. There were no ATM machines nor direct deposit of your paycheck, so you had to walk your paycheck into the bank and talk to somebody about what you wanted to do with it. The person handling your check would ask how you were and would want to know about your family. Banking was personal. Banks went out of their way to get and keep your business, and many customers remained loyal to their banks throughout their lives.

John T. Connelly is chairman of the board and former president of the First National Bank of Leesport in Pennsylvania, a mid-sized, regional institution founded as a small-town bank in 1907. Connelly tells the story of a man in Reading, Pennsylvania, who in 1960 wanted to borrow $300 to buy a truck in order to start an oil-delivery service.

None of the banks in Reading, which is located about 12 miles from Leesport, would give the man a loan. The Leesport bank, however, agreed to lend him the money. The man's business grew tremendously, and he soon had one of the biggest oil-delivery outfits in the area.

Leesport Bank had no branch offices in those days, so the man would drive from Reading to Leesport every day to make deposits and conduct other bank business. Finally, Connelly asked him why he didn't find a bank closer to home. "He told me he never forgot that Leesport gave him that first loan when the other banks turned him down," Connelly says. "He was a customer, a good customer, with us until he died."

It's harder these days to find that kind of personal service and customer loyalty in banking. You may be intimidated by the recent rash of bank mega-mergers or all the restrictions and conditions under which banks seem to operate. You might be downright confused about the type of financial institution with which you want to be associated. You may have to look around a bit to find a place that feels right for you, but don't be discouraged. It can be done.

Do You Have the Accounts You Need?

Chances are pretty good that you already have savings and checking accounts. You've probably been writing checks for years for things such as books and rent, and you probably use a *debit card*, too. There's also a good chance that you've had a savings account since before you were even old enough to know what it was. Many parents open savings accounts in their children's names and use the accounts as a place to save the money the child gets at birthdays and holidays.

Of course, there's the possibility that you've managed to get through life so far *without* checking and savings accounts. If that's the case, it's time to get them established. If you already have accounts, it's time to take a good look at them to see if you're getting the best deal on them that you can.

Checking Accounts

The concept of a checking account is simple. You keep money in an account and write checks (or use a debit card) from that account instead of paying with cash. Using checks eliminates the need to carry large amounts of cash or send cash through the mail to pay bills.

Show Me the Money

You use **debit cards**, which look like credit cards, to pay for purchases, but the money comes out of your checking account. Debit cards give you the best of both worlds: You get the convenience of a credit card without putting yourself in debt. An ATM card may or may not be a debit card. An ATM card accesses your account through an ATM machine. A debit card accesses your account from almost anywhere.

Most banks pay you no or minimal interest on the money in checking accounts, but nearly all banks impose fees and conditions on checking accounts. It pays to look at some different banks when you're considering opening or changing a checking account, because the difference in fees and conditions imposed can be significant. You might be getting a good deal on a savings account at a particular bank, but losing money on your checking account. We'll talk more about credit unions a little later in this chapter, but don't overlook them when shopping for a place to open a checking account.

There are various kinds of checking accounts. Some pay interest (although none pay very much), and others charge you a monthly fee if your balance falls below a minimum amount. Some charge you fees to open the account. Some charge you for each check you write, and others charge you if you write more than a certain number of checks each month. You get the idea.

Money Pit

Just like lunch, there is no free checking. Be careful when you see a bank that offers "free checking" when you open several accounts there. You could end up paying more fees on the other accounts or losing out on higher interest rates you could get from another bank.

Most of us don't think too much about our checking accounts. But by looking around and getting the best deal you can, you could save hundreds of dollars over the next few years. Of course, contacting 8 or 10 different banks and trying to compare every aspect of their checking accounts would be a daunting task, to say the least. But you do want to shop around. Be sure to consider the deals offered by 3 or 4 different banks before making a decision.

What you'll need to do first is figure out your habits as they relate to your checking account, and then find the plan that best suits your habits at the lowest price available. For instance, if you write only three checks a month—one to your landlord, one to pay your Visa bill, and one for your college loan—you may do well to consider an account that includes a charge for each check written. Your fee would be minimal, and there could be benefits elsewhere that offset the per-check fee. Many financial institutions provide extra services or fee waving for minimum deposits in several accounts. Check this out. You can save money. On the other hand, if you carry your checkbook with you and write checks for everything from groceries to haircuts and shoes, then you want to at all costs avoid a bank that charges for every check you write.

If you always have a lot of money in your checking account or a corresponding savings account, the bank might waive monthly fees. But if your account balance varies, or you don't keep much money in it, look out. An annoying thing that some banks do is to impose a fee if the balance of your checking account falls below a certain amount even for one day.

Suppose you have $1,000 in your checking account all month long, and now it's time to pay the bills. You write checks for the rent, the electricity, the phone, and your credit card bill. By the time you've finished, your checking account is down to $225. You're not worried though, because Friday is payday, and you'll be depositing more money in the account. Aren't you surprised when your next bank statement comes, and you've been charged $10 for a low minimum balance. It was only a couple of days between the time you paid your bills and deposited more money, but wham! your bank got you.

A better way to go is with a bank that uses an average daily balance system. That way, as long as your account balance stays above $250 (or whatever) for the month, you're not penalized. Unless you keep a ton of money in your checking account, which isn't a great idea, you probably will do better with the average daily balance system.

Be sure you find out some basic information about checking accounts from every bank you query. When you get the information, write it down carefully, and keep track of which banks have given you particular information. Things can get pretty confusing if you don't keep your information in some kind of order. Some things to ask about include the following:

➤ How much money do I need to open the account?

➤ Does the account pay interest?

➤ Is it compound or simple interest?

➤ How often is the interest compounded?

➤ Is there a monthly service charge on the account?

➤ How much money must I keep in the account to avoid a monthly fee?

➤ Does the bank use a low minimum balance or an average daily balance system?

➤ How much will I have to pay each time I need to order checks?

➤ Is there a limit on the number of checks I can write each month without having to pay a per-check fee?

➤ Will I have to pay a fee to obtain my account balance?

➤ How much will it cost if I bounce a check?

➤ Is there a feature where money will be transferred automatically from my savings account if I write a check for more than I have in my checking account?

➤ Are my canceled checks returned to me at the end of each checking period? Is there a fee if I want them?

➤ Is there overdraft protection if I overdraw my account?

➤ What's the monthly fee for overdraft protection?

➤ Are checking account fees waived if I keep a minimum balance in my savings account?

➤ Can I buy whatever checks I want, or must I get them from the bank?

➤ Can I access my account on-line?

After you've opened a checking account, or changed your account to a bank that offers a better deal, there are a few other things to keep in mind. One simple, but important, rule is to keep your checkbook in a safe place and report it immediately if it's lost or stolen.

Dollars and Sense

The average interest paid on checking accounts these days is approximately 2 percent, according to www.bankrate.com, a Web site that provides rates from banks across the country.

You must keep track of how much money you have in your account. If you don't, you risk bouncing a check. The average fee for bouncing a check these days is around $25 per check, making it a very expensive mistake. Bounce three checks, you just wasted $75.

Record every transaction immediately, or sooner or later, you'll forget about one. Record the checks you write as well as ATM and debit card transactions. Some people find it more convenient to stick a Post-it note on the outside of their checkbook and write down the basic information as soon as they write the check. Then, the information can be recorded in the checkbook when there's more time.

Even if you don't balance your checkbook to the penny, which is what you should do, make sure you know as accurately as possible how much money you have. Always look over your statement each month and confirm all deposits, ATM transactions, and withdrawals. If you notice something that doesn't look right, call your bank right away. Banks do make mistakes, and they're not always in your favor.

Balancing a checkbook requires you to first list every transaction made during the month. You add deposits to your balance, subtract out checks, and remember every ATM or debit card transaction. At month end you compare what you have with what the bank has on their statement. Should be the same. The easiest way I've found is by keeping the checkbook on the computer.

Dollars and Sense

There are some good software programs to help you balance your checkbook and take care of other basic financial tasks. Check out Quicken Basic 98 or Microsoft Money. Or look in your library or local bookstore for books to help in these areas.

To help you avoid bouncing checks, find out about your bank's check-hold policy. Banks may hold any local check of $5,000 or less for two business days and certain other checks, such as those for large amounts, for up to eight business days. That means that you could deposit your paycheck or the birthday check from Aunt Mary and still not have money in your account for two days or more. You'll be in for a shock when you use your debit card at the grocery store only to be told that you're suffering from the dreaded insufficient funds.

Also, find out what time of the day your bank stops handling transactions. If you make a deposit at 3:30 p.m., you may have missed the transaction cutoff for that day, and your deposit won't be processed until the next business day. Don't hesitate to ask the teller whether your deposit will be made that day.

If you ever find yourself considering a stop payment on a check you've written, consider what it will cost you. Say you write a check for $50 to your friend Rob because you just bought his old in-line skates. Two days later, Rob tells you he lost the check. He's not sure if he threw it out along with a stack of papers, or if he dropped it somewhere between your place and his. What to do?

You could call the bank and request a stop payment on the check. You'll need to provide the bank with all the applicable information about the check. The problem is, a stop payment will cost you somewhere around $20, and your check might be safely resting in a landfill someplace, never to be seen again. Or it might be somewhere on the sidewalk between your place and Rob's, waiting to be found by someone who just might try to cash it. It's a judgment call, and you'll have to decide what to do.

Savings Accounts

A lot of the same points we discussed about checking accounts apply when you're looking for a place to open a savings account. You'll need to figure out your savings habits and find a bank that has a deal that will best suit your habits.

Most banks will charge a monthly or quarterly maintenance fee and maybe an additional fee if your balance falls below a required minimum. In addition, you might be required to keep a savings account active for a specified time, or face penalties.

Review the list of questions suggested in the section on checking accounts, and ask those that apply to savings when you're looking for a place to set up your account. You'll also need to ask a few other questions that apply to savings accounts:

➤ Does the bank use a tiered account system? A tiered account system means you'll earn higher interest if your account balance is consistently over an amount as set by the bank, usually at least $1,000, but many times higher. There are exceptions, but generally it's better to have your money somewhere other than a savings account if you have a large amount. Still, it's nice to know what you'll be earning on the money in your savings account.

➤ Will I be penalized if I close the account before a certain time?

➤ Is the account federally insured?

➤ How much interest will I get on my savings?

Although many banks don't pay interest on checking accounts, all banks pay interest on savings accounts. Banks used to pay 5 percent interest on all savings accounts because it was a federal regulation. Then along came banking deregulation in 1986, and interest rates haven't been the same since. Deregulation allowed banks to offer different kinds of accounts, which became competitive with each other and earned substantial interest. The higher interest on those accounts resulted in savings account interest rates being lowered.

Still, it pays to shop around because the amount of interest varies from bank to bank. In addition to www.bankrate.com, financial magazines such as *Money* publish lists of the highest-paying bank accounts each month.

Other Useful Accounts

Money market accounts and certificates of deposit are two other kinds of bank accounts you can have. These accounts are explained in detail in Chapter 13 if you want more information than is presented here.

Dollars and Sense

The average savings account earns about 2 percent interest, similar to an interest-bearing checking account. Not much to get excited about, is it?

Money market accounts (MMAs) were created in 1982, and, in those good old days, you could earn 10 percent or more interest on them. For some reason, banks in Atlanta at this time offered interest rates of 25 percent on MMAs. Of course, it was too good to last. Atlanta's rates came down fast (as you might imagine), and rates elsewhere also fell. During the next 10 years, MMA interest rates bobbed up and down like a small boat on rough seas, but they never got back to the early rates. MMAs, which are considered to be a type of savings account, generally pay a bit more interest than regular savings accounts, and you can write a minimum number of checks (usually three) on the account each month.

If your savings account balance becomes substantial, that is, containing more money than you think you'll need anytime really soon, consider putting some of it in a certificate of deposit (CD). With a CD, you deposit money for a specified amount of time, usually from three months to a number of years. The longer you leave your money in the account, the more interest you should get on it. Interest rates on CDs are higher than those on savings accounts and money markets accounts, but there's usually a penalty if you need to get the

Money Pit

If you write only a couple of checks a month, a money market account might be worth considering. But there's usually a hefty fee ($10 to $20) if you write more than the number of checks permitted. Any additional interest will quickly be chewed up if you have to pay for extra checks.

money out of the account before the agreed-upon time. Although there are variable (changeable) late CDs, usually CD rates are set for the term of the certificate, while money market rates are changeable at any time.

All Banks Are Not Created Equal

Take a look around the area where you live sometime, and notice the difference in the financial institutions. There are probably quite a few, ranging in size from something as big as the $300 billion-dollar Chase-Chemical bank to a small, local bank. When you look a little closer, you'll even find some places other than banks that will handle your money for you.

Pocket Change

The U.S. banking system is federally operated, but it has 50 state jurisdictions, each with its own regulatory and operating procedures.

Generally, there are three types of financial institutions: banks, thrifts, and credit unions. Although commercial banks handle about three-quarters of the total amount of assets within the entire financial system, many people prefer thrifts or credit unions. Let's take a look at each type of institution and some of the differences between them.

Commercial Banks

Commercial banks, sometimes called full-service banks, are the most widely used financial institutions in the United States. There are somewhere around 13,000 different commercial banks operating. That's down considerably from the banking heyday of the 1920s, when there were about 31,000 different banks.

Banks first became regulated in 1863, smack in the middle of the Civil War. Today's regulations are still based on that 1863 legislation, called the *National Banking Act*. The act was instated to cover five areas of banking: deposit taking, foreign exchange trading, lending, issuance of notes, and negotiating or discounting promissory notes. Other areas of regulations have been added since the original banking act, and some of the original regulations have become obsolete.

Show Me the Money

Commercial banks are the segment of the U.S. banking system that provide the majority of financial transactions services. They hold about three-quarters of the total assets within the banking system, and provide a variety of services.

Commercial banks are permitted to take deposits, loan money, and provide other banking services. They can have either a federal or state charter and are regulated accordingly. Those with federal charters are regulated by the federal Comptroller of the Currency. Federally chartered banks must be members of the Federal Reserve system and the Federal Deposit Insurance Corporation (FDIC), which the bank pays to insure individual bank deposits.

Those with state charters are regulated by banking authorities in the state in which they're incorporated. However, those that meet specific guidelines can apply to be members of the Federal Reserve system and the FDIC.

Commercial banks vary greatly. They can be huge mega-banks that have been springing up during the past several years or small, community banks. The 300 foreign banks that operate in the United States are technically commercial banks. They must comply with federal regulations, but many of them do not offer the banking services that an average customer would require.

Dollars and Sense

The name of a bank can help you figure out whether it's state regulated or federally regulated. If it's federally regulated, its name will include "National" or "N.A."

Credit Unions

If you want an alternative to commercial banks, you can consider a *credit union*. Credit unions offer many of the same services as commercial banks: checking accounts, savings accounts, vacation clubs, ATM services, and calendars at the holidays. They generally can offer better rates on loans and savings, however, because they don't pay federal taxes.

Credit unions are non-profit organizations that were imported to the United States from Germany in the early 1900s. They were regulated in 1934 by the Federal Credit Union Act, which limits membership to "groups having a common bond of occupation or association." Groups from particular geographical areas also were eligible to join credit unions.

Show Me the Money

Credit unions were first established in this country in Massachusetts. They were defined as "a cooperative association formed for the purpose of promoting thrift among its members."

Membership limits were expanded in the early 1980s, however, mostly to accommodate small businesses that didn't have enough employees to establish their own credit unions. These small businesses were allowed to join existing credit unions, causing much dissatisfaction among banks. Banks and credit unions have been sparring over the relaxed membership requirements, with banks claiming that credit unions have an unfair tax advantage. The Supreme Court recently ruled on the side of the banks, saying credit unions have been allowed to add members that shouldn't have been eligible to join.

Pocket Change

Credit union membership has extended far beyond people who work for a particular business or industry. There are credit unions organized by ethnicity, such as the Polish–American Credit Union, and even by family name. There are seven Lee Credit Unions, supported by the approximately 100,000 people in the United States with the last name Lee.

Show Me the Money

Thrifts are the collective name for savings banks and savings and loan associations. They generally accept deposits from, and extend credit primarily to individuals.

If you're interested in joining a credit union, find out if you're eligible for membership through work. If not, you might be able to join one based on membership in a professional organization or club. If you need more information about how to join a credit union, you can call the Credit Union National Association in Madison, Wisconsin. The number is 800-358-5710. Before joining a credit union, make sure it's a member of the FDIC, which guarantees deposits. Some credit unions are not FDIC members.

Thrifts

Thrifts are the financial institutions commonly known as savings and loans (S&Ls). Savings and loans have had a tarnished reputation since the late 1980s, when many of them failed and had to be bailed out by Uncle Sam (that is: taxpayer dollars). The cost of the bailout continues, and experts say it could ultimately cost taxpayers as much as $500 billion.

Although the thrifts have lost some of their allure during the past decade, they provided an excellent service when they were first started in the 1930s. The idea of the savings and loans was to promote individual home ownership, and many people borrowed from S&Ls in order to realize their share of the American dream.

Recent legislative changes have greatly improved the quality of thrifts, making them again a good options for depositors. Make sure your deposits are insured by a sign in the window that says SLIC, on bank material, or ask a bank employee, and who knows? You might be able to grab onto a little small-town banking atmosphere at a savings and loan.

So, What's a Percentage Point or Two Among Friends?

For most people, interest rates are among the most important, if not *the* most important, reason they choose a particular financial institution. Although it's not always smart to choose a bank based solely on its interest rate, the interest rate definitely *is* important.

Say you have $1,000 in a savings account that you're going to let sit for a year. At 2 percent interest, you'll have $1,020 at the end of the year. But if you put the $1,000 in a CD, you might earn 4.75 percent. At the end of the year, you'd have $1,047.50. A percentage point here and there adds up. And, as you get more money, it makes even more of a difference.

Another New Bank Fee?

We've already covered a lot of material in this chapter about fees imposed by banks, credit unions, and thrifts. It might seem like every time your monthly statement comes, there's an additional fee. Banks are able to do this because customers let them. Don't you think that if every single customer of a particular bank showed up at the door to protest the latest fee, the big shots of that bank would think twice before adding another one?

Nickel and Diming

Bank fees might seem like pesky little charges that customers have to pay. Make no mistake about it, though, banks are making big bucks off these nickel-and-dime charges. Many banks count on fees to boost their bottom lines. An extra 50 cents on your monthly service charge won't kill you. That averages out to six dollars a year, about the cost of a lunch. But think of six extra dollars from every bank customer, and the amount seems more sizeable.

The best thing to do is to go to your bank and get a copy of its fee disclosure statement. Look it over carefully, and see how many of the fees apply to you. If it seems like too many, you might want to think about finding a new bank.

The Great Interest Versus Bank Fee Dilemma

You find a bank that's offering an interest rate that's higher than any other bank around. You can't wait to get your money into it. Well, you might have found a good deal, but you might be getting pulled into something you'll regret. Be sure to take a careful look at the fees this bank charges before you march in with the contents of your savings account. Banks sometimes try to lure in customers with high interest rates.

> **Pocket Change**
>
> It used to be that most of the profits financial institutions realized came from the spread between interest they'd pay on deposits and interest they charged on loans. But now more than 50 percent of the average bank's earnings comes from fees.

Although you think you're getting a good deal on interest, a bank could be charging you much higher fees than you'd pay at the one down the street. And it's very likely that the "special interest rate" that drew you to the bank in the first place won't last for more than three or six months.

On the other hand, don't automatically reject a bank because the interest rate is a bit lower. If the fees are substantially lower, too, you still might end up saving money.

Banking restrictions and regulations can be complicated, but try not to be intimidated. Don't be afraid to ask questions, and don't worry about making a pest of yourself. After all, you work hard for your money, and it's smart to look for the best deal you can find.

Stop at the ATM, I Need More Cash

If you're like most people, you can't imagine life without automated teller machines (ATMs). They're so convenient and easy-to-use. Studies show that in 1996, the average ATM user visited machines 72 times. Consider though, that there is another class of ATM patrons: heavy users. Heavy users, who account for about one-sixth of all ATM card holders, banked an average of 156 times at ATMs.

Automatic Teller Machines or Automatic Theft Machines?

As convenient as ATMs can be, they can be expensive. Some cynics have stated that, considering the fees levied at cash machines, ATM should not stand for automated teller machine, but for automated theft machine. Some banks charge as much as $3 for you to withdraw money (keep in mind that it's *your* money), transfer funds, or get an account balance. If one of those heavy users pays $3 for every transaction, he could be end up paying $450 a year just to access his own money!

ATMs have been around for about a quarter of a century, but they have proliferated during the past 15 years or so. ATMs are now found anywhere you might need some cash: restaurants, bars, coffee shops, department stores, movie theaters, and gas stations.

The banking industry tells us that ATMs are wonderful because they're accessible 24 hours a day and are more convenient than having to go to a bank and wait in line for a teller. The truth is, the banking industry loves ATMs because they save the industry a lot of payroll costs and generate a lot of cash through fees.

Money Pit

Banks encourage customers to use ATMs, where customers are charged substantial fees. To add insult to injury, some banks charge a fee (a dollar or so) to customers who would rather come to the bank and deal with a teller! You can't win!

Tips to Cut ATM Fees

If you use ATMs—and who doesn't?—follow these tips to save yourself some money on fees. And don't forget to retrieve your card before leaving the machine!

➤ Use your own bank's ATMs whenever possible. Most banks still don't charge a fee for customers to use their machines.

➤ If your bank's ATM machine is "down" when you try to use it, note the time and place and call your bank the next day business day to report it. It should credit your account for the amount you had to pay to use another bank's machine. If it doesn't, find another bank!

➤ If your bank or credit union doesn't have a machine that's convenient for you, shop around to find a machine with the least expensive fee. Fees vary as much as $2 per transaction.

➤ Use your debit card at the check-out line of the grocery store and get cash back. Many stores will let you get extra money, usually a maximum of about $50, when you use your card to buy groceries. This strategy makes more sense than paying $3 to withdraw $50 from an ATM.

➤ If you have to withdraw money at an ATM, think ahead and get enough so you won't be back in a day or two. It doesn't make sense to pay $2 to get $10 out of your checking account. Limit your visits to the ATM to once a week, or maybe even twice a month.

We're not saying that ATMs don't have lots of advantages. But be aware of the differences in fees from machine to machine, and try to find yourself the best deal you can.

The Least You Need to Know

➤ Understanding your options in financial institutions will help you make a good choice when deciding where to put your money.

➤ Banks, credit unions, and thrifts (savings and loans) are the three most common types of financial institutions.

➤ You've got to know the questions to ask when trying to find the best checking and savings accounts.

➤ Being aware of the fees associated with ATMs can save you some money.

Credit Cards and Debt

What a wonderful invention credit cards are. With credit cards, there's no need to carry cash, and they're much more convenient to use than having to write checks. They're easy to get, and you can use them almost everywhere. Department stores, grocery stores, doctors' offices, gas stations, restaurants, bookstores, and even some laundromats will gladly take your credit card instead of cash. So what's the problem?

There is no problem, as long as you can use your card wisely and pay back what you owe each month. Credit cards are convenient, no question about it. They also come in very handy when you want to reserve a hotel room or a car, order from a catalog, buy an airline ticket, or cash a personal check. But they also can be very dangerous and have been the tool for financial ruin for millions of people.

Everybody Wants a Credit Card—Until They Have One

By this point in your life, you probably have at least one credit card. And you can be sure if you have one, you'll be offered more.

Credit card companies in this country send out almost 2.5 billion offers for cards a year. That's 10 offers for every man, woman, and child in America. And then there are the companies that will find credit cards for those who have had serious credit problems and can't get conventional cards.

Credit cards are a huge business in this country, but it wasn't too long ago that credit cards didn't even exist. Sure, people gave and got credit. It was called having an account. A shopkeeper would record a customer's purchases in a book, and the customer would pay his debt, either at a prearranged time or when he or she got the money. Sometimes a shopkeeper would refuse credit to someone who hadn't settled up for a while, generating some hard feelings between he and the customer. Credit was primarily given as a courtesy, although some shopkeepers no doubt charged a little extra to those buying "on time."

Dollars and Sense

Credit card companies began hitting on young people in the 1980s, when they realized they'd completely saturated the baby boomer market. Even high school students who have just turned 18 are, in many cases, offered credit cards.

Show Me the Money

Revolving consumer debt is the balance on a credit card that is carried over from one month to the next, incurring interest as it does.

All that changed in the 1960s, when, at the tail end of the baby boom, the Bank of America introduced the first bank credit card. The idea caught on quickly, and Americans were soon charging up a storm. What a novelty it was to simply pull out a card and be handed your purchase. Consumers furnished their homes, clothed themselves and their children, and went on vacations with their credit cards. Everyone wanted a card. Unlike now, nearly everyone paid off their balances each month in those days. It was considered almost a disgrace to owe on a credit card. Cards were fun and convenient, but the balance on them was rarely carried over to the next month.

Many people, especially those who had lived through the Great Depression, were mistrustful of credit cards. Having already seen what happens when financial disaster strikes, they weren't taking any chances by running up debt. Times changed, however, and like most things in this country seem to, the use of credit cards kept expanding. Somewhere along the line, the stigma of owing money on them lessened and eventually disappeared. Today, it's estimated that about 70 percent of cardholders carry a balance from one month to another. This balance is called *revolving consumer debt*, and it's on the rise.

This revolving debt can quickly cause trouble among credit card holders. When you don't pay off your balance, the bank or credit card company starts charging interest on what you owe—a lot of interest. The interest rate can vary greatly, depending on who issued the card, but the average credit card interest rate is about 17 percent. If you carry over a $2,000 balance, you'll pay $340 in interest charges per year, $28 for one month. If you have $2,000 in a savings account, you'll earn about $40 interest over a year.

Getting a Card If You Don't Have One

Now that you know about the history, advantages, and potential pitfalls of credit cards, you probably still want one. And you probably should have one. As mentioned earlier, credit cards are necessary to do things such as rent cars and hotel rooms, get airline tickets, and cash personal checks. Some banks won't even let you open an account if you don't have a credit card, and it's important that you acquire credit in your name for use later on. When used properly, credit cards are valuable tools. But never forget that, if mishandled, credit card debt can become your worst nightmare.

If you don't have a card, you can find applications at your local bank. You also can find them in a magazine or by accessing a bank that offers credit cards, such as Citibank or Chase, on the Internet.

Normally, if you have no credit history, but are at least 18 years old with a job, you'll be able to get a card with a limited amount of credit, usually $500 to $1,000. If you don't have a job, but you have a parent who is willing to be a co-signer or guarantor (see the next section), you can still get a credit card.

If you are diligent with your payments, you'll probably be able to have your credit limit upped after about 12 months. The amount of the increase is dependent on your income or your ability to repay the line of credit.

Money Pit

More than 60 million households in the United States have balances on their credit cards that they're carrying over from month to month, and the average amount of this revolving debt is between $6,000 and $7,000. The only way to avoid mounting debt like this is to pay off any debt you have now and not incur anymore.

Pocket Change

I know people who will spend hours, even days, shopping around for bargains. They'll never buy anything that's not on sale, yet they'll let their credit card debt accumulate and pay nearly 20 percent interest on it. Even if they find a bargain to buy, they're still losing money by having to pay those high interest rates on their credit cards.

Co-signers and Secured Cards

If you have no credit history and your earnings are low, or you already have a bad credit history, you might not be able to get a card in your name alone. You may need to apply for a secured card or get someone to act as a *co-signer* or *guarantor*. A co-signer, or guarantor, is someone who agrees to assume responsibility if you can't, or don't, pay off credit card debt.

Show Me the Money

A **co-signer** or **guarantor** is someone who assumes responsibility if you can't pay off credit card debt.

A secured card or credit account is when the bank or credit card company requires a deposit that serves as *collateral*. The deposit is equal to the amount of credit allowed on the card. So if you got a card with a $500 credit limit, you'd have to make a $500 deposit. There are often other fees charged to open a secured account, although, as more companies offer these types of cards, some are dropping the fees in order to get an edge on the competition.

Show Me the Money

Collateral is something of value put up as security for a loan. It is to assure that the lender will not lose the money loaned.

Some companies will pay you a bit of interest on your deposit, but don't expect it to be very high. You, on the other hand, will pay between 17 percent and 21 percent interest on unpaid balances. But if you want a card and want to begin a credit history, a secured card might be the way you'll need to go.

A big word of warning here: Be very wary of companies that offer credit cards, either secured or unsecured, at fabulous rates or to people who haven't been able to get a card. There is a rapidly growing number of unscrupulous companies that target people with poor credit ratings or nonexistent credit ratings, who can't get approved for credit cards through traditional issuers. The Internet is full of offers for people who previously couldn't get cards. Some of these offers are pretty unbelievable.

Money Pit

The old saying, "if it sounds too good to be true, it probably is," definitely applies to ads for credit cards. You can get yourself into a lot of trouble if you make the mistake of dealing with a disreputable company. So many of the cards have initial balances (really substantial fees) on which you pay interest with very minimal monthly payments.

One Internet site touted "two unsecured credit cards guaranteed" to anyone who is at least 18, makes $95 a week, has a valid social security number, and has been at a current job for at least six months. That's all it takes to get two credit cards. If that sounds good, consider that when describing this great service, the author of the material on the Web site wrote (this is copied exactly as it was written on the Web site):

"Thats right credit cards are a big part of our lives

now. You can't even cash a check without having a credit card now a days! And when you do you have to have 3 or 4 pieces of ID and have all of your personal information like SS number phone number address, things you realy don't want people to have. Now on the other hand all you need with a credit card is the credit card. So now ask yourself what is better a check? That you need a ton of stuff to cash it, the time you spend writing it out in the checkout line. Or a Credit card? That you swipe through and sign and Now You can Get TWO UNSECURED CREDIT CARDS. Thats right TWO UNSECURED CREDIT CARDS."

Pretty unbelievable, isn't it? Would you, under any circumstances, want a credit card from this company—whatever or whomever it is? Unfortunately, there are many of these fly-by-night operations around, so use caution.

If you do get a secured card, be sure you find out when your account can be converted to a standard account. At that point, you should get your full deposit back, provided you've made timely payments and don't owe any money on your credit card.

The following are a few of the institutions that offer secured credit cards:

➤ Chase Manhattan Bank USA, Wilmington, DE, 800-482-4273

➤ Orchard Bank, Beaverton, OR, 800-688-6830

➤ Citibank, Sioux Falls, SD, 800-743-1332

➤ BankOne, Phoenix, AZ, 800-544-4110

➤ Marine Midland, Wilmington, DE, 800-962-7463

If you need a guarantor to get a credit card, the person must be an adult with a good credit history. Usually, a parent will take this role, although it could be someone else, depending on circumstances.

If you have a co-signed credit card, remember that it isn't just your gig. Your dad's name (or the name of whoever is your guarantor) is on the line along with yours. If you miss a payment, chances are you'll get a phone call about it. If you don't show them the money, the next call is to Dad. Miss a second payment, and they won't even bother calling you. That call goes right to you-know-who. This should give you some added incentive to get the card paid off and not overspend.

How Many Credit Cards Does One Person Need?

Once you get a credit card, it's easy to get more. Unless you screw up royally, your mailbox will be home to many credit card applications. You'll learn to recognize them right away. Fancy envelopes, often gold or silver, stamped with words such as "low annual percentage rate," "no annual fee," or "preapproved." Unless there's a good reason that you need more than one or two credit cards, you'd do well to toss these envelopes into the trash unopened.

There's no reason to have a separate credit card for every department store, gas station, and electronics store in town. Having multiple cards in your wallet merely encourages you to use them and run up more debt. Nearly all retailers that accept credit cards take Visa and MasterCard. It's a lot easier to keep track of one credit limit (or two, if you really feel that you need a backup) than a dozen cards from all over the place.

Be aware that there are different kinds of credit cards. Some distinctions include:

Charge cards. These are not really credit cards because you're required to pay off your balance at the end of each billing period. Charge cards are good because you have no interest charges, but they may come with an annual fee, and if you charge more than you can pay all at once when the bill comes, you're in trouble. The American Express card is the most well-known version of a charge card, but department stores also offer charge accounts. If you don't pay your balance, you are assessed a late fee. If the balance remains unpaid, your account is sent to collections.

Fixed-rate cards. These credit cards have a fixed rate of interest. Some people like knowing exactly what interest they're paying at any given time, but these cards typically have the highest interest rates and have fallen out of favor in the past few years.

Variable-rate cards. The interest rate on these cards changes periodically based on the rate charged by the lending institution holding the card. The rate is often tied in to the bank's prime rate, with six percentage points added on. These cards became popular a few years ago when the interest rates on them became lower than on fixed-rate cards. More than half of all cards in circulation today are variable-rate cards.

Gold, Platinum, and Titanium cards. These status cards offer some advantages, such as buyer protection plans or cash back after you spend a certain (high) amount. They also can offer perks like emergency roadside service and insurance on newly purchased merchandise. They offer high credit limits, but they sometimes carry high annual fees. They generally are available only to people with established credit reports. These cards aren't necessary for most people, who can get a sufficient credit limit with a regular card. The cash back feature can put money in your pocket, but beware of the amount you are charging, so you don't get in trouble at month end.

Keep It (Your Credit Card) in Your Pants

An important thing to remember about credit cards is that just because you have them, you don't have to use them to rack up a lot of debt for stuff you don't need. As gratifying as it might be to throw a bunch of bags onto the back seat as you leave the mall, your spending will catch up with you at the end of the billing period. And you know what they say about payback.

Knowing When to Use Your Credit Card

Say you're driving four hours to visit an old college buddy for the weekend. You're about two-thirds of the way there when you notice your car's temperature gauge is on the rise. The needle keeps nosing up, and pretty soon you notice little wisps of steam coming from under the hood. You pull over; you know when you're beat. There's obviously a problem with the car, but you have no idea what it is.

Somebody stops and offers to call for somebody to help you. The Good Samaritan is a local guy, and he gives you the name of a gas station down the road that does repairs. He says he'll stop by the station and have a tow truck sent up for you. Great, you say, because by now your car won't even start. You hang around until the tow truck comes and then accompany your car to the service station.

It doesn't take the mechanic long to figure out that there's a hole in your radiator the size of Iowa, and when he starts muttering about hoses, you see the dollar signs mounting up in your mind. You finally get the bill for the tow and the repairs, only to learn you're out $247.93. You have just $60 in your wallet, and you're still hoping to get to your friend's house for the weekend. This definitely is a situation in which you should use your credit card and be grateful that you have it. Emergencies such as this are when credit cards are at their finest.

Dollars and Sense

Credit cards are necessary if you run into an unexpected emergency expense, so don't leave home without one if you're traveling.

They're also great when you order something from a catalog. It's a lot easier to call a toll-free number and give the operator your order and your credit card number than it is to fill out the order form, figure out the tax and the shipping costs, and then write a check for the grand total. Of course, it's also easier to order that little something extra if you don't have to pay for it right away!

It's great to have a card number when you call to make a hotel reservation and the front desk person says, "Would you like to secure that with your credit card?" Ditto for renting a car or reserving a plane ticket.

Sometimes Cash Is King

There are times and places, though, where you should forget you even have a credit card. Many financial advisers will tell you to never use a credit card to buy anything that depreciates. This includes clothing, shoes, gas, meals in restaurants, groceries, and so on.

That's good advice, but it's pretty tough to follow. Of course, there are exceptions to this rule. For example, what if you're on vacation and you see a cool pair of sandals that you just love. The best part is that they're 40 percent off because it's getting near the end of the summer and the shopkeepers are trying to clear out their stock. If you pay cash for the sandals, you won't have enough cash for the rest of the vacation, so you buy the sandals and put the charge on your credit card.

As long as you know you'll have the money to pay for the sandals when the bill comes in, I don't see any problems with buying them on credit. Sure, they'll depreciate. But you'll get a couple of summers' wear out of them. There is, however, a rule that I think should never be broken: Never use a credit card to pay for something that will be gone when the bill comes.

This rule goes for food at the grocery store, tickets at the movie theater, dinner at the Outback, a T-shirt for your boyfriend, merlot from the wine store—you get the idea. Using a credit card for these types of purchases encourages you to spend more than you would ordinarily, and it's downright annoying to have to pay for groceries that have been long since used and forgotten.

Finding a Better Deal on Your Credit Cards

If you're going to use credit cards—and it's a very rare person who isn't—you might as well get the best deal on them that you can. Credit cards cost you money, make no mistake about it. But there are ways to minimize those costs.

Annual Fees

Intense competition among card companies has forced most of them to lower, or even drop, their *annual fees*. A research company in Maryland reports that more than half of all credit cards are available without an annual fee or that the fee will be waived if you ask.

If you are paying an annual fee, it shouldn't be more than about $20, unless, for some reason, you happen to have a gold card. Those fees usually run about $35 a year or more. If you do have a gold card, ask yourself why. At this stage of your life, do you really need it, or is it an ego thing?

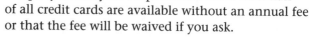

Show Me the Money

An **annual fee** is a charge you pay to the bank or credit card company for the privilege of holding its card. An **interest rate** is the amount the bank charges you to use its money to finance what you buy with your credit card.

Interest Rates

Interest rates are what make credit cards interesting, that's for sure. The *interest rate* is what the bank charges you to use its money to finance what you buy with your credit card.

When you charge a pair of boots for $125, for instance, the store from which you got them collects its money from the bank that issued your credit card. The bank, in turn, gets its money back from you along with 18-or-so percent interest if you don't pay the $125 back within a specified time. You usually have a *grace period*, which is a certain amount of time you have to pay off your purchases before you start getting charged interest.

If you pay off your credit card every month, which is the best way to do it, you won't incur any interest charges. Then your credit card is simply a convenient alternative to paying with cash. If you're like most people, however, you won't pay off your bill in full each month. That's where the trouble starts.

If you owe $1,000 on your credit card, and you make only the minimum payment each month, it will take you years to pay off the money you owe, and you'll end up paying nearly as much in interest as you owe on the loan. In plain language, it's a really bad idea to let the interest keep building up on your credit card debt. Those $125 boots could end up costing more than twice that amount if you pay them off $10 a month at 18 percent interest.

Dollars and Sense

If your credit record is good, and you're paying an annual fee on your credit card, write to the company or bank (the address should be on your bill) and ask to have the fee waived. If the bank won't waive it, write again (or call, but it's better to have a written record of everything) and say you're going to switch to another company. Betcha the bank will drop the fee rather than lose a customer.

The average credit card interest rate has been about 18 percent for a while, but fierce competition among card companies is forcing it down. Some banks offer credit cards at rates as low as 8.25 or 8.5 percent. You might even see one now and then for as low as 6.5 percent interest. Sounds good, huh? Be careful. Usually those rates only apply for six months, after which time they go up.

There are cards available for 10 or 12 percent, though, so if you're paying 16 or 18 percent, now's the time to look around for a better rate. For a list of comparative credit card rates, try one of these organizations:

Money Pit

Be sure you know what the **grace period** on your card is. The traditional grace period used to be 30 days, but it's getting shorter and shorter. The average grace period is now about 18 days.

➤ Contact Ram Research at 800-344-7714. Or send $5 to Ram Research Card Trak, Box 1700, Frederick, MD 21702. You can get the list for free on the Internet at http://www.cardtrak.com.

➤ Contact Bankcard Holders of America at 540-389-5445. Or send $4 to Bankcard Holders, 524 Branch Drive, Salem, VA 24153.

When you locate a card with a good rate, go ahead and apply. If you've had a card for a while and you've maintained a good credit record, you should qualify for a better rate. If you've only had a card for a short time, though, it might be harder to get approved for a low interest rate. Still, it can't hurt to try. There's a lot of competition for cardholders, and some places are willing to give you a lower interest rate to keep your business. All you have to do, in some cases, is ask. If you haven't had much time to build up a credit record, and you're not approved for a lower interest rate, be diligent about keeping up with your payments and try again in a year to get a better rate.

Fees and More Fees

As bad as the annual fee and the interest rates are on credit cards, it's the other, lesser-known fees that can really add up. No matter how boring and complicated it may seem, make sure you read all the fine print that comes along with your credit card policy. If you don't understand it, call the card company and ask for customer service. Insist that someone answers all your questions. Many people don't fully understand their policies, and they end up paying all kinds of hidden charges as a result.

Some other fees to look for on your own credit card, or when you're checking out an offer for a card, include the following:

Late fees. You'll be charged a fee if your payment is late. That's in addition to the interest charges for not paying off your balance by a specified time. Not all banks charge the late fee, so make sure you find out when you apply for the card.

Cash advance fees. These are nasty fees, and because they are, you should try to never take a cash advance. When you borrow cash against your credit card, most cards forget about the grace period and start charging you interest right away. About 50 percent of the card companies out there will charge you 2 percent to 6 percent more interest on a cash advance than on other charges not paid off by the end of the billing period. There's also usually a one-time fee of between 2 and 5 percent for cash advances.

You could be getting hit not once, not twice, but three times on cash advances. So you see why it's a good idea to stay away from them. But life seldom works exactly the way we'd like it to, and sometimes you're up against the wall. I once had an important meeting in New York City, about three hours from my home. I was running late and got to the bus terminal about five minutes before departure, only to find out that no credit cards or personal checks were accepted for payment. I didn't have enough cash with me to buy the ticket, and the driver wasn't going to wait for me. Thank goodness there was a machine in the terminal from which I could get a cash advance on my Visa card.

If it's an absolute emergency, you might have no choice but to get a cash advance against your credit card and suffer the fee consequences. At least be sure you pay the money back promptly to avoid possible higher interest rates. You can pay the balance on your credit card between regular payment dates by calling the company and then sending them a check.

Discretionary fees. These fees, imposed on you to pay for things such as credit life insurance or a shopping service that you never ordered, are at the discretion of the card company, not you. Be sure to read your bill carefully, and don't pay for anything you didn't order.

Two-cycle billing. Two-cycle billing is extremely unpopular among consumers and rightly so. This billing method penalizes people who pay off their cards every month for a while, but then get behind and carry a balance. The bank will charge you an extra month's interest every time you begin a balance. This could result in you paying as much as four extra months interest for a year. It's a terrible system, but some experts see it as a growing trend. If you notice any strange charges on your bill, get on the phone immediately and find out what's going on. If your card company uses two-cycle billing, start looking for another company.

Penalty interest rates. If your payment is late, you exceed your credit limit, or do anything else to annoy your card issuer, you could be slapped with penalty interest rates, which could add 3 to 10 percent to what you're already paying.

Make sure you read each bill carefully when you get it, and look for any charges you can't account for. If you feel you've been charged for something to which you didn't agree in advance, by all means pick up the phone and talk with someone in customer service. The intense competition between credit card issuers is forcing them to be responsive to consumers' needs and complaints. Make sure you take advantage of it!

Timeliness Is Next to Godliness: Paying Off Your Debt

You've already learned about late fees, but you might be surprised to know that your payment only has to be one day late in order for that fee to be issued. The typical late fee is $15, but some issuers are charging up to $25. That means you could end up paying a good piece of change because you forget to drop your envelope in the mail-box on your way to work.

If you're ever charged a late fee and your payment was only one day overdue, give a call and ask to have the charge revoked. It might not work, but then again it might. The best thing to do, though, is to make sure you pay your charge card bills on time. If you're running late, send your payment by priority mail. It will get your check to the card company in two days, and at $2.95, it will cost you a lot less to do that than to pay the late fee on your bill. You could hurt your chances significantly of getting a lower interest rate or having your annual fee dropped if you have a history of late payments. And such a history could make it more difficult to get a different card.

The Least You Need to Know

➤ Credit cards have been around for a while, but their use has greatly increased, along with the debt people carry on them.

➤ Credit cards are great when used responsibly, but they can cause financial nightmares when they're used to buy things you can't afford.

➤ A person with a poor credit history or no credit history can get a secured credit card or have a co-signer or guarantor for a credit card.

➤ It makes sense to use a credit card in certain situations, but not in every situation.

➤ If you're paying high fees and interest rates on your credit cards, it's time to look around for another card.

➤ Paying off your credit card bill in full and on time each month is the best way to go. If you can't, paying as much as you can, on time, is the next best plan.

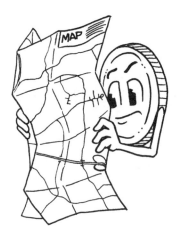

Chapter 5

Finding a Place with the Right Zip Code

In This Chapter

➤ Establishing your criteria for the perfect place to live

➤ The best ways to look for an apartment

➤ How much up-front money do you need?

➤ The pros and cons of living with roommates

➤ What about renter's insurance?

➤ Tightening the reins on living expenses

Novelist Thomas Wolfe (author of *Look Homeward, Angel,* and other books published in the '30s and '40s, not to be confused with the contemporary writer Tom Wolfe) said you can't go home again. For many of us, Wolfe's assessment is accurate.

If you liked the freedom of being away at a college or other school or wherever you happened to be living, you're likely to find it very difficult to move back home, under the watchful eyes and ears of your family. You might find their well-meaning attention stifling, when all you want is to be left alone. You resent being asked to help out with household chores when you're busy, although you know you should pitch in. You could even put up with that, though, if you could only get a little privacy. Your phone calls are screened, your mail scrutinized, and it's driving you crazy.

Although the situation may put a crimp in your once free and easy lifestyle, you should know that more Gen Xers are staying at home longer these days, due primarily to financial considerations. There comes a time, though, when you have to move out.

Doing the Apartment Thing

Most people find that renting an apartment is the way to go when they first move out on their own. There usually are plenty available, (unless you get caught up in a housing crunch, as happens sometimes, especially in cities) and they come in a wide range of prices. You can get a studio or one-bedroom apartment if you'll be living on your own or get an apartment with two or more bedrooms if you'll be sharing it with one or more roommates.

There are nearly as many kinds of apartments as there are people to fill them: brand-new apartments in huge complexes, complete with gyms, pools, and social buildings; lofts in old factories; and oddball apartments that appear to be quirks of zoning, stuck in residential neighborhoods. There are beautiful, old homes that have been converted into units and basic brick apartment buildings that are products of the '70s.

With all those options and more to choose from, how do you find an apartment that

➤ You'll like and be comfortable living in

➤ You can afford

➤ Is in a safe area

➤ Is convenient to work, shopping, and your friends?

Apartment hunting can be confusing, but if you get organized and follow some basic rules, you'll do just fine.

Dollars and Sense

Be sure to consider the costs of getting to work or to other places you go frequently if you choose to live in an area that's not close to those places. The cost of gas or public transportation can add up quickly.

Scouting Locations

If you've got to live in the 90210 zip code (or any other particular zip code), you're really narrowing your choices to find an apartment that you like and can afford. Location, however, *is* important. Maybe you want to live in a certain area because it's close to your work and not too close to your parents. Maybe you've got some good friends who live there and have told you how great it is. There are all kinds of reasons you might want to live in a particular area, and if you do, that's where you should begin your apartment search.

There are several good ways to find an apartment:

➤ **Word of mouth and personal knowledge**. These are probably the best ways of finding an apartment that's right for you. Say you know somebody who lived in the Riverloft apartments and loved it. You thought the place was great when you visited your friend, and you know it's within your budget. By all means, call the Riverloft office and see whether any apartments are available.

➤ **Classified ads.** Using the classifieds is more of a shotgun approach than targeting a place directly, but it can be effective because you can get multiple listings for many different kinds of apartments in varying price ranges. The classifieds method will require some time to call and run around to check out these places.

➤ **The phone book.** An often-overlooked tool, the phone book will give you listings of apartment facilities. If you don't know anything about them, you'll have to call each one for information and visit them to narrow your search. Also, the phone book probably only lists the larger facilities, so you won't get the full picture of what's available. Still, it can be a starting point.

➤ **A real estate agent.** Real estate agents have lists of available apartments, and it shouldn't cost you anything to access them (the owner pays that charge). Real estate agents normally get lists of rentals from people who own lots of properties and will know about all the complexes in the area. They won't, however, have access to every available apartment because many landlords don't list their properties with a real estate agent.

➤ **Road trip.** Get in your car and head for an area in which you think you'd like to live. Drive around—or better yet, get somebody else to drive so you can look—and see what's available. This is a great way to see apartments that aren't listed in the phone book or with a real estate agent, and it allows you to pinpoint areas you like and concentrate on them.

➤ **University housing office.** If you're still in college, or you're planning to stay in the town or city where you attended college, check with the housing office for lists of apartments and landlords.

Dollars and Sense

One enterprising apartment hunter narrowed his search by figuring out a 40-minute-drive radius from his office. He knew he didn't want to drive more than 40 minutes, and he made sure to find an apartment within that circle around his office.

Signing Your Life Away

When you've found an apartment you like, there are still more things to consider before you sign the lease. To start with, the landlord will want some information about you. He or she will probably do a credit check and verify your employment. You may also be asked to give some referrals, and he or she will want to know whether you have any pets.

Money Pit

Never take an apartment without seeing and signing a contract between you and the landlord. Make sure the landlord signs it, too, in your presence. If a landlord tries to tell you that you don't need a contract, get out fast. He or she could change all the conditions you agree upon verbally, and you'd have no way of proving it.

Show Me the Money

A **lease** is a legally binding agreement between a landlord and tenant. It contains the names of the landlord and the renters, the amount of rent and payment schedule and other rules and regulations that pertain.

You have to figure out whether you can afford the apartment and whether it includes the things you need. Is there a washer and dryer in the apartment or somewhere on the premises? Or will you have to lug your stuff to the Laundromat? Is there a grocery store nearby, or will shopping entail a trip across town? Will your landlord get someone to repaint the purple bedroom, or will he or she let you paint it? Don't take anything for granted. If you're not sure about something, or if it's not specified in the lease, ask.

If the *lease* seems overly complicated or confusing, you may want to get a lawyer or real estate agent to check it for you before you sign. Experts say that rent agreements are becoming increasingly complicated, with all sorts of obscure conditions that you might easily overlook.

Some things to look for in the lease, or ask your prospective landlord about, include the following:

➤ What is the term of the lease?

➤ What are the provisions for renewing the lease?

➤ Who pays the utilities (such as heat and hot water)?

➤ Who's responsible for removing snow and ice in the winter or garbage all year round?

➤ Can you sublet the apartment if you move?

➤ How much notice must you give the landlord before you move?

➤ What rules apply to the rental?

➤ Are any appliances included (refrigerator, stove, and so on), and what happens if they break?

➤ Is a discount available if you do maintenance yourself?

➤ When is the rent due?

➤ What happens if you're late paying the rent?

Don't ever let a landlord pressure you into signing a lease before you're ready to. If he or she tells you there's someone else ready to sign and you'll lose the apartment if you don't put your name on the dotted line, take a chance on losing it, even if you love it. The landlord may be trying to rush through with the deal before you notice that the lease doesn't work in your best interests. Be sure you ask the landlord for a copy of his rental policy, if he has one. Such a policy would list all rules that apply.

Up-Front Costs

You should spend no more than 25 to 30 percent of your monthly gross income (your income before taxes are deducted) for rent. So if you're making $30,000 a year ($2,500 a month), you shouldn't be paying more than $625 a month for your rent, using the 25 percent calculation. The following table will help you figure out approximately how much you should be spending for rent.

Maximum Amount You Should Spend for Housing

Annual Income*	Annual Housing Cost	Monthly Housing Cost
$20,000	$5,600	$466.67
25,000	7,000	583.33
30,000	8,400	700.00
35,000	9,800	816.67
40,000	11,200	933.33
45,000	12,600	1,050.00
50,000	14,000	1,166.67
55,000	15,400	1,283.33
60,000	16,800	1,400.00
65,000	18,200	1,516.67
70,000	19,600	1,633.33
75,000	21,000	1,750.00
80,000	22,400	1,866.67
85,000	23,800	1,983.33
90,000	25,200	2,100.00
95,000	26,600	2,216.67
100,000	28,000	2,333.33

Gross Income

The cost of renting an apartment varies greatly from region to region and even among communities. The same two-bedroom apartment could cost twice as much in the suburbs as it does in a not-so-great area of downtown. Or you might pay top dollar to live downtown in a nice area of a large city. Scan the real estate section of your newspaper to get an idea of what apartments are renting for and decide what your options are.

Another thing to keep in mind is that you're free to negotiate with an owner concerning the rent he or she is charging. You'll probably be more successful trying this with a private rental, as opposed to an apartment complex where rents are established. If you've found a place you like that's a little out of your price range, go ahead and ask the landlord to drop the rent by $25 or $50 a month. Depending on the rental market in the area, you may or may not get the results you want. Saving $50 a month in rent adds up to $600 a year. It's worth asking about, don't you think?

When you find an apartment you can afford, it's not quite as easy as handing over your first month's rent and moving in. Your landlord also may require the following:

➤ An extra month's rent (usually used to cover your last month)

➤ A *security deposit* equivalent to one or two months' rent

So if you find an apartment for $500 a month, you could end up having to pay out $2,000 before you even move in.

Show Me the Money

A **security deposit** is the amount of money you pay to the landlord to protect against damages that occur to the apartment while you're renting it. He or she should give you an itemized list of deductions to your security deposit. If you fulfill the terms of your lease and leave your apartment in good repair, your money should be refunded.

The extra month's rent and your security deposit should be kept in an escrow account, which is an account specified for the purpose of holding your money until it is either used or returned to you. Some states, but not all, require that security deposits are kept in interest-bearing accounts for the tenant.

All that up-front money can be pretty discouraging news, to be sure, and it is one reason Gen Xers are hanging out longer with Mom and Dad. It's also a reason why many people choose to rent with another person or group of people.

Three's Company—or a Crowd

If you decide to go with a roommate, you can cut your up-front costs by splitting them. Instead of $2,000, you'd need only $1,000. You can cut costs even further by renting with more than one person, but make sure you find out about any restrictions the landlord might have concerning the number of tenants per unit.

In addition to helping out financially, a roommate can be great company and make you feel more secure if you're a bit uncomfortable living by yourself. Be sure, however, that you consider any disadvantages or potential disadvantages before moving in with a roomie.

If it's someone you know well, you already have an idea of his or her personal habits, interests, and personality. Suffice it to say, though, that living with someone is a lot different than spending time with them occasionally or even frequently. If the room-mate is someone you don't know well or a stranger, get as much information about the person as you can before you move in. If it becomes apparent that the two of you aren't going to get along, it's best to get out before you're legally involved.

Once you sign a lease, thus agreeing to pay up-front costs and rent for a specified amount of time, you are legally obligated to do so. If you find out you can't live with your room-mate and you've already signed the lease, it could be very difficult for you to resolve the legal aspects of the situation.

Look for other people who know your prospec-tive roommate, and try to get a feeling for what the person is like. Don't be afraid to ask the roommate any questions you feel are applicable, either. Some people conduct extensive interviews with prospective room-mates and have the roommate agree to certain conditions before moving in.

An Orlando, Florida woman said she's had so much trouble with roommates that she now does extensive background checks before agreeing to live with somebody. She checks references, both from work and other places the person has lived, and contacts the sheriff's department to see whether the person has an arrest record. She screens potential roommates by telephone and then conducts a personal interview.

The Orlando woman isn't just paranoid. She said she's been burned by roommates several times, including the time a roommate stole one of her personal checks, forged her signa-ture, and cashed it for $500. She also had a roommate who walked out on the lease, leaving her stuck with the entire rent, and one whose rent checks consistently bounced.

Having a roommate is a great way to cut rental costs and can be a very rewarding experience. You and your roommate might end up as best

Money Pit

If you find out your prospective roommate smokes two packs of cigarettes a day and likes to have wild parties every weekend, and you can't stand smoke, and you like to relax with a good book on a Saturday night, call off the deal before it's made. If you sign a lease, you're legally obligated and will be held financially responsible for your share of expenses.

Dollars and Sense

If you get into legal trouble with a roommate, your best bet is to consult an attorney. If your room-mate walks out on the lease, talk to your landlord and explain what has happened. He or she may be sympathetic and try to work with you. Meanwhile, an attorney can best advise you on what to do.

friends, but unfortunately, there's no guarantee. Do your best to scope out a potential roommate carefully before agreeing to share an apartment. Even if it's someone you know, be sure you agree on basic rules for living together. Remember that renting an apartment is a legally binding agreement. If you default on the agreement, or get caught in the middle of a problem with a roommate who defaults, it can negatively affect your credit rating and cause you problems for years to come.

Renter's Insurance

After you've found an apartment and moved in, you might want to consider buying renter's insurance. Although you're not responsible for damages to the building (unless you directly cause the damage), you have personal property to protect in case of fire, theft, or water damage. Renter's insurance also protects you against liability in the event that someone is injured in your apartment. It can even protect you from personal liability if you rent a boat or jet ski.

If you have an apartment full of expensive electronic equipment or a valuable collection or extensive photographic equipment, you should consider renter's insurance. Be sure to get replacement coverage, which, for about 13 percent more in premiums, will give you 100 percent of the replacement cost on items that are damaged or stolen. Some landlords will require that you have renter's insurance, especially if you have a waterbed or aquarium that could cause serious water damage if it were to leak. Make sure your policy would cover those sorts of accidents.

Pocket Change

Some reputable insurance companies that offer renter's policies include Nationwide Mutual, Prudential, Allstate, Liberty Mutual, Erie Insurance, and State Farm. Check your phone book for agents who sell these brands.

If you do decide to purchase renter's insurance, make sure you shop around at reputable companies to get the best rates. Every insurance company has its own rate system, so the company that gave your friend the best rate might not be the best outfit for you. Rough estimate of cost is $80 to $100 per year. Quite inexpensive considering the expense of what would need to be replaced if damaged or stolen.

Full House

Sometimes, especially if you want to live with a group of people, it makes more sense to rent a house than an apartment. A house gives you more space and, probably, more bedrooms. This means you'll have more privacy than if you'd have bunked with somebody. You might even get a yard with room to throw a football around if you rent a house rather than an apartment. Of course, a house—even one you rent—requires more upkeep than an apartment. Be sure you know what's expected. Will you have to mow the lawn? Shovel the driveway when it snows?

If you decide to rent a house, remember that the same rules apply as when you rent an apartment:

➤ Always read a lease *completely* before signing it.

➤ Consider consulting a lawyer or real estate agent if there's anything in the lease that you don't fully understand.

➤ Never let a landlord pressure you into signing a lease that you haven't thoroughly inspected.

➤ Make sure the landlord signs the lease in your presence.

➤ Have the landlord let you know, in writing, the amount of up-front money you'll need and what the money is for.

➤ Document any existing damage to the property. Take photographs, if possible, and make two copies: one for you and one for the landlord. If you have an attorney, feel free to send another copy to him or her.

➤ Ask the landlord whether your security deposit will be kept in an escrow account and whether the account is interest-bearing in your name.

Dollars and Sense

Don't overlook the possibility of renting a condominium: there are lots of them around. Many older people live in condos until they can no longer live on their own, then move to an assisted living center or in with a relative. Many younger people buy condos as starter homes, then move out when they can afford another type of dwelling. Also, many persons purchase a condo as an investment property, the purpose is to rent. If you can find one that's in the market to be sold, you might be able to get a good price on your rent. Of course, you'll have to be prepared to move if it sells.

When you start looking for roommates to fill the house, keep the following things in mind:

➤ Get a feeling for what the prospective roomie is like by contacting people who know or work with him or her.

➤ Don't be afraid to ask your potential roommate a lot of questions.

➤ Get all the financial matters in writing. How will the rent be split up? At what time of the month must the rent be paid? What if someone wants to move out? How much will each person contribute to the security deposit? How will costs like food and utilities be paid for? Will one person write a check and be reimbursed by the others? When will the reimbursement occur? Leave nothing to chance.

➤ Don't feel you have to accept someone as a roommate just because he or she has asked to move in. Bad roommate scenarios are not uncommon. Maybe your roomie won't be as bad as Jennifer Jason Leigh in *Single White Female*, but if you have a feeling it won't work out, trust your gut.

What Am I Gonna Sleep On?

You're finally out on your own. You've got your own apartment, and you can't wait to move in. You pack up your stuff, get somebody to help you move, and you're all set, right? But wait a minute. Where are you going to sleep tonight? A sleeping bag is great for camping trips, but seven nights a week on the bedroom floor can get a little rough.

Most first-time apartment renters don't have a moving van's worth of furniture to bring with them. Many don't even have a pickup truck's worth. And anybody who's been in a furniture store lately will tell you that it's an expensive venture to furnish an apartment.

Say you go to a decent furniture store to buy the basic stuff you need for your apartment. Nothing out of the ordinary, just a sofa, a chair, and a bed. Because you're attuned to your personal finances, you make sure the store you go to is having a sale. Get out your calculator, and let's total up the cost of this hypothetical shopping trip. You ready?

Sofa: $699 (marked down from $1,299)

Loveseat: $675 (marked down from $1,249)

Coffee table: $329

End table: $249

Table lamps (two): $99

Entertainment center: $1,399

TV and VCR: $529 (you've got to have something to put in the entertainment center)

Bed: $399

Mattress and box spring: $478

Dresser: $499

Mirror: $149

Nightstand: $249

Farmhouse dining table with four chairs: $499

Grand Total: $6,252

Pretty astounding, isn't it? And these prices are conservative for new furniture from a quality store. Plus, we didn't even mention a stereo system, a desk, rugs, curtains, and all the other extras you might want. If you're not prepared or able to spend that kind of money on sofas, chairs, and accessories, don't worry. There are other ways to do it.

Furnishing Your Place Without Spending a Fortune

The first thing to do is decide what you really need. Not everything you want, just what you need. Maybe you think you need the bed, mattress, and box spring, a dresser, a sofa, a coffee table, and the dining table and chairs. Good. You've cut back, big time. The trouble is, those basics, purchased new from the furniture store, will still cost you almost $3,000 at the prices listed.

It might be time to lower your expectations and start looking for hand-downs. Maybe your older sister has moved on to bigger and better and will donate the couch from her first apartment. Your parents might let you take the desk or the bookcase from your old bedroom. Even Aunt Kay might have some treasures in her basement. Ask around; you probably know several people who would be happy to give you some furniture or accessories to help you get started in your new digs.

If not, check your phone book for second-hand stores in your neighborhood. You might get lucky and find some high-quality furniture in these places at great prices. Or maybe you'll at least find something affordable that you can live with for a while.

Going to private auctions or auction centers can be fun ways to find used furniture at good prices, too. If you're not crazy about having furniture that belonged to someone else, you can check out outlets or discount furniture stores in your area. Or jump on the Internet and look for places such as Ikea (www.ikea.com) or Pier 1 Imports (www.pier1.com) for neat stuff at moderate (not cheap) prices.

Pocket Change

Some home items, including furniture and appliances, are available by mail at wholesale prices. Call 1-800-242-7737 to order the Wholesale by Mail catalog.

Quality Is Key

As tempting as it might be to buy inexpensive furniture to fill up your apartment, remember that you get what you pay for. Even cheap furniture is going to cost you some bucks, and you'll end up replacing it before you've gotten your money's worth. We live in a hate-to-wait society, but buying cheap furniture will turn out to be no bargain in the long run. Try to be patient and wait until you can afford to buy what you really want.

Dollars and Sense

Some furniture stores will let you put a deposit on that sofa you love and give you six months or so at no interest to pay off the rest. Just be sure you'll be able to pay it off before the interest kicks in. If not, you'll owe the entire interest that was deferred for the grace period, and it's likely to be a hefty rate.

Consider buying one or two good pieces that will last and filling in the rest with used, begged, or borrowed pieces. After all, when you add a nice tablecloth and some candles, who's going to care that your dining table is a card table with folding chairs?

I Gotta Pay for That, Too?

Just when you think you've got your financial situation pretty well under control, you start getting these pesky little bills. Nothing too big—$30 here, $19 there. When you add them up, though, you've got some significant expenses.

We're talking utilities: heat, electricity, cable TV, water, telephone, and gas. Make sure you have a clear understanding of what your rent includes before you move into an apartment. Some landlords include heat and water and electricity with the rent; others don't. You don't want to work out a budget and then be surprised when unexpected bills start coming in each month.

Electricity

Ever since Thomas Edison invented electricity, people have been paying for it. Electric bills can be pretty daunting, especially if you're paying your own heat and/or air conditioning.

If electricity isn't included in your rent, take steps to control what you use. Keep your apartment a few degrees cooler in the winter and wear a sweatshirt. Keep it a few degrees warmer in the summer and go sleeveless. Be sure to adjust the temperature if the apartment will be empty, and turn off all your lights and appliances before leaving.

If you pay your electric bill, ask your landlord to show you the meter. Check the connections to make sure you're paying for only your electricity, not for you and your landlord who lives on the first floor.

Money Pit

When ordering phone service, consider carefully whether you really need call waiting, caller I.D., and other extras that the telephone representative will try to talk you into buying. These costs can add up fast on your monthly bill.

Phone

We could write a chapter comparing the qualities of various phone companies. But you no doubt hear more than you need to about MCI, Sprint, and AT&T every time you turn on your TV or radio. Every company will offer you a deal to come on board, but when you're tempted, try to look at the big picture as far as your phone bill is concerned.

If you're in Phoenix, and you call your boyfriend in New York every night and talk for an hour, your phone bill will be high. It doesn't matter if it's Sprint, MCI, or AT&T—you're going to have to pay big bucks. If, on the other hand, the only long-distance charge you have is a 10-minute call to your mother every Sunday, your phone bill will be reasonable.

Compare the costs for basic service and get the lowest one. Then control your costs by limiting long-distance calls and other extras. As tempting as it might be to call your college roommate and tell her you just heard that the guy she dated her senior year just landed a job with Microsoft, it's cheaper to e-mail. Or do the retro thing and write a letter. It still costs less than a local call on a pay phone to send a long letter from New York to Los Angeles, and there's something special about getting a handwritten note in the mail.

I Want My MTV

In the past 50 years, television has gone from small black-and-white, three-channel sets with rabbit ears on the top to color, giant screen, surround sound, with 100-plus-channels. People can spend hours debating the pros and cons of TV, but there's no arguing about one thing: watching TV has gotten expensive. Even basic cable service can cost upward of $30 a month. Throw in a couple of premium channels, and you can be billed more than $50. If you're looking to cut expenses, cut out a premium channel and you'll save about $100 a year. If you're looking to really cut expenses and have a lot more reading time, as well, opt to go without cable.

Charges for utilities can add up, there's no question about it. In addition to the basic electric, phone, and cable, keep an eye on what you're spending in some other areas:

➤ **Internet connection.** Different Internet service providers offer varying plans and rates, so shop around to make sure you're not buying more than you need. If you only spend a couple of hours a month online, it makes no sense to buy an unlimited plan.

➤ **Cell phones.** There are as many plans as there are types of phones, so look around to make sure yours is what you need, and not more than what you need. Remember it's a lot cheaper to pull over and stick 35 cents in a pay phone than it is to use your cell phone while you're driving. Save the cell phone for emergencies, unless you must use it for business.

➤ **Pagers.** Unless you're a brain surgeon or have a job that keeps you away from the office, this expense is probably one you could do without.

The fewer bills you have to pay each month, the more money you'll have to put in a mutual fund, use for a vacation, or pay off your college loans. It's easy to overlook these monthly charges, but when you add them all up, you might be surprised at how much you're spending.

The Least You Need to Know

➤ You need to consider a variety of factors when looking for an apartment that's right for you.

➤ Your rent isn't the only cost you'll have when you first move into an apartment.

➤ Having a roommate can cut costs, but beware of potential pitfalls.

➤ Buying furniture doesn't have to put you in the poorhouse.

➤ Your utility bills might be costing more than you realize, but there are ways to cut down the costs.

Chapter 6

Road Rules

In This Chapter

➤ Is America's love affair with automobiles ending?

➤ Getting around without a car

➤ The difference between buying and leasing a car

➤ Buying new versus buying used

➤ The added expenses of car ownership

Cars, trucks, sport utility vehicles, vans—Americans have had a great love affair with automobiles since Henry Ford cranked out that first Model T in the early 1900s. We talk about cars extensively. Traditionally, we've admired them, spent hours washing and polishing them, and to a point, we've identified with the cars we drive. Let's face it, many of us would feel better about ourselves while driving a new Saab than a rusty old Escort. Cars are a source of status, and a person's car can provide some interesting insights into his or her personality.

You probably know some people who keep their cars immaculate. They wouldn't dream of leaving a chewing gum wrapper on the dashboard, much less a month's worth of Big Mac wrappers, french fry cartons, and Coke cans on the back seat. Washing the car is a Saturday afternoon mainstay, and waxing it every spring and fall is something of a ritual. Then there are those who look at their cars as additional living space. They've got everything they need in there: jackets, umbrellas, food, water, flashlights, blankets, and so on.

How about the folks who decorate their cars? They display collections of stuffed animals, baseball caps, or other oddities on the space behind the back seat, or hang all sorts of memorabilia from the rearview mirror. Although interior decorating is important to some, exterior decorating is the name of the game for others. Have you ever seen a car with bumper stickers that not only cover the bumper, but most of the back of the vehicle, as well?

This chapter takes a look at cars and the advantages and disadvantages of buying and leasing and doing without. Your car probably eats up more money than you realize, and as Gen Xers seem to have figured out, you can save a lot of money by lowering your car expectations. So park yourself somewhere and get ready to learn some interesting stuff about vehicles and driving.

Cruising the Auto Industry Landscape

We've always taken our cars pretty seriously in this country. Yet there are indications that the times might be a changin', and people in their 20s and 30s are the ones who are making the changes happen. A large marketing firm in Oregon recently polled Generation X consumers about what they felt were their most significant purchases. Guess what? Only 10 percent listed a new car purchase as a high priority. They were more interested in home electronics, such as stereo equipment. Computers were way up there, too. But new cars? No thanks.

Not that people in their 20s and 30s don't want cars. Many of them still want flashy and fast cars. But more and more people your age are saying yes to used cars that will get you around, but don't have to look great or have leather seats or top-of-the-line sound systems.

Marketers and car manufacturers are understandably perplexed and nervous about this emerging attitude. They've done extremely well over the past decades at getting us to think we had to have the latest models, that bigger and fancier was better, and that the cars we drove were indicators and extensions of who we were and how much money we made.

If all that changes, car manufacturers and other industries will be in big trouble, and they know it. The American economy depends heavily on Americans buying new cars every three or four years. That habit greatly influences and affects industries such as steel, rubber, and electronics. If the habit changes, those industries and others will suffer.

The auto industry already was stung by reduced car prices in 1998. For the first time in 20 years, the average price of a new car was lower than the previous year—not much lower, but lower. *Money* magazine reported that consumers paid an average of 0.6 percent less for new cars in 1998 than in 1997, but some sticker prices were down as much as 8 percent.

Some of the factors cited for the decrease include:

➤ A strong U.S. dollar compared with the Japanese yen allows Japanese companies to sell their cars for less in the United States. American manufacturers are forced to compete by keeping their prices down.

➤ New car sales are suffering in Asia, where the economy has been faltering, so manufacturers such as Honda and Toyota are concentrating on American markets. To sell their cars here, they've got to keep the prices down.

➤ Seventeen new models were manufactured in 1998, but consumers aren't buying new cars as quickly as they had been. So there's increased supply and lessened demand, and that situation forces prices down.

➤ Car companies such as Saturn are offering basic, non-negotiable prices for new cars. By doing so, they cut their overhead and expenses and are able to pass on the savings.

All this is good news for consumers. This good news, though, should be kept in perspective. We still need cars, and they're still expensive.

Planes, Trains, and Automobiles

The best thing about having a car at your disposal is the freedom it gives you. You can go wherever you want. Just pick a destination and hop in the car, and you're off.

Other than that, there's really not that much about having a car that's so great. They're expensive to buy and to maintain. They break down occasionally, leaving you sitting by the side of the road in a thunderstorm. They require time and attention, and by the time you pay for them, they're hardly worth the metal they're made of. But most of us still can't imagine life without our wheels. Our lifestyles would change dramatically if we were to go carless.

Yet plenty of people get along perfectly fine without a vehicle of their own—no car, no truck, not even a scooter to hop on and ride across town. Some of these folks hitch a ride with somebody else when they need one, or they walk where they want to go. Others use something collectively known as *public transportation,* which includes the buses, trains, subways, and trolleys that carry people across town and across the country every day.

Taxi cabs are available for those without vehicles, as are bicycles, inline skates, and airplanes for longer trips. Our country is fairly unique in its "a car for every driver" attitude. In other countries, cars are still pretty much seen as luxuries, and a family would never aspire to have more than one.

Show Me the Money

Public transportation is the collective name for a system of buses, trains, subways, and the like that carries people to and from their intended destinations.

Not Everybody Needs a Car

If you live out on a farm in Iowa, you probably need a car or truck to get you from one place to another. The nearest store might be 15 miles down the road, and you'll have a long, long wait for the transit system bus to come along.

Dollars and Sense

If you use public transportation regularly, be sure you check out commuter passes, which allow you to buy quantities of bus, train, or subway tickets at reduced prices.

On the other hand, if you live in the middle of New York City, you probably don't need a car. Keeping a car in the city is terribly expensive, and it's a hassle. With abundant public transportation, you can easily get where you want to go without your own vehicle.

If you live in the suburbs, you probably think you need a car, and you're probably used to having a car. If you don't have one, though, you no doubt could get along without it. It would be an adjustment, but most suburbanites have access to public transportation, which could transport you to work and the other places you need to go.

Renting a Car When You Need One

If you don't own a car, either by chance or choice, you can still get around. Public transportation, as mentioned earlier, is a viable option and in many areas is being expanded to serve more people.

Still, taking a bus when you leave New York City to go to visit your college roommate in Washington, D.C. can be a hassle. It can turn a 225-mile, less-than-four-hour car trip into an all-day adventure, depending on how many stops you make along the way.

Dollars and Sense

A three-day rate for a Budget rental car from New York City is $151 (economy with unlimited mileage). A round-trip Amtrak ticket from New York to Washington, D.C. is $145. Greyhound will take you from New York to D.C. and back for $58, but you never know who you'll end up sitting next to.

And sometimes you're just not in the mood to chat with the person in the next seat, who just found out her husband is having an affair and is going home to her mother.

The thing to do in that case is to rent a car. Extravagant, you say? Not really. Rental rates vary tremendously, and they change depending on availability and other factors. To rent a car in New York City would cost about $52 a day or $150 for a three-day weekend. More than Greyhound? Yeah. More than Amtrak? About $5. If you're traveling with somebody else, then renting a car becomes an even more viable option.

Some people live in the city without a car and rent one when they need it for business purposes. Hopefully, your employer will reimburse you for that expense if you find yourself doing that. The point is, it's not always necessary to own a car.

The Great Debate: Buying or Leasing

Although it might not be necessary for everyone to own a car, facts are facts; most of us do. Owning a car means paying out a lot of money to get one.

Even with prices holding about steady from 1997 to 1998, cars are expensive. Even if you're not looking for anything fancy, you'll pay a lot of money for a new car. Just pick up the Sunday automotive section and have a look at these 1999 models:

➤ Toyota Camry: $17,790

➤ Jeep Cherokee: $23,160

➤ Taurus sedan: $16,495

➤ F-150 pickup: $17,989

➤ Nissan Altima: $15,790

➤ Chrysler Neon: $13,820

If you're going to buy a car, there are several ways to do it. You can walk into the dealership, plunk down $17,989 on the counter, and drive off in your brand spankin' new truck. Yeah, right. Or if you're like most people, you can do what most people do, and finance your car.

Financing Your Car

Most dealerships offer car financing. They really want to sell you a car, and they'll do whatever they can to make sure you buy it. However, dealer financing normally costs at least one or two percentage points more than a bank or credit union. Also, if the car dealers control your loan, they could try to talk you into buying a more expensive car than you would normally by assuring you that they'll give you the extra money you need to cover it.

A better way to finance your car is to get a loan from a bank or credit union. You'll probably get a lower interest rate, and you won't be at the mercy of the dealership. In fact, if you walk into a car dealership with a pre-approved car loan, it puts you in a great position. Here's why:

➤ You know how much money you have, and you buy within that amount.

Money Pit

Stay away from finance companies that offer guaranteed, same-day loans and other ploys to get your business. The rates these companies give you are virtually always higher than what you'd get from a bank or credit union. Most of these companies cater to people with bad credit, who would have trouble getting a bank loan.

➤ The car salesperson knows you're serious about buying, and he'll do everything he can to make sure you buy from him.

➤ You're not at the mercy of the dealership to get your loan. Instead, the dealership has to work on your terms.

Shop around for interest rates when you're looking for a car loan. Traditionally, credit unions offer the best rates on car loans, more than one and a half percent less on average than a bank loan. That difference can save you a lot of money over the length of the loan.

Consider these issues when getting a car loan:

➤ Instead of an installment loan, go for a simple interest loan, which lets you pay interest only on the remaining amount of your loan. The bank will figure out the total interest on your loan and set up a plan where you'll pay the same amount each month for the life of your loan. That's better than a front-end installment loan, which requires that you pay interest each month on the full amount of the loan. Even after you've paid off $6,000 of a $12,000 loan, you're still paying interest on $12,000, which is definitely *not* a good deal!

➤ Put down as much money as you can. The more you put down toward your car, the lower your interest rate will probably be. Plus, you'll be financing less, thereby paying less interest overall. You're usually required to put down between 10 percent and 20 percent when you buy a new car, but sometimes a bank or credit union will give you a loan for the total price.

➤ Use rebates (money the car manufacturer offers you as an incentive to buy its cars) to make your down payment bigger. If you're offered a rebate on a new car, by all means take advantage of it. But don't buy a more expensive car just because you get a rebate. If you get a $1,000 rebate, add it to your down payment. You'll reduce your monthly payment and the total cost of your loan.

➤ Take the shortest loan term you can manage. Don't pay back a loan over five years if you can do it in three. Even though your monthly payment will be smaller on the five-year loan, you'll be paying interest for a longer time and will end up paying more in the long run.

➤ Pay off your loan early if you can. Some lenders let you pay off a loan early, but others will penalize you. Be sure to find out about that before you sign on for the loan. Don't take out a loan that won't permit you to pay it off early.

➤ The interest you pay on a car loan is not tax-deductible, but the interest on a home equity loan is. If you own a home and need to borrow money for a car, look into getting a home equity loan to use instead of a car loan.

Leasing

Leasing, the practice of paying a specified amount of money for a specified time for the use of a product, has been gaining in popularity over the past several years, and many people swear by it. It's a little tricky though because determining whether it's a better deal than buying is difficult. Basically, when you lease a car, you pay for the estimated depreciation that's occurring to the car while you're driving it. You pay only for the part of the car's value that you use plus interest.

When you begin a lease agreement, the dealer will estimate what the car's *residual value* will be at the end of your lease. If you have a closed-end agreement, you simply come to the end of your lease agreement and turn in your car.

If you have an open-end lease, you can buy the car for its residual value at the end of the lease. This might be the way to go as long as the street value of the car has remained above the residual value determined by the dealer. In that case, you'd buy the car for less than you could buy it on the street. If the dealer overestimated the car's residual value, however, and you bought it at the end of the lease, you'd be paying more for it than you could buy it somewhere else. See what we mean about leasing being a tricky business?

There are some good reasons to lease a car, but there are some good reasons not to, too. One major consideration is that you'll never pay less overall for leasing than you do for buying because you'll always be paying, but you'll never own the car. It's sort of like renting a car for an extended period of time.

Still, many people like leasing for one reason or another. For instance, my neighbors leased a Jeep Grand Cherokee for three years. These are middle-aged suburban folks, who don't need a four-wheel drive for everyday driving, but they didn't get the Jeep because they wanted to jump onto the SUV bandwagon, either.

Dollars and Sense

Don't put extra money toward a 9 percent car loan if you have an 18 percent credit card bill outstanding. The extra money will go a lot further if you use it to pay off the Visa bill.

Show Me the Money

Leasing is the practice of paying a specified amount of money over a specified time for the use of a product.

Show Me the Money

Residual value is what your car will be worth at the end of the lease. It's what it would cost to buy the car, used, at that time.

Pocket Change

One way to look at leasing is like long-term renting. You shouldn't expect to own anything when you're finished.

The Jeep was appealing to them because their daughter plays basketball for a college located about three hours from us. They go to nearly all of her games, most of which are played over the winter. Because interstate driving in snow and ice is not considered good sport by most people, including my neighbors, they leased the Jeep so they'd have a rugged, dependable vehicle to get to and from their daughter's games, regardless of the weather. In their case, leasing makes sense, because their daughter will graduate at the end of the three-year lease and they won't need the Jeep anymore.

To check out whether you're a likely candidate for leasing, circle an answer for each of these questions:

1. Would you like to trade in a car for a new one every few years?
   Yes No

2. Do you like to drive a new car?
   Yes No

3. Would you drive a more expensive car if you could afford to?
   Yes No

4. Do you drive 15,000 miles or less a year?
   Yes No

5. Do you need the money you'd be required to put up as a down payment on a car for another reason?
   Yes No

If you answered yes to most of those questions, you're probably a candidate for leasing. If you have mostly yes answers to the following questions, then you probably should buy your car:

1. When you get a car, do you intend to keep it for a long time?
   Yes No

2. Does the thought of paying every month on a car you'll never own really bug you?
   Yes No

3. Do you like the feeling of owning your car?
   Yes No

4. Do you drive more than 15,000 miles a year?
   Yes No

5. Do you have enough money to make a substantial down payment on a car?
   Yes No

You're probably getting the idea by now that leasing makes sense for some people, but not for everyone. Before you decide to lease, however, consider some of the pros and cons.

Pros

➤ Many leases don't require a down payment or at least not a very high down payment.

➤ You probably can lease a more expensive car than you'd be able to buy.

➤ When your lease ends, you don't have to worry about getting rid of your car. You simply give it back.

Cons

➤ The total cost of leasing is almost always more expensive than buying a car with cash and is usually more expensive than financing a car.

➤ When your lease ends, you're out of a car.

➤ Most lease agreements impose mileage limits. If you go over the number of miles allowed, you'll have to pay a penalty.

➤ Leasing doesn't cover insurance or maintenance, so you don't save costs.

➤ You might have to pay for the dealer's cost of auctioning your car when your lease expires. This cost is called *disposition charges*.

Show Me the Money

Disposition charges are just a fancy name for the dealer's cost of auctioning your car.

If, after considering the pros and cons, you decide to lease a car, there are some things that will be important to remember. The number one rule is to do your homework. There are as many lease deals as there are kinds of cars. If you're not familiar with what's available, how are you going to find the best deal?

In addition to the tips provided here, you can check out other information sources about leasing:

➤ **Intellichoice.** This site provides a wealth of information about leasing, buying, car values, and so on. You can find it on the Internet at www.intellichoice.com.

➤ **Lycos Community Guide: Leasing.** This site has lots of tips on leasing. You can find it on the Internet at www.spry.lycos.com.

➤ **Car Buying and Leasing Tips.** At www.bookspring.com on the Internet, you can find helpful advice for buying or leasing a car.

➤ **Insider Auto: Tips and Tricks.** This site has lots of good stuff on how to get the best value. You can find it on the Internet at http://members.aol.com/gsxelipse.

➤ **Your local bookstore.** There are a variety of books that will give you good tips on car buying and leasing.

When you feel that you're sufficiently prepared to negotiate a lease, go back and review all the information once more. Keep these tips in mind:

1. Always get a closed-end agreement. This type of agreement allows you to turn in your car and say adios. If you fall in love with your leased vehicle, you can negotiate for it, but you won't be obligated to buy it.

2. You're still responsible for repairs when you lease a car. Make sure you know in what condition you're expected to return the car. If your definition of "good repair" doesn't meet that of the dealer, you could be in for some penalties.

3. Negotiate the highest residual value on the vehicle that you can. If you decide to buy it, you can negotiate. If you don't buy it, you'll end up paying less for the part of the car's value that you've used.

4. Be up front with the dealer about how many miles you plan to put on the car each year. If you exceed the dealer's limit (usually around 15,000 miles a year), you'll be fined, big time. Some dealers charge 10 cents a mile for every mile over the limit that you drive. Ten cents a mile can add up fast! You'll pay more up front for additional mileage, but not as much as the penalty at the end.

5. If you drive 10,000 miles a year or less, ask whether there is a low-mileage discount available. Be persistent if the dealer is reluctant to give it to you.

6. Check out the manufacturer's warranty on the car. The *warranty*, a written guarantee for the condition and performance of the car that makes the manufacturer responsible for repairs of replacement, is a good guide as to how long your lease should be. You don't want to end up paying for costly repairs.

Show Me the Money

A **warranty** is a written guarantee for the condition and performance of the car. It makes the manufacturer responsible for the repair or replacement of defective parts.

Show Me the Money

Gap insurance can be included in your lease agreement. It pays the difference between the value your insurance will pay if your leased car is stolen or wrecked and the amount you owe when you terminate the lease.

7. Don't sign a lease for longer than you'll want the car. For instance, if there's a possibility you'll be transferred to Singapore for work in two years, don't sign a three-year lease. You'll be penalized for breaking the lease.

8. Find out what happens if you lease a lemon. Cars you buy are covered by lemon laws. Make sure there's a provision if you lease.

9. Make sure the lease has gap insurance. Ask to have it included in the agreement with no additional charge. *Gap insurance* pays the difference between the value your insurance will pay if your leased car is stolen or totaled and the amount you're obligated to pay to terminate the lease.

10. Don't let a dealer talk you into a lease agreement that's shorter than what you want. The dealer is anxious to get you back into the show room to look at another car. Some dealers will push for very short leases for that reason, and it could end up costing you more than necessary.

Lease agreements are notorious for being complicated pieces of confusing legalese, decipherable only by a Harvard Business School Ph.D. But if you know what to look out for, you can approach the whole process with a lot less aggravation.

The more you know about leasing and lease agreements going into the showroom, the less likely a salesperson will be to take advantage of you and give you something you don't need or want that will cost you money. Remember these definitions:

> **Capitalized cost** The price you pay for the car.
>
> **Finance charge** The interest you pay on the car.
>
> **Residual value** According to the dealer, the amount the car is worth when the lease is over.

Compare these numbers in every agreement you look at. Read up on leasing, be prepared with questions, and don't be intimidated into getting something you don't want. If you decide to lease, and you follow those guidelines, you'll do just fine.

New or Used, Big or Small?

Regardless of whether you decide to buy or lease a car, you need to consider the value of the car you're getting and what you can realistically afford to pay for a car. Sure, you might be able to borrow $25,000 to buy that Toyota Camry, complete with all the options, but why would you? If you want a new car, look at what's available.

Dollars and Sense

A smaller economy car will cost you less to operate than a bigger one because it will use a lot less gas during the time you have it.

Dollars and Sense

Besides saving you money on the purchase price, a used car will be cheaper because your insurance will cost less.

Pocket Change

The average car loses 65 to 70 percent of its value during its first five years. Some estimates say it loses between 20 percent and 30 percent during the very first year. It doesn't take long for a new car to become a used car!

Consider this. If you borrow $25,000 at 10% for a Camry and pay it back over four years, you'll pay about $634 a month. If you borrow $15,000 at 10% for a Honda Civic, you'll pay about $381 a month. That's a difference of $253 a month. If you put that $253 into an investment that averages an 8 percent annual interest every month for 35 years, guess how much money you'd have? More than half a million dollars! No kidding. You'd have $580,000.

Think about it this way. If someone came up to you when you were 25 years old and said, "Hey, if you drive a Civic instead of a Camry for 35 years, I'll give you half a million bucks when you're 60," what would you say?

To get a better idea of how much specific cars cost, check out Intellichoice (www.intellichoice.com), a Web site loaded with all kinds of car stuff. It lists best overall values for cars of various sizes, and its categories are divided into price ranges.

You're probably going to buy several cars before you hang up the keys for the last time. Money you save now and invest will buy you a lot more car and give you the means to buy other extras you might want later on.

And who says you need a new car? Yeah, you're taking a chance if you buy a used car out of some guy's front yard, but many reputable car dealerships offer a good selection of used cars, complete with warranties. These cars can be had for a fraction of what they'd cost new, and if you take good care of yours, it should give you years of service.

If you buy a used car for half of what a new one costs, you can afford to pay a greater percentage of the cost up front and have to borrow less. Your monthly payments will be less, giving you more money for other things. If for some reason you think you must have a new car instead of one that's been used, consider that the minute you drive the new car off the lot, it's lost a percentage of its value. It's already a used car, and you haven't even gotten it home yet!

Your Car Costs You More Than You Think

The initial purchase of a car is a big expense. Adding insult to injury, the car keeps on costing you money once you have it! Cars are expensive, there's no getting around it.

Maintenance

Your car is finally working just the way you think it should. It's great. It's giving you a smooth, quiet ride, and everything appears to be in good running condition. You're set.

But no sooner are you cruising comfortably down the open road when you start hearing a little ping from somewhere under the hood. Soon it's turned into a major clanking noise, and you know you'd better pull over. "Hello, AAA? It's me again."

Some car repairs are unavoidable. But you can ensure that your car will be at its best by keeping up with routine maintenance. Change the oil, or have it changed, regularly. Remember to check little things such as the fluid levels and air pressure in your tires. Have your alignment checked as soon as you notice it seems a bit out of balance; bad alignment can ruin your tires. Common sense will go a long way in keeping major repair bills to a minimum. It's a lot more cost-effective to pay $20 for an oil change than it is to replace a burned-out engine.

Money Pit

Don't feel compelled to have your car maintained by the dealer from whom you bought it. It might be more expensive than having it done by an independent mechanic. Ask some people who have the same kind of car where they go for maintenance. A good mechanic whom you can trust might not be the easiest thing to find, but it's worth it to spend some time locating one.

Insurance

Auto insurance is expensive, but you can't afford to be without it (in fact, in many states, it's illegal to be without it). We discuss insurance in much more detail in Chapter 15, so you'll learn then what you need to have and what to look for when you go to buy it. You can save money on your auto insurance by keeping up a good driving record, buying a car that will hold up well in an accident, and *not* buying the latest hot car.

The Total Cost

There are other costs associated with owning a car, as well. Parking fees, tolls, fuel, and routine expenses such as washing the vehicle add up over the life of the car. It's estimated that the total annual cost of owning a vehicle, including the price of the car over the period of time you own it (known as capitalized cost), the *finance charges*, insurance, maintenance, gas, oil, inspections costs, and licensing costs, is more than $6,000 a year. And that estimate doesn't include the *capitalized cost*, the actual cost of buying the car!

Show Me the Money

Finance charges refer to the amount of interest you pay on your car loan. The **capitalized cost** is the actual amount you pay for the car.

Carpooling can cut your costs significantly, saving you money on tolls, gas, and parking. Estimates show that in medium-large cities, carpoolers can save about $1,500 a year. That's a good start to a down payment on your next car! If you have to pay regular tolls, say for a bridge crossing, look into the possibility of buying a booklet of tickets at a reduced rate.

Studies have shown that premium-grade gasolines probably aren't worth the extra money they cost you at the pump. Unless it's mentioned in the owner's manual, you do not need a higher grade, regular unleaded gas should suffice. AND NOTE, with the new electronic devices engines possess, you might be hurting your engine by using an incorrect octane.

Cars cost a lot of money. In many cases, it costs more to buy a car today than it did to buy a house 30 years ago. Maybe Gen Xers will be the ones to stop the my-car-is-an-extension-of-who-I-am mentality and get society grounded when it comes to vehicles. Until then, do your homework and know what to look for when getting a car, regardless of whether you buy or lease and whether you get a new or used vehicle.

The Least You Need to Know

➤ Americans have traditionally loved their automobiles, but recent statistics indicate that the love affair might be cooling off.

➤ For many people, a car is not essential; other modes of transportation can get you where you want to go.

➤ There are advantages and disadvantages to both buying and leasing vehicles. Be sure to do your homework before doing either one.

➤ Buying a less expensive car can yield huge savings for your future.

➤ Buying the car is the first expense, but car expenses don't end there. It costs thousands of dollars a year to operate a vehicle.

Part 2

On Your Own and Loving It

So things are looking up, are they? You have a job that you like (most days), a car that runs, and a place to live with some pretty good friends. Sure, there are some rough spots along the way. Your salary's not what you think it should be, and the car's not exactly a BMW. Your apartment is sort of drafty, and things get a little testy sometimes between a couple of the roommates.

You're trying to stick to your new budget, but it's such a drag! Even though you know you should have saved that extra $20 last week, the thought of a night out with your pals was too hard to resist. As long as you're confessing, there's that little balance you've been carrying over from month to month on your credit card, too.

All in all, though, life is pretty good. This is a time when you're establishing habits that will affect your personal finances for the rest of your life. This section gives you lots of ideas and suggestions for getting into good habits, which, hopefully, you'll carry with you.

Chapter 7

What Do You Have?

In This Chapter

➤ Dealing with a salary that's lower than you'd like

➤ Remembering other benefits of working

➤ Understanding your net worth

➤ Looking past the obvious for financial assets

You're on your own and loving it. Your apartment is great, and you've even found some furniture for it. Okay, so the couch from Mom and Dad's basement wasn't exactly what you had in mind, but it will do for now. Your car is running, even if it's not that Volkswagen Jetta you have your eye on. You've got a credit card or two, a job, and a bunch of friends to hang out with. Life is good.

Let's talk a little more about your job. Maybe you've been incredibly lucky and landed a job that gives you personal satisfaction, great benefits, and $40,000 a year. If so, congratulations! You should know, though, that you're definitely in the minority.

Most starting jobs don't pay $40,000. Some don't even pay half that much. But these aren't jobs that you'll keep until you're 60 or 65. You'll be moving up, leaving your first and second and third jobs to someone else. In the mean time, you've got a job that, handled properly, will lead you to another job. You're meeting people, making contacts, and gaining experience. You're getting benefits, such as health insurance, life insurance, and paid vacations.

Starting out on your own is an exciting time, but it is generally not the easiest time financially. In this chapter, we're going to take a look at what you have, which may be more than you realize. We'll talk about your income, which, incidentally, includes more than your salary. We'll also talk about other, less tangible assets you have in connection with your job.

That's My Salary? You've Gotta Be Kidding!

There are conflicting reports out there concerning Gen Xers and jobs. On one hand, we're told that our shift as a society to a service-based economy is forcing young people (even some with college degrees) to take low-paying jobs just to have an income. On the other hand, we're told that young people have more opportunity than ever for high-paying jobs in fields such as engineering, computers, and health care.

On one hand, we're still fearing corporate downsizing, which rode roughshod through American workplaces earlier in this decade. On the other hand, we're hearing that employers are desperate for workers, and now is the time for employees to negotiate for better salaries and job conditions.

One thing we do know is that although Generation Xers have been portrayed by the media as a group of lazy, whining 20-somethings, a closer look reveals something very different. Studies show that nearly 80 percent of Gen Xers are employed full time, and another 15 percent work part time or are full-time students. Only 5 percent are unemployed.

Overall, you're not doing too bad in the salary department, either. The average yearly salary for 25-to-34 year olds who have college degrees and full-time jobs is $34,000. Of course, there are many workers without college degrees who are making significantly less money. The median income (half make more, half less) for Gen Xers is about $23,000, according to a *USA Today*/Gallup Poll.

Pocket Change

Talk about a Gen X success story! Jerry Yang and David Filo started the Yahoo! Internet site in 1994 when they were engineering graduate students at Stanford University. In just four years, Yahoo! has made Jerry and David worth a billion dollars.

Although $23,000 sounds like a lot of money—and it is—we all know that money goes fast, and there are an awful lot of things to spend it on. Hardly anyone who works thinks that they make enough money. It's no surprise that the most frequent complaints about jobs are not about bosses (although those probably run a close second), but salaries.

If you have a job you like, but not the salary you'd like, there are several things you can do:

➤ You can (gulp) ask for a raise.

➤ You can look for a higher-paying job.

➤ You can stay in the job you have and hope you'll advance.

Of these choices, the first two are definitely more proactive and require more courage than sticking it out and seeing what happens. It takes a fair amount of guts to march (or tiptoe) into your boss's office to ask for a raise. And it takes a lot of energy to start a job hunt, especially if it hasn't been too long since you've been through one. If there's an indication that there's room for advancement in your current job, the best thing to do might be to hang out, do your very best, and see what happens. But if your salary is so low that you can't get by or you're forced to live paycheck to paycheck without being able to save a cent, you might have to take some action.

Asking for a Raise

Gen Xers have grown up with downsizing. You've seen your parents, aunts, uncles, and friends lose jobs at companies where they'd worked for years. Employers were more likely to be handing out pink slips than pay raises. As a generation, you've learned (and rightly so) a general distrust of companies and employers. No job was guaranteed, and being employed one day didn't mean you'd be employed the next. The tide, however, seems to be turning.

There are fewer entry-level workers now than in any time during recent history. Fewer people mean fewer workers, and employers are starting to sweat. If you're in a field that's starting to feel the pinch, and you're a good worker, you very well might be able to squeeze a little more money out of your boss. Some companies are starting to hand out raises, even to people who don't ask for them.

If your plan is to ask for a raise, make sure you're in a position to do so. Obviously, if you've only been working for the company you're with for a few weeks or months, you won't endear yourself to anyone by asking for more money. Be honest with yourself. Have you been doing a good job? Have you been willing to do more than you have to or asked for additional assignments? If you've recently been disciplined for being late or any other infraction, now's not the time to ask for a raise.

Pocket Change

Figures released by the National Census Bureau say that the number of people between the ages of 20 and 29 will be about 34 million in 2000. That compares to 41 million in 1980. No wonder employers are getting nervous!

Another thing to consider is your market value. Never go to your boss and complain that the guy in the next cubicle is making more than you are for doing the same job. Bosses hate knowing that employees talk about their salaries, and opening that kind of conversation definitely will not put you in her good graces. Instead, if you know you're underpaid, point out what other people doing your job on the open market are making.

Trade publications and some professional associations do regular salary surveys and can be good sources of information. Or scan the Sunday classified ads for jobs similar to yours and their salaries. You also can check out JobSmart, a Web site with links to 150 salary surveys. Access it on the Internet at www.jobsmart.org.

Once you determine you're in a position to ask for a raise, go for it. But be prepared:

➤ Talk to your boss with confidence. Remember that she probably doesn't like to talk about money any more than you do.

➤ Emphasize the extra things you've done and what you've accomplished in your job.

➤ Point out that your salary is less than what people doing similar jobs for other companies are making.

➤ Be polite and respectful, even if your boss says no.

If you're in a position to do so (for example, if you've been approached by another company about taking a job), you could tell your boss you'll have to quit if you can't get a raise. Be careful, though. You might get a big raise. Or your boss might call your bluff and tell you to not let the door hit you on the way out.

Looking for Another Job

If you're really unhappy with your salary and you know there's no chance for a raise anytime soon, you might be tempted to go out and look for another job. But what kind of job should you look for? If you're a good worker, and you have the right kind of degree or certification, you probably won't have too much trouble finding a good job with a competitive salary.

Surveys showed that many 1998 engineering and computer science majors were looking at job offers with starting salaries as high as $50,000. There has been a sharp decrease in the number of these majors, and the result is a great demand for students trained in technology.

Pocket Change

Liberal arts majors who graduated from college in 1998 were looking at an average starting salary of $28,875, according to the National Association of Colleges and Employers.

But if you're not an engineering or computer science grad, don't despair. A survey conducted by the National Association of Colleges and Employers (NACE) showed that liberal arts majors are enjoying a trickle-down effect of the technology boom. "Liberal arts majors are attractive to employers because they come prepared with communication skills and the ability to learn technical skills," said Camille Luckenbaugh, director of employment information at NACE.

As the employee pool dwindles, employers are less likely to insist on a particular degree for a particular job. They'll be more likely to look for someone who is smart, versatile, willing to work, and able to work independently. This gives you a lot more flexibility if you decide to job hunt. Don't feel that you're stuck in a particular field just because that's what your degree or certification is in. You may be able to go from one career to another that interests you without much problem. In fact, it's estimated that the average worker will have about 11 jobs and three careers over his or her working life.

Although there are other factors besides growth potential to consider when you think about a job you'd like to have, it's an important consideration. It makes no sense to get into a career that won't be around much longer. The U.S. Bureau of Labor and Statistics has identified six job areas as those that will be the fastest growing into the 21st century.

1. **Health care.** There will be 76 million, 50-something baby boomers in this country as we enter the next century. This large aging population will lead to great increases in demand for health care and related industries.

2. **Robotics.** Robots might still seem futuristic, but those who know about such things predict we'll use far more of them as we enter the next century, and they'll be much more sophisticated than the ones in use today. Robotics engineers, installers, technicians, and repair people will be in demand.

3. **Computer graphics.** Jobs in computer-aided design and computer-aided imagery will greatly increase as we approach the year 2000. Industries from manufacturing to fashion to video are using computer graphics.

4. **Information technology.** Fiber optics, the Internet, telecommunications, and other fast-growing areas will mean a far-reaching expansion of opportunities in this field.

5. **Biotechnology.** This brave new world will offer opportunities for people with backgrounds in biology, chemistry, and engineering.

6. **Lasers.** With lasers being increasingly used in areas such as communications, health care, and manufacturing, workers with knowledge about them and their use will be in demand.

The following jobs were cited by the Bureau of Labor Statistics as those that will add the most openings by 2006:

➤ Chefs, cooks, kitchen help

➤ Home health-care aides

➤ Cashiers

➤ Food and beverage service workers

➤ Systems analysts

➤ Computer scientists

➤ General managers and top executives

➤ Truck drivers

➤ Registered nurses

➤ Retail salespeople

➤ Teacher aides

➤ Nursing, psychiatric aides

Not all of these jobs are high paying, but indications are that they'll be available. If you're thinking about changing jobs, these may be some to consider. Of course, make sure you look for something in which you're interested and, preferably, passionate about. Although Gen Xers want to make a lot of money, they've also cited personal satisfaction as an important goal.

Dollars and Sense

There is a shortage of mid-level lawyers these days, studies show. One legal recruiting firm was looking for corporate lawyers to fill 140 spots in New York City. Imagine, not enough lawyers! Might be a career opportunity to investigate!

Although we once looked to big corporations for good jobs and job security, predictions are that small businesses, which can act quickly to implement new ideas and technology, will become increasingly important as employers. And guess who is starting up many of these small businesses that are going to be so important. Right! Gen Xers see owning their own business as a sign of success, and many are making the dream a reality. A recent report by IBM showed that one of five small businesses today is owned by someone under 35 years old. So don't neglect the small businesses when conducting your job search. Who knows? You may get inspired to create your own business.

If you're thinking about changing jobs, consider using the Internet to help. It's becoming increasingly important as a tool for job hunting. If you're ready to hop online, try some of these sites:

➤ The Online Career Center is a nonprofit consortium of major U.S. corporations. Access the site at http://www.occ.com.

➤ The CareerPath.com site contains the classified ads of several major newspapers. Access it at http://www.careerpath.com.

➤ The Monster Board site contains job opportunities and many other career-related subjects. Access it at http://www.monster.com.

➤ E-Span is a source of job ads and extensive employment-related editorial content. You can access this site at http://espan2.espan.com.

➤ The Career Mosaic site is loaded with ads, company profiles, and advice on writing resumes and other topics. Access it at http://www.careermosaic.com.

If you can't reconcile your salary problem, looking for another job just might be the answer. It looks like it definitely will be an employee's market during the next few years. Job hunting might never be this much fun again.

Sticking It Out

If you can't get a raise in your current job, and you're not inclined to go looking for a new one, your only choice is to stick it out, and there are several reasons why you might choose to do that.

Maybe you have a job you love that just doesn't happen to pay very much. Certain professions, social work and child care, for instance, are notoriously low-paying. Nobody going into these fields expects to get rich, but, thankfully, there are dedicated people willing to do these kinds of very important, but underpaid, jobs. If you have a low-paying job that you love, you'll have to decide whether to stay where you are. If you decide to keep it, you'll have to adjust your standard of living to mesh with your earnings.

If, on the other hand, you're staying in a low-paying job because you're too scared or unmotivated to go after a better one, you're dealing with a different issue. Reread the previous section about the job market, and give it a shot. You've got nothing to lose but a low-paying job.

Money Pit

It's easy to overspend when you're around people who have more money than you do. Resist spending more than you should in order to keep up, and leave your credit card at home when you're out with your friends.

There's More to a Job Than the Money

Regardless of how much your salary is, there's more to a job than the money you make. Jobs hold many opportunities, which savvy employees will learn to recognize and take advantage of. Did you ever wonder why some people seem to get ahead at work so much more easily than others? It might be that they're smarter or better workers, but often it's just that they're better at taking advantage of opportunities. Make the most of your job, even if it's a low-paying, entry-level position.

Contacts

Any job you have gives you opportunities to make contacts that can help you advance within the company or get a better job somewhere else. Think of all the people you meet because of your job. Unless you're stuck in a room by yourself all day, forbidden to emerge or to talk to anyone, you probably have many chances to meet people at your own level and people at levels above yours.

The trick is to take advantage of the opportunities. If you're in the elevator, for instance, and the company president gets in on the eighth floor, heading for the first, you have eight floors' worth of time to meet this guy and to make an impression. Don't just stand there staring at the buttons—do something! Extend your hand and introduce yourself. Tell him what department you're in and what your primary duties are. Don't hesitate to do a little self-promotion, either. If you recently were named employee of the week for your department, be sure to mention it.

Contacts can be anyone from the company president to the custodian, and they don't have to be strictly business. If you happen to meet someone along the way who manages that exclusive apartment complex you'd love to live in, by all means go ahead and tell her you're interested. Who knows? There might just be an unexpected opening.

Experience

Getting into the job market can be a frustrating experience. You're told you can't have a job until you have experience, but you can't get experience without having a job. When you've got a job, no matter how underpaid you might think you are, think of it as a source of experience that will help you greatly when you go to get your next job. Take advantage of all the experiences you can. Volunteer to take on extra projects, and let your boss know you're interested in doing what it takes to move up. When you go to get your next job, a prospective employer will be more impressed by someone with a wide range of experiences than someone who's done only what needs to be done to get by.

Benefits

Things such as health insurance, pension or 401(k) plans, or a company car aren't called benefits for nothing. Even if you think your salary stinks, take a minute and think about the extras you're getting. Do you have two weeks' vacation and five paid sick days a year? Maybe you have a couple of personal days on top of that. Do your medical benefits include dental coverage? Does your employer match part of what you contribute to a 401(k) plan? All those things have monetary value and should be considered as part of your total compensation for your work.

Some companies pay a supplement of up to 40 percent of an employee's salary. If an employee was earning $30,000, for example, the company would be paying $42,000 in salary and benefits for that employee. The average company pays a 25 percent supplement for benefits.

Even if your company doesn't have the greatest benefit package in the world, and you have to pay for part of your health insurance, you're probably getting it for a lot less than what it would cost to buy your own. If you've got great benefits that include eye care, dental care, a gas allowance, expense accounts, tuition reimbursement, a 401(k), and the like, your total compensation is much more than what your salary indicates.

Many big corporations and small companies are cutting back on benefits, but some are going the other way and increasing benefits and perks in order to attract the best and brightest of the shrinking pool of employees. Timberland Group, a Michigan-based insurance company, recently built a new office building complete with a gym and driving range for employees. A California company that develops computer games not only allows its employees to bring their dogs to work, but supplies pet treats. A software developing firm in California gives its employees laptops and tells them to work wherever they like. Granted, these perks are out of the ordinary, but they're out there.

Dollars and Sense

If you had to buy your own health insurance, it would cost you somewhere around $65 a month, assuming you're healthy and have no dependents. If you need to buy your own health insurance, be sure you shop around; rates differ greatly. You could pay more than double that $65 if you get the wrong policy!

So before you declare your job totally hopeless, think about the benefits you get. You might conclude that it's not as bad as you thought.

Assessing Your Assets

If you've got a job, you're probably bringing home a paycheck. Very few people show up at the office every morning just because they love to be there. The paycheck at the end of the week (or every two weeks) might not be the only thing you like about your job, but it's pretty high on the list, right?

Even if your salary isn't as much as you'd like it to be, it's probably still your primary source of income. When you begin to consider your *net worth*, or financial situation, your salary is very important. For most of us, salary pays the bills, boosts savings accounts, and sets up emergency funds.

Show Me the Money

Your **net worth** is what you get when you add up all your financial assets and then subtract all your financial liabilities.

When you examine your financial situation, however, you might be pleasantly surprised to find out you have more than you realize. There could be money you've overlooked. To determine your *net worth*, you have to know exactly what you have and exactly what your expenses are. After you've thought carefully about all your sources of income, and any money you might have in the form of savings, bonds, mutual funds, or whatever, take a minute to fill out this net worth worksheet. It should help you to get a better understanding of exactly what you have, and what you're worth. Who knows, you might be pleasantly surprised!

NET WORTH WORKSHEET

ASSETS

Bonds	$	
Cash accounts	$	
Certificates of deposit	$	
Limited partnerships	$	
Mutual funds	$	
Savings bonds	$	
Stocks	$	
Tax refunds	$	
Treasury bills	$	
Cash value life insurance	$	
	Subtotal	$

Personal Property

Businesses	$	
Cars	$	
Personal property	$	
	Subtotal	$

Real estate

Mortgages owned	$	
Residence	$	
Income property	$	
Vacation home	$	
	Subtotal	$

Retirement

Annuities	$	
IRAs	$	
Keogh accounts	$	
Pensions	$	
	Subtotal	$
	TOTAL	$

LIABILITIES

Current Liabilities

Alimony	$	
Child support	$	
Personal loans	$	
	Subtotal	$

Installment Liabilities

Bank loans	$	
Car loans	$	
College loans	$	
Credit-card bills	$	
Furniture loans	$	
Home improvement	$	
Life insurance loans	$	
Pension plan loans	$	
	Subtotal	$

Real estate liabilities

Residence (include second mortgage/ line of credit)	$	
Income property	$	
Vacation home	$	
	Subtotal	$

Taxes

Capital gains tax	$	
Income tax	$	
Property tax	$	
	Subtotal	$

Other liabilities

_____

_____

_____

TOTAL ASSETS	$
TOTAL LIABILITIES	-$
TOTAL NET WORTH	$

Think carefully about what you might have. Are there any savings accounts that were set up for you when you were a kid? What about savings bonds? Some families are great at buying U.S. savings bonds for birthdays. Have you put aside money someplace for emergencies? Do you have money saved for a car or a house?

The interest you earn on a savings account counts as income (and is taxed as income), although you probably don't regard it as such. If you have any bonds, the interest on them also counts as income. Your income tax refund, bonuses, and any monetary gifts you receive also count as assets and must be counted when considering what you have. If you have a *cash value life insurance* policy, the amount of cash value is counted toward your net worth. Generally, though, when we talk about income, we're primarily talking about your salary.

Show Me the Money

Cash value life insurance is a type of insurance policy, purchased for the long term, that sets aside funds within the policy for future payment of premium. The accumulated funds can be borrowed by the policy-holder and thus, counted as an asset for net worth purposes.

Your Secret Stash

Most people start working pretty much from the ground up when it comes to accruing money. When you first start on your own, it usually isn't very hard to figure out what you have. Sometimes, though, you might overlook money you've accumulated or that other people have accumulated for you. Hardly anybody has a long-lost rich uncle who dies and leaves behind a fortune, but many people do have well-meaning relatives who try to help them along by setting up bank accounts or buying bonds in their name.

Accounts

Be aware of any savings accounts that might have been set up for you when you were a kid. There are many cases of relatives establishing accounts in a child's name and depositing a small (or in rare cases, a large) amount of money. Sometimes, for one reason or another, the account remains open, but overlooked or forgotten. A lot of money in banks is unaccounted for. So ask your parents if there might be any bank accounts in your name that you wouldn't know about. It seems too much to hope for, but you never know.

Mutual Funds

If you have any *mutual funds*, these should be included when figuring out your net worth. There are many kinds of mutual funds, including money market funds, stock funds, bond funds, hybrid funds, U.S. funds, global funds, international funds, index funds, and specialty funds.

Don't be confused by all the names—you may not even know what type of mutual fund you have. But if you get statements from a company such as the Vanguard Group, Charles Schwab & Company, Jack White & Company, or Fidelity Investments, you have mutual funds to consider when figuring out what you have.

Stocks (Equities)

Some families give gift shares of stock to children to introduce them to the stock market, get them started in a financial venture, or just for fun. Disney stock is hugely popular for gifts because the certificates carry the images of Mickey, Minnie, Goofy, and other favorite characters. When you're figuring out your net worth, be sure to include any shares of stock you might have acquired along the way.

Show Me the Money

Mutual funds allow you to pool your money with that of a large group of investors. Professionals invest the pool of money in stocks, bonds, and other securities, and you own shares that represent the investments. We'll go more in depth about mutual funds in Chapter 13.

Bonds

Bonds are often given as contest prizes, birthday presents, or as part of scholarship packages in schools. There are many kinds of bonds, including savings, municipal, treasury, GNMA, or corporate bonds. If you know of any bonds you have, or think you might have, track them down and include them in the "what you have" category of your personal finances.

Emergency Money

Everyone should have some emergency money set aside. Unfortunately, an emergency fund is not high on the priority list for many people who are trying to pay the bills and maybe save for a house or car.

If you do have an emergency fund, include it when tallying up your assets, but don't touch it unless absolutely necessary. In addition to, or perhaps instead of, an emergency fund, you might have some money saved somewhere toward a new car or a house. That money should be included when you add up your assets.

Dollars and Sense

Financial experts recommend keeping an emergency fund of three to six months salary. The money would be used if you lose your job, or get sick and can't work, or face other emergency circumstances.

Basically, what you need to do is consider any sources of income, and all other financial assets. When you've added them all up, you've determined what you have. In the next chapter, we'll look at what you owe, also called your financial liabilities. Only when you've fully explored what you have and what you owe, can you determine your net worth.

The Least You Need to Know

➤ Nearly everyone thinks they should be paid more for their job than they are.

➤ If you're dissatisfied with your salary, you need to decide what you're going to do about it.

➤ If your salary isn't what you'd like, it helps to remember your job is giving you experience, contacts, and benefits.

➤ Your net worth is all your financial assets, less all your financial liabilities.

➤ When you think carefully, you might discover overlooked financial assets.

What Do You Need?

Now that you've got a better understanding of what you have in terms of your personal finances, it's time to take a look at what you need. If you're the kind of person who must have every cool thing you see advertised or buy everything that your best friend buys, this chapter may make you decidedly uncomfortable. Why? Because we're going to tell you that you don't need to buy the $500 digital camera. And unless you're going to use it as a substitute for a car, you don't need the $700 mountain bike, either.

This chapter is about recognizing and separating what you want from what you need, and it might not be what you want to read. You should, however, keep reading, because recognizing the difference between what you want and need and learning to postpone immediate gratification are two of the best things you can do for your financial health.

Your Financial Lifestyle

Take a few minutes and think about your financial lifestyle. This lifestyle has nothing to do with whether you're single or married, gay or straight, or into the bar scene or the church scene. Your financial lifestyle is everything you do that affects your pocketbook.

To help you get started, we've prepared a simple quiz. Answer these questions honestly by circling Yes or No, and you'll better be able to evaluate your financial lifestyle:

1. Do you go out to dinner often?
    Yes No

2. Do you spend a significant amount of money, maybe 10% or more of your income, on movies, at happy hours, dinners at restaurants, or other leisure activities?
    Yes No

3. Do you love to shop for new clothes, even when you don't need them?
    Yes No

4. Do you wear only certain name brands, such as J. Crew or Polo?
    Yes No

5. Are you intrigued by all the latest electronic stuff, and do you own more of it than you need?
    Yes No

6. Do you look at cars as status symbols, making the kind of car you drive very important to you?
    Yes No

7. Are your vacations usually trips to trendy, "in" spots?
    Yes No

8. Do you have a closet full of gear you've bought for various activities such as skiing, hiking, rock climbing, or biking?
    Yes No

9. Do you regularly buy new CDs, videos, or computer software?
    Yes No

10. Do you spend a lot of money in a short time and then are you unable to recall what you bought once the money is gone?
    Yes No

Here's what your answers mean:

➤ If you answered yes to seven or more questions, you've got a financial lifestyle that will land you in the poorhouse when you're 65. Don't worry, though. You can change it.

➤ If you answered yes to between four and seven questions, your financial lifestyle is on shaky ground, but it's fixable.

➤ If you answered yes to three or fewer questions, you can just skim the rest of this chapter. Your financial lifestyle is in good shape.

If your financial lifestyle needs some work, don't worry. That's what we're here to do. Let's first take a look at why you might have adopted your particular financial lifestyle. Then, we'll look at some ways to change it, if it needs changing.

Pocket Change

Gen Xers buy 46 percent of all audio equipment sold and 48 percent of all athletic shoes. Marketers know this, and they target your age group with advertising for these products to get you to spend even more of your money to buy them.

Evaluating Your Expectations

If this is starting to read like a self-help book for breaking bad habits and changing the way you live, stay with us. We're about to get to the financial point. If you have an unhealthy financial lifestyle, it's important to realize what causes it. Although there are exceptions, the most likely reason your financial lifestyle is not where it should be is because you have unrealistic expectations.

If you expect that your first apartment is going to look like one of those amazing *Real World* pads in New York or Miami, you've got unrealistic expectations (unless you've got a rich uncle or somebody else who's just looking for ways to spend his money on you). If you expect that your first car is going to be a new BMW, again, your expectations are unrealistic.

It's time to evaluate your expectations and, if they're too high, to adjust them to what is realistic. That's not to say you shouldn't set lofty goals for the future. Maybe it's realistic to expect that in seven years you'll be driving a new BMW, and in 20 years, you'll be living in a 15-room house in Malibu. For now, though, a used Chevy and a two-room walk-up with a tub in the kitchen might just have to be your reality.

Why, as a society, do we have such high expectations of what we should have? That's a no-brainer. From the time we're kids watching cartoons in the living room on Saturday mornings, we're sent a clear message that we need

Money Pit

Advertising has taken on a new dimension now that companies use the Internet to showcase their products. Sexy Web sites that serve as advertising forums can be hard to resist, especially because manufacturers make it so easy to order their products right away. Beware of this high-tech advertising. It's mighty tempting stuff.

stuff, lots and lots of stuff. If you believe that you should have everything you want and have it now, you've fallen right into the trap that advertisers have set for you. They have you exactly where they want you.

At first it's just the small stuff: toys, cereal, and cookies that you're told you gotta have. It all looked cool, and it was kind of fun to watch the ads and then put the pressure on Mom when you were in the grocery store to see whether she'd buy the Lucky Charms instead of boring old Corn Flakes.

When you got a little older, comic books gave you a whole new reason to spend your paper route money. Sea Monkeys ran rampant, and gag gifts were the rage. At night, you tuned into *Happy Days* and saw ads for Coke, Pepsi, and Calvin Klein jeans. It probably took a little more pressure to get Mom to buy you this stuff, but eventually, she usually gave in.

Pocket Change

Psychologists tell us there are all kinds of reasons we spend money. Some people spend to boost their self-esteem, to make other people like them, or to make up for what they perceive as deprived child-hoods.

By the time you're old enough to start looking at cars, cameras, and computers, Mom isn't footing the bill. Still, you think you should get exactly what you want because you always have. The ads are still pretty convincing, even though you're not a kid anymore. So you figure if Mom won't buy you the new Compaq, you'll get it yourself. Next thing you know, you've got a great computer, but you've run up a $3,000 credit card bill because you expected to get that computer as soon as you decided you needed (read *wanted*) it.

The advertising industry is pretty successful in doing what it's supposed to do: sell. But you're smart. You know that just because Nike has cool ads, you don't have to buy their $139 shoes. You don't need them. There's nothing wrong with lowering our expectations for material things.

As a society, we've gotten so bogged down with stuff that we don't know what to do with it. Drive around sometime on a Saturday morning and look at all the stuff for sale on people's lawns or in their garages. Flea markets are a big business, as people try to unload some of the junk they have stashed away. If you've ever helped someone move or cleaned out a house after someone died, you probably have a good appreciation for the excess stuff that most of us have.

Looking at What You Need and What You Don't

Most of us have too much stuff, but there are certain things that we all need: a place to live, food to eat, clothes, and shoes to wear. Many of us need cars to get where we need to be. Some of us need things such as medicine on a regular basis, glasses, or contacts. We need a telephone, a heater, and a fan. Some things are necessary; there's just no getting around it.

Nobody is going to argue that you shouldn't buy the things you need. It makes no sense to put money in the bank that you should have used to buy yourself a pair of glasses. Our argument is with thinking, as so many of us do, that you need everything you see or everything that someone else has and buying it. All that does is make you have too much stuff and jeopardizes your financial future.

The Bare Necessities

These can't-avoid-them expenditures are guaranteed to take your money:

Dollars and Sense

When you find yourself wanting something, and the credit card is in your hand, do yourself a favor. Put the card away, go home, and sleep on it. Think about what you're going to buy and how it will affect your more long-term dreams and expectations. The mountain bike might not seem so important in the morning.

➤ **Taxes.** Federal taxes, state taxes, local taxes, social security contributions, occupational privilege, and the like are a necessary, although unsavory, expenditure. Nobody likes them, but we've all got to pay them. To decide not to would be a really bad move, to say the least.

➤ **Shelter.** You have to live somewhere, and unless you find somebody who will let you live with them for free (hello Mom and Dad!), you'll have to pay for it. If you own instead of rent, you'll have to pay property taxes and the costs of keeping the home in good repair, in addition to your mortgage.

➤ **Utilities.** Gas, electricity, oil, water, trash pickup, and phone all are costs associated with renting or owning a home or apartment. You can control them by monitoring and cutting back, but you can't escape them.

➤ **Food.** You can stop eating, but only for a little while. Even Mom and Dad will get tired of you showing up for dinner every night. There are lots of ways to save on food costs, such as cooking for yourself instead of buying prepared foods or going out to eat. All in all, though, food is another controllable, but necessary, expenditure.

➤ **Transportation.** Maybe you don't need a car, but everybody needs to get from place to place. If you don't own a car, you'll still have to pay for public transportation or chip in for your carpool. If you do own a car, you'll rack up costs for gas, insurance, and maintenance as well as for the vehicle itself.

➤ **Debt.** If you owe, you have to pay. College loans, car payments, and credit card payments can eat a big hole in your paycheck. Much of that debt can be eliminated by not buying so much on credit. But once you buy, you'll owe, and you have to pay it back. It's smart to get high-interest debt (credit card debt) paid off as quickly as you can. If you owe $3,500 on a credit card at 18% interest when you're 30, and you pay the minimum amount due each month, you'll finally pay off the credit card when you're 70. You also will have paid $9,431 in interest, which is almost three times the amount of the original bill.

➤ **Health care.** Insurance payments or copayments, medicine, doctor visits, dental care, vision care, and other medical costs are necessities. Hopefully, at this stage of your life, your health care costs are minimal. But if a filling falls out of your tooth, you've got to get it fixed. First, it's not healthy not to, and second, it will cost you more in the long run if you let it go.

➤ **Education.** If you're finished with college or vocational school, your educational costs will be low, excluding repayment of any educational loans you have. If you're working on an advanced degree, you've still got big bills, unless your employer pays. Don't forget about the self-education that should continue throughout your life. Every time you buy a book like this one, you're investing in your education.

➤ **Clothing.** This is a big area for potential overspending, but you do need clothes. Fortunately, many businesses are getting increasingly casual, eliminating the need for expensive business clothing. Still, it's nice to look good, and all clothing is pretty expensive.

➤ **Insurance.** Insurance is another of those expenditures you wish you could do without, but probably can't. If you have a house or drive a car, you have to have insurance. And it's not cheap.

That pretty well covers the basic necessities that will cost you money, except for one: regular contributions to a savings account, retirement fund, or other vehicle to assure your future financial health. This is the most overlooked, neglected financial necessity there is and a huge source of regret among people who didn't do it.

The temptation to skip this last necessity is great. You think you're doing just fine. You're paying your bills and paying back some of the money you owe for college loans and credit cards. But what about the future? What about the house you want to buy someday? How about expenses you'll have if and when you get around to having kids? What about the master's degree you're thinking about?

If you can foresee expenses down the road, money to pay for them should be included in your "what you need" category. They won't pay for themselves, and the sooner you can put some money away for specific goals in the future, the better off you'll be.

It's hard to defer buying now in order to save for a future goal. It defies our society's mindset of getting what we want when we want it. But if you pass on the leather jacket and invest the $250, you're on your way to sending a child to college someday or getting out of the apartment and into your own house.

Far-sightedness is a quality that must be developed—most people aren't blessed with it at a young age. Once you acquire it, though, it will serve you well. A big regret of today's retired population is that they didn't start putting away earlier for retirement. "It's just silly that I didn't start saving earlier, but I never really felt like I had the money to do so," Robert Feeney, 80, a retired engineering professor from Claremont, California told *Money*.

Niceties or Necessities?

Now that we've covered the necessities, we'll have a look at some things are often thought of as necessities, but might not be:

➤ **Household furnishings.** Nobody wants to live in an empty house or apartment. Some furnishings are nice, but are the curtains that match the bedspread necessary or is that need really a want? Expensive artwork, decorative rugs, the state-of-art microwave, and the solid cherry entertainment center that houses the big-screen TV are not essential to your existence.

➤ **Cable TV.** Many people claim they couldn't live without TV, but we'll go out on a limb here and assert that they can live quite nicely without HBO. Cable TV is expensive, and the extras can send your bill through the roof. Look at this area carefully when determining what you need.

➤ **Restaurants and bars**. Food is necessary, but eating in restaurants is not. Although it's nice to get together with friends after work or on weekends, you can spend a lot of money on a few drinks in the bar. If everyone agrees, maybe a rotating happy hour at someone's apartment makes better financial sense than the bar. Cooking at home can be a relaxing activity that will save you big bucks over eating frequently in restaurants.

➤ **Wheels.** If you need a car to get back and forth to work and to the other places you go, it's a necessity. But there are many cars to choose from, and some cost a whole lot more than others. We have a whole chapter (Chapter 6) on buying and leasing cars, so reread it if you need to, and think about how to distinguish want from need when it comes to your wheels.

➤ **Bad debt.** Some kinds of debt are worse than others. A mortgage, college loans, and even a car payment are understandable,

Money Pit

A college-age friend was horrified recently when her boyfriend, who had had too many beers while hanging out in the local bar, threw his American Express card down and told the bartender to get a round for everybody. Had she not grabbed the card and escorted her boyfriend out, he could have been looking at a large and completely unnecessary expense at the end of the month.

necessary debt that you'll have to repay. But if you're paying 18 percent interest on a fancy dinner at a restaurant that you charged to your credit card three months ago, that's really bad debt. Same with that sweater you got on sale, the tickets to Splash Mountain, or the groceries from that time you didn't have enough cash and used your Visa instead.

➤ **Drugs and personal items.** There's lots of gray area in this category when it comes to want versus need. You need vision care and glasses, but do you need designer frames? You need skin care products, but do you need a basketful of cosmetics in every color produced? You need medicine for your headache, but doesn't the store brand work just as well as the higher-priced Tylenol? Evaluate the shampoos, hand lotions, and all the other stuff that accumulates in the bathroom closet or medicine cabinet. Look at ingredients and make your buying decisions based on how the product works, not the brand name. Sales for the cosmetic company, L'Oreal, skyrocketed when the company started using its "you're worth it" slogan. It was a classic example of consumers buying a name, not necessarily the best product for the price.

➤ **Classes and instruction.** Financing an education is one of the best expenses you'll ever have. There may be a time, though, when you'll have to defer on classes and instruction until you're better financially equipped to pay for them. If you need a master's degree to advance in your job, then by all means go ahead and work toward the degree. But the philosophy course that you thought sounded interesting will be offered again next year, and it might be a good idea to wait until then to take it. You also might want to hold off on the flower arranging course, the personal trainer at the gym, and the bassoon for beginners program. Personal enrichment is a wonderful thing and is to be encouraged. But it's not a good bet that your landlord will look the other way on this month's rent, even if you do give him a beautifully arranged bouquet of flowers.

➤ **Fashion.** You need clothes. You don't need Nautica. You need shoes, but you don't need more pairs than you can fit into your closet. If you can get away with not wearing a suit to work, you probably don't need clothes that have to be dry-cleaned. Many people have closets full of clothes they don't wear, on which they've spent hundreds, even thousands, of dollars. You may want to look stylish, but buying more clothes than you'll ever wear is not a necessity.

➤ **Entertainment.** Some people will disagree, but we say with conviction that leisure and recreation are necessities. Regardless of what you do, you need leisure time and fun activities with which to fill it. The problem is, leisure can be very expensive. Although you need entertainment, you don't need the fancy cruise you booked to the Bahamas or tickets for two to *Rent*. These things are nice and should definitely be included in your goals, but they're wants, not needs.

➤ **Extras.** You say you need exercise, and you're right. You could get sufficient exercise by running and working out with some weights at home, but you want to take the spinning class at the gym where everybody goes after work. And the leggings that you love to wear because they make your legs look longer? That's a want, not a need. The expensive salon haircut, the gift you got for your girlfriend last week, the watch that cost a third of your weekly salary, the daily cappuccinos, and the you-name-your-favorite weakness are wants as well.

When you separate your needs from your wants, you'll have a much clearer picture of how to pay for both those categories. You'll know exactly where your money needs to go. You wouldn't think of skipping your rent payment to go on vacation, would you? That's because you recognize that the rent is a need, but the vacation is a want. Some spending decisions aren't so obvious, however.

A good thing to do is to make a list of your needs and make another list of your wants. Be honest with yourself, but not indulgent. Don't underestimate your needs, because you must know what they are to determine how much money you'll need to pay for them. On the other hand, if you confuse wants with needs and think you need more than you actually do, you'll become frustrated that your paycheck can't stretch that far.

After you have a clear picture of what you have and what you need, you'll be able to strike a balance between the two. Obviously, what you need can't exceed what you have. If it does, you might have to re-evaluate your needs to see whether some of them are wants. Once you know exactly what you have and get your needs and wants prioritized, you're on your way to a healthy financial lifestyle.

If it gets to the point where you can't finance your needs, you need to make some pretty drastic lifestyle changes. If you live by yourself, maybe you need to get a room-mate to cut housing costs. After all, living alone, by choice, is a luxury. Or maybe you need to trade in that new Honda for a used one. As long as it gets you where you need to go, does it really matter if it's a '99 or a '96? The next two chapters go into detail about budgets and saving money, so read on for lots of suggestions about how to better handle your money.

The Least You Need to Know

➤ It's easy to confuse needs with wants, but they're two very different things and must be treated differently as far as your money is concerned.

➤ If your financial lifestyle is not healthy, it's time to change it.

➤ It might be necessary to lower your expectations if you want to improve your financial lifestyle.

➤ There are some things that everybody needs; among these needs are shelter, food, clothing, and money for taxes.

➤ As a society, we're encouraged to think that we need much more than we really do and that we need it immediately.

➤ When you understand what you need, as opposed to what you want, you'll be able to prioritize your finances.

Chapter 9

The B Word: Budgets

In This Chapter

➤ Why nobody likes a budget

➤ Accepting that a budget is the way to go

➤ Using software to help prepare and maintain a budget

➤ Knowing what to include in your budget

➤ Deciding whether you need to earn more or spend less

Mention the word *budget* when you're with a group of people, and you're likely to hear a collective groan. Used as either a noun or a verb, the B word is not a favorite in most people's vocabularies. Making a budget or sticking to one probably ranks right up there among life experiences with going to the dentist or buying a new transmission for your car.

Why is that? Why do we hate budgets so much, and why do so many of us refuse or neglect to use one? Businesses use budgets. Can you imagine Microsoft spending millions of dollars and not keeping track of where it was going? Schools use budgets. Governments use budgets (or at least claim to). It's clear that budgets are sensible, necessary things to have. We'll even go a step further here and say that budgets are desirable because they keep us out of trouble, if used properly.

Why Budgets Have Such a Bad Rep

A budget is simply a schedule of income and expenses. It's a way of keeping track of the money you earn and planning how you spend your money. See, that's not so bad, is it?

Show Me the Money

A **budget** is a schedule of income and expenses, usually broken into monthly intervals and covering a one-year period.

Money Pit

By age 25, Americans average $6,000 in debt. With that amount of debt, your chances of being able to save much money in the next five years or so are slim. That's why it's important to avoid accumulating that much debt.

If budgets are sensible, necessary, and even desirable, then why do they have such a bad reputation? Why do your friends groan and roll their eyes when the word comes up in conversation? The reason is that making a budget, or working within a budget, implies having to use restraint or, worse yet, having to do without. As a society, restraint and denial are things that we have a lot of trouble dealing with.

If you have a certain amount of money budgeted for clothes, for instance, and you've already spent it for the month, you won't be able to buy that cute sweater you saw at the mall, at least not this month. You'll have to pass on the movies Friday night if you want to have enough money left to go out to dinner Saturday. You might even have to say no thanks to the weekend at the beach that your friends are planning.

To deny yourself something that you want flies right in the face of all the advertising with which you're constantly bombarded. Practically from the minute you get up in the morning until you crawl into bed at night, ads in magazines, newspapers, billboards, on the sides of buses, on the Internet, and on television urge you to be a consumer. Credit card companies, too, tell you to go ahead and get what you want. Buy it now and worry about it later is a pervasive attitude in our society.

If you're working within a budget, you can't do that. A budget forces you to look at what you make and to pay attention to what you spend. A good budget will tell you to the dollar how much you can spend on things such as food, restaurants, clothes, makeup, drinks with friends, and movies.

Most of us don't like the restrictions a budget imposes. We'd rather buy that great coat and figure out how to pay for it later. Well, prepare for a change in attitude.

Everybody Needs a Budget

I have to assume that you're interested in getting your personal finances organized and healthy, or you wouldn't be reading this book. You want to avoid the traps that so many people fall into: too much debt, too little savings, too much spending. To do that, you've got to have a budget. There's no way around it. Unless you've got a photographic memory and a calculator for a brain, you can't possibly keep track of your income and expenditures in your head.

Think of the last time you went to Wal-Mart. Can you remember everything you bought? It's easy to forget about buying little things such as lipstick, CDs, gum, film, and magazines, but they can eat up a lot of your income if you're not careful.

It will take a little time to set up a good budget that's comfortable for you to use, but it's well worth it to get a clear picture of your financial situation. You can use the sample budget we've included in this chapter as a guide or adapt it for your purposes, but know that there's no one way to set up a budget that's perfect. It depends on your needs and how detailed you want your budget to be.

What Your Budget Should Include

You can start your budget simply by identifying spending categories and listing all the money, either estimated or exact, that you spend in each category each month. Try to include everything you spend money on, right down to toothpaste and Juicy Fruit.

Just do some free-flow thinking, and write down everything that comes to mind. Spend some time on it, because you want to list everything you possibly can on which you spend money. Remember, the better you're able to identify your spending, the easier it will be to find places to cut down. Take a look at this sample budget to see just where your money goes. Feel free to revise it to best suit your needs.

Where Your Money Goes: A Sample Budget Worksheet

Item	Estimated	Amount/Worth
Housing		
Mortgage/Rent		$
Utilities		
Phone		
Cable		
Furniture		
Appliances		
Maintenance		
	Total:	
Transportation		
Gas		
Maintenance		
Tolls		
License/taxes		
Public transportation		
Insurance		
	Total:	

continues

continued

Item	Estimated	Amount/Worth
Taxes		
Federal		
State		
Local		
Social Security		
Luxury		
	Total:	
Debt		
Credit card		
Car loans		
Student loans		
Personal loans		
Line of credit		
	Total:	
Entertainment		
Movies, concerts, and theater		
Vacation		
Hobbies		
Pets		
Magazines and books		
Videos and music tapes		
Restaurants		
	Total:	
Personal		
Food		
Gifts		
Clothes		
Shoes		
Jewelry		
Dry cleaning		
Hair/makeup		
Health club		
Other		
	Total:	
Health Care		
Co-payments		
Drugs		
	Total:	

Item	Estimated	Amount/Worth
Insurance		
Car		
Home		
Disability		
Life		
Health		
Total:		
Children		
Day care		
Babysitters		
Toys		
Clothes		
Other		
Total:		
Charity		
Donations		
Grand Total:		

Non-Routine Expenses

Although certain things, such as your rent, groceries, and clothes, will be obvious expenditures as you start preparing your budget, make sure you include a category of less-obvious expenses. Things such as Christmas or Hanukkah gifts, the birthday party you want to give your boyfriend in May, and wedding and baby gifts are known as *non-routine expenses*. They aren't exactly unexpected—I mean, Christmas and Hanukkah do roll around every year—but they're not expenditures that come up each month, so you're more apt to overlook them.

Car repairs also are non-routine expenses. If you don't budget for them, they can be devastating financial news. It's hard to anticipate when your muffler is going to drop off onto the highway, but you must have some money budgeted for a new one when it does.

Or what if you've budgeted money for routine checkups with the dentist, but learn during one

Show Me the Money

Routine expenses include the more obvious expenditures, such as rent, insurance, food, and entertainment. **Non-routine expenses** are expenditures that people often overlook because they don't have to pay them regularly. They include car repairs or medical expenses.

Dollars and Sense

Anticipating and saving for non-routine expenses is a concept reminiscent of banks' Christmas clubs or vacation clubs. In case you haven't heard of them, they were savings clubs that banks offered (some smaller banks still do) to their customers. Money was earmarked for holiday or vacation spending and deposited into a special account, where it earned interest. When the holiday or vacation came, the club money could be withdrawn, and the primary savings account would be left untouched.

of those checkups that you have a loose filling in your back tooth that needs to be taken out and replaced? A little procedure like that could set you back more than $100 and wreck your monthly budget.

The way to anticipate non-routine expenses is to figure out all that you've had in the past year. Include car repair bills, big gifts, unexpected medical bills, the weekend at the ski resort that came up unexpectedly, and any others you can think of. Add up the cost of all those things, and then divide the total by 12. That's how much you should set aside each month for non-routine expenses.

If you're just out of college and starting out, estimating your non-routine expenses will be difficult because you probably won't have much of a history of these types of expenses to work from. If that's the case, ask someone to help you. Maybe you have a friend who's been on his own for a few years and can give you an idea about these types of expenses. Or perhaps a family member can advise you on car repairs and other expenses.

Routine Expenses

First items to list are known as *routine expenses*. You'll need to have the following in your budget:

➤ **Housing.** Your rent or mortgage will make up the biggest chunk of your housing expenses, but don't forget the other things that you pay for, too. How about your phone bill, your utilities bill, and the sofa and loveseat you bought? Consider the set of dishes you got at Ikea and the washer and dryer. How about your cable bill? If you're paying costs for upkeep, such as having the carpets cleaned, windows washed, or painting done, be sure to include that, too. If you're still living with Mom and Dad, consider possible expenses connected with that. Do you contribute money for rent? Buy things for the house? Help out with bills?

➤ **Debt Service.** This is probably another big expense category, unless you've been very frugal or very lucky. Include in the debt category everything for which you owe money: your car, your student loans, your credit cards, and so on. Do you have a line of credit opened anywhere? What about personal loans? If your dad loaned you $1,500 for a security deposit and the first month's rent on your apartment, include that in your debt category. If you still owe your brother $50 from when you were in 11th grade, you might as well put that down as well. Include both principal and interest payments.

➤ **Insurance.** Include any insurance you pay for in this category: auto, health (don't forget your co-payment if you're partially insured by your employer), renter's, and so on.

➤ **Taxes.** If you don't own property, you probably don't pay many taxes other than those deducted from your paycheck. If you do own property, you'll need to include the local property taxes, even if you put money in escrow and your mortgage company makes the payment for you. Also include the taxes that are deducted from your paycheck: federal, state, social security, occupational privilege, and any others.

➤ **Transportation.** If you don't own a car, your expenses in this category will be what you spend on public transportation. If you own a car, include routine maintenance costs (such as oil changes) and what you spend on gas and car insurance. Don't forget those pesky little expenses for your license and car registration. If you pay tolls regularly when driving, include those, too.

➤ **Health care.** Hopefully, these costs are minimal. But don't forget to budget for dental costs if your insurance doesn't cover them, eye exams, glasses, prescriptions, and routine doctor visits.

➤ **Entertainment.** If you're like most people in their 20s and 30s, this category will contain considerable expenses. Make sure you include everything, for this is one of the first areas we'll be looking at in which to cut costs. This category covers a variety of expenses, such as vacations, restaurants (even fast food), and the cost of drinks if you go to bars, clubs, or coffee bars. Think about movies, concerts, museums, cover charges, and any costs associated with hobbies (golf, bowling, skiing, or whatever). Don't forget pet costs, magazines and books, video rentals, the money you spend on CDs, tapes, and CD players, and any other expenses related to entertainment. Be honest when you list expenses in this category. Many people don't realize how much money they spend on entertainment until they sit down and add it all up.

➤ **Personal.** This category includes food, clothing, shoes, jewelry, dry cleaning costs, your health club fees, all fitness expenses, and money spent on hair stylists, manicures, makeup, and toiletries. Don't forget the money you spend in the office football pool and on the trip to the casino.

➤ **Children.** If you have kids, you already know they're expensive. If you don't have kids, but plan to someday, it doesn't hurt to know what costs are involved. Include expenses incurred for baby-sitters and day care, toys, clothes, diapers, and shoes (those baby Nikes are cute, but can cost $35).

➤ **Giving.** List money you contribute to your church, synagogue, or charities.

➤ **Vacations, Recreation.** List money that needs to be put aside for planned vacations and hoped-for vacations.

After you've listed your expenses, add them all up. Think about any categories you might have to include that aren't listed here, and don't forget to include the non-routine expenses we talked about earlier.

Trimming the Fat: Analyzing Your Expenses

You already have your expenses organized into spending categories; you now can break them down further into *fixed expenses* and *variable expenses* and *non-discretionary expenses* and *discretionary expenses*. When you have all your expenses categorized, it will be easier to see how you can control your budget. Analyzing different ratios within your budget will also help you determine where you should be cutting back your expenses.

Some of your expenses are fixed and others are variable. Fixed expenses include the following:

➤ Rent

➤ Car payments

➤ Any other payments that don't vary in amount, such as dues or club membership fees

➤ Your mortgage, if you have one

While these expenses may be necessary, like rent or mortgage payments, they often can be scaled down. If your rent is more than you can afford, you might have to move to a smaller place, or get a roommate. Or perhaps you could refinance your mortgage for a lower interest rate (be sure to consider the expenses involved in refinancing before deciding to go ahead). You may really like the club you've joined, but if the membership fees are too high, you may have to consider dropping out. And, we've already discussed the varying expenses of car ownership in Chapter 6. Still, fixed expenses are not the easiest ones to scrimp on. Let's take a look at the variable expenses.

Variable expenses include the following:

➤ Food

➤ Utilities

➤ Entertainment

➤ Vacations

It's probably easier to cut back on variable expenses such as these than on fixed expenses. Utilities can be adjusted to save money, and you can pass up the

Show Me the Money

Talk about picky! You can break down your expenses into **fixed expenses**, which are fixed expenses such as rent and car payments, and **variable expenses**, such as food and entertainment. Don't stop yet! These categories can be further broken down into **non-discretionary expenses**, which are things you can't do without, such as food and rent, and **discretionary expenses**, which you can do without (vacations and entertainment).

lobster tails and eat chicken instead. Entertainment costs are among the easiest to curtail (read Chapter 10 for ways to do so), and a camping trip can replace a stay in an expensive hotel when it's time for a vacation.

After you break down your expenses into variable or fixed, you can add another category: discretionary or non-discretionary. *Non-discretionary expenses* are things you must pay for or buy, including the following:

➤ Food

➤ Rent or mortgage

➤ Car payments

➤ Utilities

Non-discretionary expenses can't be avoided, but they may be able to be controlled, as discussed earlier. *Discretionary expenses*, on the other hand, are those that aren't necessary, including the following:

➤ Vacations

➤ Entertainment

➤ Club memberships

These discretionary expenses are the most obvious ones to curtail if you're trying to cut back on expenses. Basically, there are two ways to use this information to save money: You can control your discretionary expenses (skip the vacation this year) or limit your non-discretionary expenses (find a roommate or move into a smaller apartment).

Now you can organize your expenses by how they fit into both sets of categories. The following are fixed, non-discretionary expenses:

➤ Rent or mortgage

➤ Car payments

Variable, non-discretionary expenses are as follows:

➤ Food

➤ Utilities

Your fixed, discretionary expenses include the following:

➤ Club dues

➤ Membership fees

Your variable, discretionary expenses include the following:

➤ Vacations

➤ Entertainment

Spending Ratios

When it comes to figuring out where you need to cut expenses, you'll find spending ratios to be useful tools. A *spending ratio* is simply the percentage of money, as it relates to your gross income, that you use for a particular area such as housing or entertainment. If one area of expense becomes too great, you'll see that ratio is too high and begin to cut back.

Show Me the Money

Spending ratios are used to determine the amount of your gross income that goes toward a particular expenditure area. They can be used as tools in cutting expenses.

Show Me the Money

Your **savings ratio** is the opposite of your spending ratio. It is the percentage of your gross income that you are able to save within a given time.

To figure out your housing payment ratio, which is one kind of spending ratio, add up all your housing costs (rent or mortgage, insurance, property taxes, and so on). Compare that number to your total income. If your housing costs are more than 28 percent of your gross income, you're paying too much for housing and should look for ways to cut your costs.

To figure your total debt ratio, add up all your monthly payments, including car, credit card, rent, and so on. Compare that number to your total income. If it's more than 36 percent of your income, these expenses are too high, and you should look for ways to cut them.

Finally, you can figure out your *savings ratio*, which is the percentage of your gross income that you save. Compare the amount of money you save each week or month to your income for that period. You should be aiming for 8 percent a year. If you're not saving that much, you should look for ways to cut expenses and save more.

There are other ratios, too, but these are good ones with which to start. Don't get too hung up on these ratios. If your housing costs are 29 or 30 percent instead of 28 percent, it doesn't mean you should immediately sublet your apartment and move back home with Mom and Dad. But if you find your ratio is up to 35 or 40 percent, you ought to think about downsizing.

One Job, Two Jobs, Three Jobs, Four

After you've figured out how much you're spending, you'll know exactly how much money you need to pay for that spending. You'll also have a clear picture of what you spend your money on; you might be surprised at the amount you're spending unnecessarily.

If you are spending too much, look closely at your expenses in the entertainment and personal categories. These categories are where most people find they have the most unnecessary expenditures. There are lots of tricks to saving money, but most of them are just common sense and a little restraint. We talk a lot more about ways to save money in Chapter 10.

After you've figured out what you have and the amount of money you need to spend, take a good, hard look at how you're doing. If you're able to meet all your expenses, make regular payments on any debt you have, save a portion of your income, and have some money left over for discretionary purposes, good for you. You're in good financial shape.

If, however, you're spending everything you earn and not saving anything, or you're spending *more* than you earn, you've got to change your ways. If you have credit card debt that never gets paid off, or you're over your head with car loans or other debt, your financial condition is shaky.

There are two ways to handle that situation: You can either spend less or earn more. Those who are in a real financial bind may very well need to do both of those things. For many people, it's easier to change their spending mindset and cut down their spending. Some hard-core spenders, however, would rather try to earn more than spend less.

If you fall into the hard-core spender category, and you don't see a big raise in your future any-time soon, you need to figure out a way to get more

Pocket Change

According to the U.S. Dept. of Labor and Statistics, in 1996, 6.1 percent of the general population held second jobs. More Generation Xers (6.5 percent) held second jobs than any other group.

Pocket Change

I know a woman who works full time during the week in a doctor's office. She also works from 5 to 9 Monday night and all day Saturday at a local drugstore. She only earns minimum wage at the drugstore, but she pays someone to clean her house because she doesn't have time to do it. She pays the cleaning person almost as much as she makes working an entire Saturday for minimum wage!

money. You can do something illegal, but that's definitely *not* recommended. You can play the lottery every night, but statistically, your chances of getting ahead that way are pretty slim. You can hope for a big inheritance or some other windfall, but you'll probably wait for a long, long time. If you can't cut down on spending, you'll need to get another job; there's no getting around it.

If you think you need a second job, look carefully at what you'll make and the possible expenses that you'll incur because of the job. If you'll be earning $8 an hour on a second job, but spending more money on transportation costs and clothes for the job and eating dinner out every night because you're too tired or don't have time to make something at home, it just might not be worth your time and effort.

Money Pit

Many relationships fail because one person becomes unavailable or unapproachable because he or she works too much. When working becomes (or appears to become) more important than the relationship, you can bet there will be trouble.

Dollars and Sense

Some people use the jar or cigar box system to help them measure how well they're sticking to their budgets. This system simply entails collecting receipts for everything you buy and putting them in a box or jar earmarked for a particular category. At the end of the month, you tally all the receipts to determine your expenses. Low-tech? You bet. But this system has worked for lots of budgeters.

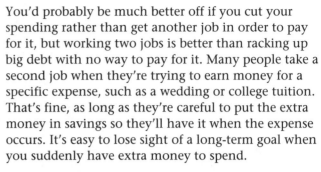

You'd probably be much better off if you cut your spending rather than get another job in order to pay for it, but working two jobs is better than racking up big debt with no way to pay for it. Many people take a second job when they're trying to earn money for a specific expense, such as a wedding or college tuition. That's fine, as long as they're careful to put the extra money in savings so they'll have it when the expense occurs. It's easy to lose sight of a long-term goal when you suddenly have extra money to spend.

If you do decide to take a second job, consider carefully what it will do to your life. What activities would you have to give up? Golf games? Tennis matches? Church or synagogue activities? How much less time would you have to spend with family and friends? It's a personal decision, but being able to buy a lot of things is less than ideal if you don't have time to enjoy them.

Sticking with It

After you have your budget written up, you need to keep track of how you're doing compared with the budget. Many people have drafted great budgets, only to give up on them after a few months. Your spending habits aren't the same every month, so you need to keep track of your expenses for several years to get an accurate picture of what you're spending over the long term.

Many people who neglect to budget for non-routine expenses get discouraged and quit using their budgets when they're hit with a car repair or other major expense. That's why it's important to include money for those types of expenses.

If you slip up one month and overspend, don't be too hard on yourself, and don't give up on the budget. It's like when you're trying to lose some weight. Just because you overeat one day doesn't mean you should quit the diet and eat whatever you want the next day, too. Go back to the plan, and you'll reach your goals.

Software and Web Sites for Budgeting

People in their 20s and 30s are more attuned to computers than any other generation. As the first generation to grow up with personal computers, Gen Xers use PCs as often and comfortably as older people use telephones. Computers are everywhere from college dorm rooms to coffee shops. They serve as sources of information, entertainment, and communication. They also perform a variety of tasks, from searching for book titles on a particular subject, to finding a date, to getting information about caring for your dog or hurricanes that have occurred over the past century.

Dollars and Sense

If you're online, check out www.outpost.com for more software that's recommended for personal finance needs. Or call Outpost at 800-856-9800.

As you would expect, there are a number of software programs that can help you with a budget and other aspects of your personal finances. The following are some of the most widely used Windows-based programs for personal finance management:

➤ MECA Managing Your Money

➤ Balance Point

➤ Check Free

➤ Money Counts Personal

➤ Microsoft Money

➤ Quicken for Windows

➤ WinCheck

Web sites that offer advice on setting up budgets and handling other financial matters are plentiful. Check out these sites to start:

➤ The Household Budget Management site gives advice on how to prepare a practical, useable budget. You can access it at http://www.netxpress.com/users/hadap/budget.html.

➤ The Current Budget site provides a detailed example of a budget. You can access it at http://www.efmoody.com/planning/budget.html.

➤ The FinanCenter: Budgeting Center site provides budget and financial calculation tools. You can access it at http://www.financenter.com/budget.htm.

➤ Your Household Budget is a site that explains how to use a budget as part of a bigger financial plan. You can access it at http://www.merrill-lynch.ml.com/investor/budgetprintform.html.

119

➤ Creditech Computerized Household Budgeting provides a sample monthly budget. You can access it at http://www.creditech.com/mobudget.htm.

➤ Makeover: Budgeting is a case study of how a budget could be improved. You can access it at http://www.abcnews.com/sections/business/DailyNews/makeover0227/index.html.

A computer and some fancy software might make budgeting easier and more fun, but they aren't necessary. You can easily make a budget yourself. The most important ingredients of successful budgeting are a willingness to make a budget and to stick to it after it's made.

The Least You Need to Know

➤ Nobody likes to think about budgeting, much less do it, but you can and should do it.

➤ You can use computer software or cigar boxes, but everyone should have a budget to know exactly how they spend their money and how they are implementing their plan.

➤ After you have a handle on what you have and what you need, you can assess your financial condition.

➤ If your earnings aren't greater than your expenditures, you've got to earn more or spend less.

➤ If you're tempted to take a second job in order to earn more money so you can spend more, consider cutting expenses instead.

Chapter 10

Getting Into the Swing of Savings

In This Chapter

➤ Determining your financial personality

➤ Saving and spending: Habits to learn or unlearn

➤ Saving a little can result in a lot

➤ A savings mindset is a good start

➤ Learning to save on just about everything

Remember when you were a kid and your Uncle Jimmy sent you $30 every year for your birthday and again at Christmas? Once you recognized the handwriting on the envelope, you'd have it ripped open before you got it out of the mailbox. There was always a card, but you never took time to read it before you opened it to make sure the cash was there. Sound familiar?

There's a point to this little trip down memory lane. What we need to know is, what did you do with the money after you took it out of the card? Maybe your parents made you put it in a bank account or stash the bills someplace for safe keeping. Or maybe you were allowed to spend half of the money. Or maybe you took the $30 and bought that video game you'd had your eye on for the past three months.

The way you handled Uncle Jimmy's birthday gift might give you some pretty good insights into your financial personality. Sure, you may have changed as you've grown up and become less (or more) impulsive and more (or less) practical. Basically, though, there are two kinds of people: savers and spenders. In this chapter, we'll take a look at these financial personalities and help you determine in which category you belong. Get ready—you might discover a few things about yourself.

Are You a Saver or a Spender?

If you know to the nickel how much money is in your wallet or purse at this moment, keep track of exactly how much you spend and where you spend it, buy only clothing that doesn't need to be dry-cleaned, and eat pasta three times a week to stretch your food dollars, you're probably a saver.

If, on the other hand, you simply *must* eat at that little bistro with the great wine selection twice a week, can't imagine life without your $140 Nikes, haven't a clue as to where you might have spent that $50 you stashed in your wallet Saturday morning, and haven't had your Visa paid off for more than a year, chances are you're a spender.

Pocket Change

If you had saved all of the $30 gifts Uncle Jimmy sent you from your first birthday through your 20th in a savings account at 4 percent interest, you'd have more than $900!

Show Me the Money

Pre-tax means the earnings or returns on income are exactly as received. No income taxes have been paid or calculated on the sum.

After-tax (post tax) is considered a net amount, taking the initial sum and deducting all amounts paid for income taxes.

Although we'll talk more about it in Chapter 14, your return on your savings and investments can be calculated *pre-tax* and *after tax*. After tax obviously means after you pay income tax on the earnings; however, this figure can be difficult to determine since we all have different tax rates. Thus, all returns in this book, unless specified otherwise, are assumed to be after tax figures.

Most of us probably fall somewhere in the middle of the saving/spending continuum, but plenty of people go to extremes. My brother-in-law hasn't bought a new cassette (he doesn't own a CD player) for 10 years. If he can't find it at the flea market for $2 or less, he figures he can live without it. He pays cash for his cars, never charges anything, and wears his clothes until they're worn out. He's a great guy and perhaps the best example of a saver that I've ever met.

A friend, on the other hand, takes his kids, who live most of the year with their mother, on extravagant vacations annually. When I say extravagant, I mean two weeks in a beachfront home with its own pool, hot tub, and every other extra you can imagine or a ski vacation to Aspen, complete with private lessons, first-class restaurants, and new ski clothing. He buys them everything they ask for, charging everything to his credit card. With the vacation and all the extras, he runs up a bill that takes the rest of the year to pay off. He's a great guy, too, and perhaps the best example of a spender that I've ever met.

Evaluating Your Financial Personality

When we talk about your financial personality, we're not making any value judgments. Whether you're a saver or a spender is part of your personality. It's sort of like whether you're outgoing or reserved or whether you love Indian food or hate it. It's just something about you.

Being a saver or a spender isn't good or bad on its own, but either personality can cause problems if it's not managed properly. You probably won't need to look too closely at your own habits to determine whether you're a saver or a spender. If you're not sure which you are, answer these questions:

1. Do you carry balances on any of your credit cards?

   A. No

   B. Yes

2. Why do you use your credit cards?

   A. For convenience

   B. To buy things I don't have enough money for

3. Do you ever use your credit cards to get cash advances with which to pay your bills?

   A. No

   B. Yes

4. Does your credit card bill normally contain charges for things that are past and forgotten, such as dinners out or movie tickets?

   A. No

   B. Yes

5. Are you able to put some money from each paycheck into savings?

   A. Yes

   B. No

6. When do you shop?

   A. When I need something

   B. When I'm bored or depressed

7. When you go to the grocery store, how much do you buy?

   A. Only what's on my list

   B. Twice as many items as I intended to get

8. When you see something you want to buy, what do you do?

   A. Wait a couple of weeks to see whether it is going to be marked down

   B. Buy it regardless of whether it's on sale

9. How much do you spend on entertainment?

   A. A moderate amount

   B. A lot

10. What are your long-distance phone habits?

    A. I wait until the rates go down to make personal calls

    B. I call whenever I get an urge to talk

If your answers to these questions were mostly A's, you're a saver. If your answers to these questions were mostly B's, you're a spender. If you're a saver, good for you. It doesn't necessarily make you a better person, but you have a great start on managing your personal finances.

If you're a spender, don't despair. There's something to be said for living the good life. The only problem is, too much of the good life now is likely to mean less of the good life later. Your financial personality ties in directly to your financial situation, so spenders have to learn to exercise some self-control.

Some people spend everything they earn, and don't hesitate to use credit cards to pay for things they want, but can't afford. I have a friend, John, whose father died of a heart attack in his 40s. John, who's 35, smokes at least a pack of cigarettes a day, drinks regularly, and drives a Harley Davidson. He's convinced (and possibly with good reason) that he also will die young.

Because of this belief, John has adopted a live-for-the-moment mentality, which includes his spending habits. He spends everything he earns and has credit card debt that would scare most people half to death. John gets his credit card bills each month, pays the minimum due, and keeps on spending. He's digging himself into a huge hole, but John fully intends to die with that credit card debt. But what happens if John inherited his mother's longevity genes and ends up, despite his convictions and his lifestyle, living into his 70s? He's in for a long, rocky financial future.

If John does die when he's relatively young, he's leaving behind a nightmare for his wife and family. When a person dies with more debts than assets, the executor of his estate usually has to sell the assets (house, motorcycle, car, and so on) to pay for the person's funeral and to pay the expenses of settling

Dollars and Sense

If you spend a dollar a day for a soda or coffee, think about this: Investing a dollar a day earning an average 8 percent return for 40 years would give you over $100,000 at the end of that period.

Money Pit

John is extreme in his spending habits, but he's not alone. About 80 percent of the general population in this country live paycheck to paycheck and have very little, if any, savings.

124

the estate. Then, the people to whom he or she owes money (hello credit card companies!) swarm in like vultures to grab a share of whatever money is left. If there's not enough money left from the assets to pay back all the debt, each person who's owed money has to write off some of the unpaid debt. This mess is known as an insolvent estate situation, and it must be settled in court. Also, if John's wife, Karen, is named as co-owner on any of John's debt, guess what? She's responsible for paying it back.

Savers Have It Made (Almost)

If you've determined that you're a saver, give yourself a pat on the back. Managing your personal finances probably will be a little easier for you. Now, get ready to assess your savings habits. Could you be saving more? Are you saving smart? Are you saving in the right places? Are you saving *too* much?

We've all heard the stories of elderly people who die in one-room apartments with few comforts, who, unknown to everyone, had savings and investments of a million dollars or more. They were saving their money to give to their children, or their church, or the local animal shelter. For whatever reasons, some people choose to forego comforts and even necessities (heat, air conditioning, even food) in order to save their money.

It makes no sense, of course, to save so much money that you don't have the things you need and some of the things you want. After all, that's why we work. It's a rare person who would continue to show up at the job every day if the paychecks stopped coming.

There are no guarantees in this life, and unfortunately, some of us won't even make it to retirement age. It would be tragic to deny yourself everything you want in order to save money for a day that never comes. It's important to strike a balance between extreme frugality in the name of saving money and a devil-may-care spending spree that compromises your financial future. You'll learn more about saving and investing for the future in the upcoming chapters on investments and retirement funds.

Spenders Have to Work a Little Harder

If you're a spender, you can console yourself with the fact that you're far from alone. Most people find it much easier to spend money than to save it. From the time we're children in America, we're sent a clear message: Go ahead—spend. Whenever we watch TV, pick up a magazine, or get on the Internet, we're bombarded with advertising telling us to spend. Buy cars! Buy beer! Buy shampoo! Buy jeans! Buy anything, but buy!

One hundred years ago, people made a lot less money than they make today. They spent a whole lot less, too. One reason was that there was simply less to buy. There were no malls, no television shopping clubs, no luxury vacation condos, and not many expectations.

Money Pit

Try this exercise: Choose one room and identify all the things in it that are unnecessary and unused. Then, estimate the cost of each item and add them up. When you've finished, multiply the total by the number of rooms in your house. If you invested the total you just came up with, you'd no doubt enhance your retirement fund nicely. Think about that the next time you're in Pier One.

Did you ever walk through a 150-year-old house? If you did, you probably were struck by the pronounced lack of closet space. "Where did they keep all their stuff?" was likely the question that came to your mind. Compare the tiny closets (or, in many rooms, no closets at all) of those century-plus houses to the huge walk-ins found in new homes. Some of these new closets are bigger than entire rooms of the old houses. Even houses built in the 1950s and 1960s have noticeably less closet space than new homes.

After we've filled up all the closet space and packed the basement and attic full with our indoor stuff, we turn to our garages. Many of the garages in my neighborhood won't hold a car because they're too jammed with stuff, and nearly every house has an outdoor storage space to hold the overflow. Some people have to use storage rental places to hold their extra stuff.

We are part of a society that pushes spending and consumerism, and we're bombarded every day with the message that spending money is good. Is it any wonder so many of us do?

A Penny Saved Is More Than a Penny Earned

We've all heard the expression, "a penny saved, is a penny earned." When it comes to saving money, we don't think much in pennies anymore, unless you're a kid with a piggy bank. We think in dollars, or tens of dollars, or hundreds of dollars. And that's part of the problem for many people who have trouble saving money. They feel that it's not worth saving a few cents or a few dollars, so they don't. They spend a little here and a little there, not realizing how quickly those little bits of money add up.

Think about the money you spend each day on incidentals: a cup of coffee and a bagel at the Dunkin' Donuts on your way to work, a sandwich and a Snapple at the deli at lunchtime, and a bottle of shampoo at the drugstore on your way back to work. Your friend calls after dinner, and you meet at Starbucks for a cafe latte. No big deal, it's just an ordinary day. When you add it all up, though, you'll see that this ordinary day cost you more than $10 in incidentals.

Multiply the expenses for a typical workday by five, and you're spending $50 a week on incidentals. By the end of the week, you have nothing to show for your spending but half a bottle of shampoo and a caffeine habit, and the weekend is just beginning.

Of course, nobody is telling you to cut out all incidental spending. You do need shampoo, and coffee drinkers might argue that even shampoo is secondary to the Starbucks blend. But what if you cut that incidental spending in half? For instance, you could make your coffee at home and carry a sandwich to work. Would saving $25 a week make a difference in your long-term savings? You bet it would! If you saved that $25 each week, at the end of a year you'd have $1,300.

Yeah, $1,300 is a lot of money, but maybe you're still not convinced to cut back at Starbucks. If you invested the money at a 10 percent return, you'd quickly see that a penny saved is much more than a penny earned:

➤ Investing $25 a week in a mutual fund with an average after tax annual return of 10 percent for 5 years would give you $8,400.

➤ Investing $25 a week in a mutual fund with an average after tax annual return of 10 percent for 10 years would give you $22,300.

It's hard to imagine that cutting out a cup of coffee and a sandwich each day will make that much difference to your savings, but it does. Interest, especially compound interest, can give you big returns on small investments. What's the difference in types of interest, you ask? Let's have a look.

Simple interest, which is what we normally just refer to as interest, is a method of calculating what you earn on your money by applying the stated rate on only the actual balance on deposit for the exact period of deposit. For instance, if you invest $2,000 in an account for one year at 5 percent interest, the bank would pay you $100 at the end of the year. Not bad, huh? You get $100 just for letting your money sit there. But if you were earning compound interest on your $2,000, you'd be in even better shape.

Compound interest is paid on an initial deposit plus any accumulated interest from period to period. Compound interest gives you interest on your interest. It's definitely the way to invest. Compounding interest at 5 percent over a year wouldn't make a great difference on a $2,000 deposit, but it still would give you a couple of dollars more for your money. When you get into big investments at higher interest rates, compounding interest really becomes significant.

Dollars and Sense

Some financial advisors advise paying for every purchase with bills, and saving all the change you get. At the end of the month, take all the change to the bank for deposit. You'll be surprised at how it will add up.

Show Me the Money

Simple interest is a method of calculating what you earn on your money by applying the stated rate on only the balance on deposit for the exact period of deposit. **Compound interest** is paid on an initial deposit plus any accumulated interest from period to period.

Interest is generally compounded in one of several ways: continuous, daily, weekly, monthly, quarterly, or annually. The more often it's compounded, the better off you'll be. Look for banks that compound interest continually or daily. When your money starts growing, you'll be pleasantly surprised.

Look how saving $10 a week with 12 percent compound interest adds up:

➤ If you start saving when you're 25, you'll have $43,041 when you turn 45. ($10,400 is your investment; the interest earned is $32,600.)

➤ If you start saving when you're 25, you'll have $153,957 when you turn 55. ($15,600 is your investment; the interest earned is $138,400.)

➤ If you start saving when you're 25, you'll have $520,506 when you turn 65. ($20,800 is your investment; the interest earned is $499,700.)

Sounds pretty amazing, doesn't it? This is the power of compound interest and why a penny saved is a lot more than a penny earned. Even if you save just $10 a month with an 8 percent return, you'll have a lot more money than your initial investment in 20 or 30 years:

➤ If you start saving when you're 25, you'll have $5,900 when you turn 45.

➤ If you start saving when you're 25, you'll have $15,000 when you turn 55.

Dollars and Sense

Remember that it's very important to find out how often interest is compounded before choosing a financial institution in which to invest your money. Review Chapter 3 for other suggestions!

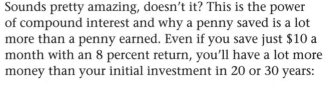

Getting Into a Savings Mindset

Trading a spending habit for a saving habit isn't easy, but it can be done. Being aware of your spending habits is an important first step. You need to realize that you're spending close to $10 a day on coffee, bagels, and shampoo before you can decide to cut out the bagel and save a little money.

If you're a saver, you already realize the importance of putting money away for all the things you'll want or need in the future, such as a house, cars, college, and retirement. Even if you haven't started saving yet, knowing that it's important puts you on the right track.

Dollars and Sense

For 2 weeks try keeping a list of everything—from a pack of gum to a new suit—that you buy. This will give you a better picture of where you're spending your money.

If you're a natural-born spender, don't despair. You have plenty of company. Don't think, though, that overspending is something you can't change, like being born short or tall. You can't change your height, but you can change your spending habits.

If you want to save money, it's easy to get started. There are many ways to save, and once you start, you'll see it's not that hard. Almost everyone can find at least one area in which they can cut back and stash the money they save into some kind of account. First, though, you need to examine your priorities and how you look at spending and saving money.

If you're spending every dollar you earn, or, worse yet, borrowing money or running up your credit cards in order to buy everything you want, you're heading for big financial trouble. A $30 blouse or sweater that you'll wear for a season or two is not an investment—it's an expenditure that you probably could do without.

Dollars and Sense

Practice what we talked about in last chapter's discussion on budgeting, and find an area of non-essential spending. Examine it carefully, and find expenditures that you can eliminate.

As a society, Americans are financially pretty well-off. Yes, there are people in this country who don't have enough to eat. There are kids who don't get winter coats or new shoes when they need them, and elderly people who die during heat waves because they're afraid they won't be able to pay their electric bills if they turn on their air conditioners or fans. And there are homeless men and women who spend cold, winter nights huddled over heat vents in the sidewalks. All things considered, however, *most* Americans have it pretty good.

Our average incomes (after adjusting for inflation) have more than doubled over the past 40 years. Our homes keep getting bigger and bigger, and we take for granted things that people a few generations ago would never have dreamed of owning. The problem is, we lose sight of how well off we are when we compare ourselves to someone who's richer or has more.

Pocket Change

Two-thirds of people throughout the world have a standard of living that is just 20 percent of that enjoyed by the average American.

Nobody feels like they have much money if they compare their financial situations to the dynasties of Bill Gates or Malcolm Forbes. But take a minute to consider these statistics that have been making the rounds on the Internet:

➤ If the earth's population was condensed to a village of 100 people, with all of the existing ratios remaining what they are now, 80 of those people would live in substandard housing.

➤ Fifty would suffer from malnutrition.

➤ Only one person would have a college education, and nobody would own a computer.

➤ Fifty percent of all the wealth would be in the hands of just 6 of those 100 people. Those six would all be Americans.

It's difficult to maintain a global perspective if you've always lived comfortably. It's easier to compare your financial situation with that of your friends, family members, and people you read about in the newspaper or hear about on TV.

This ties directly in with our mindsets concerning saving and spending. If you're determined to keep up with your friends, and you buy more and more so that you'll have what they have, you trap yourself into the mindset of spending. If you don't concern yourself with what your friends are buying, and think about what you have and what you need, however, you can develop a savings mindset. If you can achieve the mindset that saving money is good, and is something from which you'll benefit greatly in the future, you'll find it a lot easier to pass up on things you want in order to keep your cash.

Of course, people spend money for many different reasons, not just to keep up in the great game of possessing. Some people spend because it makes them feel better if they're disappointed, hurt, or angry. Some people enjoy spending money so much that it becomes an addiction. "Shopaholic" is a word that many people use jokingly, but an addiction to spending is a real and serious problem for some people. Of course, other addictions, such as drugs or gambling, also can take huge tolls on your personal finances. Anyone with an addiction of any kind should seek help as soon as possible.

Dollars and Sense

If you think you have a spending addiction, help is available. Check your phone directory to see whether there's a chapter of Debtors Anonymous (DA) in your area. DA uses a 12-step program, similar to Alcoholics Anonymous, and has helped many people from all social and economic backgrounds to overcome spending addictions. If you can't find a local chapter of DA, you can get more information by writing to: Debtors Anonymous, P.O. Box 800, Needham, MA 02492, or by calling 781-453-2743.

Tips for Saving Money on Almost Everything

Many people have a perpetual plan to start saving money, but they never do. They swear they'll start saving 10 percent of their salary, just as soon as they've got the new car, computer, boots, mountain bike, guitar, bracelet, or whatever. If you want to save money, you have to make a firm commitment and stick to it. That means you won't be able to buy the mountain bike this month or next month. You might not even be able to buy it this year. Besides deferring expenses, another good way to save money is to get the best deal on purchases you do make. This section provides tips on how to do just that.

Food

Even if you pass up the cappuccino and buy only the basics, food is expensive. It seems that every trip to the grocery store costs more than the previous one.

Everyone seems to have an opinion about what's the best way to save money on food. Some people claim that using manufacturer's coupons saves money; others say coupons only encourage you to buy things you don't really need. Some food shoppers drive from store to store, hunting out bargains; others say the cheapest way to buy is to get everything at once in one place. Some people swear by Sam's Club, buying enough fish sticks at one time to feed a cafeteria full of school kids; others say it makes better financial sense to buy only what you need at the moment.

Dollars and Sense

If you must have the mountain bike, check out some of the used gear shops that are gaining popularity. They're stocked with used, but good, sports or recreational gear, electronic equipment, musical instruments, exercise machines, and so on. Check your phone book to see what's in your area. You could save some major dollars.

You'll have to use your best judgment and make up you own mind about those issues. There are, however, some basic guidelines to consider if you're trying to save money on your food bill:

➤ Never, unless it's an absolute emergency, buy food at a mini-market or convenience store. You'll almost always end up paying a whole lot more than in a regular grocery store.

➤ Buy soda, juice, water, and beer in multipacks. Think about the can of Diet Coke you buy at work every day. What does it cost? Fifty cents? Sixty? Seventy-five? Now, think about the cost of a case of Diet Coke on sale at the grocery store: 24 cans for around five dollars. You can do the math. It's a lot cheaper to buy the case and take a can to work with you.

➤ Pack a lunch. Make your own turkey and Swiss and grab an apple. Put them in one of those insulated bags with an ice pack, and you're set to save big bucks over buying a sandwich and chips at the corner deli.

➤ Buy store brands instead of name brands. These products sometimes come from the same sources and are essentially the same thing with different labels. Yet, the store brands can cost a third less because there are fewer costs, such as advertising, involved in their production.

Pocket Change

If you pack lunch three days a week, saving $5 each time, you'll save $450 in one year, just on lunches.

131

➤ Think about what you eat and adjust your menus to save money. If you're eating fresh tuna on Monday, filet on Wednesday, and organically raised squab on Friday, you're spending a lot more than necessary on food. Designate two or three nights a week as meatless nights, cut down on convenience and frozen foods, and limit high-priced snack foods.

➤ Avoid buying foods that aren't in season where you live. Fresh strawberries in January are terribly expensive and probably not that good. Visit a farm stand or pick your own strawberries when they're in season and stock your freezer, instead. It's better for your local economy and your wallet.

➤ Don't browse in the grocery store. There are dozens of new items in the store every time you go, and many of them look mighty tempting. Take a list and buy only what's on the list. It's too easy to walk in to the store for 6 items and walk out with 12.

Eating in Restaurants

Eating in restaurants or getting takeout is generally more expensive than cooking and eating at home, so you should think of restaurants and take-out meals as luxuries. When you do go out to eat, keep these things in mind:

➤ Drinks are expensive. Many restaurants charge $5 for a cocktail and a good glass of wine can cost $7 or $8. Even a cup of coffee can be upward of $1.50, so plan accordingly. Why not have a drink and appetizer at home before going to the restaurant or return home for coffee and dessert?

➤ Pasta with shrimp might sound like a bargain at $9.95, but if you have to pay $3.50 extra for a salad and $2.50 for garlic bread, all of a sudden your dinner has gotten pretty expensive. Watch out for hidden costs.

➤ That fresh sea bass with the tomato cream sauce special sounds great, but how much will it cost? Don't make the mistake of ordering a daily special without first asking how much it will cost. "Special" often doesn't refer to the cost of the item.

➤ Find a good, inexpensive restaurant. Many ethnic or health food places offer meatless meals that won't break your bank. Or you might be able to find a place that offers smaller portions of food at reduced prices, thus helping your waistline and your wallet.

Dollars and Sense

Think of all the restaurant meals you've eaten that were only so-so, or worse. You often can do better grabbing something at home—and save a lot of money, too.

➤ Don't be fooled into thinking that fast food is cheap food. Add up what you spend the next time you eat at a fast-food restaurant. You can easily end up spending $5 or more for a totally unmemorable meal.

➤ If you get takeout to eat at home, provide your own beverages and dessert. These items can greatly increase your take-out bill.

➤ Invite friends over for dinner instead of going out. You can buy what you need to make a nice dinner for four people for half of what you'd spend for dinner for two at a good restaurant. Hopefully, your friends will return the favor.

Clothes

Take just a minute and visualize your clothes closet. If you're like most people, you probably have far many more clothes than you need or wear. If you're spending too much on clothing, consider some of these tips:

➤ Never use a credit card to buy clothes. You'll have a better handle on what you're spending if you use cash, and you'll avoid getting a bill for something that you've worn a few times and already designated to the back of the closet.

➤ Shop for clothes only when you need (need, not want) something specific. Buy that item and leave before you spot the silk blouse that would be perfect with your black suit.

➤ Minimize your accessories, which can be quite costly. How many black belts do you really need?

Dollars and Sense

When you're tempted to buy clothes that you don't really need, try leaving the garment in the store. If you really love it, you can come back the next day. Chances are, though, a lot of things won't seem as enticing the next day.

➤ Avoid clothes that must be dry-cleaned. Dry cleaning bills add up.

➤ If you see something you really like, ask a salesperson if the item will be put on sale soon. Many stores have sales every weekend. If you've bought something and then see it's been put on sale shortly afterwards, take it back with your receipt and ask to have your cost adjusted to the sale price.

➤ Buy clothing that matches items you already own, and buy classic styles that won't be outdated by the next season.

➤ Consider borrowing clothing from a friend or family member if you need something special for a one-time occasion.

➤ Buy 6 or 12 pairs of socks or pantyhose at a time. You often can save money by buying in quantity.

Fitness

Sure, you want to be healthy and look good. But if gym fees are taking too big a chunk out of your budget, you might have to find another way to stay in shape:

➤ Look for special rates at gyms or fitness centers. These are often offered when a facility first opens or at certain times of the year, such as New Year's and just before summer.

➤ Walk or jog in your neighborhood or on a school track. The only cost involved is a good pair of shoes.

➤ Don't get carried away with exercise clothing. It might look good, but it's expensive, and it doesn't improve the quality of your workout.

➤ Look in the classified ads or at yard sales for used exercise equipment and exercise at home. The cost of the equipment will quickly be offset by what you save in gym fees.

Grooming

Haircuts, perms, hair coloring, makeup, lotions, nail care—the cost of these things can add up. It's understandable that you want to look your best, but think about some ways to save in this area:

➤ Get a good haircut from a stylist and use cheaper places for in-between maintenance.

➤ Do your own nails or arrange with a friend to do each others' nails.

➤ Look for store brands or less expensive name brands in shampoos, face creams, and other grooming items. Check the ingredients. They're often the same as the more expensive name brands.

Vacations

Vacations are great, but they can undo your budget if you're not careful. Plan carefully and think about ways to save money before you make reservations:

➤ Drive instead of fly, when possible. It takes longer, but it can save you hundreds of dollars, especially when there's more than one person traveling.

➤ Use discount coupons for hotels, car rentals, and restaurants. These coupons are available from a variety of sources and can be found in your Sunday newspaper, magazines, and even your telephone book—be on the lookout for them.

➤ Use the Internet to find the least expensive airline seats. There are sites that will notify you of bargain rates to places you want to go. Try Independent Traveler's Bargain Box, a feature of the America Online service. Hit keyword "Bargain Box." Or try Shoestring Travel at www.stratpub.com/shoe1.html.

➤ Share a vacation with some friends. Get a group together and chip in for a house near the beach or ski slopes. Just make sure they're people you get along with well.

➤ Consider low-cost vacations, such as hiking or camping trips or a week at your aunt's beach house. Even if this kind of vacation is not your first choice, it will give you a chance to get away and relax.

Pocket Change

Check out these places to get up to 65 percent off hotel rates in certain cities:

Accommodation Express: 800-444-7666 or on the Internet at www.accommodationexpress.com

Hotel Reservation Network: 800-964-6835 or on the Internet at www.80096hotel.com

Household Expenses

We love our comforts. We like our homes to be warm in the winter and cool in the summer. We throw our clothes in the dryer and zap pre-made meals in the microwave to eat while we watch premium channels on our TVs. The trouble with all these comforts is that they cost money. There are, however, some things you can do to cut down the costs:

➤ Get comfortable cooler. Set your thermostat at 68 instead of 72, and you'll save about 12 percent on your heating bill. Crank it way down at night and pull on an extra blanket.

➤ In the summer, set your air conditioning thermostat at 78 instead of 75, and you'll see some savings. Make sure to turn the thermostat up a few degrees when no one is home for an extended period.

➤ Get rid of HBO or another premium channel. You'll save close to $100 in a year.

➤ If you live in an area where you can hang laundry outside, give it a try. You'll save on dryer costs and your wash will smell great. If you live in a condo or townhouse, though, check first. Some associations prohibit hanging laundry.

Dollars and Sense

Try going for one day, or even an evening using no electricity, gas, heat, or the like. This will greatly increase your appreciation for the conveniences we take for granted.

Every Little Bit Counts

Little things you don't think about have a way of adding up fast. Here are some ideas for cutting back on some of those sneaky costs:

➤ Borrow books from the library instead of buying paperbacks. Not only will you save a lot of money, you won't have to worry about where to keep them when you're done reading.

➤ Wait for movies to reach the "cheap" theaters or rent videos instead of going out to movies.

➤ Ride a bike or walk short distances instead of using your car. You'll be surprised at the gas you won't have to buy over time.

➤ Cut subscriptions to magazines or other periodicals that you don't have time to read or have lost interest in. Use the TV directory that comes with most Sunday newspapers instead of buying *TV Guide*.

These little savings on food, clothes, energy bills, and the other areas we've discussed can add up to big savings over time. Keep a record of all the things you don't buy and the ways you've saved money. You'll be surprised at your total.

The Least You Need to Know

➤ Some people are more naturally attuned to saving money than others; however, saving can be learned.

➤ Natural savers have a head start when it comes to successfully managing their personal finances.

➤ You'll be surprised at how fast even little savings add up over time.

➤ Once you put yourself in a mindset to save money, you won't mind as much doing without some of the things you'd like to have.

➤ There are dozens of ways to save money on everything from food to exercise equipment.

Chapter 11

Your Credit: Use It, Don't Abuse It

In This Chapter

➤ Knowing how your credit history affects your life

➤ Avoiding problems with credit and debt

➤ Getting help for credit and debt problems when you need it

➤ Fixing your credit and debt problems

➤ Learning about your credit report

➤ Accessing your credit report

Getting a credit card and knowing how to use it wisely, topics covered extensively in Chapter 4, are the first steps in establishing good credit. Anybody who has ever been turned down for a car loan or mortgage can tell you how important it is to get and maintain a good credit history. Many people, however, take their credit rating for granted, never really understanding how it works or why it's important. It's something they never think about until it goes bad.

Say you apply for a new credit card or a car loan, and you get a big surprise when you're turned down because of problems with your credit report. Unfortunately, that's the point at which most people start thinking about their credit history and personal credit record. By that time, though, it could be too late or an extreme hassle to fix whatever the problem is.

Many people don't even understand that their credit history is carefully documented in a *credit report*, which, by the way, usually contains some very personal and specific information. So let's start at the beginning and see exactly what a credit history is, how you build it, and what it's used for. Then you'll be able to understand why it's so important and how it can affect many areas of your life.

Building a Credit History

Your *credit history* is the record of everything pertaining to any credit you've ever had or applied for. If you want to borrow money for a car, a house, a vacation, debt consolidation, college, or a business, you'll need credit.

If you go to a bank to borrow money, and there's no history of you ever having any credit, you don't stand a good chance of getting the loan. The bank will be reluctant to take a chance on you because it has no indication of whether you'll pay back the money or default on the loan.

Show Me the Money

Your **credit history** is a record of all the credit you've ever had or applied for. Details of your credit history are documented extensively in a **credit report.**

Dollars and Sense

Establishing a credit history can be a classic catch-22. If you can't get credit because you have no credit history, how will you establish a history so you can get credit?

It used to be that you could go to your neighborhood bank, and the banker would lend you money because he'd known you and your family for 35 years. He'd done business with your dad—helped him to get his shoe store up and running, in fact. Your mom and his wife played bridge together every Tuesday, and you and his kids had been on the same teams in school. Mr. Banker was happy to give you a loan. You'd gossip a little bit while you filled out the application, which was really just a formality. After all, if you didn't pay back the loan, all Mr. Banker had to do was talk to your dad about it. He knew he'd get the money back one way or another.

Today, you'd be hard-pressed to find a bank that has anything much left of the personal touch, although some try to lure you in on that pretense. Banking is big business, and there's not much room for taking risks by giving loans to guys and gals just starting out. Because most of us will need occasional loans to finance our dreams and endeavors, we need credit histories in order get those loans.

It's not hard to establish a credit history these days. Credit cards are plentiful and available for the taking. The trick is to develop and maintain a healthy credit history.

Knowing When Enough Is Enough

You want to establish a credit history because you're looking ahead and you know that you're going to need some loans. The old car you've had since your freshman year isn't going to last forever. You'd eventually like to trade in your apartment for your own house, and you think that somewhere down the road you'd even like to start your own graphics business.

Pleased with your forward-looking plan, you start collecting credit cards. Soon, you've got Visas, MasterCards, Discover cards, gas cards, and phone cards. You've got cards for Sears, J.C. Penney, Bloomingdale's, and Marshall's. You have more cards that you know what to do with, and pretty soon you have more bills than you know what to do with, too.

Well, you're establishing a credit history all right, but it's not the kind that's going to get you a loan to help start your own business. If you can't keep up with the payments on all your cards, your credit history will show you as a bad risk. When you go to apply for those loans, you won't be regarded as a good candidate. And you will have unnecessarily put your credit rating in jeopardy. Having too many open lines of credit (credit cards) can be harmful to you when you apply for a loan—let's say a car loan. Lenders want to feel secure that your debt is under control—that you are managing your finances responsibly.

You're much more likely to be approved for a loan if you have a good record of paying off debt on a few credit cards, or even one card, than you would after you've been bogged down with a dozen cards that got away from you. Keep in control of your credit cards and your debt and make sure your payments are on time. Know when enough is enough and establish a good, responsible record of paying back debt.

Oops! I Think I'm in Trouble

Debt and credit card trouble can sneak up on you gradually or can suddenly appear, seemingly out of nowhere. You'll know trouble's coming when you can no longer pay off your debts at the end of the month with the money from your paycheck. If you have to dip into your savings to pay off your debts, sit up and take notice, because your spending habits just might be spiraling out of control.

Consider this potentially embarrassing scene: You go into the department store and come out of the dressing room an hour later with two pairs of

Money Pit

In 1996, the average total debt in this country for people in their 20s, excluding mortgage debt, was nearly $11,000. That was up from a $6,600 average in 1994 and was nearly as much debt as the average for older adults. The scary thing, though, is that the 20-somethings were earning only about half as much as people in their 50s with similar debt.

139

jeans, a sweater, a jacket, and a pair of boots. You throw them onto the counter along with your trusty Visa card, only to be told that the sale is denied because you've exceeded your credit limit.

If the credit card company has put a stop to your account, you're probably already over your credit limit. The general rule is when you have exceeded your limit by 10 percent, your card will be frozen from further use until you make a payment to get the balance down below your limit. You could request an increase in your limit, but that's jumping from the frying pan into the fire, isn't it? Besides, most credit card companies are reluctant to increase your limit after you have exceeded it. If you need to increase your limit, do it before you max out your cards.

Recognizing Credit Trouble

A big sign of credit trouble, as we mentioned previously, is when you can no longer pay your bills out of your regular income. If you're dipping into your savings account or looking for money elsewhere to pay off credit card bills or other debts, you're heading for trouble fast, if you're not already there. Even if you still have money in the bank, you're probably still heading toward a financial crisis.

Some people get so far into debt trouble that it's extremely difficult to fix. If you think you're having trouble managing your debt, it's very important to acknowledge the problem early and to take immediate steps to fix it.

Dollars and Sense

The rule of thumb is that your total debt at the end of the month should not be more than 36 percent of your monthly gross income. Total debt service (amount you are required to pay monthly to keep your debts/loans current) includes payments for rent or mortgage, car payments, college loans, and charge card (the kind you must pay off every month) payments. If your debt is more than 35 percent of your income, you'd better take a closer look at what you're spending money on.

Knowing When to Get Help

We've discussed extensively how our society encourages us to buy and to spend. We're big-time consumers, doing just what advertisers and marketers want us to do.

People buy things and spend a lot of money for many different reasons. Some are compulsive spenders, buying more and more because it fills some need within them. Studies show that many women try to gain affection by financially supporting men. They are trying, in effect, to buy love. People who were abandoned or ignored as children sometimes try to fill that emotional void with things and buy whatever they can.

People who grew up with little money and few material comforts sometimes try to make up for their deprived pasts all at once. It's easy to get a credit card and use it to try to buy yourself some happiness. Unfortunately, when the bills start coming in and there's no money to pay them, reality comes back very quickly.

Remember Hans Christian Anderson's sad story of the poor little match girl? In the story, the little girl sells matches to make a few pennies in order to survive. On New Year's Eve, she is alone and cold, with nowhere to go and no one who loves her. While huddled out in the cold, she starts lighting the matches one by one. While each one burns, she imagines she is in a beautiful, warm place. When the match goes out, she is back in the cold street. She begins lighting matches faster and faster, until they are all burning and she is transported to a wonderful, cheerful, loving place. When all the matches burn out, the little match girl dies in the cold street.

Okay, so the match girl story is a little bit dramatic as an example. But people who buy things they can't afford in order to make themselves feel better for a short time are going to burn out just like the little girl's matches when the creditors start banging on their doors. There are many reasons why people don't control their money and their spending. If you're one of those people, you shouldn't be ashamed, but it's important to realize when you need some help.

If you're not sure whether you have a credit problem, consider these questions from Debtors Anonymous (DA)—copyright credit to Debtors Anonymous General Service Board, Inc., and reprinted by permission. Similar to Alcoholics Anonymous, DA uses a 12-step program to help people stop their debt problems. If you answer yes to eight or more of the following questions, you're headed for (or already have) a big problem with debt:

1. Are your debts making your home life unhappy?
   Yes No

2. Does the pressure of your debts distract you from your daily work?
   Yes No

3. Are your debts affecting your reputation?
   Yes No

4. Do your debts cause you to think less of yourself?
   Yes No

5. Have you ever given false information in order to obtain credit?
   Yes No

6. Have you ever made unrealistic promises to your creditors?
   Yes No

7. Does the pressure of your debts make you careless of the welfare of your family?
   Yes No

8. Do you ever fear that your employer, family, or friends will learn the extent of your total indebtedness?
   Yes No

9. When faced with a difficult financial situation, does the prospect of borrowing give you an inordinate feeling of relief?
   Yes No

10. Does the pressure of your debts cause you to have difficulty sleeping?
Yes No

11. Has the pressure of your debts ever caused you to consider getting drunk?
Yes No

12. Have you ever borrowed money without giving adequate consideration to the rate of interest you are required to pay?
Yes No

13. Do you usually expect a negative response when you are subject to a credit investigation (such as when you apply for a credit card or car loan)?
Yes No

14. Have you ever developed a strict regimen for paying off your debts, only to break it under pressure?
Yes No

15. Do you justify your debts by telling yourself that you are superior to the "other" people, and when you get your "break," you'll be out of debt?
Yes No

If you think you can't stop spending, and you're incurring more debt than you can handle, get some help. You can contact Debtors Anonymous at the General Services Office, P.O. Box 888, Needham, MA 02492-0009. The phone number is 781-453-2743. Or access it on the Internet at www.debtorsanonymous.org. There are also counselors who specialize in financial recovery. Some of them work for nonprofit organizations and their services can be obtained at no cost. Check your phone book for local listings.

Dollars and Sense

Try putting your credit card in a deep freeze to avoid using it when you shouldn't. Put it in a container of water in the freezer, and thaw it out when you want to use it. Waiting around while it thaws allows you time to consider the purchase and whether it's a good idea. If you do this, remember that it's against the rules to use the microwave to thaw out the water!

Repairing the Damage

If you determine that you have a problem with your credit and debt, there are steps you can take on your own to fix it. The most immediate step is to stop incurring more debt. To do that, you might have to get rid of your credit cards completely. "What?!" you shriek. "Live without credit cards? Impossible!"

Guess what? It's not impossible. It won't be easy, but if you can't resist racking up debt on your credit cards, you're better off without them. If you can trust yourself, keep one to use when you want to rent a car or reserve a hotel room. Otherwise, cut them up and call the credit card company to cancel your accounts. Then, plan carefully to pay for whatever you buy with cash, check, or a debit card.

When you stop piling up more and more debt, you can start working to get rid of what you already have:

➤ Take a close look at what you owe and to whom you owe it. Record all the information, and pay special attention to any bills marked past due. If you're in the middle of a credit card billing cycle, call the provider and ask for your balance. You need to know exactly where you stand.

➤ Contact those creditors to whom your payment is overdue. Let them know that you acknowledge your debt, and you will work in good faith to pay it off. Ask if you can work together to come up with a plan that will allow you to pay off the debt in a manner that you can afford. Most creditors will work with you if you are up-front and acting in good faith. After a payment plan is established, stick to it! You can't afford to screw up any more than you already have.

➤ Think about possible sources of money. As difficult as it might be to go to a family member or friend, confess your sins and ask for a loan; it may be the healthiest thing for you to do, financially.

➤ If you have any money in a savings account, break into it and pay off what you can. It's practically a sure bet that you're paying more interest on your debts than you're earning on your savings account.

➤ If your debt is serious, consider borrowing from your retirement account at work. Ask the benefits department at your company if you're permitted to borrow from your account balance. If you are, find out what the interest rate is. It's usually reasonable, and as you pay off the loan, the interest goes back into your account.

➤ Sell assets. Sell any stocks you may have or sell a collection. Downsize your car from the one of your dreams to a Hyundai. Do whatever is necessary to get caught up.

➤ Consider getting a second job.

Be honest with yourself when assessing your debt. If you're afraid you might have a problem, you probably do. But unless you've had the problem for a long time and have ignored it, you probably can figure out a way to fix it before it gets completely out of hand.

It's sort of like your weight. If you notice you've gained five pounds, and you decide to eat less and exercise more, you can take care of the problem without too much trouble. If you wait until you've gained 25 pounds, however, you're talking about nothing but Lean Cuisine and aerobic classes for months to come. It's better to face the problem early on and go about fixing it before it becomes too serious.

Your Credit Report

When you applied for your first credit card (probably back in high school or college), your name and a lot of personal information got zapped into a computer, and your personal credit report had begun. Since then, every time you applied for another credit card or a store card, took a vacation loan from your bank or credit union, or applied for a car loan, information was added to your report.

There are three big, nationwide credit agency companies, and each of them probably has the same information about you and your credit history. They get it from banks, finance companies, credit card suppliers, department stores, mail order companies, and various other places that have had the pleasure of doing business with you. Smaller, regional credit bureaus supplement the information.

Your personal credit report includes information such as your name, social security number, date of birth, your address from the time you first got a credit card until now, everywhere you've worked during that time, and how you pay your bills. Whenever you apply for a loan or for credit, the place at which you applied will check out your report with a credit agency. In turn, it will give the credit agency any additional information that it's picked up on you.

Say you want to buy a Jeep, and you apply for credit with the car dealership. Before Jack's Jeep Company approves your application (which, incidentally, will contain all sorts of personal information), somebody from the company calls up Equifax to check you out. Equifax employee Jenny pulls up your credit report on her computer, makes a printout, and faxes the information to Jack's Jeep Company. In turn, Jack hands back the additional information you volunteered about yourself on the application.

Pocket Change

The three largest credit agency companies are Equifax Credit Services, Trans Union Credit Information Services, and Experian.

Money Pit

When you understand how much credit information is floating around out there, it becomes easy to see how mistakes are made with that information. Human error is a big factor, and somebody who misreads some information about you can screw up your credit report royally.

Pretty soon, a whole bunch of information about you is floating around out there, ready to be handed out to who-knows-who whenever you go for a loan or apply for a credit card or mortgage. If you find it a little unsettling that all this personal information about you is available, you might find some comfort in knowing that not just anyone can get access to your credit report.

The Fair Credit Reporting Act limits who can see your credit report. Of course, the list is pretty long, but it does set some guidelines. Your credit report can be released by a reporting agency under the following circumstances:

➤ In response (God forbid!) to a court order or a federal grand jury subpoena

➤ To anyone to whom you've given written permission

➤ To anyone considering you for credit or collection of an account

➤ To anyone who will use the report for insurance purposes

➤ To determine your eligibility for a government license or benefits

➤ To anyone with a legitimate business need for the report in connection with a business transaction with which you're involved. This includes your landlord when you apply to rent an apartment.

When you realize how often your credit report can be accessed, then you can begin to see how important it is that you keep it clean. But even if your credit record is perfect, your report might not be. A study showed that one out of four people who took the time to thoroughly review their credit reports discovered a mistake that eventually was corrected. Be aware that every time an inquiry is made for your credit report it is automatically logged into your report. Although this isn't necessarily bad, numerous inquiries may need to be explained to a potential lender.

You're going to learn more about why it's important to keep an eye on your credit report and exactly how to go about getting a copy of it. But first let's see what a credit report looks like.

How to Get a Copy of Your Credit Report

Even if you don't plan to apply for a car loan, a mortgage, or a credit card anytime soon, it's a good idea to take a look at your credit report. You can get a copy of your report from any of the three largest credit agencies:

Equifax Credit Services
P.O. Box 740241
Atlanta, GA 30374
Toll-free: 800-685-1111
http://www.equifax.com

Dollars and Sense

If you ever apply for a job in an area such as defense, banking, or the medical field, you can expect that your prospective employer will take a look at your credit report before deciding whether to hire you. If you're turned down for the job because of something in the report, you're required, under federal law, to be notified of your right to get a copy of the report at no charge.

Dollars and Sense

Experts recommend that you scan your credit report carefully about once a year, especially before you apply for credit or when you know that the credit report will be checked (as when you rent an apartment). This is the only way to be sure that no mistakes have been made that will damage your credit record.

Pocket Change

You have a legal right to submit a letter up to 100 words long to the credit agency, disputing something you've discovered on your credit report. The letter must be included in your file. If you do this, make sure your letter is clear, concise, and to the point.

Trans Union Credit Information Services
1561 E. Orangethorpe Ave.
Fullerton, CA 92631
Toll-free: 800-916-8800
http://wwwtransunion.com

Experian
P.O. Box 949
Allen, TX 75013
Toll-free: 888-397-3742
http://www.experian.com

If you've been turned down for a mortgage, loan, or credit card, you're entitled to get a copy of your credit report for free at your request. If you want to get a copy of your credit report to check it over, there will be a fee ($8 in most states). Call one of the companies listed here or contact it by mail with an enclosed check or money order. Be prepared to provide your name, address, social security number and maybe your date of birth as ID.

When you have the report, look it over carefully. If you discover a mistake, take the following steps to correct it:

➤ Contact all three credit agencies by certified mail and inform them of the mistake you've discovered. Request that they investigate.

➤ If you don't get a reply within 60 days, send another letter. Remind the companies that they are required by law to investigate incorrect information or provide an updated credit report with the incorrect information removed.

If you see information you don't like on your credit report that, unfortunately, isn't a mistake, don't despair. The Fair Credit Reporting Act mandates that negative information on your report be removed after a certain period of time. Even if you (gasp!) declare bankruptcy, that information is supposed to be removed from your report after 10 years. The trick, of course, is keeping your credit report healthy and in good shape. In this case, preventive maintenance works best.

The Least You Need to Know

➤ It pays to be aware of your credit history because it affects many areas of your life.

➤ It's not how much credit you have, but how you handle it, that affects your credit history.

➤ Recognizing and acknowledging credit and debt problems early can stop the situation from getting out of control.

➤ If your credit problems are more than you can handle, there are places that can help.

➤ You should know what your credit report contains and how you can get a copy of it and correct mistakes when necessary.

Part 3
Coasting Along

"Wow! I'm making some pretty good money, here." We're hopeful that you're to the point where this statement is accurate. If not, we hope it will be soon. Things get a little more comfortable after you get a few raises or maybe even a better, higher-paying job. You can think about doing some things that weren't in your vocabulary just a little while back. Things such as vacations, investments, emergency funds, and your own apartment.

With this better financial position, however, comes added decisions and responsibilities. You need to know what types of investment vehicles are available and which ones are best for someone in your situation. You need to resist the temptation to spend your extra cash and realize that it's not too early to be thinking about saving for the future.

Chapters 12 through 15 will tell you all about things that will begin to affect and influence your personal finances at this stage of your life, things such as investments, taxes, and insurance. But it's not all serious, grown-up stuff. You're earning money and getting ahead—it's a great time to have some fun, too. Part 3 will examine how to strike a balance between living well now and starting to look to the future.

Chapter 12

Movin' On Up

In This Chapter

➤ Planning ahead while you're moving ahead

➤ Setting aside some emergency money

➤ When to keep your car and when to trade it in

➤ Is there a higher degree in your future?

➤ Taking vacations and other fun stuff

➤ Ditching the roomies for a place of your own

Getting started was pretty tough, but things are looking up for you now. You've gotten a couple of raises at work, and it seems that your future in the industry is looking pretty good. You even had people from that competing company calling a few months ago to see whether you might consider working for them.

You're feeling good that you're not in a paycheck-to-paycheck situation any more, and you've managed to save some money. You're watching your credit card debt and trying to keep your balance down. Your car loan is paid off, and you're up-to-date with college loan payments. You think you're pretty much on track financially.

You don't have to wonder anymore if you'll have enough money to go out to dinner with your friends on Friday night, and you were able to fly out to Los Angeles to be with your sister and her family during the Christmas holiday. You're even thinking about taking a long weekend in Bermuda with some friends when February rolls around. You're not rich, but spending money isn't in as short supply as it was a few years ago when you were just starting out and worrying about how you'd pay for everything. Life is good.

Congratulations! You've come a long way in a short time, and you're on your feet, financially speaking. But before you start patting yourself on the back, you still have a lot to learn, and many of the things we haven't talked about yet will cost you money. Now is the time for you to start setting financial goals. Think about what you'll need in the future and how much those things will cost.

You may feel like king of the hill now, but you can bet that your lifestyle will change during the next 10 years or so. Perhaps you'll get married; maybe you'll even have a child or two. You might want to buy a house, and your car won't last forever. What if you find out you can't get that promotion at work unless you get an advanced degree? You've also developed a strong interest in scuba diving, but, unfortunately, the best dives are nowhere near your home in Peoria.

All those things, and many more that will come up, will cost you money. Go ahead and enjoy your new-found financial comfort. Live a little. Don't get carried away, though. Remember that financial security for the future requires good planning and some self-control and sacrifices today.

Emergency Funds

Just when you think you have some fun money, we're going to tell you to stash it away in case of an emergency. Sorry to burst your bubble!

An emergency fund is essential. If you lose your job (we still live somewhat under the specter of downsizing) or run into dire straits from another direction, you'll need some money to tide you over until you get reorganized.

Money Pit

Be careful not to use your emergency fund as a convenient means of money if you run a little short at the end of the pay period. The intent of an emergency fund is to keep you afloat if your income is interrupted. If you're not careful, you could easily deplete your emergency fund before an emergency occurs.

Some people need to have an emergency fund to tap into, because of the unsteady income provided by their jobs. If you're in a business where you earn a lot of money sometimes and very little or no money at other times, you might need emergency money to use during the lean periods. Of course, it's important to set up a budget so that you don't spend more than you should when you have money coming in.

If you don't have an emergency fund, and you lose your job or get into financial trouble, the temptation might be to use your credit card. You could live perfectly well on your credit cards for several months, depending on your credit limits. Nearly everyone, from your doctor to your grocery store, will take your plastic instead of your cash, and your credit card issuer will be delighted. But if you end up with $4,000 or $5,000 in credit card debt at the end of that time, you'll be the one who's sorry. It will take you a long time to get back on your feet again.

Establishing an emergency fund should be a priority in your personal finances plan. Build the funds within a money market fund, which will give you accessibility and liquidity, as needed. You'll learn more about money markets in Chapter 13.

Finding Another Car

Just when you think you're sailing along financially, the odds are that you'll run into some rough seas. It's practically a rule, almost as certain as death and taxes. For many people, these financial setbacks pop up in the form of car problems. As long as you own a car, you're not immune to the problems that go along with it.

Dollars and Sense

Three to six months' salary is the rule of thumb for what you should have in an emergency fund. If you have other sources of emergency money such as family or a 401(k) plan that you could call on for a short-term loan, you probably can get by with less. If you have no other sources of money, try to save a little more.

You're driving along one day, and you hear a strange noise. It doesn't last long, and you promptly forget about it until a day later, when you hear it again. Pretty soon, the noise is too loud to ignore, and you reluctantly get the car to the repair shop. Sure enough, the mechanic tells you that the entire exhaust system is shot, and it's going to cost you $329 to have the thing fixed.

Now, if this were the first big bill you'd had on the car for a while, you probably wouldn't be so upset. But the cooling system went out before this, and you had to replace a couple of hoses before that, and there was a problem with the timing belt before all that, so now you're really annoyed.

Your car is eight years old, and you've been pretty hard on it. You've put well over 100,000 miles on it, and you're at the point where you don't feel like sinking any more money in it. Everybody says you won't get anything when you go to trade it in, but you're thinking it's time to get rid of it. What to do?

Knowing When to Trade It In

There's no set formula that can tell you exactly how long you should have a car before you trade it in for a new one. It would be helpful to

Money Pit

Unless you know and trust your mechanic, it's a good idea to get a second opinion. I once had a mechanic tell me I needed an entire new exhaust system. When I took it a garage that specialized in exhaust systems, the mechanic told me he could replace one section of pipe, and it would be as good as new. I would have been out a couple of hundred dollars without the second opinion.

your financial planning if you knew that every six years to the day you would need to trade in your present vehicle for another one. But there are far too many variables involved to come up with anything like that. Consider the following:

➤ If you've kept your car meticulously maintained, it should last longer than a car that's only had two oil changes since you brought it home.

➤ If your car was used when you bought it, you know how old it is and how many miles are on it, but you can't ever know for sure how it was treated before you had it. It could have been taken care of like a second child, or it could have been abused.

➤ The climate in which you live can affect the life of your car. Wet, salty air, for instance, can build up on car parts and shorten their life span.

➤ If you had an accident with your car, it could have damaged something that you're unaware of. That something could eventually cause problems and shorten the life of your car.

➤ If you can fix the car yourself, you might be inclined to keep it long after someone who can't fix it would.

➤ Maybe you just like driving a new car and tire quickly of your current set of wheels. This can make your car seem pretty unattractive, even if there's nothing wrong with it.

As you can see, determining the ideal time to trade in a car can be difficult. But if you're constantly shelling out money for repairs and your car has become undependable, it might be time to kiss it good-bye.

If you decide it's time to trade in your car for something different (whether brand-new or used), there are some things to remember when negotiating with car salespeople to assure you get the best deal possible:

➤ Clean up your car. Investing a little bit of money in your car can pay off big time when you go to trade it or sell it. Clean it thoroughly, or have it cleaned, and get it waxed, as well. Be sure you lift up the seats and collect the gum wrappers and coins that have been accumulating there since you owned the car. Buy new floor mats. Clean out the glove compartment, and clean the ketchup stain off the back seat. If there are small, mechanical problems that need to be fixed, have that done, too.

➤ Don't let the car dealer know you have a car to trade in until after he's made you an offer. That way, he can't factor in the trade with the price of the new car. The dealer might not be too happy with you if you do this, but he'll get over it.

➤ To work out a deal with the car salesperson, you should know exactly how much the dealership paid for the car you want (the invoice price). You can get this information from the Consumer Reports Auto Price Service. Call them at 312-347-5801. There's a small charge, but this company will tell you what the dealer paid for the car, plus each option. Figure out the options that you want, add them to the basic cost of the car, and make that number your first offer to the dealer.

➤ When the dealer tells you he can't possibly give you the car for that price, be prepared to negotiate. He'll make a counteroffer, at which time you should make your own. Make your counteroffer about 2 percent higher than your original offer, and never pay more than 5 percent over what the dealer paid.

➤ Know what your car is worth. Look up its value in the "blue book," that is, the National Automobile Dealers Association (NADA) guide. Your library will have a copy, or you can access the information from the N.A.D.A. Official Used Car Guide Company's Web site at www.nada.com. After you know what your car is worth, and you have an offer on the new car you want, all you have to do is subtract the value of your car from the price of the new one.

➤ Don't ever let a car dealer tell you that the value of your car depends on the cost of the car you're buying. The two should have nothing to do with one another.

➤ Have pre-approved financing from a bank or credit union before you begin to negotiate. That prevents the salesperson from using financing as a bargaining tool.

You probably can get more money for your car if you sell it privately than if you trade it in when getting a new one. Again, you need to know exactly how much your car is worth and decide how much higher you think you can go when you put it up for sale. Remember to leave some room for negotiating. Most people will ask you to come down on your original price. Check out some of the auto seller magazines at your newsstand to see what others with similar cars are asking.

If you do sell the car privately, make sure you thoroughly clean it, and you have all the applicable papers (warranties, service records, owner's manual, and so on) together for the next owner. This will make a good impression on prospective buyers in addition to being

Dollars and Sense

If you decide to privately sell your car to someone you don't know, be careful about how you're paid. If you have any reason to think a check you get for the car is no good, check with the bank first before agreeing to take it and never give the prospective buyer the car keys until you do so. Better yet, take only cash or a bank check.

155

helpful to whoever ends up with the car. Write up an agreement detailing the price and leave room for the names of the buyer and seller and the date of the sale. Make sure the agreement contains the words "sold as seen" or "as is" and have the buyer sign it.

Knowing When to Keep It

Only you can decide exactly when you're ready to trade in your car for a different one. We've all seen cars that are 15 years old with more than 200,000 miles on them that look as though they won't make it to the corner. Somehow, though, they keep running for years and years.

On the other hand, we know people who have a car for a few years and then get a wandering eye. Suddenly, nothing about their car is right anymore. Little rattles become huge annoyances. Just having the oil changed seems like a big imposition. They're ready to move on to something new. Remember though, that having no car payment is better than having a car payment, and that money you don't have to pay each month on your car can be used for other things—an emergency fund, perhaps.

Back to School

If going back to school is part of your plans, now might be a good time to start thinking about it. If you're still paying off college loans, you might be reluctant put yourself further into debt for more schooling. But if you think you need an advanced degree to get ahead in your career, you might as well get it as early on as possible to increase your chances of advancing earlier and earning more money before you retire.

Another thing to think about is your schedule. As busy as you think you are now, believe me when I tell you that it doesn't get any better. If you're still single, but planning to get married some day, you probably have more free time now than you will after the wedding bells have rung. If you're married with kids still in the future, you'll have much less time for school or anything else when your house is filled with cribs and diapers.

If you decide you need a graduate degree, and that it makes sense to get it now, look into your options before committing yourself to a program. The fastest way to get a degree is to go back to school full time. Most people, though, can't afford to do that. School has to be something that's done in addition to and around the schedule of your work.

Colleges understand this and have gone to great lengths to make their graduate programs appealing to working men and women. Classes are scheduled at night and on weekends, catering to those with nine-to-five commitments.

Pocket Change

Graduate school is expensive. The New York State Higher Education Services says the average under-graduate student in that state owes $30,000 after graduation. Tacking on a graduate education can boost the total to more than $100,000.

An option that is relatively new, but quickly gaining in popularity, is online learning. Also called distance learning, this virtual education gives students their courses electronically, via the Internet, e-mail, satellite, compressed video, and other technologies. If you haven't yet heard about distance learning, you will. It's becoming more widespread all the time and is employed by schools as traditional as Duke University and the University of Virginia.

The University of Phoenix was one of the first schools to adopt online learning, and its program is considered to be a model. At this university, more than 2,000 online students undertake six-week courses in varying subjects. They're mailed textbooks before the course begins, and they receive their instructors' lectures by e-mail, which they can download onto their computers. They communicate with the instructor and their classmates by e-mail, writing weekly summaries of what they've learned. Even exams are taken online.

Educators praise online learning, saying it makes education more accessible and convenient. To find out what's available, access the Web site of the college in which you're interested, or call the school for more information.

If you decide to go for an advanced degree, make sure you check with the school you'll be attending to see what financial aid programs might be available. You might have a better shot of getting some aid if you're doing your graduate work at the same school you received an undergraduate degree from. Many employers will reimburse you for educational expenses if you receive a grade of C or better for the course. Check with your company's human resources or benefits department to find out what might be available. Keep in mind that money spent on education that can help you to advance is a good way to spend money, even if it means you'll be incurring some more debt.

Dollars and Sense

Try to tailor your advanced degree to a particular career opportunity, if you can. For example, if you have a psychology degree, and you're interested in working with industry, look for something such as a master's program in industrial and organizational psychology.

Life Is Better in the Tropics

When your financial situation improves a little bit, it's tempting to start thinking of all the fun things you want to do and all the places you'd love to visit. Vacations are great, but unfortunately they can be very expensive. If your tastes run to fancy resorts in tropical destinations in the middle of February, you'd better be prepared to drop a significant chunk of your income on your vacations. Just remember that when you come home, you'll still have to pay the rent and the electric bill.

There are lots of ways, though, to take vacations that won't wreck you financially. All you have to do is be creative. Think about it. If you're vacationing with a group of

Dollars and Sense

Remember that a driving vacation is almost always cheaper than if you have to buy airline tickets, especially if there's more than one person. Several people sharing the cost of gas and tolls can cut travel costs significantly.

friends, won't you have a good time just about any-where you go? There are plenty of vacations that won't cost you a month's salary. Consider camping or getting a bunch of people to split the cost of a house near the beach.

It's easier than ever to find bargain vacations. If you and your friends are flexible, you can get some great discounts by signing up for a trip midweek and going that weekend. Put the money you save into your emergency fund.

Some airlines will notify you by e-mail of bargain fares. Check out www.travelnavigator.com to sign up for notice of discount fares from Air Tran, Air Canada, America West, American Airlines, Cathay Pacific Airlines, Continental Airlines, Northwest Airlines, Trans World Airlines, United Airlines, and US Airways. For last-minute bargain airfares, try Cheap Tickets at 1-800-377-1000 or contact these airlines at their Web sites:

➤ Air Tran at www.airtran.com/specials

➤ Northwest Airlines at www.nwa.com/travel/cyber/cyber

➤ Trans World Airlines at www.twa.com/html/flights/faresale

➤ US Airways at www.usairways.com/travel/fares

If cruises are your thing, you can find some discounted prices on well-known cruise lines by checking out the following sites:

➤ Cheap Cruises at www.cheap-cruises.com

➤ Cruise Web at www.cruiseweb.com

➤ Cruise Bargains at www.cruisebargains.com

➤ Worldwide Travel Service at www.wwts.com/openseas

For discounted rates at major hotel chains, check out these Web sites:

➤ Hilton at www.hilton.com/specials/values

➤ Inter-Continental Hotels and Resorts at www.interconti.com

➤ Radisson at www.radisson.com/low-res/hotdeals

➤ Hyatt at www.hyatt.com/hotdeals

Aren't These Computers Cool?

People in their 20s and 30s have grown up with technology. It's part of your lives and integral to your work and your leisure. We all know that technology is advancing at a phenomenal rate, which makes it hard sometimes to keep up with everything new. Our TVs are changing, our cameras are changing, our means for communicating with one another are changing, and our computers never stop changing.

If you're tempted by every new technological gadget that comes along, you'll be spending a lot of money on grown-up toys. As awesome of some of the new stuff is, it doesn't come cheap. Only you can judge what you need and what you buy just because it's so cool you think you can't do without it. Expensive electronic stuff is a good purchase to put off for a day or two and re-evaluate before you buy.

Do you really need a $329 hand-held fax reader that plugs into your cell phone, allowing you to receive, read, and send faxes while you're on the road? Are you going to use the $250-dollar wristwatch that has a tape recorder built into it?

No matter what it is that you're going to buy, make sure you do some comparison shopping. Look at ads in magazines to compare different brands, or check out a trade show where many items are displayed at once, and buy it only when you've saved enough to buy it. The expensive "toys" can be budget busters. Plan, dream, and save for the day you will own the first digital TV on the block.

Pocket Change

Somebody 70 years old today has come from a world without TV to a world of amazing computers and other practically unimaginable technology. No wonder some people have trouble keeping up!

Getting Your Own Place

If you've been living with roommates or are even still at home with Mom and Dad, you might be getting ready to look for your own place. You'd like a little more privacy, or maybe you have to bring work home at night and it's hard to get it done because of the noise.

For whatever reasons, if you move from a roommate situation to a non-roommate situation, you'll probably find that living expenses will cost you more. Even if you move to a smaller place, paying the full rent on an apartment by yourself will probably cost more than sharing rent. You'll also have to come up

Dollars and Sense

Be sure to reread Chapter 5 before moving out by yourself. It has a lot of tips for getting the best place for your money.

with the up-front costs of a security deposit and a couple of months' rent when you first get your own place. And even if you've accumulated some furniture and household items by now, it's likely you'll have to get more because you won't have Bob's or Stephanie's stuff to supplement your own.

If you're absolutely determined to live on your own, go ahead. Just keep the following suggestions in mind:

➤ Don't be brainwashed into believing that you have to live in a certain area because it's popular at the moment. Rents are likely to be a lot cheaper in a non-trendy section.

➤ Be ready to give up some things you may have grown accustomed to having. Maybe you won't have your own parking space when you move out on your own because you won't be able to afford an apartment that provides one. Be prepared to make some trade-offs.

➤ Negotiate for your rent. You don't necessarily have to hand over whatever rent your landlord requests. Request that he or she lower the rent (before you move in, of course), and after you're in the apartment, negotiate to lower rent increases, as well.

➤ Don't invest in a lot of furniture and household items to fill up an apartment you might not keep very long. Sure, you'll need to buy some things to make it livable, but try to keep your purchases to a minimum. You'll find a better use for that money later.

➤ Think about how moving in by yourself will affect your long-range plans. If the extra costs associated with living on your own are going to prevent you from realizing goals such as buying a house in five years or getting married in two years, perhaps it's time to re-examine your priorities. Roommates can be a hassle, and privacy is nice. You just have to weigh whether living alone is worth the additional costs.

The expenses discussed in this chapter are only some of the things on which you'll be spending your money. We're not going to tell you to invest every penny you make and never have any fun—what kind of life would that be? A word of advice, though: Weigh the value of things you spend money on today against the value of things you hope to acquire in the future.

Is an extra trip to the ski slopes this winter going to be worth having to wait six months longer to get a house when you're ready to buy? Will buying the new computer mean you'll have to delay starting a retirement fund? It's hard to postpone what we want today in exchange for the promise of financial security tomorrow. If you want that security, however, you have to be willing to do just that.

The Least You Need to Know

➤ It's tempting to spend more money when you're making more, but it's important to remember your future financial needs.

➤ As soon as you start earning money, establishing an emergency fund should be one of your first financial priorities.

➤ Cars are a reoccurring expense, but there are ways to keep the costs down.

➤ If you're going to go back to school, you'll need to figure out when it makes sense to do so.

➤ Vacations and grown-up toys are fun, but they can take a big bite out of your budget.

➤ Living by yourself might be appealing, but you have to evaluate whether the extra cost is worth it.

What's All This Talk About Investments?

If you're like most people, you believe that investments are a good thing. Having money to invest means that you have savings that you want to put to work for you. Everybody should have some investments so that their funds earn money. Good investments grow over time which help you keep up with inflation and help assure your financial security when you retire. Investments must be important because people spend a lot of time talking about them. Turn on the radio, and you're likely to hear a stock market report. Or, put a couple of people who own stocks together and, sooner or later, the topic will come up.

Although most people see investments as desirable, investing itself intimidates them. Investing implies taking action and moving money around to different places. Investing must be learned, and it sounds mighty complicated. Investing is a risky business that can result in you losing money that you've been saving for years.

If you want to have investments but are reluctant to do much investing, you're in good company. A good portion of the general population has no clue about how or where to invest money. As a result, they keep money in low-interest accounts, effectively denying themselves the money they could be earning.

Investing money baffles many people, but it doesn't have to be that difficult or scary. A lot of folks are intimidated because they hear investment talk on the news that they can't decipher or look at incredibly small print in the newspaper that they know deals with investments, but seems to mean nothing. Or they think they wouldn't have enough money to invest anywhere. So they maintain their financial status quo, missing chance after chance to increase their net worth.

This chapter will not tell you everything you'll ever need to know about investments, but it will give you basic information about various kinds of investments and tell you which ones make sense for new investors. We can't guarantee that after you read this chapter, you'll never make a mistake when it comes to investing your money, but you'll be better prepared to avoid mistakes that result from poor judgment or greed. You should be able to invest your money responsibly and understand why you're putting it where you do.

If you've been reluctant to learn about investing because it seems too boring or complicated, relax. It might not be as much fun as a night out, but we promise it won't be too agonizing.

Starting Small

Many people think they just don't have enough money to invest it anywhere. Or they think they'll need to pay a financial advisor to direct them to where they should invest their money and that will cost more than they have to invest in the first place. Neither of these ideas is true.

Money Pit

Don't even think about investing money if you owe credit card debt. Making 10 percent or 12 percent off an investment pales in comparison to paying out 17 percent or 18 percent on your Visa. Pay off the plastic first. You can't get ahead while you're carrying a load of debt.

You don't need a ton of money to start investing. You can begin investing with just $50 (we'll tell you how to do that a little later in the chapter). You don't necessarily need a financial advisor or a salesperson to tell you where to put your money either. Many investments can be purchased without a salesperson, and if you do your homework carefully, you'll be able to figure out on your own the best places to put your money at this point in your life.

Almost everyone who starts investing starts small and builds up their investments over time. If you work carefully and patiently, you'll do the same. It's fun to watch the growth, particularly when you remember that you started small.

How Much Do You Have to Invest?

No, you don't have to be rich to invest, but you do need to know what money you have available to invest. Just because you have $10,000 sitting around in various accounts doesn't mean you have $10,000 to invest. Think carefully about the money you have and what your goals for that money are.

For instance, if you have the equivalent of three months' salary set aside for emergencies, that's not money that you want to tie up in a long-term investment. You need to be able to get it when you need it in case there *is* an emergency. It's the same with the money you've been saving for a down payment for a house. You sure can't afford to take much risk with that money, because you're going to need it in a couple of years.

As you learn more about investment vehicles, you'll find out which ones are good for short-term investments and which ones to go with for the long haul. That's important, because you don't want to tie up money for 20 years that you might need in two. How you invest your money depends largely on how long it can remain out of your reach. It also depends on how much of it you can afford to lose. Some investments are a lot riskier than others, and you need to know what you're getting into before you throw your money into the pot.

To figure out what kind of risk-taker you can afford to be, think about having $1,000 invested for one year. If you think you can afford to lose no more than 6 percent of that money ($60), then you're a low-risk type of investor. If you could stand to lose up to 15 percent ($150), you're a moderate-risk type of investor. If you could stand to lose as much of a quarter of your money ($250), you're a high-risk type of investor.

Of course, this $1,000-invested-for-a-year scenario is terribly simplified. Your stakes would be a lot higher if you were talking about many thousands of dollars. It's easy to say you could afford to lose $150, but if you had $50,000 invested, you'd have to decide if you'd be willing to lose $7,500.

Before we begin there's a simple rule that helps you know, at a given rate of return, how long it will take you to double your money. It's the Rule of 72. For example, if a CD pays 10 percent interest, your money will double in 7.2 years (72 divided by 10). It gives you an idea of how well you're doing on your investments.

Pocket Change

Generation X investment clubs are popping up all over the place, as young people realize their investment money goes farther when it's pooled. A group of eight friends in the Seattle area are members of the Green Machine Investment Club. They each throw in $50 a month for a mutually agreeable stock. In less than three years, their assets bounded from $4,500 to $13,000, and they figure barring any major problems with the stock market, they'll be worth a collective $2.3 million come retirement.

What's Out There?

It's important to know which types of investments will keep your money safe and sound while earning you a little bit of interest and which have the potential to make you a lot of money, while playing roulette with your investment. If you're just learning about investments and investing, there's no question that it can be intimidating. Stocks, international stocks, money markets, mutual funds, annuities, real estate, precious metals—there's a lot to swallow. It's almost enough to make you stick your money into a savings account and keep it there, earning its lowly 2 percent interest a year.

Savings accounts are a form of investment, and a very safe form, but you can do better than that. The following sections discuss some good investment vehicles for people who are just starting: mutual funds, money market funds, and certificates of deposit (CDs). We'll get into detail about a lot of other kinds of investments in Chapter 19. For now, though, we'll stick with the basics.

Mutual Funds

Mutual funds are the most common investment vehicle for individuals because they don't require a lot of money to get started. They carry some other advantages, as well.

What are mutual funds? They're investments that pool the money of many people and place the cash into stocks, bonds, and other holdings. When you put your money into a mutual fund, you're throwing it into a pot with another couple hundred million dollars or so. Some mutual funds can go as high as a billion dollars or more.

Show Me the Money

Mutual funds are investments that pool the money of many investors and place it in stocks, bonds, and other holdings. The money is managed by a **portfolio manager** and team of researchers.

The money is managed by a *portfolio manager* and a team of researchers, who are responsible for finding the best places in which to invest the money. While a portfolio is a group of investments assembled to meet an investment goal, a portfolio manager is someone who is paid to supervise the investment decisions of others. The fund managers get paid for their services from a fee within the fund, usually a percentage of the value of the fund. Although you don't see this fee, you should remember that it exists. The terms "portfolio manager" and "money manager" are terms used interchangeably. Both handle the management of a portfolio, be it for individuals or for a mutual fund. They are paid on a percentage of the assets under management.

Mutual funds can offer you some great advantages:

➤ No-load mutual funds let you avoid paying a sales commission on your transactions. The companies that offer no-load funds have toll-free phone numbers that you can call for recommendations of what funds to buy. Load funds charge a sales commission. Usually, how your financial adviser is paid determines the type of fund you're shown as a possible investment. (Chapter 19 will discuss how to identify a mutual fund that is right for you in more detail.)

Load funds are sales commissions paid to a broker, financial adviser, insurance consultant, etc. No-load funds are shown by advisers who receive compensation otherwise, often an hourly rate. If your mutual fund has a load, know how much it is and how you pay it. Load funds have front-end loads, deferred sales charges, or back-end loads:

➤ Front-end loads are fees paid up front. A 5 percent front load means you pay 5 percent of every dollar invested as a fee, and you invest the remaining funds. $100 invested means that $95 goes in the fund and $5 goes to the salesperson.

➤ A deferred sales charge permits the load to be postponed, and gradually declines over a period of years until the sales charge is 0. Thus, if you invest $1,000 in February in a mutual fund with a 5 percent deferred sales charge, you would pay 5 percent if you sell the fund the first year, 4 percent the second year, and so forth until the sixth year, when you could withdraw all the funds without a fee.

➤ A back-end load means you pay a set fee upon sale of the mutual fund. An example is if you purchase and then sell a fund within too short a time, certain funds will charge a back-end fee. Fund loads/fees should be reviewed by the salesperson and stated in the prospectus (paperwork) sent from the company.

➤ Money can be taken directly from your bank account each month and transferred into a mutual fund. This makes investing nearly painless.

Money Pit

Be careful when you buy a no-load mutual fund. You won't pay any commission, but you could be charged fees for marketing and promotional costs, fees for reinvesting your dividends, and other hidden fees. Make sure you know what fees will be charged before you agree to buy.

➤ Mutual funds can offer *diversification*. If you are diversified and one or more of your investments hits a slump, you can rely on your other investments to boost your total portfolio. You could, for instance, divide your money among three or four different types of stock funds (we'll talk about the different types of mutual funds in Chapter 19), assuring that you'd always have some money invested in a profitable area of the market. Part of diversification is also investing in stocks and bonds, as well as just different types of stocks. It would be difficult for you to plan that diversification on your own, which is why people look to mutual funds to diversify their portfolios.

➤ It doesn't cost much out of pocket to have mutual funds. If you purchase a no-load fund, you do not pay a sales charge to buy the fund. Brokerage for the investments within the mutual fund, the cost of buying or selling shares of the stocks or bonds, are generally far lower than standard brokerage because the fund managers buy or sell so many shares of a security at one time and buy and sell frequently. Having this power enables them to negotiate trades for a lot less money than you could on your own. Many people assume that mutual funds do not pay to trade securities, but that's a false assumption. Fees occur whenever a security is traded; although, they are usually lower inside a fund, due to the large number of shares traded.

➤ The Securities and Exchange Commission (SEC) oversees the records and expenses of all mutual funds.

➤ You can direct almost any amount of money to where you want it. If you're into a mutual fund for the long haul, you can direct your money to funds that invest more heavily in stocks instead of directing your money to the more conservative bond funds.

If you're looking for mutual funds that don't require a lot of money to open or to be contributed each month, consider the following options. They all were given high ratings by *Morningstar Mutual Funds*, a newsletter published twice a month by Morningstar, Inc. in Chicago:

American Century: 800-331-8331

Columbia Funds: 800-547-1707

Fremont Funds: 800-548-4539

Homestead Funds: 800-258-3030

Invesco Funds Group: 800-525-8085

Preferred Group: 800-662-4769

Show Me the Money

Diversification is investing your money in different securities in different industries, hoping to protect your investment against one or more companies undergoing financial disaster. **Securities** are investments that represent evidence of debt, ownership of a business or the legal right to acquire or sell an ownership interest in a business.

T.Rowe Price: 800-638-5660

Smith Breeden Associates: 800-221-3138

Strong Funds: 800-368-1030

Vanguard: 800-523-7077

Show Me the Money

A **money market fund** is a mutual fund with a nonfluctuating $1 investment fee per share. Your return on these investments is in the yield—what a bank or financial institution pays on your money, including compounding.

One final advantage of mutual funds is that they carry almost no risk of going bankrupt. Due to diversification within a fund, a mutual fund is very unlikely to lose its entire value. You can invest $5,000 into XYZ Computer Company, and within 5 years, the value could drop to $0, but $5,000 dollars invested a diversified general mutual fund should follow the ups and downs of the stock market, not just one stock.

Take a careful look at mutual funds as you begin to think about investing your money. They're a great place to start investing and are an excellent vehicle in which your money can grow.

Money Markets

A *money market fund* (MMF) is a mutual fund with a nonfluctuating $1 investment value per share (that is, per unit that you purchase). Like a savings account, if you put $500 into an MMF you'll get $500, plus interest, out—"dollar in, dollar out." Although money market funds aren't insured or guaranteed, most mutual fund companies try to keep them safe enough so that the fund value is never a problem. Your return on these investments is the *yield,* the amount your financial institution pays on your money.

Note that money market funds are different from the money market accounts we discussed in Chapter 3. *Money market accounts* are accounts held with banks, and thus, insured within FDIC guidelines. *Money market funds* are held within mutual fund companies. They are not insured. Their safety is dependent upon the safety of the investments within the funds. An example is a U.S. Treasury Money Market Fund, which is very safe because the Treasury Notes are insured even though the fund itself is not. You can have a money market account with a brokerage house or a mutual fund company, although most of them are usually associated with banks. Some brokerage houses have insured money market accounts, and these accounts are associated with banks. If the bank is FDIC-insured, the money market account is insured and is thus guaranteed, unlike a money market fund.

Money market funds are a good, safe choice for short-term investments. Your original investment is fairly secure while you earn competitive interest rates. They're not the most exciting investment vehicle, but if you have money that you need to keep at a constant value, you might want to give them a look.

Money market funds typically pay a bit more interest than savings or checking accounts, and like money market accounts, most of them allow you write up to three checks a month to a party other than yourself for free. The check has to be for at least a minimum amount (often $250).

There are various types of money market funds. Some are invested in only U.S. Treasury obligations and are not subject to state income tax liability. Some are invested in municipal bonds and similar investments, so they are known as tax-free investments. If you purchase a tax-free mutual fund that participates only in investments within your state, the fund is called a triple tax-free fund (no federal, state, or local income tax). If you are in one of the higher tax brackets, this kind of money market fund might be a way for you to go.

CDs—We're Not Talking Compact Discs

In the world of music, CDs are compact discs. In the world of personal finance, they're *certificates of deposit*. CDs (the financial ones, not the music ones) require that you deposit your money for a certain amount of time. It could be days, months, or years, depending on the type of CD you choose. The financial institution that holds the CD agrees to pay you a certain interest rate and yield for the time that it has your money.

Show Me the Money

A **certificate of deposit** is an investment that pays a fixed interest rate on your money if you keep it in for a specified amount of time.

CDs are investments for security. If you pick an insured bank or savings & loan, etc., your investment is guaranteed to be there when the CD matures (comes due). The most popular CDs out there are the ones for six months, one year, two years, three years, four years, or five years. Normally, the longer you keep your money in a CD, the more interest you'll get. This increased interest rate is the financial institution's way of rewarding you for allowing it to keep your money for that period of time.

If you don't hold up your end of the bargain and take your money out of the account before the specified amount of time has expired, you'll be charged a penalty. The amount of the penalty varies, but it can be pretty hefty. If the circumstances are right, you could even end up with less money than you started with for pulling your money out early. You'd lose not only whatever interest you had earned, but part of your principal as well.

Interest rates vary, but most CDs pay more than savings accounts or money market accounts. Most pay fixed rates, but some offer variable rates, meaning that the interest rate can change. The choices are as varied as the bank's imagination. The interest rates on CDs vary not only from bank to bank, but they change within a bank, as well. Rates are contingent on many factors (watch for CD specials), but they tend to mirror the interest rates in the general market. Most bank CDs are tied to the Treasury Notes and

Treasury Bill rates. Treasury rates are the rates offered by the Federal Reserve when they issue Treasury obligations. Treasury obligations are the debt of the federal government. If the two-year Treasury Note pays a good rate, interest rates on the Bank's CDs tend to be at a good rate, too. The inverse applies, as well.

If rates are low, purchase shorter-term CDs and wait for rates to rise. This eliminates you tying up your funds for long periods of time. Some banks, however, might allow you to add money to a CD account at the interest rate of that particular day. That way, if you opened the account on a day when the rate was low, you can boost your earnings by adding money at a higher interest rate, later.

Dollars and Sense

Some CDs advertise no penalties, but they probably have many stipulations. CDs are required by law to charge a penalty if the money is withdrawn within the first seven days, so there really can be no such thing as a no-penalty CD. A CD that's advertised as having no penalty is probably a money market account in disguise.

If you're going CD shopping, don't just start and stop at your local bank. Check out the rates at savings and loans and credit unions. Credit unions typically pay up to half of a percentage point higher interest on CDs. Savings and loans generally pay more than banks, but less than credit unions.

Before you put your money in a CD account, ask some questions. Include these on your list:

➤ What's the minimum deposit to open the account?

➤ What's the interest rate? The yield?

➤ How often is the interest compounded? Remember, the more frequently it's compounded, the better it is for you. Continuous compounding is best.

➤ Is the interest rate fixed or variable?

➤ How long will the interest rate be effective?

➤ Can you add to your fund at a higher interest rate if the rate goes up while your money is invested?

➤ What's the penalty for early withdrawal?

➤ Does the financial institution offer any incentives, such as waiving fees on your checking account or ATM transactions in return for investing in a CD with them? If so, what is the minimum requirement for the waivers?

If the financial institution to which you're directing your questions can't give you fast, clear answers, look elsewhere. Loads of institutions offer CDs, and you want to deal with one that knows what it's doing.

CDs aren't the most exciting investment you'll ever make. But if you have some money that you can afford to be without for a specified period, they might be worth

Money Pit

Beware of accounts with names like step-up CDs or bump-up CDs. Banks will try a lot of tricks to get you to invest your money with them, and these types of CDs might have more disadvantages than advantages. Be sure you understand exactly what's involved before signing on to a "special" CD offer.

Show Me the Money

A **401(k)** is a type of retirement savings plan that allows employees to contribute a portion of their paychecks to a company-sponsored investment plan. A **pension plan** is an employee-sponsored retirement plan in which a retiree receives a fixed, periodic payment.

your consideration. There are many different kinds of CDs, so be sure to do your homework before plunking down your money.

This chapter was only a crash course on places to invest your hard-earned money. Before you start seriously investing, you should check out some other resources for more detailed information. See the appendix in the back of this book for some suggestions.

401(k)s

It's a weird name for a retirement plan, but *401(k)*s have arguably done more to get young people investing for their futures than anything else. The 401(k) savings plan was introduced in 1982 as a way for employers to save money they had been putting in *pension plans.*

There have always been retirement plans. Employers used to (some still do) provide pension plans for employees. Pensions were good for workers because they basically were additional job benefits. They didn't cost the workers anything. What they did, though, was make it hard for employees to leave their companies. If employees wanted their full pensions, they had to stay with the company until they retired.

In contrast, 401(k)s allow employees to contribute a portion of their paychecks to a company investment plan until they leave the firm or retire. At that time, the employee's money can be either left where it is, rolled over into another retirement account, or claimed by the individual, who usually will face some penalties and an income tax liability for taking the money early.

The 401(k) accounts (if your employer is a nonprofit organization, you'll have a 403(b) plan instead of a 401(k)) have been criticized for putting too much of the responsibility for saving on the employee and leaving the employer off the hook. Still, employers are not obligated to provide a defined benefit plan pension, and if they don't, 401(k) plans are an effective way of assuring you that you'll have money available when you retire.

In addition to allowing flexibility, 401(k)s may offer a great savings incentive by way of an employer match. The amount of the match varies from company to company. If you're really lucky, your employer will match dollar for dollar your contribution up to a certain percentage of your paycheck. The most typical match is for every dollar an employee contributes up to 4 percent, the employer will throw in 50 cents. By taking advantage of the match, you get an automatic 50 percent return on your money. It doesn't take a financial wizard to figure out that that's a good deal!

What happens to your money once it goes into the 401(k)? You get to decide where your money should be invested by choosing from a list of various investment options provided by your employer through the plan. If your employer has the 401(k) account in various mutual funds or a family of funds (which provide a variety of fund choices within the same company), you could divide your money between stocks and bonds with perhaps some fixed-interest rate investments or money market funds thrown in for good measure.

Understandably, selecting investments can be a daunting proposition for someone who knows next to nothing about investments. But experts say that the process of choosing these options has served as a crash course for a lot of young people who would otherwise know nothing about investing money. They say that selecting investments is not that complicated if you choose to keep it simple.

Employers have been reluctant to offer advice regarding their employees' 401(k)s because they're afraid if their advice turns out to be wrong, they might be liable. Financial advisors, however, have come up with some guidelines to direct employees in investing their 401(k) plans. Most suggest that a conservative investor put at least 60 percent of the money in a large company U.S. stock fund (such as Vanguard's U.S. Growth Fund). The rest, they say, could be divided between international stocks, small company stocks, and bonds. Your employer should provide meetings about the various investment choices and how they pertain to you. If it doesn't, ask to have the service provided. You must understand your choices; your future depends on it.

Dollars and Sense

Mary Rowland, the author of a book on 401(k)s, says that workers aren't taking advantage of employers' offers to match funds up to a certain percentage of employees' pay. It's estimated that employees are leaving $6 billion of employers' money untouched by not contributing the maximum allowable amounts to their 401(k)s, Rowland says. Don't miss out on what could be a wise financial move on your part.

Dollars and Sense

If you want a more detailed explanation of 401(k)s, check out Mary Rowland's book *A Commonsense Guide to Your 401(k)*. Rowland is a former personal finance columnist for the *New York Times* and author of another book on mutual funds.

Keep in mind that your 401(k) money is long-term money that you shouldn't plan to use until your retirement. This makes it conducive to equities, what most people consider the stock market, where you have to accept that your money is in for the long haul and be willing to ride out the ups and downs of the market.

Another great advantage of 401(k) plans is that the money you put into them is both pre-tax money and tax-deferred money. That means you win twice. Your 401(k) contributions are taken out of your salary before your salary is taxed for federal income taxes. The contributions are still subject to social security taxes, and some states subject the contributions to state and local income taxes. Still, not having to pay federal income tax on the money you contribute is a great benefit.

The money you contribute is also tax-deferred, which means you don't pay any tax on it or the money that it earns for you until you withdraw it during retirement. An individual in the 28 percent tax bracket will pay 28 cents less tax on every $1 invested into a 401(k). (You'll learn about tax brackets in Chapter 14.) Here's another way of looking at it: If you are a person in the 28 percent tax bracket who invests $100 per month into your 401(k), your federal tax liability will be $336 less per year than if you didn't invest in the 401(k).

Many people in their 20s and 30s balk at the idea of putting away a significant portion of their income in a retirement fund. Retirement is still 35 or 40 years down the road, and they fear their money will be locked away somewhere, never to be seen until they leave work for the last time.

Often, your employer will let you borrow against your plan, and deduct the repayment from your paycheck. The money you repay goes right back into your account, and you pay yourself, not a bank, with the principal and interest. If your employer doesn't have such a loan program, you'll be unable to withdraw funds from the 401(k) unless you leave your employer. You'd have to change jobs in order to gain access to your funds, which seems harsh but helps guarantee the funds are there when you retire. There are withdrawals from 410(k)s for hardship, but you must show your employer need or hardship. One note about 401(k)s is that there may be a lapse of several months between the time you leave a company, and when the money in your 401(k) becomes available. This is due to the administrative work to calculate your share, it's growth, etc. by your employer's 410(k) administrator.

If you take your 401(k) money before you're 59.5 years old, expect to pay some stiff penalties. You'll pay 10 percent, and the money will be taxable, which can be a signifi-cant blow at tax time. The IRS directs that people who withdraw funds from their 401(k) plans have 20 percent withheld from the money to be used for tax payment. The problem is, that amount usually isn't enough money to pay for both the penalty and the taxes owed on the withdrawal.

For example, if you withdrew $5,000 from your 401(k) plan and had the standard 20 percent withheld ($1,000), you would receive $4,000. But if you're a taxpayer in the 28 percent bracket, you'd owe $1,400 in taxes, plus $500 for the penalty for a total of

$1,900. The 20 percent taken out wouldn't cover those costs, and you'd be $900 short on April 15th. Not a nice surprise! Still, the 401(k) is your money, and you can get it if there is a real need and if you're willing to pay the penalties.

The 401(k) plans continue to gain popularity and are giving many people incentive to start saving for retirement. One thing to watch for: Some employers make you wait a year until you can start contributing to a 401(k), so check with the company's benefits department if you have questions.

Quick note—403(b) is similar to a 401(k) except the retirement plans are only offered by hospitals, schools, and nonprofit employers. 403(b) assets are usually held with an insurance company in an annuity format. Participants can contribute up to 15% of their salary to an annual maximum ($10,000 in 1998).

Pocket Change

At the beginning of 1998, 22 million Americans had a collective $750 billion dollars in 401(k) plans, according to Mary Rowland.

Vesting

You may hear about vesting of funds when your employer discusses your 401(k). *Vesting* is the amount of time you are required to work in a company before you are entitled to the funds your employer has put into your retirement account on your behalf.

Cliff vesting (usually 5 years) means you must work for your employer for 5 years before you are entitled to the matching fund placed in your 401(k). If you change jobs after only 3 years, and your company has 5 year cliff vesting, you will only have your contributions available to move elsewhere. This portability is what makes 401(k)s so popular. If you leave this employer after 5 years, you receive all the employer's match.

A consideration when you change jobs— change now or wait until you are vested. Always know how much of your retirement plan is employer match and how much you have to lose if you leave.

Show Me the Money

Vesting is the amount of time required for an employee to work for a company before he is entitled to the employer's contributions to the plan. There are two types of vesting, cliff and graduated.

The second way for an employer to vest is via graduated vesting. You are partially vested after 3 years, but you must stay with your employer for 7 years before you are 100 percent vested. The schedule goes as follows:

Years Employed	Percent Vested
3	20%
4	40%
5	60%
6	80%
7	100%

When you change jobs, whether you are vested or not you have your contribution to your 401(k). These funds can be withdrawn (oh, my gosh—let's remember income tax liability and penalty), rolled over into an IRA, or even possibly rolled over into your new employer's 401(k) plan.

If your new employer has a 401(k) plan see if you can transfer directly from one employer's 401(k) plan to another. If you can't, roll the funds into a separate IRA for any others you have, then roll it into our new 401(k) later, if permitted. If you can't do that, you will have an IRA to manage.

The Least You Need to Know

➤ People think you need to have thousands of dollars to invest, but it's not true. You can begin investing with $50 or less.

➤ Investing your money will be a less daunting task if you start small and learn what investment opportunities are available before you start putting out money.

➤ The very popular 401(k) plans offered by employers these days are a great incentive for retirement saving.

➤ Mutual funds offer diversification and are a great place to start investing.

➤ Money market funds are generally safe places in which to place funds, although not too exciting as investment vehicles.

➤ CDs can be good investments, but they require a little homework.

Chapter 14

A Taxing Topic

In This Chapter

➤ Understanding what taxable income is

➤ Reducing your taxable income

➤ Checking out your tax bracket

➤ Preparing your tax returns

➤ Using personal computers to help you prepare your tax returns

For most people, taxes are an annoyance to be dealt with at various times throughout the year. They get the most attention in April, when people line up at the post office minutes before the mid-month deadline to get their federal income tax returns in the mail on time. But taxes aren't restricted to the springtime. They bug you in the form of the pesky tax bills that show up in the mail, and they annoy you every time you see them deducted from your paycheck.

Federal income tax is the biggie of the taxes, but there are also state taxes (unless you live in Alaska, Florida, Nevada, South Dakota, Texas, Washington, or Wyoming; these states don't impose income taxes), school taxes, county taxes, and occupational privilege taxes to pay. The list goes on and on. The trouble with taxes is that you can complain about them all you want to, but you've still got to pay them. Not only that, you've got to go to a lot of trouble (or pay somebody else to go to the trouble) to figure out how much you're supposed to pay and exactly what it is you're paying on first. Talk about adding insult to injury!

Still, Uncle Sam frowns on those who don't pay taxes, and you can just imagine what happens when Uncle Sam gets mad. He just might send out an Internal Revenue Service (IRS) agent to knock on your door and see what's going on. Nobody wants that, so the taxes must be paid.

There are ways, though, of reducing the taxes you pay, and one of the goals of this chapter is to educate you on these methods. We'll tell you about ways that you can make less of your income taxable, which will reduce your overall tax rate. There's nothing magic (or illegal) about it; it's just a matter of getting a better understanding of how the tax system works and using it to your best advantage.

Nobody from the IRS is going to call you to say you're paying more in taxes than you need to and offer to let you redo your tax returns. Once you file, you've filed. A more thorough grasp of the system, however, will help you understand exactly what you're required to pay and what you're not.

What's Your Taxable Income?

Before we begin the process of understanding taxes, take a look at the theory of how we calculate our taxes, below:

To Calculate Taxable Income:

Add all Taxable Income
(Subtract Adjustments)
Total is know as Adjusted Gross Income (AGI)
(Subtract Standard Deduction or Itemized Deductions)
(Subtract Number of Exemptions × $2,450)
Total Taxable Income
Calculate Tax

Show Me the Money

Your **taxable income** is the amount of your income on which you begin calculating your final tax liability. **Non-taxable income** is income that is excluded from taxable income.

Taxable income is the amount of your income on which you pay taxes. Yeah, we know. You thought for sure you were paying taxes on every cent you make, or your taxes wouldn't consume such a large chunk of your income, right? Well, if it seems that way, you're right. We work for a good part of the year just to make the money that we pay in taxes, and it can be mighty discouraging if you dwell on it.

But you're not going to dwell on it. Instead, you're going to figure out how to make less of your income taxable. You're still going to pay taxes, don't get us wrong. But you might be able to whittle them down a little bit and give yourself a little more money for other things.

You have to pay taxes on the money you earn by working, but as you'll remember from Chapter 7, your income may come from sources other than your paycheck. For instance, the interest you earn on the money in your 401(k) plan is income, but it's not taxable income. This income is referred to as *non-taxable income.* You get to earn it for free (for now, anyway). Theoretically, you could make all your income non-taxable. Of course if you did that, you wouldn't have a salary or any money to live on. But at least you wouldn't be paying any taxes!

Let's have a look at what's taxable income and what's not. Taxable income includes the following:

➤ Your salary, with the exception of money you may have deducted and put into a 401(k) plan

➤ Interest earned on savings and checking accounts

➤ Interest on all bonds except municipal (tax free) bonds and dividends on investments

➤ Bonuses, severance pay, and sick pay from your employer

➤ Unemployment compensation

➤ Tips

➤ Capital gains on mutual funds and other investments (Capital gains are the amount by which proceeds from the sale of a capital asset exceed the cost. They're the profit you make.)

➤ Bartering, royalties, and gambling winnings, including lottery winnings

➤ Most withdrawals from an IRA or annuity

Non-taxable income includes the following:

➤ Money you contribute to certain types of retirement accounts

➤ Gifts from your grandmother or any other gifts

➤ Disability income on benefits you paid for with after-tax dollars

➤ Child care paid for through a plan at work

➤ Return of invested capital—that is, your money invested that is returned to you

➤ 401(k) money that's rolled over into another 401(k) or IRA when you change jobs

➤ Child-support payments

➤ Money you've lent that is repaid

Use this information about taxable and non-taxable income to help you to be smart when it comes time to figure out what to do with the money from your salary that you don't need to cover your expenses.

How to Make Less of Your Income Taxable

Once you have calculated your taxable income (totaling lines 1 through 22) of your federal income tax return (1040), you may be able to take off what are call adjustments. *Adjustments* from gross income are such things as IRA deductions (a tax-deductible contribution to an IRA account), moving expenses, etc. Here are two kinds of adjustments in more detail:

➤ **Moving expenses.** If you move because you get a new job that's at least 50 miles away from your previous employer, you can deduct the cost of moving your things from your old home to your new home, plus the miles driving, at a rate of 10 cents a mile. You can't, however, deduct meals, house-hunting expenses, or costs of temporary living.

➤ **Student loan interest.** The Taxpayer Relief Act of 1997 allows taxpayers who pay interest on certain higher education loans for themselves or their spouses to deduct interest paid during the first sixty months in which interest payments are required on the loan. The amount of deduction increases from $1,000 in 1998 to $2,500 in the year 2001 and after. The interest deduction is available to taxpayers regardless of whether they itemize their other deductions. Married couples must file a joint return to claim the deduction, and the deduction has certain income limitations. This item is especially helpful since it comes directly off your gross income rather than being lumped in as a deduction.

When you have totaled your taxable income and subtracted your total adjustments, you have what is known as your adjusted gross income (AGI). Once you have your AGI, you're ready to take your deduction.

To make less of your income taxable, you can contribute to accounts where it won't be taxed, such as 401(k)s and child care plans through your employer. Or you can increase your itemized deductions of income, which lowers the amount that's subject to taxes.

Pocket Change

The latest statistics show that the average American works until after May 1 just to pay his or her taxes.

Deductions are perfectly legal, but it's up to you to find out which ones apply to you. There are tons of deductions, but you can't just help yourself to them like you would at a smorgasbord. For instance, you can't take a deduction on your mortgage interest if you don't own a home. The IRS frowns on that sort of thing, and we don't want to see our readers paying large fines or worse. The idea is to lower your taxable income by putting as much as you can into tax-sheltered accounts and by taking all the deductions that apply to you.

There are two methods for figuring out your total deductions:

➤ Standard deduction

➤ Itemized deductions

The good news is, you can figure out which method gives you a better deal, and go with it.

Standard Deductions

Most young people take the *standard deduction,* which is the amount allowed by the IRS, because their financial situations are reasonably simple, and they're not eligible for a lot of deductions associated with owning property and other investments. If your income is not exorbitant, and you rent rather than own where you live, you'll probably be better off taking a standard deduction. It's set right now at $4,250 for single people and $7,100 for married couples filing jointly.

If your financial life is a bit more complicated, you should figure out whether you'll do better by itemizing your deductions. You need to get a copy of Schedule A of the IRS form 1040 on which to itemize. You also might want to itemize your deductions if you've had an unusually large number of medical bills during the tax year, a high amount of charitable contributions, or significant loss because of theft, fire, or natural disaster. Check out page 323 for a sample Schedule A.

Show Me the Money

A **standard deduction** is the lump-sum amount of allowable deductions that you can subtract from your total taxable income. The IRS sets this amount. **Itemized deductions** are deductions that you list separately if you've incurred a large number of deductible expenses.

Itemized Deductions

You have to know exactly what deductions you can take as *itemized deductions*, and that's where many people go wrong. They don't keep records of things they buy that could be counted as deductions, so they have no idea how much they can deduct.

These expenses can be itemized:

➤ **Taxes.** You can deduct state and local income taxes, real estate taxes, foreign taxes, and personal property taxes.

➤ **Interest expenses on home mortgages, home equity loans, and points charged when buying a home.** The catch with this one is that you've got to own a home. Points are those pesky fees that you have to pay to a mortgage lender to cover the loan application fees. Chapter 24 explains how owning a home affects your taxes, so you'll read all about it then. For now, we'll just say that if you've bought a home, you're in for some tax advantages.

➤ **Charitable work and contributions (money or property) to tax-exempt organizations.** If you drive for Meals on Wheels or deliver baskets to shut-ins for the Salvation Army, you can deduct your mileage. The standard charitable mileage deduction is 14 cents per mile, plus tolls and parking fees. You'll need to use your odometer for each trip, and keep a log of the miles you've driven. As with all itemized deductions, thorough documentation is essential. You can't just say you've driven 864 miles for charitable organizations. You've got to be able to come up with something showing that you did. If you donate property like an old couch, loveseat, or end tables to a charitable organization such as Goodwill, you can deduct the furniture at its current *fair market value*. Fair market value means what it's worth at the time you donate it, not what you paid for it. When you drop off the furniture, be sure you get a receipt showing the charity's name and a description of the property. You must keep a list of the property you gave, along with its fair market value.

Show Me the Money

The charity to which you donate property usually will indicate the **fair market value** of your donation based on what it's worth when you drop it off (not what the original cost was). If not, you can estimate what the value is, unless it's valued at more than $5,000. If it is worth more than $5,000, the IRS requires a qualified appraisal. If you donate property valued at more than $500, you'll need to attach a special form to your tax return.

➤ **Home office expenses.** If you work from your home, you can deduct a portion of your utilities and home real estate taxes, and you can depreciate a portion of the costs of your home. You can only do this, however, if your home office is your only place of business. If your boss lets you work from home every now and then, you can't claim deductions on a home office. Your home office must also be an area of your house that is used only for business, and it must be used regularly. If your computer is on one end of your dining room table, and you eat at the other end, you're going to have a hard time convincing the IRS that it's a home office. Still, if you do work exclusively out of your home, the home office deduction is worth looking into. You also can deduct business expenses, such as computers, fax machines, and the like.

➤ **Gambling losses.** You can deduct these up to the amount of gambling winnings (are you surprised?).

➤ **Job search expenses.** You can deduct these expenses if you're looking for work in the same trade or business in which you're currently employed, but not if you're looking for a different line of work (nobody ever said tax laws make a lot of sense). You also can deduct job-hunt-related travel expenses and costs such as having a resume prepared, postage, and so on. You don't need to get the job in order to deduct the expenses.

➤ **Nonbusiness casualty and theft losses.** Such losses would include storm damage to your home or the theft of your brand-new computer. The amount of the deduction can be no more than 10 percent of your adjusted gross income. You can figure out your *adjusted gross income* by subtracting all allowable adjustments from your taxable income.

➤ **Impairment-related work expenses for people with disabilities.** This would include, for example, the cost of a special handicapped-accessible desk or computer.

Lowering of you taxable income is done two ways. The first is called an adjustment (student loan interest, moving expenses, etc.), and the second way is a deduction. You should know that an adjustment is subtracted directly from your income (no minimum) while deductions must total more than the standard deduction before they begin to be helpful.

You can itemize the following expenses if they total more than 2 percent of your adjusted gross income:

➤ **Job-related car expenses.** Car deductions include the cost of gas, oil, maintenance, insurance, repairs, car registration, licensing, and so on. You also may be able to take a depreciation allowance if you own your car, but only if your car is used for business purposes.

➤ **Business expenses not covered by your employer.** These expenses can include travel and entertaining.

Show Me the Money

Your **adjusted gross income** is all your taxable income, less certain permitted adjustments. Examples of adjustments are moving expenses and contributions to an IRA.

➤ **Educational expenses.** These expenses are deductible if you spent money to maintain or improve skills required by your job or by law. For instance, insurance agents are required to take continuing education courses in order to remain licensed. If you decide to go back to school in order to change careers, however, or because you think an advanced degree will help you along in your career, those expenses are not deductible.

➤ **Professional dues, tools, uniforms, and legal expenses incurred to collect income.**

➤ **Tax preparation fees.** If you wimp out and decide to have your taxes prepared for you, you can deduct the cost of the work. Most people with fairly simple financial lives, though, are able to prepare their own tax returns.

➤ **Investment fees.**

➤ The cost of a cellular phone used for business.

➤ **A passport fee.** You can deduct this fee only if the passport was necessary for business travel.

➤ **Safe deposit box fees.** These bank fees are deductible as long as you use the box to store taxable bonds or stock certificates.

➤ **Subscriptions to job-related magazines, newspapers, or services that provide investment information or advice.**

➤ **The cost of a home computer.** You must be able to prove that the purchase was necessary for your job.

You can also deduct medical and dental expenses that you paid for you, your spouse, or any dependents, if they total more than 7.5 percent of your adjusted gross income. After you reach this 7.5 percent mark, you can start deducting expenses for things such as contact lenses, weight-loss and stop-smoking programs (if they're recommended by your doctor), childbirth classes, travel to Alcoholics Anonymous meetings (if the meetings are recommended by your doctor), and remedial reading classes for a dyslexic child.

Money Pit

Remember, if you itemize your deductions, you must have documentation for each one. Don't deduct the cost of that computer you bought in September unless you can prove when, where, and why you bought it and how much you bought it for. If you would happen to be audited and had no documentation, let's just say it wouldn't be pretty!

You can't deduct these things:

➤ Political contributions

➤ Trash collection fees

➤ Homeowners association charges, except the portion used to pay real estate taxes, and, perhaps the portion used to pay interest

➤ Water bills (unless they're for a business)

➤ Estate, inheritance, legacy, or succession taxes

➤ Credit card interest (except for a business)

➤ Car loan interest

➤ Interest on loans where proceeds are used to purchase tax-exempt investments

➤ Points if you are the seller of the property

If you qualify for these types of deductions, you can significantly reduce the amount of your taxable income. If you don't have a lot of itemized deductions, take the standard one and be glad for the $4,250 for singles or the $7,100 for married people filing jointly.

After you've deferred all the money you can into non-taxable accounts, used as many adjustments as possible, and taken all the deductions you're eligible for, you're ready to go compute your taxable income.

Fitting In: Tax Brackets

If your salary isn't as much as you think it should be, and you're having a hard time getting your boss to give you a big raise, you can comfort yourself by knowing that you're paying less in taxes than Mr. Big Shot down the hall who makes $10,000 more a year than you do. You're paying less not only because you don't have as much taxable income, but you're also being taxed at a lower rate because your income is lower.

Pocket Change

The tax system makes no sense when it comes to taking standard deductions for single and married people. Why on earth do you have to take a smaller standard deduction if you're married and you choose to file jointly? It's almost enough to make you defer nuptials, thank you very much!

Of course, it's good to make more money. Nobody's going to argue with you on that point. However, if you nudge up just over the cut-off point and your tax rate increases, you will increase the rate of tax on the excess earnings. Bummer! That situation doesn't happen very often, though, so it's not worth losing sleep over.

Something most people don't realize is that every taxpayer filing as a single person is taxed at 15 percent on the first $25,350 of taxable income. It doesn't matter whether you earn $1 million or $35,000 a year, your first $25,350 is taxed at 15 percent. For some people, 15 percent is the tax rate for all their income because they don't make more than $25,350.

When your taxable income is more than $25,350, the money beyond that amount is taxed at a higher rate (28 percent). So if you earn $50,700, you pay nearly twice as much tax on your last $25,350 dollars of earnings as you do on your first $25,350. Refer to the tax bracket chart to get an idea of how your taxes increase as your income gets higher. Notice that the biggest jump, by far, is that from 15 percent to 28 percent. Just when you're starting to get somewhere, wham! you're socked with a much higher tax rate.

Such is the way of the American tax system. The tax rate that you end up paying, based on your income dollars beyond $25,350, is called your *marginal tax rate*. If you earn $35,350 a year, for instance, your marginal tax rate is 28 percent, which you're paying on the last $10,000 of your income. By knowing the amount of your marginal tax rate, you can figure out any additional taxes you'd have to pay if your taxable income were to increase. Reviewing the total amount of taxes you pay per year and dividing this amount by your adjusted gross income will give you your average tax rate.

Marginal tax rate is tricky to grasp because of how taxes are deducted from paychecks. If you have the same salary throughout the year, the amount of state and federal income tax taken from your check each pay period will be the same. So it appears that all your income is being taxed at the same rate, even though it's really not.

Show Me the Money

Your **marginal tax rate** is the tax rate that you pay on your next dollar of income. Your highest income tax bracket.

Preparing Your Tax Returns

April 15 is fast approaching, and you have taxes on the brain. You know you have to get a return prepared and in the mail, but you've been putting it off. Preparing a tax return is one of those things we tend to build up in our minds as a big deal, when it doesn't have to be. It's like painting the living room. You know it's a one-day job, but the longer you think about it, the bigger a task it seems to be. Eventually, it's like a monster looming over you. When you finally get around to painting the room, you wonder why you turned it into such a project in the first place.

I Can Do That!

If your financial situation is not very complicated, you probably can prepare your tax return yourself. In fact, it's probably a good idea to do it yourself, because it forces you to learn a little about the tax codes and to become more familiar with your personal finances. Seeing in black and white what you earned, what you invested where, and what deductions you're eligible for can give you a better understanding of where you stand financially.

The IRS tax return contains an introduction that gives you basic directions on how to fill out the return. If your return is not at all complicated, you should be okay using just those instructions. If you want more information, you can get it for free from the IRS.

If you want more than IRS information, plenty of books are available to help you with your taxes. We've listed a few here, but you can find many more in your library or local bookstore. Be sure you get the most recent books you can find, because tax laws keep changing all the time.

Dollars and Sense

For an IRS booklet on preparing an individual tax return, call 800-TAX-FORM and request Publication 17, *Your Federal Income Tax*. Find the IRS online at www.taxadmin.org.

➤ *The Complete Idiot's Guide to Doing Your Income Taxes* by Gail Perry and Paul Craig Roberts.

➤ *Kiplinger Cut Your Taxes* by Kevin McCormally.

➤ *Taxes for Busy People: The Book to Use When There's No Time to Lose* by Robert A. Cooke.

➤ *Your Tax Questions Answered 1998: A CPA with Over Twenty Years of Experience Answers the Most Commonly Asked Tax Questions* by Ed Slott.

➤ *Pay Less Tax Legally: The Tax Preparation Guide* by Barry Steiner.

A word of advice for those of you doing your own taxes: Don't wait until the last minute! You'll only end up frustrated and maybe filing for an extension.

If you don't think you can figure out your return on your own, or you just don't have time, or you messed it up last year and you're scared to death you'll do it again and end up getting audited, you can hire somebody to prepare it for you.

Help! I Need Somebody (Not Just Anybody)

If you decide not to do your taxes yourself, there are plenty of people around who will do it for you. If you look in the Yellow Pages, you'll see the names of a bunch of people who will prepare your tax return. But they call themselves different things. There are tax preparers, enrolled agents, certified public accounts, and tax attorneys. How do you know who to pick?

Different people who work with taxes have different levels of expertise, beginning with a tax preparer and ending with a tax attorney. The more expertise someone has, the higher his or her rate generally will be. If you're filing a simple tax return, there's no reason you need to hire a tax attorney to do it for you.

Let's have a quick look at the different categories of tax help, so you can decide which one is right for you:

➤ **Tax preparers.** As a group, tax preparers have the least amount of training. They don't need to be licensed, and many of them work part time. H&R Block is a well-known company that prepares taxes. The people that work for Block are tax preparers. Preparers are normally reliable if your tax return is fairly straightforward, and they won't break your budget. They usually charge about $100 for a basic tax return.

Money Pit

Nearly everyone has a friend or relative who prepares taxes. Maybe you know a CPA or someone who works part-time during tax season for H&R Block. Don't assume, however, that just because you know somebody who works with taxes, he or she *is* qualified to prepare *your* taxes. Good friends do not necessarily make good tax preparers. And do you really want your friend or relative to know all the personal financial information that your tax return includes?

➤ **Enrolled agents.** Enrolled agents are licensed and can represent clients in front of the IRS in the event of an audit. Enrolled agents generally have more training than tax preparers, and they're required to participate in continuing education. As a group, they charge more than tax preparers. If your return is a simple one, you probably don't need an enrolled agent.

➤ **Certified public accounts (CPAs).** CPAs undergo a lot of training and must pass an exam to receive their credentials. They have to complete continuing education courses each year in order to remain certified. If your taxes are complicated because you have your own business or for other reasons, you might need a CPA. CPAs usually charge about $100 an hour, so you could be looking at a hefty bill.

➤ **Tax attorneys.** You probably will never need a tax attorney to complete your tax return, unless your financial life gets incredibly complicated, with all kinds of legal ramifications. If you do need one some day, be prepared to pay, big time! Many tax attorneys charge up to $300 an hour.

Dollars and Sense

If you hire someone to do your taxes and you feel that they're not doing a good job for you, get someone else to look at their work. Anyone, even a hot-shot CPA, can make a mistake, and, unfortunately, her mistake could become your problem.

If you find someone that you like and trust to prepare your taxes, consider yourself lucky. There are many excellent people around, but finding one makes your life a little easier. Once you find someone, try to stick with her, if you can. She'll have your files in case you ever get audited, and there's a lot to be said for continuity.

Web Sites and Software That Can Help You Prepare Your Taxes

An increasing number of Americans are relying on their personal computers to help them complete their tax returns. There's more and more tax-preparation software coming out all the time, and it can provide some real advantages.

The tax forms you need are contained in the software, so you don't have to zip down to the post office to get them, only to find out the post office has been out of them for a week. Some software allows you to file your return electronically, with the IRS sending you a confirmation when it's received.

Tax-preparation software programs generally aren't very difficult to work with. They merely require you to enter the information requested, and the programs zap your info into the appropriate tax form. The two most popular tax software programs are Intuit's Turbo Tax (MacInTax for Macintosh), and Block Financial's Kiplinger Tax Cut.

Here are some Web sites to check out for information and tax advice:

➤ Tax Return Help on the Web at http://ocean.st.usm.edu

➤ The Tax Center at www.qfn.com/taxcenter

For online tax preparation programs, go to this site:

➤ Secure Tax, located at www.securetax.com

Pocket Change

Don't overlook your state income taxes when working online. There are software programs for state taxes, too.

If you're looking for free tax forms that you can download onto your PC, check out the IRS site at www.irs.ustreas.gov/prod/cover.html.

Regardless of how you decide to prepare your tax returns, make sure you check everything before you send them in. According to the IRS, a high percentage of completed forms contain mistakes. Also, make sure you start far enough in advance, so you don't end up in a panic on April 15.

The Least You Need to Know

➤ Not all of your income is taxable income.

➤ You can reduce your taxable income by taking advantage of certain investments and deductions.

➤ Not all of your income is taxed at the same rate.

➤ You can prepare your own tax returns or hire someone to do them for you.

➤ More and more software programs are available to help you prepare your tax returns.

Chapter 15

Looking Out for What You Have

In This Chapter

➤ Understanding how insurance works

➤ Thinking big is the way to go

➤ Knowing what kinds of insurance you need and don't need

➤ Shopping around to get the best rates

➤ Fighting back for fair treatment

Insurance is one of those things most people don't like to think about, much less sit around and discuss with friends. It's sort of an unsavory area of life. First of all, you have to buy the darn stuff, and it's expensive. Even as you're shelling out the bucks to pay for it, you're hoping you never need it. If you do need it, something bad has happened. Let's face it, insurance can be a drag.

Still, it's better to have insurance than not to. You never know when something bad—an illness, a car crash, a fire, a terrible storm—is going to happen. Because we can't see ahead to what losses will befall us (and who would want to?) we need to protect ourselves against possible catastrophic losses. Insurance is a method of sharing risk among a large group of people.

That's not to say you need to insure yourself and your possessions against everything that could possibly go wrong. I know people who insure their china, their crystal, their jewelry, their washers and dryers, their garden sheds, and even their dogs and cats. This is probably going overboard.

If you learn one thing about insurance from this chapter, let it be this: Insurance is meant to protect the important things in your life, such as your life, your health, and your home, against big losses. If you somehow manage to break every piece of china you own, you can save up and go out and buy another set. If the Waterford decanter and glasses set you got as a wedding present crashes to the floor and shatters into a million shards of glass, you can use a Tupperware pitcher and paper cups. They won't be as pretty, but they'll serve their purpose.

If you get sick and can't work, though, you'd better have insurance to cover your lost income, even if you're supporting only yourself. If you have a house and it burns down, you'd better have insurance to rebuild and replace the stuff you lost. Whenever you walk outside and get into your car, there's the potential for an accident, and you need to be insured just in case.

Dollars and Sense

It's been estimated by the National Insurance Consumers Organization that 90 percent of Americans have the wrong kind of insurance, in the wrong amounts, from the wrong companies. Sounds like we all could use some insurance education! Read on to find out what's right for you.

Pocket Change

It's estimated by the National Insurance Consumers Organization that 1 out of every 12 dollars Americans spend is to pay for some kind of insurance.

Welcome to the Insurance Jungle

There are more kinds of insurance policies available to Americans than you probably can imagine, and we buy tons of it. Most people, though, don't understand the insurance industry or even what kinds of insurance they should have.

The insurance industry is huge, and it commands a large chunk of our nation's economy. There are tens of thousands of insurance companies in this country, and one and a half million people are employed in the industry. Insurance is a powerful industry, as well. It has an extremely strong lobby that exerts tremendous pressure on the government agencies that are supposed to oversee it. As a result, it has become a formidable force in our society.

Think about the ramifications involved with insurance. People in hospitals have died because their insurance company wouldn't cover a certain procedure. People have died at home because they didn't have insurance to go to the hospital in the first place. The insurance industry, in the past several decades, has exerted enormous control over our entire society. Businesses have shut down because they couldn't get or couldn't afford the necessary insurance. Governments knuckle under to demands of the insurance industry, and people grow increasingly nervous about their futures as they relate to insurance. Insurance is an issue we all need to think about, because we need to have it.

Insurance 101

Most insurance is sold through agents or brokers, who work for insurance companies such as Allstate, State Farm, Nationwide, Liberty Mutual, and thousands of others. The agents earn commissions from the insurance companies, based on how much and what type of insurance they sell. Certainly, insurance agents aren't the only people out there who work on commission. Real estate agents do, and many other types of salespeople do, as well. There's nothing wrong with a commission system, but you should be aware that's how the insurance industry works.

If an agent is going to get a big commission for selling a certain type of policy, you can be sure he's going to knock himself out trying to sell it. That's how he makes his living, and some agents are really good at convincing you that you need something that's completely unnecessary. If you know someone well who sells insurance, pick his or her brain sometime about how it's done and what considerations are involved. If it's someone you know well, and you trust, ask him or her to tell you about how the commission system affects the sale.

Money Pit

Some analysts say that nearly 50 percent of insurance agents and brokers try to sell you policies that generate the highest commissions for them. If you don't know what you want or need, you could be suckered into buying unnecessary coverage while lining the pockets of the agent.

If you don't know anyone who sells insurance, you'll have to take your chances with a referral or someone you find on your own. Choose someone with a CLU (Chartered Life Underwriter) or ChFC (Chartered Financial Consultant) designation, which demonstrates the agent has taken courses to further educate him or herself about the industry. It also implies that the agent has affirmed to practice ethically. As we'll discuss later, these designations show an educational commitment and ethical pledge to do the best for the client.

Show Me the Money

A **premium** is the amount of money you pay, at regular predetermined intervals, for a certain insurance policy.

After you read this chapter, you'll have a better understanding of what you need and don't need. Don't let an agent talk you into buying something you don't need, for which you'll end up paying a large premium. The *premium*, by the way, is the amount of money you pay for a particular insurance policy. Be sure he or she understands your situation so that you get the kind of coverage you should have.

Sometimes You Need It, Sometimes You Don't

You've already learned to think big when it concerns insurance. Forget the little stuff, even if it's tempting because it doesn't seem to cost very much. Sure, it's more likely that your computer will break down than it is you'll get run over by a bus while crossing the street in front of your office, but how much is it likely to cost to fix your computer? No, you won't like paying to have it fixed, but it won't cause you to seek out the advice of a bankruptcy lawyer.

Dollars and Sense

Insurance companies pay out an average of 60 cents in benefits on every dollar they pull in for premiums. Some policies, though, such as repair plans, average less than half of that amount. Skip the little stuff and worry about the big stuff.

If you buy a lot of little insurance policies, hoping to cover every possibility for loss, you'll end up spending a lot more on the policies than you would fixing the things that go wrong. If your computer does break down, by the time you pay the deductible, spend an hour or two filling out the claim, and try to cut through the inevitable red tape, you're probably better off having it fixed on your own. Instead, spend the time and energy finding a dependable, reasonably priced computer repairperson. Then, when your Gateway goes belly up, you can make a phone call and get somebody you trust to fix it for a fair price. You'll be back to work or cruising the Net a lot faster than you will if you wait for the extended warranty claim to be processed.

The types of insurance you need depend on where you are in your life. A thumbnail sketch of who needs what follows:

➤ **Single with no dependents.** At this point of your life, you need health insurance, auto insurance, and homeowner's insurance. If you rent, consider getting renter's insurance (see Chapter 5 for more details). Disability insurance also makes sense for you now.

➤ **Married with no kids.** Now you'll need some life insurance, especially if your spouse doesn't work or if you own a home. Auto and homeowner's or renter's insurance is necessary, as are health and disability insurance.

➤ **Married with kids.** Kids bump up the amount and types of insurance you need. If you didn't get life insurance yet, you'll definitely need it now. Term life insurance, where you pay a certain amount per year, and your survivors receive a certain amount if you die (more about this later in the chapter) is probably your best bet. You'll still need health and disability insurance too, along with auto (pay special attention to that one once the babies get to be teenagers and start driving!) and homeowner's insurance. It's a good idea at this point to re-examine all your policies to make sure you're adequately covered. Having kids makes you responsible for them, and you want to make sure they'd have sufficient resources if you were to die or become disabled.

➤ **Married with grown children.** You're getting older, so you should take a good look at your health and life insurance policies. If your life insurance doesn't cover debts, such as funeral expenses and estate taxes, you might want to consider additional coverage. You should talk with someone about the pros and cons of trading your term life insurance for a cash value policy which combines a protection plan with some benefits of a saving plan (more on this later). Try to determine how comprehensive your health insurance is, and if you've got considerable assets you'd like to protect, think about buying some long-term care insurance. Senior citizens often are eligible for discounts on their auto insurance, and if you've traded in the family home for a smaller one, your homeowner's insurance should be less expensive.

We're going to concentrate on the types of insurance necessary for people in the first two categories: single with no dependents and married with no kids. We'll also touch briefly on what you need if you're in the third category, married with kids.

Health Insurance

Everyone, from tiny babies to the very oldest members of our society, needs health insurance. Unfortunately, not everyone has it, and that's wrong. There's no justification for someone who happens to have a job that provides good health insurance to get better medical care than someone who doesn't work, is self-employed, or whose employer doesn't, or can't, offer the same benefits.

What's equally disturbing is that some people can afford to pay for health insurance, but choose not to. They rationalize the decision by thinking they won't get sick or hurt, and if they do, they figure the system will take care of them somehow. Not having health insurance if you're able to buy it is incredibly short-sighted. You're setting yourself up for huge hassles, potential financial losses, and inadequate health care. Plus, you're less likely to seek medical advice early on if you don't have health insurance. This reluctance can lead to a little problem becoming a big problem by the time you get around to doing something about it.

If you get health insurance through your employer, breathe a big sigh of relief. Even if you have to kick in for a *co-pay* (a plan in which you contribute a portion of your salary to offset the employer's cost for your insurance plan), you're better off than buying it on your own. If you do need to buy your own health insurance, be sure you get a plan that covers the big stuff. You need to be covered for hospitalization, physician costs, and charges for things such as X-rays, lab tests, and diagnostic tests. If you're a woman who plans to have a baby in the not-too-distant future, look for maternity benefits, too. If you're leaving a job where you have an insurance plan, look into the possibility of extending your coverage when you leave. COBRA (Consolidated Omnibus Budget Reconciliation Act of 1985) requires your employer to continue your

Show Me the Money

A **co-pay** is a plan that enables you to contribute a fixed portion of your salary to help offset your employer's cost for your insurance plan.

Dollars and Sense

If you're buying your own health insurance, take the largest deductible you can afford, which is an amount you'll be required to pay before the insurance company will pay a claim, to keep the cost down. Also, consider a co-payment option, in which you'd pay a percentage of your health costs. Make sure the co-pay option includes a maximum out-of-pocket limit, though.

Show Me the Money

Health maintenance organizations (HMOs) and **preferred provider organizations** (PPOs) are health plans that restrict your choice of health care providers. As a result, these plans generally cost less than those which don't restrict providers.

health coverage after a job loss, death of an employee, divorce, or age (as when a child reaches an age when he or she is no longer covered under the plan). Your employer is required to offer COBRA coverage for eighteen months after you quit your job or thirty-six months for other situations (such as divorce).

You can probably get a better rate on a *health maintenance organization (HMO)* or *preferred provider organization (PPO)* plan, both of which limit your choice of health care providers, than a plan that lets you see whomever you want. Many HMOs and PPOs probably include your current doctors, so don't reject them right away. Ask to see a list of which doctors are included as providers.

Check out the big health care insurers such as Blue Cross and Blue Shield if you're shopping for a policy. They can get better rates from health-care providers and are more stable than many smaller companies. Look for a plan that has the highest lifetime maximum benefits you can find and is guaranteed to be renewable.

Auto Insurance

You must have car insurance, because the liability risk if you're in an accident is too great to ignore. Auto insurance is expensive, but it's required by law in nearly every state. Even if it weren't, you couldn't afford to be without it.

Different types of coverage are associated with car insurance, but the one that's required by almost all states is liability. Liability coverage is twofold: bodily injury and property damage. The bodily injury liability coverage protects you against lawsuits in the event that someone is injured in an accident in which you're involved. Most states impose a minimum amount of bodily injury coverage, usually $25,000 a person and $50,000 per accident. If you lend your car to someone else to drive, remember that insurance follows the car. Thus, your coverage is the primary insurance in the event of an accident.

When you rent a car, your policy provides coverage unless it states otherwise. Read your policy and always call before you go on a trip. Also, verify whether your policy is comprehensive or collision (for an older car, for example). If your deductibles are high, you should purchase coverage from the rental company.

The property damage liability covers damage to other cars and property that's caused by your car. It would not only cover the cost of fixing a car that you hit, but it would pay to repair or replace the fence you ran over, too. Most states require a minimum of $10,000 in property coverage.

If you have a loan on your car, you'll need collision and comprehensive coverage, as well. Collision coverage pays for damage to your car if you're in an accident or pays to replace a car that's totaled. Comprehensive coverage protects you from car theft or weird things that could happen to your car, such as a tree falling on it or it being damaged during a riot, fire, or flood.

The following table shows you the auto coverage for a 1993 Mazda as an example. Note the coverages, limits, deductibles, and premiums:

Money Pit

Although $50,000 sounds like a lot of bodily injury coverage, experts say that to protect your assets in case you're sued, you should have up to $300,000 in coverage. If you buy only the minimum amount, it might not cover all your liability in event of a lawsuit.

Pocket Change

Certain vehicles are more likely to be stolen than others, according to police statistics. Honda Accords and Jeep Cherokees are two vehicles frequently targeted by thieves.

1993 Mazda

COVERAGE	LIMITS	DEDUCTIBLE	PREMIUM
Automobile Liability Insurance—Full Tort			
➤ Bodily Injury	$300,000 each person $300,000 each occurrence	Not Applicable	$101.00
➤ Property Damage	$100,000 each occurrence	Not Applicable	$74.00
Medical Expenses	$5,000 each person	Not Applicable	$30.00
Uninsured Motorists Insurance	$300,000 each person	Not Applicable	$22.00
Full Tort/ Stacked Limits	$300,000 each accident		

continues

197

continued

COVERAGE	LIMITS	DEDUCTIBLE	PREMIUM
Auto Collision Insurance	Actual Cash Value	$500	$201.00
Auto Comprehensive Insurance	Actual Cash Value	$500	$68.00
Total Premium for 93 Mazda			**$529.10**

DISCOUNTS Your premium for this vehicle reflects the following discounts:

Multiple Car	$102.00	Renewal	$125.00
Automatic Seat Belts	$6.00	Prior Insurance	$159.00

SURCHARGES Your premium for this vehicle reflects the following surcharges:

Accident Involvement	$55.00

RATING INFORMATION

This vehicle is driven over 7,500 miles per year, 3–9 miles to work/school, with no unmarried driver under 25.

If you get hit by someone who doesn't have insurance (this isn't as unusual as you might think), you'll need uninsured motorist coverage. This insurance covers your medical expenses and lost wages in the event you're injured by an uninsured motorist.

There's a big difference in auto insurance rates, so be sure you look around. Be aware that a poor driving record will dramatically increase your insurance rates. Look for cars with good safety records (a Volvo anyone?), and stay away from hot sports cars or convertibles if you're interested in keeping your rates down.

If you're over 25, you'll generally get a better rate than someone who is younger. Also, being married, living in what is considered a safe neighborhood, and having a relatively short work commute (driving less than 7,500/year, not using your car for work) will lower your insurance rates.

Property Insurance

You're required to buy property insurance before you can get a mortgage, so if you own a home, you already have homeowner's insurance. But do you know what type of insurance you have and exactly what it covers? For instance, one type of homeowner's insurance will cover damages if your house is struck by lightning, but won't cover damages if your roof collapses under the four feet of wet snow on top of it.

Homeowner's coverage protects you from what the insurance industry calls "perils," which are all the things that could happen to wreck your house. The 11 most common perils, covered by a basic homeowner's policy, are the following:

1. Fire or lightning damage
2. Smoke damage
3. Broken glass
4. Damage from aircraft
5. Damage from rioting
6. Damage from vehicles
7. Vandalism to your property
8. Property loss
9. Theft
10. Damage caused by an explosion
11. Damage from a windstorm, hailstorm, or hurricane

More extensive policies will cover things such as damage caused by electrical surges (we all know those surge protectors can't guarantee that your computer monitor won't succumb to the effects of a good lightning strike), roof collapse due to ice or snow, damage resulting from burst water pipes, damage from a tree falling on your house, or damage from your heater going bad and spewing oil all over your house.

Your homeowner's insurance should cover not only damage to the structure but damage to your belongings, as well. Usually, personal property coverage is equal to 50 percent of the coverage you have on the structure. Make sure you understand the provisions of your policy, and make sure you document what is in your home. Videotapes are an effective way of doing this, but you can also take photographs and write descriptions of items. Include the serial numbers and purchase dates of anything applicable.

As silly as it sounds, take a look in your drawers, and either photograph or write down what's inside. If your home were destroyed by fire, you'd no doubt be stuck to think of everything you had stored away. Check closets, cabinets, and other storage areas as well.

Money Pit

Make sure your homeowner's policy contains a guaranteed replacement cost provision, which will cover the total cost of replacing property that is lost or damaged. If it doesn't, your insurer could balk at paying the full cost of rebuilding your house if it's more than your policy coverage.

Homeowner's insurance doesn't cover floods and earthquakes, and although the possibility of one of these calamities wrecking your home might be remote, it's still a possibility. You can't get flood insurance unless you live in a flood plain, and it's only offered through the federal government. If you do live in a flood plain, you definitely should have flood insurance.

The Allentown/Reading/Lancaster area of Pennsylvania, located west of Philadelphia, has been hit by earthquakes several times in the last decade. Although they haven't been major disasters, some of the earthquakes have resulted in considerable property damage because they caused large sinkholes to open up. Reading is also located along the Schuylkill River and has been the site of extensive flood damage in the past. The point is, just because you don't live in California or along the Mississippi River, it doesn't mean a flood or earthquake can't or won't occur in your neighborhood. Each company has different coverages in different states. You should verify whether your company covers hurricane damage. If not, shop around.

We've seen all kinds of weird weather phenomena during the past several years, due primarily to the effects of El Niño. Unless you can afford to replace your home and everything in it, or you could walk away and forget about it if it's destroyed, flood and earthquake coverage are worth looking into.

If you're renting an apartment, you'll need renter's insurance if you have a lot of stuff you want to protect. Damage to the building is not your responsibility, but if your TV or VCR is stolen or damaged, you'll need insurance if you want to replace it. If you have a bunch of good computer equipment or a rare coin collection, you definitely should look into renter's insurance.

If all you own at the moment is some hand-me-down furniture and a couple of beer mugs lifted from the frat house, you can skip the renter's insurance, unless you're worried about one of your buddies falling from the chandelier and suing you. Liability is always a consideration in our litigious society.

Disability Insurance

What would happen if you had a serious accident while skiing that resulted in a head injury? Pretty gruesome to think about, huh? Still, nobody is immune to accident or injury, and if you were hurt and unable to work for a long period of time, you'd be out of luck. You have a greater chance of being disabled by age 65 than dying, after all. You'd be a little less out of luck, though, if you had disability insurance, which would provide you with an income to live on until you could work again.

Most large companies provide disability insurance to employees who are unable to work because of a physical or mental *disability*. But if you work for a small company or are self-employed, you might have to buy it on your own. If you can't afford to be without a paycheck for an extended period of time, you'd better have disability insurance. By the way, if you don't work, you can't get disability insurance.

How much disability insurance you need depends on how much money you have. If you've been living paycheck to paycheck and have no money saved, you'd better have enough insurance to cover the full amount of your paycheck. If you have enough money in the bank to live off of for six months or a year, you can skimp a little.

Disability insurance becomes increasingly important as you gain dependents. If you're married and your spouse doesn't work or doesn't earn enough to support both of you, you can't be without it. If your spouse is making enough to support both of you, then it's not as important. Once you have kids, however, you've got to have disability insurance, unless your spouse makes enough money to support the entire family for an extended period of time. Almost half of all foreclosures on homes are the result of a disability within a family.

If you can imagine how devastating it would be to deal with a serious illness or injury, think about how much better you'd feel if you at least knew you'd have some income during the recovery time. Yet fewer than half of the people working in this country are insured against disability.

Make sure you know what is included in your disability coverage if you get it through work. Many people don't take the time to find out, and you can't depend on the benefits department to seek you out and tell you that you're eligible for coverage. Most companies have short-term and long-term provisions, so if you find out you need an operation and will be out of work for a couple of weeks, be sure to check to see whether you're eligible for benefits.

Show Me the Money

Disability is not an old person's condition; it's the inability to work because of a physical or mental condition. More than one-third of all disabilities are reported among people who are under 45 years old.

Dollars and Sense

If you don't have disability insurance through your employer, you might be able to purchase it through a professional organization, in which you're eligible for membership. Groups should be able to buy insurance for less than individuals, so you should be able to get a better rate. The American Medical Association, National Education Association (teachers), Writer's Guild, CLU, and ChFC Society are all professional organizations. If you need coverage, find out if you can qualify under such a group.

Don't depend on government programs such as social security or worker's compensation to provide you with benefits in the event of a disability. If you are eligible for coverage, your benefits won't be as much as you need. Also, your chances of being injured off the job are probably as good, or better, as those of being injured at work. You need coverage in the event of any disability.

Life Insurance

You need life insurance so that your family will have financial support if you die and can no longer provide for them. If you're single without children, you probably don't need life insurance. If you're married, but have no kids, you should think about life insurance if your spouse would have to drastically change his or her lifestyle if you died. If you have kids, you need life insurance.

How much life insurance you need varies, depending on your situation, but experts say it should be for five to eight times the amount of your current salary. After you figure out about how much coverage you need, it's time to decide what kind of coverage you want. As mentioned briefly earlier in this chapter, there are two basic types of life insurance: term insurance and cash value insurance. Nearly everyone (except for those who are rolling in wealth) benefits more from term insurance than cash value insurance when they are young. Cash value insurance makes sense for older people, but for people in their 20s and 30s, term is probably better.

Show Me the Money

Term life insurance is a policy in which you pay an annual premium, in exchange for a predetermined amount of money that will be paid to your beneficiaries if you die during the term that you're insured. **Cash value insurance** combines a life insurance policy with a type of savings account, where you actually earn interest on part of the money you play into the plan.

Term life insurance is the least expensive kind of life insurance. In exchange for your annual premium, term life will give a predetermined amount of money to your beneficiaries if you die during the term in which you're insured. All you need to do is keep paying the premium. The premium, however, will keep increasing as you get older, and someday might be prohibitive. It's a good idea to review your policies periodically to be sure they make sense for you.

The other kind of life insurance, cash value insurance, combines life insurance with a sort of savings account. Your premiums not only insure that your survivors will receive money if you die, but some of the money from the premiums is also credited to an account that will increase in value as long as you keep paying premiums.

Cash value insurance might sound like a better deal because you think you'll be getting something back from it. An agent hawking cash value life insurance will tell you that after you pay on the policy for so many years (usually 10 or 20), your policy will be all paid up, and you won't have to make more payments. The problem is, that cash value insurance is much, much more expensive to buy than term, and the only reason you might be able to stop paying premiums at a certain time is that you've already paid in a great amount of premium. Agents love cash value life because they get a much higher commission from selling it than they do on term. Don't let an agent or broker talk you into buying cash value insurance. At this point of your life, it's not likely that you'll need it.

There are many different aspects to life insurance, and we could write an entire book about all of the ins and outs. But because your chances of dying in your 20s or 30s are, statistically, pretty small, we won't devote too much time to it. Suffice it to say that if you're going to buy life insurance, make sure you get it from a reputable, dependable agent and that you understand what you're buying.

You Just Don't Need It

We've already told you to think big when it comes to insurance and not fall for every policy that comes down the pike. In addition to extended warranties for your computer, washer, and hairdryer, there are some other insurance goodies you can live without. If an agent tries to get you to buy these sorts of policies, just say no:

> ➤ **Dental insurance.** If your employer offers dental insurance, by all means, go ahead and use it. If not, though, don't bother getting it on your own. It usually doesn't pay for extensive work, and it's not worth buying to cover having your teeth cleaned a few times a year.

> ➤ **Flight insurance.** This novelty insurance plays on the fears of people who don't like to fly. If your life is worth a lot of money, you'll have your life insurance up to date anyway.

> ➤ **Credit life and disability insurance.** Sold by credit card companies, these policies will pay a small amount to your beneficiaries if you die with a credit card balance. The policy only covers the debt on that one card. Don't bother.

> ➤ **Life insurance for your kids.** Life insurance is to protect income, and children generally don't have income. If your child dies, a small amount of insurance money isn't going to make things better for you.

Money Pit

Cash value insurance can cost up to eight times as much as term life insurance for the same amount of coverage. Unless there are special circumstances, like if you're very wealthy and anticipate an estate tax problem if you should die, term insurance is a better deal for young people.

Dollars and Sense

Call Direct Insurance Services at 800-622-3699 for some proposals from insurance companies that have high ratings, but low costs. You'll get an idea of what's available, but you won't be under any obligation to buy. Check out www.Ameritas. com for online information about insurance; this site will even give you quotes.

My Mama Told Me: You Better Shop Around

To keep the cost of your insurance policies down, you must comparison-shop. Costs can vary greatly.

We mentioned earlier that you should take the highest deductibles you can afford on your insurance. Of course, you'll pay more in the event that something happens, but you'll pay less on your premiums. Chances are, you'll end up paying more in premiums than you will on a higher deductible for an occasional claim. If you have a very low *deductible*, you'll end up filing claims a lot more often than if your deductible is higher.

Show Me the Money

A **deductible** is the most amount of money that you have to pay before your insurance coverage picks up the cost.

Say that your roof leaked during that last, nasty thunderstorm. It's nothing too bad, but the estimate to repair the drywall and repaint the wall was for $175. If your deductible is $100, you're going to spend a lot of time filling out claims forms and hassling with the insurance company for the sake of $75. Also, if you report every minor claim, you can bet that the insurance company will soon be hiking up your rates. If you have a $300 deductible, though, you'll save significant money on your premiums, a savings you can use to make minor repairs. Comparison-shop the premium savings and the deductible limits, and then determine what you can afford to pay out if you have a claim.

Also mentioned earlier was the advantage of getting a group rate on an insurance policy, rather than buying it on your own. Whenever possible, check out group rates through your employer or an organization you belong to for the insurance you need. You can often save significant money by doing so.

Finally, when you're shopping around, check out the rating of the insurance company you're thinking of doing business with. Various organizations evaluate and rate insurance companies, judging them on their financial stability and health. Look to A.M. Best, Standard & Poor's, Weis Research, or Moody's rating services. Directories published by these services are available in most libraries.

What Do You Mean I'm Not Covered?

Coming from your insurance agent, the words, "you're not covered," can strike fear in even the staunchest hearts. If you've filed a claim and your insurer doesn't want to pay it or wants to pay you only part of what you believe it should, don't roll over. There are things you can do to assure your best shot at getting what you deserve:

➤ **Document your losses.** If you're in a car accident, get the names and addresses of all possible witnesses. If your property was damaged, take photos or videotapes of the damage. File police reports when necessary, and get several estimates for what it will cost to repair or replace whatever was damaged.

➤ **Don't give up.** If you file a claim for $2,286 for repairs to your car after a wreck, and the insurance company says it will give you $1,500, find out why. If you don't get any satisfaction from the *adjuster*, the person who surveyed the damage and determined what you should be paid, find out who the supervisors and managers are and ask to talk to them. Ask your agent to help you.

➤ **Prepare your claim carefully.** Make sure that your policy covers the claim you're about to make and write out your claim report carefully and clearly. By all means, keep a copy of the report and document all conversations you have with anyone concerning your claim.

➤ **Get legal help.** If you've been denied coverage for a major claim that you feel you're entitled to, you might want to hire a lawyer who specializes in insurance concerns. It will be expensive, but if there's a significant amount of money at stake, it might be worth it.

Insurance is a big, powerful industry, and it's in the business to make money. Don't expect that your insurer will go out of its way to please you and make you happy. Although you shouldn't assume an adversarial position with your insurance company, you should remain alert to the possibility that you'll have to do a little haggling to get what you deserve. Good companies do, and all companies are expected to, honor their commitments and promises to their customers.

If you aren't satisfied with the service or coverage you've received, you can contact your state insurance department. Just make sure that you're entitled under your policy to whatever compensation you're seeking.

Show Me the Money

An insurance **adjuster** is a person who inspects damage and determines the amount that the insurance company should pay for repairs or replacement.

The Least You Need to Know

➤ Hardly anyone likes insurance, but we all need to have it.

➤ The insurance industry is large and powerful, and we're pretty much at its mercy.

➤ Purchase insurance to cover major losses, not to protect you against every little thing that could go wrong.

➤ There are some types of policies that almost everyone needs, and some that hardly anyone should buy.

➤ There are ways to save money when buying insurance, so it pays to know what you need and look around before you buy.

➤ If your insurer hassles you about paying a claim, be prepared to fight.

Part 4
To Everything There Is a Season

Things change. Your old pals and roommates are getting married. People are getting new jobs and moving away. A couple of your friends even have babies. It seems the only thing you can count on anymore is the fact that nothing stays the same.

You find that you're taking life a bit more seriously yourself, these days. You're not all business; you still love to have a great time. Nobody laughs at you yet on the basketball court, and you're never left looking for something to do on Saturday night. It's just that you're a bit more settled than you were five years ago. You've even met somebody that you think maybe, just maybe, you'd like to spend the rest of your life with.

Your finances reflect these changes in attitude, too. You're looking past your 401(k) plan and even thinking about getting into the stock market. You've started asking around for a good financial advisor. You're looking down the road, that's for sure.

There's an awful lot involved in these kinds of decisions, and we cover a lot of material in this section, everything from weddings to market risk. By the time you're finished reading this section, you should feel a little more comfortable with it all and ready to move ahead.

Chapter 16

The Game of Life

In This Chapter

➤ Understanding that your life situation affects your finances

➤ Being single and earning a paycheck

➤ How living together affects your personal finances

➤ How marriage affects your checkbook, your insurance, and your taxes

Remember those lazy afternoons playing board games when you were a kid? Do you remember the game called *Life?* You know, the one where you put the little pink or blue pegs into cars, spun the wheel, picked a profession, and took a chance on romance? While you were paying the "bills" and having "kids," you probably never thought twice about how that related to real life. Your mom called you for dinner, and you put the game away. No more wrong moves, no more unpaid bills, no more problems—such was the game of Life.

Off the board, things are a little different. Life is not a game of chance. It moves along at its own pace. Days pass, seasons change, and all of a sudden, you're another year older. Maybe you've done the bridesmaid thing more times than you can count during the past three or four years. You may have even been to a baby shower or two. Maybe you're finding it hard to get enough of your buddies together to shoot hoops because they're all living with their girlfriends and have stuff they need to do.

Your life is changing, too. You're probably better established in your career than you were a year or two ago, and it might seem like a lifetime ago that you left college and started working. Hopefully, your personal finances are on track, and you're enjoying having a little extra money—not only for things you want to buy, but for investing in your future, as well. Maybe you've met somebody who's really special, and you're contemplating making a deeper commitment. It's an exciting time of life, but it can get complicated. These changes require some preparation.

We spent a good deal of time in Chapter 8 evaluating your financial lifestyle and determining your expectations as they relate to your personal finances. Now, we're going to have a look at how different stages of life can affect your personal finances and how you can make the most of each of those stages.

Life circumstances dictate your personal finances to a great extent. If you're single and still sharing an apartment with your buddies, it has probably been easier (at least it should have been easier!) for you to save money than if you were already married and had two kids. If you're part of a two-income couple that lives together, you probably have more discretionary income than a recent college graduate who just landed his or her first (low-paying) job.

In this chapter, you'll see how your circumstances affect and, to a large degree, dictate your financial situation. You'll learn how to plan and execute your finances most effectively for the particular situation in which you happen to find yourself.

Footloose and Fancy-Free

If you've been out of college and working for several years, and you're still single with no intention of hooking up with someone anytime soon, you're probably making your mother very nervous. She no doubt listens enviously as her friends talk of their sons' and daughters' wedding plans, longing for the day she can shop for a mother of the bride/groom dress. She might drop some hints about how nice it would be for you to find someone and "settle down." Or maybe she's not that subtle. Maybe she comes right out and asks you what you think you're waiting for. You're not getting any younger, you know.

Pocket Change

The median age for first marriages in America is 25 for women and 27 for men. That compares with 22 for women and 25 for men in 1980. Pass that little tidbit of information along to Mom the next time she starts making comments about your unmarried status.

Sorry, Mom. It's your life, and you've got to live it according to your style. Maybe you just haven't met anybody with whom you're interested in spending the rest of your life. Maybe you have, but the feeling wasn't mutual. Maybe you're too busy getting ahead at work to worry much about your personal life. Or maybe you just like being single and on your own.

The single years can be some of the best ones of your life. You're getting your career off the ground and starting to be recognized for your accomplishments. You're meeting lots of new people and enjoying an active social life. You're not broke like you were in college and the first couple of years when you started working, so you can afford to do some things now that you couldn't do before. You're learning a little about investments, putting some money away in your 401(k) plan, and maybe even thinking about buying a place of your own.

If you're still living with your parents, you've lasted longer than a lot of people could, but you're by no means alone. Gen Xers are staying at home longer, and they say it's to be able to save money. Staying at home allows you to buy and do things that you probably couldn't afford to do if you took on the additional expenses of rent, utilities, and the like.

Of course, not all single people are financially responsible. Some not-so-young-anymore singles haven't saved a dime, and they aren't looking into the future past their next paycheck. They've been having a great time out on their own ever since they got out of college, and they see no reason to change it now. New cars, recreational equipment, electronic equipment, clothes, trips, and other previously unaffordable luxury items can be extremely tempting to those with money and few financial responsibilities. Unfortunately, all the ski equipment you continue to amass won't help you much when you retire and start looking for some money to live on.

Pocket Change

More young adults currently live with their parents than at any other time since the Great Depression of the 1930s.

We've covered some information in earlier chapters about investments, taxes, and other topics that can affect your finances and your future. Hopefully, you've learned something and are doing what you need to in order to both enjoy your single years and assure your future. At the very least, you should by now be doing the following:

➤ Paying back college loans

➤ Working to reduce (hopefully to eliminate) credit card debt

➤ Saving money in an emergency fund

➤ Putting some money into your employer's 401(k) plan or another type of tax-deferred retirement plan

We'd never suggest that you miss out on the opportunity to enjoy those great single years because you're saving every penny you make and never have any money with which to do anything. Just don't lose sight of the fact that you have a lot of life ahead of you, and all the fun you have when you're footloose and fancy-free won't finance your retirement.

She (Gulp!) Wants Me to Move in with Her!

So you've met somebody you really, really like. Okay, you're in love. You're spending a lot of time together. Actually, you're together almost all the time. You talk about a future together, but neither of you feels like you're quite ready to start shopping for engagement rings. You're just hanging out one day when it happens. She tells you she'd like you to move in with her.

Dollars and Sense

If you decide that living together makes financial sense, you're in good company. More than three million unmarried couples are living together in the United States, according to U.S. census figures.

There are many reasons why so many couples are living together these days. Some do it because it's convenient. It eliminates running back and forth between two apartments and shuffling your belongings all over town. Some couples use living together as a sort of "trial run" for marriage. They reason that it makes more sense to see whether it will work out before you get married than risk a divorce a year or two after the nuptials.

Financial considerations can also factor in to a couple's decision to live together rather than get married. Many couples set a goal of saving a specific amount of money, or paying off their student loans, or getting enough for a down payment on a house before taking the plunge. Some wait to establish their careers before getting married and live together while they do.

Whatever the reasons, plenty of couples choose to live together. Although cohabitation doesn't raise eyebrows the way it did 30 years ago, it can still be a sticky arrangement. There are financial and legal ramifications, as well as the less tangible emotional aspects to consider. You're on your own to figure out the emotional particulars of living together, but we can tell you some things you should know about the legal and financial aspects.

Financial Advantages

There are definitely financial advantages to living together. If you each had an apartment before you moved in together, you've cut your housing costs by about 50 percent by sharing your space. That makes more sense than paying rent on an apartment that was empty most of the time, anyway. You'll also be sharing costs for utilities, so you'll see some savings there. If you were living a considerable distance apart, you'll save money on transportation and phone bills, too.

You'll also realize some tax advantages by living together instead of opting for marriage. Although you're living together, you'll continue filing your tax returns as singles. That can save you some money, especially if you and your significant other earn above-average salaries. Consider that if you each earn $45,000 a year, you'll pay about $1,400 more in taxes after marriage than if you were still single.

Financial Disadvantages

Although there are financial advantages to living together, it's not all a bed of roses. There are instances in which you'd be better off financially if you were married. Consider the following:

➤ **Health benefits.** Many employers offer health and dental benefits to spouses of employees, but not to a person with whom the employee lives.

➤ **Life insurance.** If an employer offers life insurance and the employee dies, benefits automatically go to the spouse of the deceased. An unmarried partner must be named beneficiary to get the benefits.

➤ **Pension.** Many companies will pay some pension benefits to the spouse of an employee who dies before retirement. These benefits usually don't apply to unmarried couples.

➤ **Social security.** If a person dies while employed, the spouse might be eligible for some social security benefits upon reaching age 60. An unmarried partner isn't eligible for these benefits.

➤ **Memberships.** Unmarried couples usually aren't eligible for money-saving "family" memberships in clubs and organizations. You'll sometimes end up paying almost twice as much as singles.

We're not trying to turn marriage into a business transaction, but as you can see, there are financial advantages and disadvantages to living together instead of getting married. One thing to remember, though, is that marriage implies love and commitment that extends far past the savings account. If you're putting off marriage because you'll be taxed at a higher rate, you might have to ask yourself whether you're looking for an excuse to stay single.

Breaking Up Is Hard to Do

As much as you both might want the relationship to work, sometimes things go wrong. Relationships end, and sometimes it's not under the best circumstances. When that occurs, couples who lived together, but weren't married, might have a hard time figuring out where they stand legally. Divorce laws are pretty clear-cut in most states, but there are few laws that deal with break-ups of couples who have lived together.

What happens, for instance, if a man works two jobs to put his girlfriend through law school, and then the couple breaks up and the girlfriend moves out. Should he be entitled to reimbursement for her law school tuition? Or what happens to property when an unmarried couple breaks up? Even if there's not a house involved, there's likely to be furniture, maybe some art, computers, CD players, and TVs. Unmarried couples who split should try for congenial and equitable property division because there's a lot of legal gray area out there.

If you're planning to live together, we wish you all the best. But if you have a significant amount of property between the two of you, you might do well to consult a lawyer before you move in.

Will You Marry Me, Bill?

You've finally decided to take the plunge and make it official by getting married. Hearty congratulations and best wishes to you both! Before you blissfully embark on your honeymoon, though, you need to think about some financial considerations.

A large number of divorces are caused by financial problems. Sometimes these problems are a result of a gambling or other type of addiction. Often, though, financial problems occur because the couple doesn't work together on their financial health. Maybe they don't share common attitudes about money, but they never bother to work out those differences. Maybe they don't even know each other's attitudes toward money because they've never discussed it.

If you're planning to marry, it's absolutely necessary that you and your intended sit down and carefully and thoroughly discuss how you'll handle your finances after the wedding. You should establish some goals to work toward together and make sure you know about each other's debts, spending patterns, and investments.

If you've been living together, you may or may not have joint accounts. If you haven't lived together, you'll need to decide how you'll set up your bank accounts as a married couple. It's not necessary to have joint accounts, although most married couples have at least some of their money pooled. Some couples, especially when both people are earning, keep separate accounts, while also establishing joint accounts. Separate accounts give individuals freedom and independence, while joint accounts offer the convenience of allowing either spouse to sign a check. This is a decision that you and your partner need to discuss and figure out. Do whatever you agree will work best for the two of you.

Learn your partner's attitudes concerning savings and the best means for savings. Do you have 401(k) plans? Any stocks? What about savings bonds you got as gifts when you were a kid? Talk about saving to buy a house. What about saving for kids?

Talk about whether you'll operate within a budget and together plan the budget you'll use. You don't want the stresses of adjusting to married life to be aggravated by a misunderstanding of how you'll be handling your finances. Get as many financial considerations as possible ironed out before the wedding to avoid conflicts afterwards.

Money Pit

Love might be blind, but your understanding of your partner's financial situation shouldn't be. You'll be in for an unpleasant surprise if you find out your new husband owes $10,000 for something you know nothing about. If one of you does have a lot of debt or other financial problems, discuss those problems and reach an agreement before the wedding as to how you're going to handle them.

You should also discuss the following financial issues:

➤ How will your marriage affect your employer benefits? If one of you has a much better package than the other, make sure you both are covered by the better deal. Consider health benefits, retirement savings plans, and anything else that might affect your financial situation. Check to see whether either employer offers compensation to an employee who gives up benefits to be covered by the partner's plan.

➤ Figure out how much life and disability insurance you need. It costs more for two people to live than one person. If your partner dies, can you continue your lifestyle on your own earnings? Or if your partner becomes disabled and can't work, can you both live on one income? If not, make sure you have sufficient life and disability insurance. If you already have life and disability insurance, rename the beneficiary if it's not already your spouse.

➤ Start an emergency fund if you don't already have one. When you're footloose and fancy-free, you're the only one you have to worry about. Now, you have the additional responsibility of another person. You should start saving whatever you can to get three to six months' worth of living expenses in case of an emergency. We'll talk later about where to invest such money, but it should be a safe, short-term account. This is a daunting task, to be sure, but it's something you should have. You don't have to save a huge amount each week, but try to save something toward this fund.

➤ Make or update your wills. If you don't already have wills, now is a great time to get them. If you do have them, they'll need to be updated. Don't be queasy about wills. They're a piece of cake to do, and you'll benefit greatly from the peace of mind that having them brings. Contact your local Bar Association and ask for the name of a lawyer who will be able to prepare a will. Will kits are a nice way to obtain information, but any will completed through a will kit should be reviewed by an attorney. Note that in many states a will is considered invalid if a marriage has taken place after the will was signed. You want to have your assets distributed per your wishes, not by the state.

Uh, Could You Sign Here, Please?

Prenuptial agreements—those handy little plans that spell out how assets will be divided in the event that the marriage fails—used to be primarily for Hollywood types who had tons of money

Show Me the Money

A **prenuptial agreement** is a legal document that protects your financial interests. The average estimated cost of a prenuptial agreement ranges from $1,500 to $3,000.

but little staying power when it came to marriage. It's pretty clear that with 1.2 million couples getting divorced each year, many of us average Joes have lost our staying power as well.

Even if you don't have tons of money, some matrimonial lawyers and financial advisors strongly recommend prenuptial agreements, especially if one person has a child or children from a previous marriage or relationship. A prenuptial agreement also might make sense if one partner owns a business or makes a lot more money than the other. Such an agreement could also be important if one partner has major assets independently and doesn't want to risk losing them.

Whether or not to have a prenuptial agreement is something you and your intended will have to decide together. If you can't agree on the need for one, or if you feel your partner is pressuring you to have one and you don't want it, it might be a goof idea to get some financial or relationship counseling before the wedding. It might just be a matter of not fully understanding the other's concerns or wishes that's making it hard to reach an agreement.

Goin' to the Chapel and We're Gonna Get Married

Once you decide to get married, you can kiss your free time good-bye. There's just so much to do. You need to make the official announcement, pick a date, and start making wedding plans. You've got to arrange for time off from work for your honeymoon, think about where you'll live, and pick out your wedding dress and tux.

As busy as you'll be, however, you've got to spend some time doing some serious thinking about your personal finances and how the wedding and marriage will affect them. A wedding can be unbelievably expensive (almost enough to make you want to elope!), and you'll be spending money on a lot of other things such as an engagement ring and honeymoon. Let's take a look at some of the expenses you might be faced with.

With This Ring

One of the very first expenses involved with getting married is buying an engagement ring. Of course, a ring is not required, but it's traditional and quite important to many couples. It used to be that the groom-to-be would pick out and buy the ring without benefit of the bride-to-be's input. Then, he'd present the ring when he asked his girlfriend to become his fianceé. Some couples still do that, but many women like to pick out their own engagement rings and aren't shy about saying so. Picking out the engagement ring has become a two-person endeavor, although the man still normally pays for it.

Regardless of who picks out the ring, be smart about it, and don't get a ring that you simply can't afford. The two months' salary rule is archaic. An engagement ring should be a symbol of your love and commitment, not a statement of your financial situation. You'll have plenty of occasions to upgrade your ring after you're married.

Ouch! Here Comes the Bill

Traditionally, most wedding expenses were paid for by the bride's parents. But times have changed, and the way we pay for weddings has changed as well. Increased costs have forced families to re-evaluate how to pay for a wedding, which may simply be too expensive for one family to manage.

The following are some modern options for paying for a wedding:

➤ Bride and groom pay for the entire wedding

➤ Expenses are divided between the couple, the bride's family, and the groom's family

➤ Each family pays for the number of guests it invites

➤ The bride's family and groom's family split the expenses

Money Pit

Some jewelers really play on your emotions when you go to buy a ring. They might hint that you have to spend a lot of money to prove to your girlfriend that you think she's "worth it." If your girlfriend doesn't already know that you think she's the greatest, she probably won't want to marry you anyway. Don't let a jeweler talk you into buying a ring you can't afford.

Pocket Change

Reports show that a wedding with all the trimmings for 150 guests can easily cost more than $15,000, and the cost can go much, much higher.

Certain expenses have traditionally been assigned to the bride, the groom, the attendants, and the families of the bride and groom. Don't expect it to work out like this, but if it does, hey, lucky you. We've provided the breakdown for your amusement:

➤ Bride pays for: wedding ring for the groom, wedding gift for the groom, gifts for bridal attendants, personal stationery, her medical exam and blood test

➤ Groom pays for: engagement ring and bride's wedding ring, wedding gift for the bride, gifts for the best man and ushers, groom's wedding attire, bride's bouquet, mothers' corsages, boutonnieres for attendants and fathers, his medical exam and blood test, marriage license, clergyman's fee, honeymoon expenses, and bachelor party (if not given by best man)

➤ Bride's family pays for: engagement party, ceremony cost (including location, music, rentals, and all other expenses), entire cost of reception (including location, food, beverage, entertainment, rental items, decorations, and wedding cake), bride's wedding attire, a wedding gift for the couple, bridesmaids' bouquets, bridesmaids' luncheon, photography, flowers

➤ Groom's family pays for: rehearsal dinner, travel and accommodations for the groom's family, wedding gift for the bride and groom

➤ Attendants pay for: wedding attire for themselves, travel expenses, wedding gift for the bride and groom, bridal showers, bachelor party

➤ Bride and groom pay for: gifts of appreciation for parents and others

That's the traditional breakdown of expenses, but it's certainly not a hard-and-fast rule. Wedding expenses should be divided according to who is able, and willing, to pay for certain things.

The first important thing to do when planning your wedding is to establish how much you can spend. This will require talking to everyone who might be contributing and finding out how much you'll have. If you learn that you'll have $25,000—great! Go ahead and throw yourself a bash. If you find out you have $7,500, then you'll need to scale down and work within those parameters. Remember that it makes no sense to pay $5,000 for a wedding cake and $15,000 for flowers if you can't afford it.

On the following page is a wedding worksheet to guide you through the process. Setting a total budget amount, with category percentages, should help keep your costs under control. Good Luck!

Your wedding can be beautiful, elegant, and an event that people will remember and talk about without sending you into the debt dungeon for the next 10 years. Consider these suggestions for saving money, and then see whether you can come up with some others on your own:

➤ **Wedding dress.** All brides are beautiful, regardless of whether their dress cost $100 or $10,000. There are an increasing number of options available for getting a wedding dress that won't bust your budget. Some consignment shops carry wedding dresses, and there are places that rent them. Or how about borrowing your best friend's dress that you helped her pick out?

➤ **Headpiece.** Tons of these are floating around out there. Borrow one or get creative and make your own. It can save you hundreds of dollars.

➤ **Food.** You don't have to have a sit-down dinner. Nontraditional wedding formats such as a brunch, tea, or patio cocktail party can be elegant alternatives to high-priced dinners. If you're on a very tight budget, keep in mind that buffets are usually cheaper than sit-down affairs. You can also enlist some friends and make at least some of the food yourselves.

The budget for every wedding is different, because every wedding is different. This worksheet, however, gives you an idea of the way the average wedding budget breaks down, by listing the percentage for the total budget as it normally is allocated. Use these percentages as a guide to plan your wedding, so you can stay within your budget.

So, grab your calculator, and you'll get an idea of how much money you'll have to spend for each cost area.

Total wedding budget $_____

Stationery items (3%) estimated cost $_____ actual cost $_____

Bridal attire (10%) estimated cost $_____ actual cost $_____

Reception (40%) estimated cost $_____ actual cost $_____

Flowers (8%) estimated cost $_____ actual cost $_____

Music (3%) estimated cost $_____ actual cost $_____

Photographs (7%) estimated cost $_____ actual cost $_____

Gifts-attendants (2%) estimated cost $_____ actual cost $_____

Honeymoon (20%) estimated cost $_____ actual cost $_____

Misc. (i.e., special parties) (7%) estimated cost $_____ actual cost $_____

Total estimated cost $_____ Total actual cost $_____

Obviously, these percentages will vary, as you customize your own wedding. Be sure you keep track of all your wedding expenses by saving all receipts and filing them in a safe place.

➤ **Alcohol.** Be prepared to shell out more for booze than you will for food. You can save a tremendous amount of cash if you supply the alcohol yourself. Wine and beer are the cheapest option, but if you buy in bulk, you can probably afford the harder stuff. If you can't bring your own, talk with your caterer about a fixed price per person instead of an open bar. This will allow your guests to drink unlimited amounts that you've already paid for. Open bars mean wasted drinks and wasted money (and wasted guests).

➤ **Photography.** Photographers are expensive. If you hire a professional, be sure you find out exactly how she charges. Can you limit the number of shots to cut expenses? How about hiring a good amateur photographer, instead? Ask your friends to bring cameras and take lots of candid shots or leave disposable cameras on the tables at the reception and encourage guests to use them.

➤ **Facility.** It's risky, weather-wise, but an outdoor wedding can be beautiful and less expensive than renting an indoor facility. Or perhaps the wedding could be at someone's home. What about a room in your church or synagogue? Get an overview of what's available before making a commitment.

➤ **Guests.** Limiting your guest list is a good way to save money, because caterers usually charge per person. Go over your list and ask yourself if you really need to invite Lisa, whom you haven't seen since you changed jobs two years ago, just because you went to her wedding.

➤ **Honeymoon.** See the money-saving travel tips in Chapter 10, and remember that although this might be your first trip as a married couple, it won't be your last.

Uncle Sam Has a Little Wedding Present for You

Most people consider marriage to be a desirable institution, but you won't get any rewards for it from Uncle Sam. The good-old U.S. government gives married couples a real slap in the face, starting with their first tax return.

As a single person filing your income tax return, you were eligible for a $4,250 personal deduction. If you decide to file a joint return after you're married, however, your deduction will be only $7,100. Do the math, and you'll find out that it doesn't add up. If you don't file a joint return, you file "married filing separately." Your deduction is halved at $3550 each with many other limitations. It's usually the least advantageous way for a married couple to file their taxes. Thanks a lot, Uncle Sam.

The Least You Need to Know

➤ Your financial situation will be significantly affected by your life circumstances.

➤ Living single and bringing in a paycheck is a great time to save, but it's also a tempting time during which to spend.

➤ Living together without being married can affect your finances. Consider these effects before making a commitment.

➤ Getting married might involve changes to your insurance, bank accounts, and will.

➤ Everyone wants a great wedding, but you need to be sure you work within your budget.

➤ Getting married works to your disadvantage as far as taxes are concerned.

Chapter 17

Not Your Father's Pension Plan: Retirement Funds in the Modern World

---

In This Chapter

➤ Understanding why retirement savings are so important

➤ Knowing what kinds of plans are available

➤ Setting up a plan if you're self-employed

➤ Allocating your money inside a retirement account

➤ Penalties and regulations concerning early withdrawal

As a nation, we're living longer, and many of us will be around well after we reach retirement age. The bad news is that all the medical breakthroughs that allow us to live longer lives won't help us save the money we need to support ourselves in our golden years. Saving for retirement is becoming a national concern because more people are living past 65, and less money is available in social security and individual retirement funds. People just aren't realizing how important saving for retirement is.

Consider these nationwide wake-up calls:

➤ In the spring of 1998, Securities and Exchange Commission chairman Arthur Levitt led a "Facts on Saving and Investing" campaign.

➤ Also in 1998, Fidelity Investments created and sponsored a first-ever "National Pay Yourself Day," with 300 corporations joining in with support.

➤ In the summer of 1998, President Clinton called for the first national summit on saving for retirement. (Could he have some info about social security that we haven't been told about?)

Why all this concern about saving for retirement, you ask? Because too many people aren't doing it. A Merrill Lynch poll shows that baby boomers have saved only about 36 percent of what they'll need for retirement, and many haven't saved at all. When *Money* magazine asked retirees what their biggest financial mistake had been, most of them said it was waiting too long to start saving for retirement. Gen Xers, who say they have little faith in the social security system, appear to be starting to save earlier than boomers did. Still, many aren't saving enough or saving at all.

Is Retirement Planning Your Top Priority? It Should Be

It used to be that most people who worked had pensions that were provided by their employers. Between their pension checks and Social Security payments, retirees had enough money to live comfortably. Times have changed, though, and pensions are, for the most part, a thing of the past.

We have to take responsibility for our own retirement savings now. What about social security, you ask? As baby boomers reach retirement, there will be fewer workers to support the number of people taking money out of social security. Nobody knows how this situation will play out, but indications show that there's enough money in the fund to last until 2020, which means that unless something changes, there won't be any social security money left when Generation X is ready to retire. Even if the social security system is fixed and is intact when you retire, your payments will probably not be enough to live on.

People might not be saving enough, but they're retiring earlier today than they used to. Only about one-third of American men who are 55 or older are still working full-time at the job they held previously, according to the U.S. Department of Labor. Many, though, are working part-time or in different, less demanding jobs. In 1950, nearly 70 percent of that age group was still employed in their primary jobs. What this means is that a lot of people will be living for a long time after retirement, and many of them will run out of money.

Studies show that most people will require about three quarters as much money to maintain their standard of living during retirement as they required before retiring. Of course, all kinds of factors go into that estimate, and remember that it's an average. If you want to retire to a villa in the South of France and travel frequently between there and the States on the Concorde, you will need to do some fancy financial planning to fund your dream.

On the other hand, if you plan to move to the in-laws apartment in your daughter's house and spend your retirement catching up on your reading, you'll be able to live very comfortably with a portion of your pre-retirement income. At this point, though, who knows what those retirement years will bring? There's no way of knowing what your health will be like in 40 years or what other circumstances will be affecting your life.

Remember these two important things about saving for retirement:

1. The earlier you start, the easier it is to accumulate all the money you'll need.
2. Little savings can add up over the years to make big savings.

If you find it hard to believe that a couple of years makes a big difference in what you'll be able to save, take a look at this example: If you invest $5,000 when you're 25 at 8 percent interest and let it sit until you're 60, you'll have $73,900, unless, of course, something terrible happens to the U.S. economy. But if you wait until you're 35 to invest $5,000 at the same interest rate, you'll have only $34,240 when you turn 60. If you wait until you're 45 to invest the money, you'll have only $15,900.

Here are some examples of how starting early is advantageous to your retirement's good health:

IT PAYS TO START EARLY

The chart below compares the profiles of two people who invest in a diversified portfolio with the original investment made my Employee A beginning at age 21. The results assume a 10% compound rate of return with the new $2,000 investment being made on January 2 of each year. Results are as of December 31 of each year.

EMPLOYEE A

Begins at age 21

Invests $2,000 each year until he or she is 29, and does **not** put any more money in after that

Total contributions made over nine years: $18,000

EMPLOYEE B

Begins at age 30

Invests $2,000 each year, and continues to do so until he or she is 65 years old

Total contributions made over 35 years: $70,000

Age	EMPLOYEE A	EMPLOYEE B
22	$2,200	$0
27	$16,974	$0
32	$36,146	$4,620
36	$58,210	$16,970
41	$93,746	$40,766
46	$150,977	$79,083
51	$243,147	$140,794
56	$391,587	$240,179
61	$630,652	$400,238
65	$839,396	$658,015

IT PAYS TO START BUILDING WEALTH
WHILE YOU'RE YOUNG

The more time your tax-deferred savings have to grow, the more you'll have at retirement, if all else is equal.

Age Contributions Begin	Total Contributed at Age 65	Retirement Account Total at Age 65
25	$75,401	$302,090
30	60,462	202,797
35	47,575	133,732
40	36,459	85,982
45	26,870	53,224
50	18,599	30,978

Assumes: starting annual income of $20,000, 3% annual wage increases, steady 5% bi-weekly retirement plan contributions, a hypothetical 7% annual investment return, and no employer contributions. The totals shown are for illustrative purposes only. They do not represent any particular investment. Your investment performance will differ.

Source: NPI

YOUR TAX-DEFERRAL MAKES CONTRIBUTING EASIER

Here's how a 5% retirement plan contribution saves federal income taxes for someone in a 15% federal income tax bracket.

Bi-weekly Income ($)	Contribution Amount ($)	Estimated Tax Savings ($)	Reduction in Take-home Pay ($)
600	30	25.50	4.50
800	40	34.00	6.00
1,000	50	42.50	7.50
1,200	60	51.00	9.00
1,500	75	63.75	11.25

If you can't imagine that saving a couple of dollars here and there will make a difference, consider these fun facts from Fidelity Investments. All the amounts are based on saving for 30 years at 9 percent interest:

➤ If you save $300 a year by exercising at home instead of joining a gym, you'll have $44,572.

➤ If you save $7 a week by making your daily cappuccino an every-other-day cappuccino, you'll have $56,092.

➤ If you save $12 a month by renting a video instead of going to the movies (with popcorn, please), you'll have $22,134.

➤ If you save $35 a month by collecting all your change, you'll have $64,557.

If you do all those things, you'll have $187,355 in 30 years. Not a bad exchange for some little sacrifices, is it? Most of us, though, still go ahead and buy the cappuccinos.

Fortunately, the increasing popularity of 401(k)s is improving the retirement savings situation in this country somewhat. But studies show that only about 60 percent of people who have the opportunity to contribute to an employer-sponsored retirement plan such as a 401(k) do it.

Unfortunately, the IRS limits how much you can contribute annually to your 401(k) plan. The amount is at $10,000 now, but it's adjusted each year with inflation. Some employers also limit the amount of money you can contribute to the plan. Be sure you know if yours does.

Dollars and Sense

Some experts say that questions concerning the future of the social security program, and the proliferation of 401(k) plans, are causing more and more Generation Xers to start saving. We say, "Whatever it takes!"

The question is, then, if you have money to invest somewhere else, either instead of a 401(k) or in addition to your 401(k), where should you put it? The answer is that you should look at other retirement funds in which to invest your earnings. Why? Because of the tax advantages.

What's Out There?

In most cases, investing in retirement accounts is simpler than investing outside of retirement accounts. It tends to be less overwhelming because there are fewer options for investing, and you don't have to worry about tax factors because your investments aren't taxed until you make withdrawls from the accounts. 401(k)s are particularly easy because your employer does most of the work for you. But this chapter is about retirement funds other than 401(k)s, so let's have a look at what else is available. Read this section carefully, so you'll be able to explain it in detail to your friends the next time you're together at a party (yeah, right!).

Individual Retirement Accounts (IRAs)

Anybody who makes any money working can contribute up to $2,000 a year in an *individual retirement account* (IRA). An IRA is a tax-deferred type of retirement savings plan, meaning you don't pay taxes until you withdraw from the fund. Of course, this money can only be contributed if you work. If you make $3,000 a year mowing lawns and shoveling snow, but never report a penny of it, those earnings don't make you eligible to contribute to an IRA (they could, however, get you in trouble with the IRS). If you earn less than $2,000 a year, however, you can only contribute the amount you've earned to an IRA. If you earn $1,650 scooping ice cream at Ben & Jerry's, for instance, that's the amount you can stash in an IRA. If you're married, but not working, your spouse can contribute up to $2,000 a year for you, $4,000 total for the family.

IRAs used to be the hot-shot investment vehicle. Things changed, though, when lawmakers got cranky and dumped all kinds of restrictions onto them in 1986. Back in the good old days, anybody could deduct their IRA contributions. Now the money you contribute might be tax-deductible, but it might not be. Here's how it breaks down:

➤ If you're single and do not have an employer-sponsored retirement plan, you can put up to $2,000 a year in an IRA. The full $2,000 is deductible on your income tax return. It's a dollar for dollar deduction from your taxable income.

➤ If you're single, covered by an employer-sponsored plan, and your annual adjusted gross income is $30,000 or less, you can contribute up to $2,000 and deduct the full amount. If your income is between $30,000 and $40,000, the deduction is pro-rated. If you make more than $40,000 a year, you can contribute, but you get no deduction. These numbers will gradually increase to $50,000 (take the full deduction) to $60,000 (take no deduction) by the year 2005.

➤ If you're married and file jointly, have an employer-sponsored plan, and your annual adjusted gross income is $50,000 or less (thanks again, Uncle Sam), you can deduct the full amount. The figure is pro-rated from $50,000 to $60,000. After $60,000, you can't take any deduction. The numbers will increase to $80,000 (full deduction) and $100,000 (no deduction) by 2007.

➤ If your spouse doesn't have a retirement plan at work, and you file a joint tax return, the spouse can deduct his or her full $2,000 contribution until your joint income reaches $150,000. After that, the deduction is pro-rated until your joint income is $160,000, at which time you can't deduct the IRA contribution.

Even if you can't deduct the contributions, they still help out with taxes because they're *tax-deferred*. It's not as great as *tax-deductible*, but it's the next best thing. IRAs are good savings vehicles, but if your IRA contributions aren't deductible, make sure you take advantage of the programs on which you can get a tax deduction, such as 401(k)s, first.

Roth IRAs

This variation on your basic IRA is the new darling of the investor crowd. New in 1998, the *Roth IRA* is different from the traditional one in several ways, and many financial experts agree that it is better than the traditional IRA for people with the right circumstances.

For starters, your contribution to a Roth IRA is after-tax money, as opposed to the traditional IRA, in which your contribution is pre-tax money. Huh? Okay, when you contribute to a regular, deductible IRA, you put in $2,000 (or whatever) before you pay tax on that money. When you take your contributions and your earnings out at retirement, you have to pay taxes on that money.

Pocket Change

A person who has no income, but receives alimony, also is eligible to contribute to an IRA.

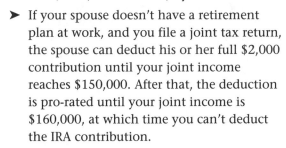

Show Me the Money

A **tax-deferred** investment is one on which you'll pay no tax on income or gain until you withdraw the money. A **tax-deductible** investment is one that reduces the amount of your current taxable income.

Show Me the Money

A **Roth IRA** is an IRA in which the funds placed into the account are non-deductible. If held more than five years, all funds withdrawn are received tax-free .

With a Roth IRA, your $2,000 contribution comes out of income you've already paid taxes on (that is, earnings). The funds contributed accumulate tax free, and if held for five years, you never pay tax on the money withdrawn. Yep, you heard it. If you follow the rules and hold the funds within the Roth for five years, you never have to pay tax on the account again. That means you get all the earnings on that $2,000 tax-free, which is a very appealing feature of the Roth.

Another great thing about Roths is that when you take the money out, it's not considered taxable income. After you've had a Roth IRA for five years and reach age $59^1/_2$, you can tap into your investment, as well as the earnings. As long as you take out your investment and the earnings, you can get the money whenever you need it. Like traditional IRAs, Roths have a $2,000 annual contribution limit.

You can get your Roth money without penalty any time after you reach 59.5 years of age, but you're not required to take it out when you reach 70.5 as you are with traditional IRAs. You can just let that money sit there if you want to, continuing to grow, tax-free. You can even leave the money and *all* the earnings there to pass on, tax-free, to your heirs.

There are income limits to Roths, though. If your income is more than $110,000 and you're single, you can't get a Roth IRA. If you and your spouse have a combined income of more than $160,000, you're not eligible for a Roth IRA.

Doing It on Your Own

Many Generation Xers are self-employed or work on contract basis as freelancers. If you're self-employed or have started your own business, you still need to think about saving for retirement. The good news is, you can set up a retirement plan that works for you, in your particular situation. The bad news is, you can set up a retirement plan that works for you, in your particular situation.

That last paragraph wasn't a typo, it really is both good and bad news. If done properly, designing your own retirement plan will give you exactly what you need. But it's going to take some careful consideration and a fair amount of work to figure out what you need and how to get it going.

SEP-IRAs

SEP-IRAs, which stands for Simplified Employee Pension Individual Retirement Account (talk about a mouthful!), are not very complicated and are a great deal for a person who's self-employed, but doesn't have employees. As with other types of IRAs, the interest you make in a SEP-IRA is not taxed until you take the money out.

If you work for yourself, you can contribute up to about 13 percent of your income or up to $22,500 into a SEP-IRA every year. The money you contribute is deducted from your taxable income, so your contribution can save you a lot on federal and, depending on where you live, state taxes. You can open and contribute to a SEP-IRA up until the very last day of your tax-filing deadline.

Show Me the Money

A **SEP-IRA** is a retirement plan for self-employed persons, in which contributions of up to $25,000 a year are permitted. A **Keogh** is a federally approved retirement program that allows self-employed workers to set aside up to $30,000, or 25% of their income.

SEP-IRAs are advantageous for people who need to save on their own. They might sound intimidating, but you can have SEP-IRA anywhere you could have a regular IRA. It just requires a little paperwork. Ask your tax preparer or financial consultant about changing your IRA to a SEP-IRA.

Keoghs

Keoghs are another retirement plan for self-employed workers. Keoghs can be tricky to set up; there's a lot of paperwork involved, and it's a good idea to get a professional to help you with it. (See Chapter 20 for more information about finding the right financial person to help you.) Keogh plans must be set up by the end of the year, with contributions made by the tax-filing deadline, including exclusions. For Keogh purposes, the owner is considered an employer.

Keoghs are the plans most frequently used by employers who have several employees. Recently, something called SIMPLE plans have been gaining in popularity for smaller companies, but they allow only $6,000 a year, per employee. Every employer should look at the advantages and disadvantages of various plans and decide what is best. For practicality purposes, you need at least 20–25 employees to efficiently offer a 401(k) plan—although there isn't any limitation by law—but even an employer with just one employee can set up a Keogh plan.

If you have your own business and have people working for you, you're required to provide coverage for your employees if you provide coverage for yourself. If you don't, you can be penalized by the IRS, which might even make your own prior contributions invalid. But don't put off starting a fund for yourself because you don't want to have to have one for employees. Some employees, such as part-timers and those who haven't

Dollars and Sense

Hopefully, you can see the value of providing a retirement plan for your employees. Sure, it's going to cost you money, so you might have to start small. But you need to look forward and consider intangibles such as loyalty and commitment, qualities that make employees want to do their best and see the business of which they're a part succeed.

Show Me the Money

Vesting schedules are formulas that require employees to spend a certain amount of time working for a company before their full retirement savings plan benefits kick in. **Vesting** pertains only to the funds contributed by your employer. Your own contributions are always 100-percent vested.

worked for you long enough, can be excluded from the plans. All qualified employees, though, must be provided with plans that allow them to contribute a percentage of their income.

There are four types of Keogh plans:

1. **Profit-sharing plans.** These plans limit your contributions to 15 percent, a bit higher than SEP-IRAs. They contain *vesting schedules*, so they're good for owners of small businesses who want to hold the reins on contributions for their employees. You contribute to them only if your business makes a profit.

2. **Money-purchase pension plans.** The main attraction of these plans is that you can stash 20 percent of your income into them. The main drawback is that you *have* to stash 20 percent. Unless you can afford to contribute $10,000 of your $50,000 income, or $8,000 of your $40,000 income, or $6,000 of your $30,000 income, this type of Keogh isn't for you.

3. **Paired plans.** Paired plans combine features of the money-purchase pension and profit-sharing plans in that you can contribute 20 percent, but you have some flexibility in the amount. Some people feel that paired plans are the best of the Keogh family, although they require some pretty extensive paperwork to set up and run.

4. **Defined-benefit plans.** If you can afford these plans, you can afford to hire someone to administer them for you. Under a defined-benefit plan, you must be able to contribute at least $30,000 a year, making them unfeasible for most people.

Annuities

Annuities are a little confusing, and many financial advisors will advise you to look into other types of retirement investment vehicles first. Like non-deductible IRAs, annuities are tax-deferred investments, not tax-deductible. Because annuities are not tax-deductible contributions, you should consider them only if you have money to invest after investing in employee-sponsored plans or tax-deductible IRAs. Unlike IRAs, there's no limit to what you can contribute to annuities. You can plunk down $2,000, $5,000, or $100,000—the sky's the limit.

Annuities are akin to life insurance in that if you stash your money in them and die before you get it out, your beneficiary (the person who receives your benefits) may be guaranteed to get your original investment. Annuities are contracts that are backed by insurance companies, so the similarities of annuities and life insurance policies make a little bit of sense.

Show Me the Money

Annuities are tax-deferred investments that offer, at retirement, a stream of equal payments at predetermined intervals.

They can supplement IRAs when you reach retirement because you're not required to withdraw (and pay tax on) your money at age 70.5, as you are with IRAs. When you retire, you can leave your annuities alone while you use the money from your IRAs.

There are two kinds of annuities: fixed and variable. A fixed annuity is comparable to a certificate of deposit in that you receive a set interest rate on your investment over a set period of time. After that, the interest rate changes, based on the contract guidelines and an underlying fixed-income security. A variable annuity is invested in a series of mutual funds, similar to the funds within a 401(k). You can choose the funds in which you want to invest.

So Where Should My Retirement Money Go?

Once you decide on the type of retirement account you're going to use, you still have work to do. You need to decide where, within that account, you want your money to go. We know. Sometimes it seems as though Harvard Business School graduates will be the only ones able to make sense out of all this investment mumbo-jumbo, while the rest of us will be doomed to live in retirement-savings darkness.

Figuring out where to put your money within retirement accounts doesn't have to be that hard. Stick to the main concepts, and don't get bogged down in every last detail. You'll do just fine.

If your money is in a retirement savings plan sponsored by your employer, then she'll provide the investment options for you. All you have to do is choose from the list. Most financial experts advise dividing your money between some of the stocks and bonds included in the options. How you invest depends on your risk tolerance and time horizon. Try using this investment guideline: To find out what percentage of your portfolio should be invested in stocks, subtract your age from 100. If you're 25, for instance, about 75 percent of your investments should be stocks. That's because you have time to ride out a rough market if that should occur. Once you decide to invest in stocks, you need to choose what kinds of stocks. Chapter 19 handles that issue.

If your retirement fund is not set up by your employer, then you get to choose where your money goes. You can work with a reputable investment company, such as

Pocket Change

There are lots of investment companies, but Vanguard, T Rowe Price, and Fidelity are three of the most respected and well-known. You can contact Vanguard by calling 800-662-7447. You can reach Fidelity at 800-544-8666. Or, get Vanguard online at www.vanguard.com. Fidelity's web site is www.fidelity.com.

Vanguard or Fidelity, which will assist you in applying for accounts and advise you in allocating your money in a manner that makes sense for you.

An important thing to remember when you're trying to figure out this retirement account business is that you don't have to do it by yourself. If your plan is set up through your employer, there may be someone in the benefits office who can help you. Or you can ask advice from an investment company. Don't allow confusion or fear to make you give up on your retirement fund.

Early Withdrawal Penalties

Retirement savings plans have one major drawback. Once your money is in one, you normally can't get it out without paying a penalty. Requirements vary on different types of plans. For instance, as we told you in Chapter 13, there are penalties for taking money out of your 401(k) before you're 59.5 years old. The money you take out will be taxable, and in addition you'll be charged a 10 percent penalty. But your employer might have a program where you can borrow from your 401(k) and pay back the money to your account. There's also something called a hardship withdrawal that applies to 401(k)s, but strict rules apply, and it has to be a genuine hardship, such as serious illness.

With a traditional IRA, you must start withdrawing your money between the ages of 59.5 and 70.5 to avoid penalties—or, more precisely, before April 1st of the year following the one in which you turn 70.5 years old. You'll have to decide on a distribution schedule, which usually is based on your life expectancy. If you have a Roth IRA, you can tap into your principal after having the account for five years, and you don't have to start taking your money out of the account at any certain age.

With an annuity, you don't have to begin withdrawing money at age 70.5. But if you try to get your money before you're 59.5, you'll get slapped with a 10 percent fine on the interest you've earned and possibly a penalty on your principal from the insurance company, and always remember, income tax on the earnings.

All these requirements, rules, and regulations concerning retirement savings plans are enough to cool anybody's enthusiasm for participation. Still, you have to look past the confusion and the red tape to the idea behind the plans. If you don't save now, you won't have anything later. It's that simple. But if you start saving now, when you have a lot of years to do so, you'll be able to plan for all those fun things you want to do when you retire at age 59 and a half.

The Least You Need to Know

➤ Most people don't start saving the money they'll need for retirement until it's too late, and many don't save at all.

➤ Various types of retirement savings plans are available, and they all have advantages and disadvantages.

➤ Always consider using a plan that is tax-deductible first, and then go to one that is tax-deferred.

➤ If you're self-employed, you can still set up a retirement plan.

➤ After you choose a retirement plan, you have to allocate your money within the plan.

➤ Make sure you understand the rules and penalties that apply to taking your money out of the plan early.

Chapter 18

Investing Beyond Retirement Accounts

In This Chapter

➤ When to start investing

➤ Determining whether you're a high-risk, moderate, or conservative investor

➤ How investments can affect your taxes

➤ How to start investing

➤ Where to learn about investing

You might reach this chapter and cheer, or you might be tempted to close the book and find a novel. Try to resist that temptation. You've come this far—you might as well give it a whirl. Investing in the stock market—the term for investing in stocks whether done individually or through mutual funds—can be fun.

Investing money in the stock or bond market is incredibly exciting for some people and incredibly daunting for others. Maybe you're the type who can't wait to get started with investing and see how you'll do. You already check the market reports each day, and you've got some pretty good ideas about what you want to do when you get going in this investing business.

Or maybe the thought of throwing your hard-earned money out into the market makes you feel sick, and the thought of learning how to get started doesn't sound like any fun at all. C'mon, it's not that bad. If you've read this far, you've absorbed more than you think, and your head is probably chock full of useful information. You should be proud of yourself!

Regardless of how you feel about investing, it's an important part of your personal finances, and it won't become less important if you stick your head in the sand and ignore it. Some people spend most of their lives learning about, predicting, and tracking financial markets. They sleep, eat, and breathe the stock market, and there's seemingly nothing they don't know about when it comes to investments. Most of us, though, want to make good, sound investments without committing the rest of our lives to studying full-time to learn how to do it.

That's the balance you'll have to find. Please understand that you will have to do some homework to even begin to grasp the concepts of investing. That may sound like a big hassle, but if you're serious about your personal finances, of which investing is a big piece, you can't avoid it.

When Is the Best Time to Start Investing?

If your credit card debt is under control, you're keeping up with your car and loan payments, you have an emergency fund, your 401(k) is loaded up, and you're contributing to a Roth IRA as well, you might be starting to think about investments outside of retirement accounts. If you've reached this point in your personal finances, you must be doing something right, and you should be congratulated for being so savvy at a young age.

Before you move on, let's just make sure you understand that it's important to take care of basic business first. If you're carrying a lot of credit card debt at 18 percent interest, you shouldn't be thinking of doing anything with your money except paying it off. High credit card debt is one of the worst traps you can get stuck in. If you're having trouble making payments on loans or keeping up with rent, you obviously shouldn't be worrying about stocks and bonds. We've also discussed how important it is have some money put aside in an emergency fund, in case you're ever caught without an income or need extra money for something fast.

You know how we feel about saving for retirement: You can never start too early. The reason we think it's better to invest in retirement funds first is because of the tax advantages they have over non-retirement investing. Any investments can be used to fund your retirement, of course, but those designated as retirement accounts will be of greater advantage to you now.

If you fall short in one of those categories, the best thing for you to do is take a couple of steps back, and take care of business. Pay off the debts, contribute to retirement accounts, and get an emergency fund set up.

All done? Okay, let's talk about what kind of investor you expect that you'll be.

What Kind of Investor Do You Want to Be?

Not all investors are created equal. Some are the aggressive, make-me-rich-quick kind that want to make a killing on their investments. They rarely do or at least not for long, mind you, but they're sure willing to give it a try. This type of investor is the person at the amusement park who has to go on every roller coaster twice, except for the really big one that loops upside down. He has to go on that one three times.

Other investors are the middle-of-the-road kind. They want something that will be kind of exciting, but nothing too dangerous. They'll risk the tilt-a-whirl at the amusement park, but say no thanks to the roller coasters.

Then there are those investors who just want a nice, safe place to put their money. They don't expect to get rich from their investments, but they want to feel confident that their money will do okay in them and the investments will provide some security down the road. These are the people at the park who love the carousel and think that the Ferris wheel is about as much excitement as there should be in life.

The following risk pyramid shows various investments and how the industry rates their risk of principal loss:

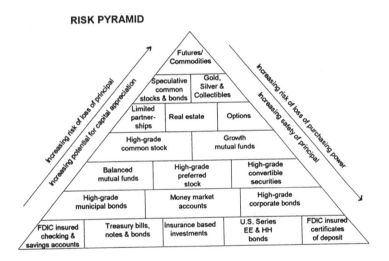

RISK PYRAMID

Each of these categories has risks and rewards. Let's have a look.

High-Risk Investors

People can be high-risk investors by choice, or as in most cases, they can be high-risk investors because they don't know enough about what they're doing. A high-risk investor is generally classified as someone who can live with losing about a quarter of his or her *investment portfolio* in a year.

An investment portfolio is the listing and value of all your investments. If you have $10,000 to invest, and the thought of losing $2,500 doesn't give you chills, you might qualify as high-risk. But even if you're a high-risk investor, you still have to do your homework and find out where your money has the best chance of earning you more. There's a big difference between high-risk and just plain stupid.

Suppose an investor chooses to be high-risk. He jumps into the stock market and buys only investments with potential for very high returns. He got a hot tip from a buddy of his that a certain industry is about to take off, so he loads most of his money into that industry stock. Even if this guy knows what he's doing, he's a daredevil. But if he's making high-risk investments because he hasn't done his homework and doesn't understand the importance of diversification or that his money should be spread around, he's risking catastrophe; he's speculating.

Speculating, like gambling, is taking chances and rolling the dice to try to make a killing in the market quickly. Getting a hot tip at a cocktail party and acting on it by putting down $5,000 is speculating. Investing is buying 100 shares of Microsoft stock after you've investigated exactly what the company does, the fundamentals (explained later in the chapter), and the company's outlook for the future.

Moderate-Risk Investors

If you're a moderate-risk investor, you won't bet the farm on a tip you overhear while you're getting your hair cut or sitting in the sauna at the health club. You're generally classified as a moderate-risk investor if you figure you can stand to lose up to 15 percent of that $10,000 in your portfolio. The thought of being out $1,500 doesn't make you jump up and down, but it won't keep you up every night either.

Conservative Investors

Conservative investors are the meat-and-potatoes people of the investment world. Keep your fancy appetizers, your cream sauces, and your puff pastry desserts. Just give these folks something they can depend on, something that won't give them any surprises, and something they don't have to worry about. They don't want to take any chances with their investments and will gladly give up even the possibility of high returns to know that their money will be there when they want it.

Conservative investors generally start having nightmares at the thought of losing even 5 or 6 percent of their portfolios over a year's time. The thought of losing $600 of that $10,000 investment sets their hair on end.

Your Timetable Is Important, Too

After you've figured out your investing personality, you need to think about your timetable. How long do you want to leave your money invested? A year? Three years? Ten years?

Your timetable has a lot to do with the way you should invest. Traditionally, investments with the potential for higher return are more likely to go up and down in value. That means you should be prepared to leave your money in those investments over a longer period of time. They're not short-term investments because you can't count on them being where you want them to be when you're ready to take your money out.

If, for instance, you're investing money that you want to use for your wedding the next year, you shouldn't buy volatile stocks that could go anywhere during the next 12 months. You'd want something safe that would allow your money to grow, but wouldn't risk your principal. It just wouldn't do for you to try to withdraw your wedding money two months before the big event and find out it was gone.

On the other hand, if you've just had a baby and want to put some money away for college, you know you have 18 years. That gives you a much better opportunity to ride out some storms and take advantage of the potential for high returns. As you can see, there are many variables when it comes to investments and investors.

Dollars and Sense

If you're investing money that you'll need within two years or less, you're generally considered a short-term investor. Investing your money for two to seven years puts you in the mid-term range. If you won't need your money for more than seven years, you're considered a long-range investor.

One thing, however, is constant. Regardless of the type of investor you think you are, you need to know what you're doing. If you depend on an investment advisor to lead you by the nose through the world of stocks, bonds, and mutual funds, you'll never be in control of your financial situation. We're not suggesting that you'll never need help with investing or in other areas of your personal finance, but to hand all the responsibility over to someone else is to relinquish your control. Presumably, you've worked pretty hard to earn your money. Why would you let somebody else climb into the driver's seat and take off with it?

There are tons of good books on investing, and lots of other information is available, too. We'll list a bunch of resources later in the chapter; the appendix of additional resources in the back of this book lists even more, so check it out.

You Can't Tax That! Can You?

We've already sung the praises of retirement accounts and the tax advantages they offer, and we hope we've sufficiently stressed that you should invest in any applicable

Money Pit

Some people are attracted to the stock market because they think it's exciting—even glamorous. We're not discouraging you from Wall Street, but remember to put your financial house in order, first. If you don't consider all the advantages—and disadvantages (including taxes)—before you invest, you could be putting your personal financial situation at risk.

Pocket Change

Although we usually don't consider them such, savings accounts are a type of investment. We'll talk more about different types of investments in Chapter 19.

retirement accounts before looking elsewhere. When you get into other types of investments, and you start earning on those investments, be prepared to pay taxes on your earnings.

To figure out how your investments will affect your tax situation, take a look at how much interest or yield you'll get from each investment. You must know your tax bracket, too (review Chapter 14 if necessary).

Say you're in the 28 percent marginal tax bracket. To refresh your memory, you're taxed at that rate if you make $25,350 to $61,400 as a single or $42,350 to $102,300 if you're married and filing jointly. If you're keeping $5,000 in a savings account that's earning 2 percent interest, you're earning only $100 a year on that money. This is the before-tax return on your investment. To add insult to injury, Uncle Sam takes 28 percent of your earnings, leaving you with even less. This is known as the after-tax return on an investment. This is your actual return on your investment. It's imperative you're cognizant of the before- and after-tax returns of all your investments. That money would be much better off in a tax-free money market fund (a money market fund for which income is not subject to income tax liability), which probably earns more than 2 percent.

On the other hand, if somebody in the 15 percent tax bracket ($25,349 or less for a single earner) puts $5,000 in a tax-free money market with a 3 percent yield, he'll be earning $150 a year, tax-free. But if he put the $5,000 in a taxable account with a 5 percent yield, he'd earn $250 a year, less 15 percent tax. Because 15 percent of $250 is only $37.50, he'd still be $62.50 better off after paying the tax than he'd be with the tax-free earnings.

Consider each investment carefully, but keep these general guidelines in mind:

➤ If you're in the 15 percent federal tax bracket, don't worry too much about the tax you'll have to pay on investment income. You'll probably come out further ahead than you would with lower-yield, tax-free investments.

➤ If you're in the 28 percent bracket, look carefully at the yield or interest before deciding whether to participate in the investment. You're likely to do better with taxable investments, but that might not always be the case.

➤ If you're in the 31 percent bracket or higher, stay away from investments that will give you taxable income. You have to hand over too great a share of your earnings. Look for investment vehicles that generate tax-free income, instead.

Once you understand the tax implications of investments, you can take a look at *capital gains,* your profits on an investment. Say that you purchased 100 shares of IBM stock at $75 per share, for a total of $7,500. Say that you sold the same shares for $120 each. Good job! You've made a profit of $45 per share or $4,500. The profit you earned is the capital gain, and guess what? You're paying taxes on it. There's an up side to the tax thing, though. If your Nike stock nose-dives and you sell it at a big capital loss, you can use the loss to offset the taxes you'll be paying on your capital gain. Get it?

If you did, get ready. Here are some more fun investment facts coming at you:

Show Me the Money

Capital gains are the profit you make on an investment.

➤ If you hold an investment for less than one year, the gain or loss from that investment is considered short-term. Short-term gains and losses are netted against each other, and short-term gains are taxed at your regular tax rate. If you're in a 28 percent tax bracket, for instance, you pay 28 percent on your gains. Short-term capital gains can be expensive.

➤ If you hold an investment for more than a year, the gain or loss is considered long-term. Long-term gains and losses are netted against each other too. If you're in a 15 percent tax bracket, net long-term capital gains are taxed at 10 percent. If you're in a 28 percent or greater marginal tax bracket, your capital gains are taxed at 20 percent. This tax advantage makes it desirable to hold assets for more than a year, particularly if your income is pretty high.

➤ There is additional netting of net short term losses against net long term gains and of net long term losses against net short term gains. Interesting, huh? Follow your tax program and know the final net figure; a gain could cost you money.

The tax implications concerning capital gains are important to keep in mind. However, you should never invest solely on the basis of tax considerations, nor should you sell stock only on the basis of capital gains or losses.

Before we leave this exciting topic, we need to cover one more area: capital gains on mutual funds. Suppose you bought 1,000 shares of XYZ Mutual Stock Fund at $30 per share for a total of $3,000. You are now the proud owner of a piece of a pie. The pie contains many different stocks: shares of ownership in various companies. If you own stock in a company, you actually own a part of the company. These stocks trade quite

Pocket Change

Mutual funds used to operate based only on their performances, with no regard for the tax implications of the capital gains and losses they generated. A new crop of mutual funds is opening, however, that takes capital gains and losses into consideration, called tax advantaged mutual funds.

regularly. The turnover ratio (how often a stock trades within a mutual fund) is an important tidbit to learn about a fund before you buy it.

Almost every time a stock trades within an account, there is a capital gain or loss. Within a mutual fund, the gains are held in a separate fund and distributed out to shareholders as cash. This distribution normally occurs once a year, although sometimes it's done more often. This cash is taxed to the shareholders as short-term or long-term capital gains, or both. Usually, you'll be able to choose whether to reinvest the capital gains or take them as a cash payment. Either way, you will owe taxes on the gains at the end of the year.

Whew! That was pretty intense. I'm hopeful that you have a handle on some of these tax matters, and you feel confident enough to move on.

Show Me the Way to the Investment Store

Beginning investors often are confused about exactly how to get started. Do you just walk into an investment firm and announce that you're ready to buy? Do you call an 800 number and commit your investments to a voice on the phone? Do you fill out an application, stick it in the mailbox, and hope for the best? Or do you jump online and throw your money into cyberspace? There are several ways to get started.

Buying Mutual Funds

Suppose you've saved $3,500, and you're ready to begin investing. You're thinking about going into a mutual fund, and you heard the guys at work talking about a cool telecommunications fund. It sounds good, and you want to know more about it. Where do you go?

You have two choices:

➤ Call a stockbroker, a professional buyer and seller of investments, and ask about the fund.

➤ Go directly to the mutual fund. Either go to the library, check out the fund online at www. morningstar.com, or find the telephone number of the fund and let your fingers do the walking.

We'll talk about different types of brokers a bit later in the chapter. For now, think about whether you know anything about this fund you're thinking of jumping into. How has it performed over the last five years? Is it considered risky? Find out every-thing you can about the fund before you decide whether to buy it.

Get a mutual fund directory and read about the fund. The report will have a toll-free number, which you can call and get information about the fund. This information usually comes in the form of a prospectus. After you have the *prospectus*, learn as much about the fund as you can. The prospectus is a detailed explanation on an investment. We'll get into more detail about this item in Chapter 19.

Show Me the Money

A detailed explanation on a particular investment is called a **prospectus**.

There are several mutual fund directories, such as the Morningstar report, that track and offer information on thousands of mutual funds. Value Line is another directory They'll be available at your local library.

Opening a new account with a mutual fund isn't exactly a stroll through the park. After you con-tact the mutual fund or the stockbroker, you'll receive a new account form. You'll need to provide all kinds of information, such as where you work, the name of your bank, your first transaction, your investment knowledge, your social security number, and many, many other things.

After you've handed over all the pertinent information and the mutual fund company has opened an account for you, all you have to do is mention that you'd like to buy XYZ Mutual Fund. The person on the phone will tell you how much it will cost, and you state whether you want in and how many shares you want. After a verbal agreement is reached, you'll get a written confirmation. Always check the confirmation as soon as it arrives to verify that the transaction is correct. If it is, immediately send a check to the mutual fund to make the deal final.

After you've bought in to the fund, you'll get either get a monthly or quarterly statement, showing you the value of the fund. It will also include what income has been paid out in the fund, whether more shares have been purchased, the price of the fund today, the share price of the fund when you purchased it which some fund statements provide, and the like. You also will get an annual statement at the end of the year and a 1099 form to use when you prepare your income tax return.

Buying Stocks or Bonds

The way you buy stocks and bonds—which, as you'll learn in Chapter 19, are different types of investment vehicles—is very similar to buying mutual funds. You work with a broker to buy or sell stock.

There are a couple different varieties of brokers. You could use a full-service broker, who would charge you about 1 percent of the value of your investment. What are you getting for your money, you ask? Hopefully, the broker you'd be working with would have good knowledge and information concerning your particular investment, and you would benefit from his or her expertise.

Pocket Change

The U.S. Securities and Exchange Commission is an independent, quasi-judicial agency that's responsible for administering federal securities laws. The agency calls itself "the investor's advocate."

Discount brokers are brokers who are paid a salary by the company for which they work, rather than working on commission. This makes them very attractive to many investors who recognize the potential for a conflict of interest among brokers who work strictly for commission.

Discount brokers didn't exist before 1975, when the Securities and Exchange Commission deregulated the retail brokerage industry. Before deregulation, all investors had to pay the same commission whenever they bought a particular stock, bond, or mutual fund. As long as the price of the stock was the same, you'd pay the same price, regardless of where you got it.

Deregulation led to some healthy competition among brokers, and many new firms opened, offering lower fees than the traditional firms such as Merrill Lynch and Smith Barney. Some analysts say you can save 50 percent or more by buying from the big discount brokers such as Charles Schwab or Waterhouse Securities, rather than from the traditional brokerages. Also, the concern that you're being sold a particular stock or bond because the broker stands to make a big, fat commission from it is lessened.

Full-service or discount broker? The choice is yours. If you feel you need advice and direction, look for a full-service broker. If you know what you want, or you have another type of financial advisor (more on financial advisors in Chapter 20), a discount broker should be fine.

Where to Learn About Investments

Where can you learn about investments? Just about anywhere, but you need to be careful of the information you'll be taking in. Everyone from Uncle Harry to the letter carrier to your friend, Jack, the banker, will have some advice for you, and sometimes it's hard to weed out the worthless from the worthwhile. Don't despair. Reliable advice is readily available, and we're going to tell you how to find it.

Books

In this age of electronic everything, we're going to start this section by listing some good, old-fashioned books that will help increase your knowledge about investments and investing. We can't provide all the information regarding investments that will be helpful to you in one or two chapters in this book. So go ahead and make a trip to your library or bookstore. As you read, be on the lookout for common themes and advice. You'll start to get a feeling for what's important.

➤ *The First Book of Investing: The Absolute Beginner's Guide to Building Wealth Safely* by Samuel Case

➤ *25 Myths You've Got to Avoid If You Want to Manage Your Money Right: The New Rules for Financial Success* by Jonathan Clements

➤ *The Truth About Money: Because Money Doesn't Come With Instructions* by Ric Edelman

➤ *The Motley Fools' Investment Workbook* by David Gardner and Tom Gardner (the Motley Fools)

➤ *Investing From Scratch: A Handbook for the Young Investor* by James Lowell

➤ *Learn to Earn: A Beginner's Guide to the Basics of Investing and Business* by Peter Lynch and John Rothchild

➤ *The Wall Street Journal Guide to Understanding Money and Investing* by Kenneth M. Morris and Alan M. Siegel

➤ *Four Easy Steps to Successful Investing* by Jonathan D. Pond

➤ *Stock Market Primer* by Claude Rosenberg

These books are all aimed at beginning investors and provide information that you may find interesting and valuable. You don't have to read all of them (unless you want to), but reading at least three of them will give you a good overview of investing. You won't be an expert, but at least you'll be able to recognize what you need to learn.

Web Sites

Now it's time to get out of the library and online. The following are just a few of the many Web sites available that contain all kinds of financial advice and information. More sites are listed in the appendix in the back of this book.

➤ The American Express financial site walks you through seven financial planning subjects. Access it at www.americanexpress.com.

➤ The American Stock Exchange site is almost as much fun as being there. Find it at www.amex.com.

➤ The S&P Equity Investor Service site offers news headlines and stock picks from Standard & Poors. You can access it at www.stockinfo.standardpoor.com.

➤ Yahoo! Finance offers lots of information on financial news, data, and stock quotes. Find it at www.quote.yahoo.com.

Newspapers and Magazines

These publications are great for keeping up with the constant changes that occur on Wall Street and other financial areas. Hundreds of publications are available, but here are a few of the good ones:

➤ *The Wall Street Journal* has been the financial standard for years. This daily newspaper gives you information on nationwide and worldwide markets and about many things that affect your personal finances. You can call the Wall Street Journal at 800-568-7625.

➤ *Money* is a monthly publication that covers areas of personal finance and money management and tells you where to find the best deals for certificates of deposit and credit cards. You can call *Money* at 800-633-9970.

➤ *Smart Money* is another monthly magazine that offers good tips on matters concerning personal finances. It analyzes investments to see which ones will be good and which ones won't.

TV Shows

Not only are there shows devoted to financial news, there are entire networks. Two of them are CNBC and CNNfn. These networks offer continual programs dealing with varying topics related to business and finance. Check out these financial shows:

➤ *Wall Street Week*, hosted by Louis Rukeyser, is on Friday nights at 8:30 on most Public Broadcasting System stations.

➤ Broadcast by CNN and hosted by Lou Dobbs, *Moneyline* gives you the latest business news, economic reports, and financial profiles. It's on every weeknight at 6:30 and 11:30.

➤ Another PBS show, the *Nightly Business Report*, is on every weeknight, but the times vary, according to the stations in your area. Check your TV listings for times.

The Least You Need to Know

➤ Make sure your savings, debt, and retirement funds are taken care of before you start thinking about investments.

➤ Just as there are different kinds of people, there are also different kinds of investors.

➤ Your investments can have a big effect on your taxes.

➤ You can buy stocks, bonds, and mutual funds on your own or enlist the help of a broker.

➤ There are good newspapers, books, Internet sites, and television shows to help you increase your financial knowledge.

Investment Options

After you have a feel for the type of investor you'll be, and you've located some materials from which to learn more about investing, you're ready to start looking at some investment options. That doesn't mean that we're going to give you a list of stocks and tell you how many of each to buy. No way.

Just in case you've been living in Bolivia lately, the stock market has been a bit, shall we say, testy. It's been losing and gaining points faster than Mark McGwire hits home runs. What's good one day could be bad the next, and nobody without a crystal ball is able to tell you what to buy. We'd never presume to give you a list of stocks and tell you that's where to put your money.

What we will give you is a basic understanding of how the stock market works. We'll also talk about other investment options, such as bonds and mutual funds. So sit back, and get ready to take an exciting trip to Wall Street.

How Does the Stock Market Work?

It's no wonder that many new investors, and even not-so-new investors, find the task of learning where to put their money to be a daunting proposition. Listen to the stock reports sometime, or try to read that impossibly tiny print they use to list them in most newspapers. They're filled with words and phrases like NASDAQ, the Dow Jones, blue chip stock, and composite index. It's enough to make any potential investor pack up his portfolio and go back to watching soap operas.

But don't be dissuaded. It's confusing, to be sure, but stick with us. We'll walk you through this investment thing, and try to give you a good, basic understanding of what all the mumbo-jumbo is about.

First, what exactly is the stock market? The *stock market* is a generic term that encompasses the trading of *securities*. This trading takes place in stock exchanges. There are three major stock exchanges in the United States:

➤ Formed in 1792, the New York Stock Exchange (NYSE) is the largest organized stock exchange in the United States.

➤ The American Stock Exchange (AMEX) was known before 1951 as the American Curb Exchange. That's because trading was conducted on the curb of Wall and Broad streets in New York City. The American Stock Exchange has less stringent listing requirements than the NYSE, so it attracts many smaller companies.

➤ Another of the major stock exchanges, NASDAQ stands for the National Association of Securities Dealers Automated Quotation System. Unlike the NYSE and the AMEX, there isn't any physical location for the exchange; trading is done by computer. The American Stock Exchange and NASDAQ have merged. Currently, they are standing as separate entities.

The overall performance of the stock market is evaluated in many different ways. The Dow Jones Industrial Average (DJIA) is one measure of the stock market, the

Dollars and Sense

Check out your local newspaper's business page for a "stocks of local interest" column. Read these stock reports daily for a week or two to get a feeling for how the local companies are doing in the market. It's sometimes easier to understand something that can be confusing, such as the stock market, if you look at how it pertains to something with which you're familiar.

Show Me the Money

The **stock market** is the organized securities exchange for stock and bond transactions. The major U.S. markets are the New York Stock Exchange, the American Stock Exchange, and the National Association of Securities Dealers Automate Quotation System (NASDAQ). **Securities** are investments that represent evidence of debt, ownership of a business, or the legal right to acquire or sell an ownership interest in a business.

standard we hear every day. There are three indices that include averages for utilities, industrial, and transportation stocks, as well as the composite averages. Each average reflects the simple mathematical average of the closing prices (prices at the end of the day) and indicates the day-to-day changes in the market prices of stocks in the designated index. Okay, what does that mean? The DJIA is a composite (group) of 30 stocks with a daily average. Tomorrow, if the stocks as an average go up in price, the DJIA goes up. If the average value of these selected stocks go down, the DJIA goes down. If market trends are moving increasingly upward, it's called a *bull market*. Market trends that are moving continuously downward are called a *bear market*.

Now that you know the major exchanges and how the market is measured, let's get down to business. How do you make money on this deal? There are two kinds of investment returns: total return and yield. *Total return* on an investment is the current income, plus the capital gain or loss. Yield is the amount of dividends or interest paid on an investment. These returns can be very different, although many people lump them together as the same thing.

Show Me the Money

When market trends move upward, it's called a **bull market**. It's a **bear market** when trends move continuously downward.

Show Me the Money

When you invest, you take a chance that you'll lose money; that's the **investment risk**. The **total return** on an investment is the current income plus the capital gain or loss.

Every investment you make involves a certain level of *investment risk*, with the chance that you'll lose the money you invest or even that the investment won't perform as well as you thought. Investments with the chance for higher returns carry greater risk than those without the return potential.

Although the terminology involved can be a bit baffling, the basic concept of investing isn't all that complicated. You can buy something with your money: a little piece of a company as shares of stock, or some real estate, or something else. Or you can lend your money to an organization and have it agree to pay you back, with interest, over a specified time. When it comes to investing, you can own, or you can loan.

When You Own

When you invest your money in a company, or in real estate, or in stamps, or Beanie Babies, you're buying a piece of something that you hope will increase in value and be profitable. Most people think of the stock market in relation to investing, and that's what we'll focus on in this section. Just so you know, it's not the only investment opportunity.

Stocks are merely investments that represent a piece of ownership in a company. The more *shares* of stock in one company that you have, the bigger piece of the company you own. Owning stock makes you a *shareholder* in the company. The word stock is commonly used interchangeably with the phrase *common stock*.

Stocks come in many flavors:

➤ **Blue-chip stock.** This phrase refers to stock of well-established companies that historically pay *dividends* in good years and bad. Some examples of blue-chip stock are General Motors, Exxon, and IBM.

➤ **Growth stock.** This stock is issued by companies that have sales, earnings, and market share that are growing at rates higher than the average company or the general economy. These stocks do not typically pay large dividends, and any appreciation goes untaxed until gain is realized.

➤ **Small cap stock.** This type of stock refers to companies which have less than $1 billion capitalization (the sum of a corporation's long term debt, stock, and retained earnings—called invested capital). These are smaller, often newer, companies.

➤ **Mid cap stock.** This type of stock refers to those with $1 billion to $10 billion capitalization in medium-sized companies.

➤ **Large cap stock.** These stocks have over $10 billion in capitalization. Some examples of large cap stocks are GE, Johnson and Johnson, and Exxon. These are the biggest of the big.

➤ **Income stock.** This type of stock historically pays regular and steady dividends and usually appreciates in value to keep up with inflation. These stocks are popular among older, income-oriented investors. Utility stocks have historically been a good example of income stocks.

➤ **Cyclical stock.** Cyclical stocks tend to prosper and grow when the economy expands, but they do poorly when the economy suffers. Types of companies that offer cyclical stocks are automobile, paper, airlines, steel, and cement.

Show Me the Money

When you own **stock** in a company, you own little pieces of that company. Stocks are sold in units called **shares**. So if you buy stock, you're a **shareholder**—you own a small portion of the company. Consider yourself lucky if you own **blue chip stock** in a well-established company. These stocks normally are good for paying you annual **dividends**, or earnings on your money.

Show Me the Money

Companies that have sales or earnings higher than the average company (or economy) are known as **growth stock. Emerging market stocks** are stocks in new markets around the world. If you have **income stock,** in a utility company, for example, you'll get regular dividends. But watch out if the economy suffers and you're holding **cyclical stock;** they suffer right along with it. As the name says, **defensive stock** hold its own against fluctuations in the economy. **Interest-sensitive stock** reacts to changes in interest rates.

➤ **Defensive stock.** This stock is relatively unaffected by general fluctuations in the economy. Examples of this kind of stock are Coca-Cola and Pepsi stock and stock in large grocery stores. People still eat and drink soda when the economy heads south.

➤ **Interest-sensitive stock.** The performance of companies that are interest sensitive are largely affected by changes in interest rates, and the stock value will react accordingly. Examples are bank and insurance company stock.

➤ **Value stock.** This is a stock in which the price is considered well below normal using valuation measures common to the market. Examples are stocks undergoing management problems, restructuring, and so forth.

A company sells stock, or little pieces of itself, to raise money. When it sells stock through an *initial public offering* (IPO), it goes public. Even small companies have stock, but the shares aren't sold to the public. When a company goes public, anyone can purchase the shares.

If you buy stock in Disney Corporation, for example, you're buying a tiny, tiny piece of a huge company. Shares of stock usually are sold in groups of 100, which are called *round lots*. Groups of less than 100 shares are called *odd lots*. If you buy 100 shares of stock from a company that has a million shares of stock outstanding, you can figure that you own one-thousandth of the company. Regardless of whether you buy 10 Disney shares or 10,000, you're still a shareholder in the company. As long as the company makes a profit, you're entitled, as a shareholder, to share and benefit from it.

Show Me the Money

When a company goes public, it offers its common stock for sale to the public. The first time it does so is its known as an **initial public offering**. After that, it's no longer a privately held company.

As a shareholder, you may get annual dividends. Hopefully, the price of the stock will increase so that if you wanted to, you could sell your stock for more than what you bought it for and make a profit. The amount of dividends a corporation pays out is a reflection of the type of company it is. The stock of a growing company will not pay out the dividends that, say, an electric company does. It's important to remember this difference if you're planning to buy shares of a company. Will you receive a good annual income from your stocks, or are you banking on profits that will occur a few years or more down the road?

Show Me the Money

Shares of stocks are usually sold in **round lots**, which are groups of 100. Groups of less than 100 shares are called **odd lots**.

What happens, though, if somebody comes up with something even more exciting than Mickey and Disney World that captures the collective imagination of the whole world? All of a sudden, people stop visiting Disney parks, watching and buying Disney movies and shows, and purchasing scads of Disney toys, clothes, and other merchandise. Even the staunchest Pluto fans are sucked into the new entertainment venture, and the whole Disney thing is just a gigantic has-been. If that happens, your Disney stock will take a nose-dive. The value will plummet faster than you can watch it fall, and you'll be left alone, wearing your Mickey ears and holding your stock certificates.

Stocks aren't the only type of investment that you can own. Many people buy investment real estate, which they rent out to receive an income or resell for a profit.

Or you can decide to invest in something else that you hope will increase in value, Beanie Babies, for example. You can get up early every Saturday and peruse the shops that sell Rover the red dog and Blackie the bear, hoping against hope that you'll discover a forgotten Jerry Garcia Beanie in a bin somewhere. You can buy 12 of each Beanie Baby ever made and hang on to them until 2035, at which point you might be able to sell each set for $2 million. Or you might be able to give them to your grandkids and tell them how much fun you had getting up early on all those Saturday mornings.

Those are some of the opportunities you have to own your investments. Now, let's look at the type of investment in which you loan your money.

When You Loan

Ownership investments aren't the only option. You also can participate in a *lending investment*. A lending investment is when you loan your money with the understanding that you'll get it back—with interest—after a specified time.

Show Me the Money

A **lending investment** is when you loan your money with the understanding that you'll get it back—with interest—after a specified time. Think of a **bond** as an IOU. When you buy a bond, you're lending your money to the company or government for a specified period of time.

We most commonly think of *bonds* as lending investments, and they are the most widely used. But there are others, as well. Some other examples of lending investments are certificates of deposit; treasury bills, notes, and bonds; municipal bonds; general obligation bonds; revenue bonds; corporate bonds; high-yield bonds; savings bonds; and government agency bonds.

These are all investments in which you give your money to a particular entity with the understanding that you'll get it back at a certain time, with an agreed-upon amount of interest added. The entity borrowing your money varies from a bank, which generally administers certificates of deposits, to the U.S. government, which offers bonds. Bonds also are offered by corporations. They borrow funds from you, in the form of a bond, giving you interest, generating income for you.

The conditions, such as length of time our money will be invested, amount of interest paid, and so forth, are different for each of these types of lending investments. In most cases, bonds offer a fixed interest rate, that is, where the rate remains steady throughout the life of the loan.

If you're holding a bond that pays 7 percent interest, and the interest rate jumps to 9 percent, you lose on the value of your bonds if you sell it. But if you're earning 8 percent interest on your bond and the interest rate drops to 7 percent, you're still entitled to 8 percent, the agreed-upon rate. In that case, your bond would have increased in value (known as a premium bond) compared to new bonds being issued. Either way, you'll get your initial investment back when the investment matures. Always make sure the bonds you buy have a clear maturity date so that you'll know exactly when you can get your money back.

The following are some of the different kinds of bonds:

➤ **Corporate bonds.** These bonds are offered by corporations, and they traditionally pay more interest than government bonds. But they're not backed by a U.S. government guarantee, so there's more risk involved than with government bonds. Also, they typically have a fairly high face value (the price you pay for the bond), which usually starts at $1,000.

➤ **High-yield bonds.** Also known as *junk bonds*, these primarily corporate bonds offer higher interest rates, but they are considered to be riskier than standard bonds. Companies may actually offer so much interest that they don't earn enough to pay it back to their investors. There are some junk municipal bonds these days, as well as corporate.

➤ **Treasury bills.** These U.S. government bonds are fully backed by the faith and credit of the federal government. They are short term, with either three-month, six-month, or one-year maturity dates. They're sold by the U.S. Treasury Department during weekly or monthly auctions, and they require a minimum investment. The minimum was reduced recently from $10,000 to $1,000 per investment.

Pocket Change

An important thing to remember about bonds is that when interest rates go up, the value of your bond goes down. When interest rates go down, the value of your bond goes up.

Show Me the Money

Corporate bonds and high-yield corporate bonds are bonds offered by corporations. Treasury bills, treasury notes, treasury bonds, municipal bonds, and government agency bonds are those offered through government agencies. Some are issued by and backed by the federal government, while others are issued and backed by other governmental bodies.

➤ **Treasury notes.** These U.S. government bonds are also fully backed by the faith and credit of the federal government. They are auctioned by the Treasury Department and have the same minimum investment as treasury bills. They generally mature in two, five, or ten years.

➤ **Treasury bonds.** These bonds have the longest maturity period, 30 years, of any of the U.S. government bonds (they are also fully backed by the faith and credit of the federal government). They're auctioned during certain months and require a $1,000 minimum investment.

➤ **Municipal bonds.** These government bonds are issued by state, local, county, and even town governments; hospitals; and colleges(nonprofit institutions) rather than the federal government. The interest payments you get on municipal bonds are not subject to federal income taxes, and depending on where you live, they might not be included in state or local taxes, either.

➤ **Government agency bonds.** These are also a form of government bonds, but they're backed only by the agency that issues them, not the federal government. The most common types of government agency bonds are Freddie Mac, Ginnie Mae, and Fannie Mae. The money with which investors buy these bonds is used to purchase huge blocks of mortgages from banks and savings and loans. Because they are backed by mortgages, which makes them long-term investments, these government agency bonds can offer higher yields than treasury bills, notes, or bonds.

Mutual Funds

We discussed mutual funds in Chapter 13, but they're such an important investment vehicle that we felt compelled to say a bit more about them. Mutual funds can be ownership or lending investments and, in some cases, are both. When you invest in mutual funds, your money can go into stocks, bonds, and other holdings, as well. Many people think of mutual funds as being strictly stocks, but they're not.

Pocket Change

More people have money invested in mutual funds than in individual stocks, probably because there are more mutual funds available to choose from than individual stocks.

To better understand mutual funds, think about them as pies. When you put down your money for mutual funds, you're getting a slice of the pie. If the value of your mutual fund goes down, the pie (and your piece of the pie) gets smaller. If the value increases, the pie gets bigger.

We discussed the advantages of mutual funds in Chapter 13 and told you about load funds and no-load funds. As a refresher, load funds are those that charge you a sales commission when shares are purchased, and no-load funds are those that you can buy directly from a company, without paying a sales commission.

Another important mutual fund distinction is between open-end mutual funds and closed-end mutual funds. *Open-end mutual funds* are the huge pies. Open-end funds can issue an unlimited number of shares to investors. The size of the fund can therefore continue to grow, as long as investors are willing to keep putting their money into them. The number of shares available to investors is limited to an initial set amount in *closed-end mutual funds*. Shares in these funds are sold like stocks and bonds.

Mutual fund companies offer different types of mutual funds for different types of investors. As with stocks and bonds, some types include more risk than others. The most common types of mutual funds are the following:

➤ Stock funds

➤ Bond funds

➤ Money market funds

Stock funds are those that invest in stocks (you probably could have figured out this one yourself). There are different kinds of stock funds, and some involve higher risk than others.

Bond funds are those mutual funds that invest in bonds (see how easy this is?). They're usually less risky than stock funds, and some of them are tax-free. Bond funds contain many, many bonds, which normally are set up so they will mature periodically.

Money market funds are those in which the value of your original investment doesn't change. They're not too different from savings accounts, but they have some distinct advantages, including higher yields and check-writing privileges. Some are tax-free. Money market funds are the safest type of mutual fund.

Here are some other types of mutual funds:

➤ **Hybrid funds.** As the name implies, these funds invest in a mixture of securities, usually stocks and bonds.

➤ **Global and international funds.** These funds invest money internationally; global funds can include U.S. companies, but international funds do not.

Show Me the Money

Open-end mutual funds are those with no size limit. They can contain an unlimited number of shares and can continue growing as long as investors keep putting money into them. **Closed-end mutual funds** have a limited number of shares, which are sold like stocks and bonds.

Show Me the Money

Stock funds, bond funds, and **money market funds** are the three most common kinds of mutual funds. They vary in risk factor, with stock funds carrying the most risk, and money market funds the least.

Show Me the Money

Hybrid funds, global and international funds, index funds, sector funds, and balanced funds are all types of mutual funds. They offer different features, and some carry more risk than others.

Show Me the Money

The type of risk that affects the entire market is called **systematic risk**. The kind of risk that affects only a single business or industry is called **unsystematic risk**.

➤ **Emerging market funds.** These markets are typically those companies in countries where the markets are not yet developed, but are poised to do so. Some emerging markets at this time are in Zaire and Thailand.

➤ **Index funds.** These funds are invested in the same stocks that make up a particular index and in the same ratio (portion). The DJIA has 30-some stocks. Exxon represents a certain percentage of this index. If you purchase units of a DJIA index fund, you are purchasing a composite of stocks including Exxon along with all the other holdings in the index. For instance, Vanguard's Index 500 fund has the same makeup of stocks as the S&P 500.

➤ **Sector funds.** These funds invest in only one type of investment, such as a health care fund or a telecommunication fund

➤ **Balanced funds.** These are funds in which similar portions of common stocks and bonds are held together; these funds focus more on income than growth and have a lower risk than other common stock funds.

Understanding the Risks

Everyone knows that investing money is never risk-free. The idea is for you to find the investments that offer the best chance for a good return, with the least amount of risk, and that takes some know-how. Some risk affects only a particular business or industry, and is called *unsystematic risk*. Risk that affects the entire market is called *systematic risk*. Both are to be managed by diversification.

First of all, there are all kinds of investment risk. The following are just some of the different types:

➤ **Business risk.** This risk comes from the way in which the business that issued the security is managed. Will it be in business in three years? Does it have a marketable product?

➤ **Financial risk.** This risk is associated with the finances of the company. Does it have too much debt, or does the company spend too much on new technology?

➤ **Purchasing power risk.** This risk is the effect that inflation might have on the value of your holding. When your 30-year, $10,000 treasury note matures, how much will $10,000 truly be worth? If there's been high inflation over that 30 years, your bond won't be worth as much in current dollars as if inflation had been low.

➤ **Interest rate risk.** This risk involves how changes in interest rates may affect your investment.

➤ **Market risk.** This risk reflects the tendency for stock to move with the market, and entire industrial group or for a particular security, as a result of factors such as economic, political, or social events—also known as systematic risk.

➤ **Default risk.** This risk is the chance that the company you've invested in will be unable to service the debt.

Show Me the Money

Business risk, financial risk, purchasing power risk, interest rate risk, market risk, default risk, and foreign currency risk are all types of risk associated with investments. Not all risk applies to every investment, but you should be aware of how your investment might be affected by different kinds of risk.

➤ **Foreign currency risk.** This risk is that a change in the relationship between the value of the U.S. dollar and the value of the currency of the country in which your investment is held will affect your holding. This is an important risk for international investing. Just ask anyone who's had money in a Thai or Russian fund during the past year. Ouch!

Reading all those possibilities for risk can be scary, but you must understand as much about risk as possible. The key thing to understand is exactly how great these risks are and where they are the most likely to occur.

For most beginning investors, the stock market is a pretty tempting place. Everybody knows stocks really pay off, right? In the long run, they usually do. But if you can't leave your money invested for a long period of time, then stocks might not be the best investment for you.

The stock market is subject to some pretty significant fluctuations and involves many possibilities for risk. If you can put your money in and ride it out for the long haul, you'll probably do okay. But if you have a limited period in which to leave your money in stocks, you risk having to take it out at a time when the market is down. If that happens, you'll lose money. Investments in real estate carry similar risks. The real estate market can be great, or it can drop pretty dramatically.

On the other hand, if you invest in something extra safe, you're almost assured to get a lower return, at least when interest rates are as low as they are today. Investors want to be rewarded for the risks they take, so junk bonds must pay a higher yield than treasuries and so forth. If it's feasible for you to have your money invested for a long time, then stocks are probably a better investment than low-risk, low-yield bonds.

Take a look at the following statistics. They'll show the chances of the returns on stocks beating the returns on bonds at different lengths of time after the initial investment:

Dollars and Sense

Mutual funds often offer built-in diversification, which makes them an attractive option to many investors. As you get to know your way around the investment arena a little bit better, you can pick and choose your own diversified investments. When you're a beginning investor, however, mutual funds make good sense.

➤ If you hold an investment for one year, there's a 60 percent chance that stocks will give you a better return than bonds.

➤ If you hold an investment for five years, there's a 70 percent chance that stocks will give you a better return than bonds.

➤ If you hold an investment for 10 years, there's an 80 percent chance that stocks will give you a better return than bonds.

➤ If you hold an investment for 20 years, there's a 90 percent chance that stocks will give you a better return than bonds.

➤ If you hold an investment for 30 years, there's nearly a 100 percent chance that stocks will give you a better return than bonds.

Probably the best way of controlling risk, as far as your investments are concerned, is through diversification. When you diversify, you put your money into different investments so that if the value of some of them decreases, the value of the others is likely to be high enough to keep your investments stable.

Where to Invest Your Money

We've told you a little bit about various investment vehicles and the risks and opportunities associated with them. Stocks generally have the potential for better returns, but they're riskier than bonds. Money markets are the safest, but you're not going to make a killing from them. So what's a new investor to do?

Safe, but Not Too Exciting

If we're talking safe, but not too exciting, we're talking bonds, dependable, safe, boring bonds. Well, that's not really fair. Bonds can be quite interesting, particularly long-term bonds with their fluctuation potential; they just don't share the glamour that we associate with stocks.

Even bonds, however, are not without some risk. When you buy a bond, you're agreeing to lend your money to a company or other agency for a certain amount of time, and they're agreeing to pay you a certain amount of interest after that time.

But what if you want to get your money back early? Or what if the company calls your bond in early? If a company is permitted to call in a bond early, there's nothing to stop it from waiting until the interest rates drop, calling in your bond, and reissuing it at a lower rate, which means you end up losing the future interest at a higher interest rate. You will be forced to reinvest at a lower rate. These are issues you need to inquire about before you purchase a bond.

Remember the bond rule: If the interest rate drops, the value of your bond increases. If the interest rate rises, the value of your bond drops. If the value of the bond increases, the bond is called a *premium bond*. If the value decreases, it's called a *discounted bond*.

If you loan the XYZ Company $10,000 at 8 percent interest for five years, and the interest rate drops to 6 percent, the value of your bond will be somewhere around $11,500. If the interest rate rises to 10 percent though, your bond will be worth about $8,000.

Money Pit

Always make sure that you know the interest rate on your bond and when it is due for maturity. In addition, make sure you know whether the company can call in the bond early. If it can, you might want to look around for something else or see if it makes sense to invest until the call date.

Show Me the Money

A **premium bond** is a bond whose value has increased. If its value has decreased, it's called a **discounted bond**.

Exciting, but Just How Safe?

Stocks keep your blood pumping with their potential for payoffs, but they also can give you an incredible, wake-you-up-at-night headache with their potential for loss. It's important to remember that there are different types of stocks, with different degrees of risk:

➤ **Growth stocks.** These stocks are reputed to be one of the easiest ways to make money because they're issued by companies that have higher-than-average earnings and profits. But they're volatile and can decrease in value, too. Be prepared to hold onto growth stocks in order to ride out any ups and downs.

➤ **Income stocks.** True to their name, income stocks pay dividends on a regular basis. They're not the flashy investments that growth stocks are, but they're more dependable and easier on the blood pressure.

➤ **Growth and income stocks.** These stocks offer the best of the two previous types of stocks. You can get capital gains from growth stocks as well as some dividends from the income stocks. Unfortunately, you might not get all the growth benefits that you would from pure growth stock.

Is Investing in Beanie Babies a Good Idea?

The answer to that question depends on how much you like Beanie Babies, or stamps, or antique furniture, or dolls, or whatever collectibles you're interested in. Investing in collectibles is not a sure thing, to say the least. For starters, you have to physically care for the stuff you're collecting. You have to do extensive research to know what to buy and what not to, and you have to work with dealers who are looking to make a profit off of you.

Pocket Change

Some people can make money off of collectibles. We know a Pennsylvania man who paid for a good portion of his new home with the money he got from selling his collection of baseball cards.

Pocket Change

Many items that become valuable are not pre-planned collectibles; they're just things that happen to catch the imagination of collectors. Take metal lunch boxes, for instance. If baby boomers would have saved those school-day remnants, complete with their images of Popeye the Sailor Man and Yogi Bear, they'd have a collectible that's worth some money today. But who would have ever thought that Yogi would be valuable?

If you ask a financial adviser whether you should plow the nest egg money into Beanie Babies, you can pretty much count on a negative reaction. Financial analysts (such as the folks over at *Forbes* magazine, who should know) have been advising wealthy clients for some time that the Beanie craze is beginning to die down. Some collectible price guides don't include Beanies at all, dismissing them as an evanescent fad destined to roll away into the mists of time like yesterday's hula hoop.

If you insist on buying Beanie Babies or any sort of collectible, you might get lucky. Maybe the Beanie Baby market will skyrocket over the next 20 years. You'll be able to sell off your collection, send both your kids to college, and have money left over for a trip to Europe. Or you might end up sitting around in 20 years with a bunch of stuffed animals, wondering whatever possessed you to buy them.

If you buy collectibles as investments, you'll need to insure them against fire and theft. Investments such as gold and silver should be kept in a safe deposit box. There are some risks involved with every type of investment, whether it's stocks, bonds, collectibles, or putting your money under the mattress. Collectibles, however, tend to be riskier than most other vehicles.

When you're getting started in investments, the thing to do is to get the best understanding possible of investment options and the associated benefits and risks. Factor in your investment timetable and how much risk you're willing, and able, to take. Then, do what feels right for you. You don't want to feel as though you're spinning your wheels and getting nowhere, but you don't want to wake up sweating at night, either.

The Least You Need to Know

➤ There's a lot of jargon and confusing talk about investments, but if you get an understanding of the basics, it won't seem so overwhelming.

➤ Stocks are investments that you buy. Bonds are investments for which you loan money and get interest back in return.

➤ Mutual funds can contain ownership and lending investments.

➤ There are risks associated with all kinds of investments, but some types carry more risk than others.

➤ Stocks are generally considered higher-risk investments than bonds.

➤ Collectibles are fun, but they're not considered great investment vehicles.

Chapter 20

We All Need Somebody to Lean On

In This Chapter

➤ How to find someone to help you with your investments

➤ The right questions to ask before you hire a financial advisor

➤ Knowing who to stay away from

➤ Some cautions concerning your financial advisor

Probably the worst thing someone who knows nothing about his personal finances can do is go out and hire a financial advisor, assuming that she'll take care of everything, and he'll never have to think about his finances again. On the surface, it sounds like it would be a good idea. It's like calling a plumber to fix that leaky pipe because you don't have a clue what's wrong with it. Or seeing a doctor about that pain in your leg, rather than thinking it'll go away on its own.

The problem with hiring a financial advisor when you have no knowledge of your own finances is that you're placing a lot of trust, and some of your most valuable assets, in the hands of a person you may know nothing about. When you go to the doctor, you're going about something you know well, your body. You tell the doctor your leg hurts, and you know what you're talking about because you've had that leg for 25 years. You know all about it. You might not know why it hurts at this moment, but you know that it hurt the same way two years ago, and it started hurting after the rugby season that time, too. You have intimate knowledge of the problem site.

When you call a plumber to fix a leaky pipe, you can ask him what he has to do to fix it, and he'll tell you. It's not that hard to figure out why a pipe leaks and what has to be done to fix it. Besides, it's a pipe. Even if the plumber messes up, and the thing bursts, it's hardly the end of the world. You can call another plumber to come in and fix the botched job. But if you hire somebody to handle your personal finances, and the person turns out to be inept or worse, you've just written your own ticket to potential financial disaster.

We've all read stories in the newspaper about shady, low-down scoundrels who bilk elderly people out of their savings through one scam or another. You've probably heard about some guy who convinces his friends and neighbors that he can get them the deal of a lifetime if they'll just hand over their money, only to go blow the savings of everybody he knows in some Atlantic City casino. This kind of stuff happens all the time.

It could be that the financial "expert" you hire is not an expert at all. Basically, just about anybody can claim to be a financial advisor. Theoretically, somebody who worked as a bank teller for a few years could pump up his credentials enough to make you believe he was qualified to handle your finances. It could take a long time for you to realize that he couldn't. By that time, it could be too late.

Finances, investments, taxation, and the like are all very complicated and complex topics that take years of education to acquire the knowledge to do the job well. Not everyone can be an expert, and it's imperative to find someone who has the knowledge that you're looking for.

Know Thy Finances, Know Thy Advisor

All of this gloom-and-doom financial advisor talk isn't meant to scare you off from hiring someone to help you with your finances. Nearly everybody can use some help sometimes. The point is, the more you know about your personal finances, the easier it will be for you to find a qualified, trustworthy *financial advisor*.

Show Me the Money

A **financial advisor** is a broad term for a professional whom you hire to help you make decisions about your finances. Anybody can claim to be a financial advisor, but that doesn't mean that person is qualified to do the job.

When you understand your finances, you'll be able to ask intelligent questions of those you're considering for the job and understand their answers. You'll know what they're talking about when they throw out phrases like "full-service broker" or "fee-only advisor." You won't feel stupid asking questions about your own money because you'll know that, generally, you know exactly what you're talking about.

Pregnant women often are advised to establish a team, with themselves as the leader, to make sure their pregnancy, labor, and delivery follow a certain plan. Ideally, the team comprises the woman, the health care provider, and the baby's father. The woman, who we'll compare to the person with the money hooking up with a financial advisor, takes charge of the situation.

She works with the other team members to assure a positive outcome to the situation. In many ways, you should think the same way when you seek out a financial advisor. Establish yourself as the team leader and use the advisor for guidance and direction to assure a positive outcome of your financial situation.

To let someone else take control over your personal finances is akin to a pregnant woman saying to her doctor, "Just tell me what you want me to do. I don't care." She would be relinquishing all control and responsibility about her own body and her own baby. That idea went out of favor with most women a long time ago, and it should do the same where finances are involved.

You can, and should, seek advice when you need it. Just be sure that you do two things:

1. Know whom you're hiring. We'll get into that issue more in the next section of this chapter.

2. Understand, and make it understood, that you're ultimately in charge of your financial situation.

Do I Need a Financial Advisor?

There are several reasons why you might need a financial advisor. Maybe you're faced with a complicated financial situation regarding the sale or purchase of a property. Maybe you want to buy some stocks or bonds, and despite the reading and studying you've done, you're still confused. You just don't feel comfortable jumping into the market without some advice. Maybe you're too busy to deal with your finances. A financial advisor can guide you in the right direction expeditiously.

Or maybe tragedy has struck your life and your parents were killed in a car accident. As the only child, you're left to figure out what to do with the estate, your inheritance, and a bunch of other issues. You don't feel strong enough right now to research all these things on your own, and you need somebody to walk you through it.

On a happier note, maybe you and your spouse are expecting a child. Although you're both thrilled, you're also nervous because you know it costs a lot of money to raise a child these days. You're looking for some sound advice about the best way to prepare financially for your child's future.

Money Pit

Some unethical financial advisors try to take advantage of people who are emotionally distraught. If you're going through an emotionally trying time and you need financial advice, be careful. Seek all the advice you need, but try to avoid making any major decisions until you've had a chance to think clearly about them.

Or maybe you've finally gotten serious about saving money for retirement, but you work for yourself and don't have access to an employer-sponsored plan. You have a couple of guys working for you, and you'd like to see what you can set up for them.

All of these are perfectly legitimate reasons for looking for some financial help. Some people are more confident than others about handling their own finances and might opt to deal with these situations on their own. If you're not that confident, though, getting some help probably makes sense for you.

The Who's Who of Financial Advisors

What are some of the different kinds of financial advisors? This issue can be a little bit complicated, because a financial advisor by any other name may, or may not, be a financial advisor.

Some of the common classes of financial advisors are explained in the following sections. Just remember that what type of advisor you'll need depends on your circumstances, and, you should never hire someone because they have a title that you think sounds impressive.

Financial Planners

The term "financial planner" often is used to describe anyone who offers financial advice or services. It also frequently is used interchangeably with "financial advisor."

Financial planners, as the name implies, are people who design financial plans of action. They may design and carry out the plan, or their clients may choose to execute the plans.

Financial planner is a very broad categorization, so if you're looking to hire one make sure you know what credentials or other titles may come along with it. For starters, financial planners can be certified—or not.

Certified Financial Planners

There's a very large fraternity of people in this country called *certified financial planners*. What they have in common is that they've earned the Certified Financial Planning (CFP) credential, a national certification. Earning the CFP credential involves working through a home-study program and passing a cumulative, 10-hour test. Designees must have three years of financial work experience and promise to adhere to a code of ethics. Work experience should include financial planning, investments, or banking. CFPs also are required to take 30 hours of continuing education courses every two years to keep up-to-date on industry happenings.

Of concern to some financial experts are CFPs who work on a commission basis. Many CFPs are employed by brokerage firms, which encourage them to sell products on which they'll earn the highest commissions. In that sense, there's an obvious conflict of interest. If a CFP stands to earn $3,000 commission on a particular mutual fund or $500 on another product, which do you think he'll be inclined to recommend to his client? Consumers must be aware of this potential for conflict and know what questions to ask before hiring a certified financial planner (stay tuned, we're getting to that). This is not to say that CFPs, in general, are not qualified, or that they should not be considered as financial advisors. Just be aware of possible hidden agendas. Also, understand that some CPFs do not work for commissions, but charge a flat fee for their services.

Financial Consultants

Financial consultants provide an overview of financial information and options in order to allow you to choose the products that make the most sense for you. They generally will not produce a plan for your finances, only information and advice. The assumption is that the planner is fee-only (he won't receive a commission on any products sold). Ask how your consultant will be paid.

Dollars and Sense

Certified financial planners (CFPs) have earned the Certified Financial Planning credential. CFPs may call themselves financial consultants, financial planners, financial advisors, or similar names, but be sure you know a person's full qualifications before you consider hiring her.

Bank Customer Service Representatives

A bank *customer service representative* (CSR) is usually trained by the bank at which he's employed. His job is to bring deposits into the bank, either as CDs, money market funds, trust accounts, or other types of accounts. He also is expected to direct clients' money to a subsidiary company that sells mutual funds or one in which the bank receives either a commission or percentage of the management fee. Unless you purchase a load fund—that is, one that charges a sales commission—you do not pay any fee to these consultants.

Certified Public Accountants/Personal Financial Specialists

More and more *certified public accountants* (CPAs) are becoming financial consultants all the time. The American Institute of Certified Public Accountants now has a special designation, called a *personal financial specialist* (PFS) for CPAs who have three years of financial planning experience and pass a six-hour test. Unless you purchase a product, CPAs usually are paid on an hourly basis. Many people depend on their CPA for financial help, regardless of whether or not the CPA is designated a PFS.

Insurance Agents

Insurance agents who specialize in financial planning usually have either a CLU (Chartered Life Underwriter) or ChFC (Charter Financial Consultant) designation or both. These are designations by the American College in Bryn Mawr, Pennsylvania, given to persons who complete and pass a 10-course program. Often, the program of study can be designed in the agent's area of expertise. ChFCs need continuing education. The designations, though not mandatory to do financial planning, show a level of expertise and experience.

Money Managers

A *money manager* is someone who, after reviewing your parameters, risk tolerance, and total financial picture, agrees to handle your funds, make trades on your behalf, and buy and sell stocks and bonds for you. A money manager normally is employed by investors who have a great deal of money. Money managers typically receive a percentage of the market value of their client's account as compensation. Most money managers have a CFA designation (Certified Financial Analyst). Look for this designation when you're thinking about hiring a money manager.

Show Me the Money

All financial advisors are not the same. A **financial consultant** (ChFC or CFP) gives you information and options so that you can choose the best products for your situation. A **customer service representative** works for a bank. A **personal financial specialist** is a **certified public accountant** who has additional financial planning, credentials, and experience. A **Chartered Life Underwriter** or **Charter Financial Consultant** are insurance agents with specialized training in financial matters. A **money manager** handles your funds, makes trades, and buys stocks and bonds for you. A **financial planner** will help you design a plan of action for your finances.

Finding a Reputable Financial Advisor

Now you know a little about the different categories of financial advisors. So how do you go about finding a good one?

You could pick up your trusty yellow pages and start dialing. Lots of people find all kinds of services from the phone listings: doctors, landscapers, lawyers, electricians, and financial advisors. If that's the way you want to do it, okay. At least you're getting started, and you'll have some names to choose from. But don't ever decide to hire someone just because you like their ad, or their name, or that their office is close to your house. You're going to have to meet with the people you call and get some information before you decide whom to hire.

A better way to find a financial advisor is with your ears. Listen to people at work when they talk about money at the water cooler and make a note if somebody's raving about an advisor with whom they've been working. Do any of your friends have financial advisors? How about your relatives? If you have a lawyer, you can ask her for the names of some good financial advisors. If you keep hearing the same name in the context of good financial help, that person is probably worth checking out.

It's important to find somebody who shares your views and philosophies on investments, so don't hire someone without first having a meeting to get to know that person. Remember that you should have some good financial information and understanding under your belt before the meeting, because you've been doing your homework and reading about investments and other financial matters that may affect you.

When you're with your prospective advisor, there are some questions you should ask. Let's get one thing very clear, though, before we start. Don't forget, even for a minute, that you're the person who will be hiring the financial advisor, and you'll be paying his fees. It's not the other way around.

Many people are intimidated by professionals because they feel stupid or uninformed around them. Hello! That's why you're meeting with the advisor in the first place. It's understood that he has more expertise in the finance area than you do, and hopefully you can benefit from his knowledge. That's the point, right? Just remember that you're the person doing the hiring. You don't need to impress the financial advisor; he needs to impress you.

Dollars and Sense

Just because your father's been working with the same financial guy for 25 years doesn't necessarily mean that you should work with him, too. Perhaps, though, that service record should point you toward the firm the guy works for, where you might find someone else that you'd like.

How Long Have You Been in This Business?

Although some of the best and brightest advisors probably are just starting out, there's a lot to be said for experience when it comes to hiring someone to help you manage your money. Plus, there's always a chance—slim, yes, but still a chance—that someone you don't know who's just hung out a shingle is some fly-by-night guy who will soon be out of business, with your money. As we said before, personal finance is a complex business. You want someone who understands the intricacies.

How Have You Prepared for This Job?

It's nice to know whether the person you're considering is a product of the Harvard Business School or of a financial course he found one night while surfing the Web. That's not to say you should only consider hiring someone with a degree from a prestigious school, but you need to make sure that he has sufficient education and experience to do his job well. Ask him for a list of prior job experiences and his educational background. With the world of finance changing every day, you should work with someone who's keeping up.

What Was Your Job Before You Became a Financial Advisor?

Look for a logical progression. Maybe she was a trust officer in a bank or a certified public accountant. You can see that moving into financial planning was a natural move, spurred by experience in a previous job. If she was, say, a physical therapist, however, you have to wonder about the progression. If she tells you she was in sales, the bells should start ringing in your head. We don't want to generalize, but you need a planner, not a salesperson.

Can You Give Me the Names of Some Other Clients, Please?

The downside of this, of course, is that the advisor can hand-pick the people he wants you to talk to, but at least you'll know he has clients, and you'll be able to get an idea from them what he is like. Understand that the advisor must be confidential about his clients; however, every financial advisor should have some clients who are willing to talk with a perspective customer. If you ask for some references, and your prospective financial advisor gets visibly agitated, turns red, and starts moving around in his chair, head for the door. Something's wrong.

Pocket Change

Some financial advisors cater to particular groups of people, claiming they can better serve their needs with specialized advice. Financial firm John Kinnard & Co. offers Womanvest, an information clearinghouse for personalized advice for women. American Express has trained some of its advisors to handle the particular financial needs of gays and lesbians. Some planners cater to ethnic groups such as African-Americans or Asians.

When you do get some names and numbers of references, think about what you'll ask before you make the call. You might ask the person to tell you what the advisor's greatest strength and weakness are. Ask to what degree the person acts on the advisor's suggestions. Has the advice made a difference in the person's financial situation? If the person had it to over again, would he choose the same advisor? Does he feel that the advisor is knowledgeable and trustworthy?

Go with the Gut

There's one more important factor when you're choosing a financial advisor: your gut. Some people click, and others don't. We've all met people who we inexplicably liked or didn't like. Although you should never hire somebody just because you like him, you probably shouldn't hire somebody whom you just don't like.

If you like somebody, and you're assured that he's professional and good at what he does, it sounds like you've got a match. You need someone who will take the time to talk with you, teach you, and be there for you. You should get a feeling fairly early in the relationship for whether the person you're considering is right for you.

If you don't like someone, it probably will be very hard to work together effectively, even if he's the best financial advisor in the business. Ultimately, the decision is up to you. Consider all the factors, throw in your gut feeling, and go for it.

Places and People to Avoid

We don't need to tell you that if you see somebody operating as a financial advisor out of the trunk of his car, it's not a good plan for you to get involved with him. Just say no. But there also are other, more subtle things to avoid when you're choosing a financial advisor: exorbitant fees, conflict of interest concerning products and services, less-than-notable track records, and a sleaze factor.

Too-High Fees

Unless you're a notable exception, you're a little short on money that you don't know what to do with. That's why you have to make sure up front what a financial advisor charges and what you get for that fee.

Find out whether the advisor is fee-only or whether she gets a commission from the financial products she sells. If you can, stick with someone who doesn't sell for a commission (more on that in the next section). Then find out what she charges as an hourly fee. Rates vary greatly, so be sure you shop around. You don't want to sign up with somebody and find out later that her rate is $250 an hour.

The following table compares a standard brokerage fee schedule and a discounted brokerage. Interesting!

Stock Commissions

	200 Shares	300 Shares	500 Shares	1,000 Shares
Full Service Brokerage	$130	$165	$225	$308
Discount Brokerage	$89	$96	$107	$124
Deep Discount Broker	$35	$41	$58	$90

Dollars and Sense

Always find out when you set up an initial appointment with a financial advisor whether the meeting is free. Many, but not all, advisors offer a free consultation for prospective clients.

If the hourly fee seems too high (expect to pay between $75 and $100 an hour), call some other advisors in your area and compare rates. Remember that fee-only financial planners will charge you every time you ask for advice or information. That's how they make their living. If you choose a fee-only advisor, make sure you're billed regularly. That will let you know exactly what you're paying for and help you to decide whether the advice is worth the money.

If your financial advisor works on commission and receives a fee from the annuity company from which she gets the products she sells, you won't know how much she's earning on your investment unless you ask. Go ahead. She should tell you the price of her advice.

Conflicts of Interest

If a financial advisor stands to make big money on commissions from selling certain types of financial products, then watch out. You might be pressured to buy products that are more beneficial to your advisor than they are to you. An advisor who does this is more salesperson than financial advisor, and that's not what you need. Some of the best financial consultants available are commissioned salespeople; you just need to understand how they are paid and ask if there is a product available with a smaller commission.

When you first meet with someone you think you might hire, ask whether he gets a commission from products he sells. If he says he doesn't, but you're getting a bad feeling, you can check him out. All advisors are required to register with the Securities Exchange Commission (SEC) in Washington or their state SEC, and they all must fill out the Uniform Application for Investment Advisor Registration (try saying that before your first cup of coffee!).

Dollars and Sense

You can contact the U.S. Securities and Exchange Commission at 800-732-0330 or by writing to 450 Fifth St. NW, Washington, D.C. 20549.

Ask the advisor for a copy of that form, commonly known as Form ADV. If he says he doesn't have one, you can call the SEC to make sure he's registered. Every advisor also must be registered with his state SEC, and you should be able to get a copy of your advisor's registration form from that agency.

I Know What You Did Last Summer

Form ADV contains information about whether an advisor has had problems in the past, such as being sanctioned or having his license suspended. If you want to check your advisor's track record, ask the SEC in Washington and your state SEC office if they have received any complaints concerning this advisor. You also could call the Better Business Bureau or even the insurance commissioner in your state.

The Sleaze Factor

Most financial advisors are diligent and honest and want to do their best for their clients. As in any profession, though, you'll find some financial advisors who are out to make a quick buck. These are the people that bring the "sleaze factor" to the profession. Unfortunately for the profession, but fortunately for the consumer, horror stories of people being cheated out of their money are usually pretty well-publicized. It's good for consumers, because it gives them an idea of what to watch for. It's bad for the profession, however, because it brings the sleaze factor to the forefront. If you keep in mind that the sleaze factor exists, you'll be more likely to avoid it.

Things Your Investment Advisor Should Never Do

There are some things your financial advisor might do that you don't like, such as take off every Friday afternoon to head for the beach or recommend that you put money in an investment that ends up in the tank. But there are some things your financial advisor should never, ever do. If he does, you need to find yourself a new advisor, and you might want to consider taking legal action.

Misrepresentation

If your advisor tells you the mutual fund you're buying carries no commission for him, but you find out later that he made big bucks by selling it to you, that's *misrepresentation*. It's also misrepresentation if the advisor tells you to go ahead and put your money in a particular investment because you're guaranteed to make 20 percent, and you end up losing most of your principal.

If he would have said, "I think this might be a good investment for you. Why don't we try it?" you couldn't charge that you'd been misrepresented. But an advisor should never tell you something is guaranteed unless he has a guarantee, in writing. Your advisor should always give you the pros and cons of an investment and tell you exactly how the risk relates to your objectives. If he doesn't, consider it a sign that he may be conducting less than ethical business.

Show Me the Money

Be on the lookout for an advisor who guarantees your investments or makes commissions off of sales that he told you carried no commissions for him. If he's doing just that, you can charge him with **misrepresentation**. Some shady advisors also move your investments all over the place, earning commissions at your expense. That's called **churning and burning**, and you don't have to stand for it.

Money Pit

Another kind of misrepresentation is personal misrepresentation. If you find out your advisor has told you he's something or someone he's not, you should ask him about it, check out his most recent ADV, and if you still fell uncomfortable, find someone new.

Churning and Burning

Churning and burning is when an advisor moves your investments around more often than you change your socks. If he's constantly trading and moving your stuff, your antennae should go up. He may be pulling down commissions at your expense.

If you suspect your advisor is doing this, confront him and find out what's going on. Don't hesitate to ask your advisor how much he stands to make on moving around your investments. If he won't tell you, start looking for somebody else to represent you. If you don't feel satisfied with his response, ask for his supervisor or the manager of his office. They'll help review the situation and are usually willing to alleviate dissatisfaction.

Ignoring Your Wishes or Neglecting to Keep You Informed

If you read about a money market fund that gives you just what you've been looking for, and you call your advisor and tell him you want to put $3,000 in it, he should go ahead and complete the transaction. Unless he's a money manager (and he should do it anyway), your advisor is obligated to follow your instructions. Now, if he feels it is an inappropriate investment for you, he should tell you why, maybe even following up with a letter; however, he should still follow your instructions.

Dollars and Sense

Arbitration is the hearing and determination of a dispute between parties by a third party. The American Arbitration Association will send you materials you'll need to prepare your own case, if that's the route you choose. Call the American Arbitration Headquarters at 212-484-4000 to request the package or write to the headquarters at 140 W. 51st St., New York, NY 10020.

He may try to advise you not to put your money in that particular fund, and if you trust him, you'd do well to listen. Still, if you insist, he must place your money where you tell him to. It is, after all, your money.

If you find out your advisor has been buying and selling your investments without your approval, you have a legitimate complaint. Terminate your relationship immediately.

If your financial advisor always has an excuse to get out of a meeting with you, or doesn't keep you informed about what's going on, you need to ask why. Your advisor should meet with you either on a regular basis or certainly upon your request.

If you feel that your financial advisor has cheated you or has done something unethical, you can look for help by contacting a securities lawyer. Or you can seek *arbitration*, which is the hearing and determination of a dispute between parties by a third party. You can do this either by hiring an attorney to represent you in arbitration, or by representing yourself in arbitration. If you go into arbitration, you and your advisor will each present your side of the matter to an arbitration panel. A three-member panel will hear the case and then decide on a solution. Its solution is final and can't be appealed.

The Least You Need to Know

➤ Although you might be able to handle most aspects of your personal finances on your own, there are times you may need someone to help.

➤ You need to know what types of financial advisors are available and where to find someone you can trust before you can choose one.

➤ Don't be afraid to ask your potential advisor specific questions about his or her experience, qualifications, and references.

➤ Avoid advisors who overcharge, look for big commissions at your expense, have poor track records, or embody the "sleaze factor."

➤ Keep an eye out for the things your financial advisor should never do.

➤ If you feel you've been cheated by your financial advisor, you may have some recourse.

Part 5
So You're Thinking of Buying a House

Ten years ago, it probably never occurred to you that you'd be a homeowner someday. Sure, you figured that some day you'd have a house, but it wasn't something you thought about on a regular basis. But now, it seems pretty important, and you find yourself thinking about it a lot. You can just imagine yourself in your own house, and you're pretty comfortable with the image.

Buying a house seems like a good idea. The problem is, it's a huge undertaking. You don't know much about getting a mortgage or paying it off once you have it. You'll need to find out about homeowner's insurance, taxes, down payments, settlement, and all kinds of other house-buying-related things.

Buying a home is a huge move, there's no question about it. But don't worry. In Part 5, we'll cover all the basics and a lot of the particulars of home buying. You'll feel a lot more comfortable with the idea of getting a house when you finish reading Chapters 21 through 25.

Chapter 21

There's No Place Like Home

In This Chapter

➤ To buy or not to buy

➤ Figuring out how much house you'll be able to afford

➤ Considering a down payment

➤ Choosing a real estate agent

➤ Looking for a house

➤ Other expenses associated with buying a house

People decide to buy their first home for many reasons. They get tired of paying out money for rent every month and getting nothing in return except a place to live for the next 30 days: no tax breaks, no security, not even a chance to hang your own curtains or change the bathroom wallpaper. Or they outgrow the rented apartment and figure as long as they have to move, they might as well buy a house. Maybe they're thinking about their personal finances and think a house would make sense as an investment. It's part of the American Dream—to someday have a house of your own.

Or, and this is a biggie, they've embraced the *idea* of having a house. They envision themselves on the couch on a winter's night, with a fire in the fireplace, popcorn on the coffee table, and a movie in the VCR. They imagine having friends over for a party on the deck on a hot, summer night or picture the family gathered around the table on Thanksgiving day, waiting for the turkey to be taken from the oven.

For whatever reason, many people buy homes for the first time each year, and maybe you think you're ready to become one of them. If so, you're on the verge of making a very important decision that will affect your life, and your finances, for a very long time. If you're already thinking about the bedspread with the matching curtains that you want for the guest room or planning how you'll arrange your computer equipment in the office, slow down! You have a lot of work to do if you want to buy a house. The first order of business is to figure out whether owning a home is right for you.

It's the American Dream—But Is It Right for Everyone?

Americans have this idea that everybody should have a home of their own, yet we probably all know people who really shouldn't be homeowners. Some people love the *idea* of having a house, but they hate the work that goes with it.

When you have a house, there's always something to be fixed, adjusted, or redone. There's painting, cleaning the rugs, redoing the grouting in the bathtub, raking up the leaves, mowing the grass, sweeping the garage, and shoveling the sidewalk when it snows. Maybe you can hire somebody to do all those things for you, so it doesn't matter whether you enjoy doing them. More likely than not, though, you'll end up doing the bulk of those chores yourself. If you can't stand the idea of doing this kind of work or having to deal with the never-ending problems that come with owning a house, then maybe you should reconsider or look at a condominium. Condos provide home ownership with the outside work done for you, of course, for a monthly maintenance fee.

Another reason it might not be a good idea to buy a house is if you know your life situation will be changing soon. None of us can know what will happen in our futures, but if you have a clue—say, your boss told you that you'll be transferred in six months to a year—then it's not a good time to think about buying a home. The same thing applies if your marriage is on shaky ground, or if your job security is threatened, or if you've just learned that you'll need an advanced degree in order to keep your job.

Pocket Change

Everyone considering buying a house should see the 1986 movie *The Money Pit* with Tom Hanks and Shelley Long.

Of course, lest we sound too pessimistic here, you should know that there are some very good reasons why you should consider buying a house:

➤ You'll build up equity in your house as you pay off your mortgage. You'll have something that is yours.

➤ Owning a home gives you good tax advantages. We discuss this issue in detail in Chapter 24, but be aware that it can save you a bundle.

➤ Owning a home makes you part of a community and gives you a stake in the well-being of that community. Even if you live in a rural area without close neighbors, you're a tax-paying member of a municipality and a school district. If you move into a neighborhood, you become part of a group of particular people, just because of where you live.

Dollars and Sense

Equity in a home is the difference between the current market value of the home and the money you still owe on the mortgage.

Only you can decide whether owning a home is right for you. The implications of home ownership extend well past the financial ones, so you'll have to examine the whole picture and then make a decision.

If you decide, after checking out the financial and other relevant implications of home ownership, that you want to buy a home, congratulations! It's certainly an exciting time. Be prepared to do your homework and talk to a lot of people to get the best information you can. You'll have many important decisions to make.

Maybe after you carefully evaluate all the information concerning buying a home, you'll decide that now isn't the right time for you to do it. If that happens, you might feel disappointed, almost as if something has been taken away from you. Your images of the matching bedspread and curtains evaporate, along with your dream of Thanksgiving dinner in your dining room and the movie you'd watch while lying in front of your fireplace.

Dollars and Sense

If you're getting ready to buy a home, it's a good idea to set up a file to keep everything organized. You'll be collecting a lot of paperwork throughout the process, and you'll need to keep it all organized.

It's okay to feel like that, but remember that postponing home ownership doesn't mean you can never buy a house. If you decide that, for whatever reasons, you're not ready to own a home, you've probably done the right thing. There will be homes for sale next year, and the year after that, and in 10 years down the road. When you're ready to buy, you'll find a house that you'll like.

Quiz

To help you decide whether the time has come to start house-hunting, take the short quiz below. But, remember, only you can make the decision:

1. Do you plan on living in the area in which you are house-hunting for the next five years?

   Yes No

2. Do you have funds available to put down as a down payment, even the minimum of 5% down?
   Yes No

3. In order to own a home, are you willing to be cash poor for several years?
   Yes no

4. Are you handy and/or do you like yard work?
   Yes No

5. Do you have your credit card debts/outstanding loans/credit under control? Will you qualify for a mortgage?
   Yes no

6. Will your finances change drastically in the years ahead? (i.e., Do you plan to return to college or attend graduate school?)
   Yes No

7. Will you need a new vehicle within a year or two and need to save the funds to purchase it?
   Yes No

8. If you are married or in a serious relationship, is it secure enough to go into home ownership at this time?
   Yes No

Each yes answer counts as one point. Score yourself as follows:

> 7–8   Sounds like you're ready to take the plunge. Good Luck!

> 5–6   Slowly look around at homes while you assess your situation.

> 4 or below   Re-sign your lease for another year and take the quiz again next year.

How Much House Can You Afford?

If you've decided that owning a home is something you want to do, and that now is the time to do it, you have to take care of a bunch of things before you can start looking at color samples from the paint store. One of the first things is to determine just how much house you'll be able to afford. You need to know how large a loan, or mortgage, you'll be able to get. (We'll talk more about what a mortgage is and where you can get one in Chapter 22.)

It's better to learn this before you start house hunting. Sure, it's great fun to drive around, looking at houses and envisioning yourself sitting on the porch or lounging by the pool. But you're setting yourself up for a fall if you get your heart set on a particular house, only to find out it's way out of your reach.

Before you apply for a mortgage, you need to get your finances in order. To improve your chances of getting the mortgage you want, do the following things:

➤ Reduce your debt. Pay off as much debt as you can before you even start shopping for a mortgage. That includes credit cards, car debts, and any other debts you might have.

➤ Start getting some money together for a down payment. We'll discuss down payments in more detail later on. For now, we'll just say that the more you have for your down payment, the less you'll have to finance on your loan.

➤ Patch up any glitches on your credit rating or get some credit established—fast!

How Much Do You Make?

To determine how big a mortgage you can probably get, the first thing to look at is how much money you make, before taxes. This amount is your gross income. The recommended guideline is that you should spend no more than 28 percent of your gross monthly income on your mortgage payment. (If you're not sure exactly what your monthly income is, gather up your last couple of pay stubs and figure it out. Or divide your gross annual income by 12 to get the figure.) The mortgage payment includes the principal, interest, real estate taxes, and homeowner's insurance.

The principal of a mortgage is the amount loaned. If you borrow $120,000, that amount is the principal, and you are obligated to repay a portion of the mortgage amount each month. You pay principal each month based on the unpaid balance of the mortgage. The interest is the fee the lender charges you to use his money. Real estate taxes are the taxes assessed by the municipality and/or school district within which you live. They're based on the value of your home. And, homeowner's insurance fees are the cost of insurance to protect the property and its contents. The four things are normally figured into each payment you'll make on your mortgage, although the taxes and insurance are sometimes paid separately.

Your Expenses

It seems that every time you turn around, your expenses have increased. When you're thinking about applying for a mortgage, you must pay close attention to your expenses as they relate to your income.

Although the recommended maximum for your mortgage payment is 28 percent of your gross monthly income, the recommended maximum for your total monthly debt is 36 percent of your income. That means that all your expenses other than a mortgage, such as your car payment, credit card bills, student loans, child support payments, and other bills, should total no more than 8 percent of your gross income.

Dollars and Sense

If you have very high monthly expenses because of high credit card or other debt, reduce the debt as much as you can before you go to apply for a mortgage. It will work against you on your application.

Your Monthly Mortgage Payment

Say you're earning $40,000 a year. That means, without going above 28 percent of your income, you could pay $11,196 a year for your mortgage or $933 a month. To keep within the 36 percent limit for total debt payment, you could spend $14,400 a year or $1,200 a month on all of your debts. The following chart gives you a better idea of how much you can afford to pay each month. Remember that a mortgage will typically include the principal, interest, real estate taxes, and homeowner's insurance. There are additional payments for PMI (Private Mortgage Insurance), mortgage insurance, etc.

Maximum Amount You Should Borrow for Your Mortgage

Annual Income*	Annual Mortgage Payment	Monthly Mortgage Payment
20,000	5,600	466.67
25,000	7,000	583.33
30,000	8,400	700.00
35,000	9,800	816.67
40,000	11,200	933.33
45,000	12,600	1050.00
50,000	14,000	1166.67
55,000	15,400	1283.33
60,000	16,800	1400.00
65,000	18,200	1516.67
70,000	19,600	1633.33
75,000	21,000	1750.00
80,000	22,400	1866.67
85,000	23,800	1983.33
90,000	25,200	2100.00
95,000	26,600	2216.67
100,000	28,000	2333.33

Gross Income

You should have an idea of how high the property taxes, also called real estate taxes, are in the areas in which you're looking at homes. The tax rate can vary greatly, depending on the makeup of the area. For instance, an area that contains affluent businesses and industry will normally offer a lower tax rate for residents, because the industry provides a strong tax base. An area that is almost entirely residential, however, generally has a higher tax rate. The tax rate can make a difference when you're deciding whether you'll be able to afford a particular home.

If you have a mortgage, you're required to have homeowner's insurance. If you put down less than 20 percent of the value of the home, you'll need *private*

Show Me the Money

Lenders often require **private mortgage insurance** (PMI) to protect them against losing their money if you should default on your loan.

mortgage insurance (PMI), as well. Lenders often require this type of insurance as protection against borrowers who may default on the loan.

Try to get an idea of what the cost of homeowner's insurance runs in the areas in which you're looking at homes. Your insurance agent or a company in the same general area will be able to give you estimates. We'll discuss homeowner's insurance in more detail in Chapter 25.

Dollars and Sense

Don't apply for a mortgage and then start trying to scrape together a down payment. Have your down payment in place well before you apply.

The All-Important Down Payment

Another very important factor in figuring out how much house you can afford is the down payment. A down payment is the amount of money you're required (or have available) to pay up front on a house. The rest of the payment for the house is financed through a mortgage. You're normally required to put down between 5 and 20 percent of the price of the home you want to buy. That's somewhere between $5,000 and $20,000 on a home that costs $100,000.

If you don't have the greatest credit record in the world, but you have a sizable down payment, many lenders will give you more serious consideration than you'd get without a substantial down payment. The bigger the down payment you make, the less your monthly mortgage payment will be. This can work in your favor in two ways:

➤ You can lower your monthly payments and have more money to invest or to use for other purposes.

➤ You could afford a more expensive house with a bigger down payment, because you'll be financing less of the cost of the home. If you buy a $100,000 home and make a $5,000 down payment, you have to finance $95,000. But if you make a $20,000 down payment on the same house, you'll be financing only $80,000.

The following charts show examples of how down payment and interest rates factor in to determining how much house you can afford. The monthly payment of $1,060 does not exceed the recommended maximum of 36 percent of a $40,000 gross annual income.

Money Pit

In addition to a down payment, you've got to consider money you'll need to pay points and settlement fees. We'll discuss these nasty little things in more detail later, but pay attention when your mortgage lender mentions them. Each point will cost you $1,000 on a $100,000 mortgage. If you don't set money aside to pay them, you could come up short at settlement.

Monthly Payment on $100,000 Home—7% Interest Rate, Different Down Payments

Down Payment Amount	15-Year Mortgage	20-Year Mortgage	30-Year Mortgage
$5,000	$853.88	$736.53	$632.04
10,000	808.94	697.77	598.77
15,000	764.00	659.00	565.51
20,000	719.07	620.24	532.25

The interest rate isn't a factor in how much you need to borrow to buy the house. It's a factor in how much you'll have to pay for borrowing the money. With interest rates currently at historical lows, individuals can afford to purchase a great deal more house than ten years ago because the monthly repayment amount is so much lower than when interest rates are higher.

Monthly Payment on $100,000 Mortgage—Varying Interest Rates, Varying Mortgage Terms

7%

15 year	20 year	25 year	30 year
$898.83	$775.30	$706.78	$665.31

9%

15 year	20 year	25 year	30 year
$1,014.27	$899.73	$839.20	$804.63

12%

15 year	20 year	25 year	30 year
$1,200.17	$1,101.09	$1,053.23	$1,028.62

If your mortgage application is turned down because you don't have enough of a down payment, you can either come up with more money or look for a less-expensive house. Hopefully, you've planned for your down payment and have enough money saved. If not, you'll want to accumulate money as quickly as possible. Ways to help you do that might include the following:

➤ Give up anything you don't absolutely need in order to save for the down payment. If you've been thinking of trading in your car, hold onto it. If you've been looking wistfully at vacation brochures, put them away. If you want to buy a home, you must make it your top financial priority.

➤ Borrow from your 401(k). If you have enough equity, and your employer allows it, you can borrow money from your 401(k) plan to supplement your down payment.

➤ Withdraw, not borrow, funds from your IRA. If you're a first-time home buyer, the money you take out isn't subject to a penalty, but you will have to pay income tax on it. The withdrawl amount may be for up to $10,000 to the first time buyer.

➤ Borrow money from a relative, if possible, and set up a schedule for repayment.

➤ Get a second job and earmark every penny for a down payment.

➤ If you already have a house, you can use any equity you have in it as part of the down payment on a new home.

➤ Look for a mortgage insured by a government agency that might not require a down payment or will allow you to put a small amount down. Examples of these mortgages are Veteran's Administration and Federal Housing Authority mortgages, which we'll discuss in more detail in Chapter 22.

Choosing the Right Real Estate Agent

After you've decided you're going to buy a house, and you've figured out about how much you'll be able to spend, it's time to look for a real estate agent. Some first-time buyers decide to do their house hunting and buying on their own without the experience and expertise of a professional real estate agent. We don't recommend this. Unless you're knowledgeable about the ins and outs of real estate, there are just too many legal and financial factors involved to try to go it alone. You could end up spending much more than you have to or, worse, finding out after the fact that you're in some kind of legal trouble. If you do decide to buy or sell a property on your own, good luck. The least you should do is have a real estate lawyer review any agreements before you sign them.

Real estate agents are abundant in almost any given area. Try these tips to find one who will look out for your interests:

➤ Get personal recommendations. If your friends just got a good deal on the cutest house, and they raved about their real estate agent the entire time they worked with her, you should hear some bells ringing. A reference like that is very valuable, and you shouldn't overlook it. On the other hand, if your friends just endured a terrible experience with a real estate agent, you probably should look for somebody else.

➤ Check 'em out. Do an interview. Ask the agent for names of clients they've worked

Money Pit

Be sure to stand firm when working with a real estate agent. Don't let her talk you into something that you don't want or don't think you can afford. Remember, real estate agents work on a commission basis and benefit from you buying a house that might be more than you can comfortably afford.

with in the past four or five months. Don't be afraid of appearing pushy. A good real estate agent will not be offended. Rather, she should appreciate the fact that you want the best help you can get when buying your home.

Dollars and Sense

If you start working with a real estate agent and discover that it's just not going to work out, don't feel compelled to continue working with her. You're entitled to change. It's not a good idea to continue working with someone you don't feel is doing a good job for you or with whom you can't get along.

➤ Call your local board of real estate agents and ask for recommendations. Or ask your local chamber of commerce to recommend a real estate agent.

As with any other profession, there are great real estate agents, good real estate agents, mediocre real estate agents, and those who shouldn't be real estate agents. You and your real estate agent will spend a lot of time together during the months that you're house hunting, arranging for a mortgage, and getting ready to move. You want someone that you get along with, but it's also important to have someone who is a professional and knows how to get the best deals possible for you.

Consider the following when you're looking for someone to help you buy a home:

➤ **Experience.** How much experience does the real estate agent have? Is she a full-time real estate agent or does she sell homes on the side? She's going to be paying for it, so you might as well get someone who's in the business full-time and is up-to-date with what's going on. The real estate agents work for the seller, meaning they must put the buyer first—unless they are a buyer's broker and then their job is to put you first. If you buy a house using a buyer's broker, your realtor will be paid a sales commission, and if you don't buy you'll be responsible to pay the broker yourself.

➤ **Diplomacy and communication skills.** You certainly want someone who will look out for your best interests, but you don't want someone who will alienate everyone she works with. You'd hate to think that your real estate agent would push so hard for your interests that the people selling the home you just have to have would sell it to someone else just to avoid working with your real estate agent.

➤ **Honesty.** Be sure to verify an agent's honesty when you talk with former clients. You're investing valuable assets with this person: money, time, and emotions.

➤ **Understanding.** If you're a first-time buyer, you'll have tons of questions, and you'll need a lot of direction. A real estate agent who is impatient or doesn't have the time you need to answer all your questions, reassure you, and give you direction, isn't the agent you need.

➤ **A feel for the areas in which you're considering moving.** A good real estate agent can give you insights about the areas you're considering. She can tell you about the neighbors, the schools, and the available facilities. If the house you're looking at is directly below the incoming flight path of the local airport, your real estate agent should tell you that, too.

➤ **Knowledge of various mortgage companies, inspectors, and other people you might need.** A good real estate agent can pave the way when it comes to finding people you need. She should be helpful and informative, but shouldn't railroad you into using people she works with frequently.

The Great House Hunt Begins

After you've taken care of everything we've discussed so far, and you have a real estate agent on board, you're ready to start house hunting in earnest. You probably have a pretty good idea of where you want to live and maybe you've even checked out some houses informally.

An important rule to remember when you're house hunting is to keep an open mind. Don't refuse to look at homes anywhere outside of the three-block area you have your heart set on, because you're sure to miss out on some good properties. The house of your dreams might be just on the other side of the creek you've set as your boundary or on the other side of town or the county.

Real estate prices vary tremendously, based on the location of the home. You may be able to afford a townhouse in the "in" neighborhood or a much larger single home with an acre of land in another area. It's a matter of getting your priorities and your finances straight.

For many people, house hunting gets to be like a sickness. Those infected by the house-hunt fever are often seen frequenting Sunday afternoon "open houses" or skulking around neighborhoods at various times of the day and night, checking out houses with "for sale" signs in the front. Consider yourself warned.

Dollars and Sense

Hunting for a house can become nearly an obsession, if you're not careful. Determine ahead of time just how many hours a week you can spend house hunting and stick to it.

Single, Double, Townhouse, Duplex, or Condo?

There's so many different kinds of homes; how will you ever find the one you want and can afford? Let's start with single dwellings. Many people who think about buying a house consider only single dwellings. To them, a single dwelling is the only option that truly is a house; the rest are somehow something less. Single homes are fine, but understand that, like many things we take for granted in this country, they're luxuries. There's no reason that every family in town needs to have its own, detached dwelling.

True, single homes tend to be larger than nonsingles and generally come with more land. So people with large families or the need for a multiacre garden might require a single. But not everyone does. If you're set on a single home, go ahead and check them out. Just remember that they're not the only game in town.

A double house is a structure with two homes that are side-by-side, sharing a common wall. Each dwelling in a double home can be quite large, and each half often includes some property. They generally are less expensive than single homes and can be a good value. If there are double homes in the area in which you're looking, be sure to check some out. Some people love having close neighbors, and others feel too confined, so think about which kind of person you are before you buy a double. Also, be sure to check out the neighbors before buying the house.

A townhouse is an attached home, commonly called a rowhome. These homes are generally less expensive than singles, unless they're in an extremely trendy area. Townhouses offer advantages such as security, community, and financial value. As with double homes, only you know how you feel about living in close proximity with your neighbors.

A duplex is another example of nonsingle-family housing, but in this case, one complete living unit is above another complete living unit. Duplexes are popular investment properties, and the owner will often live either upstairs or downstairs and rent the other unit. As with other kinds of nonsingle housing, duplexes offer financial advantages, and many people like the security of having someone near.

When you buy a condominium, you own it and part of everything else in the community. That means you normally have shared costs for maintenance and other expenses. Condos are great for people who have no time or interest in the upkeep involved with a single home and property.

Dollars and Sense

No matter what kind of house you buy, make sure you have it inspected before you agree to buy it. Home inspections can cost $400 or $500, but are really necessary to avoid possible big problems. Your real estate agent can recommend a home inspector, or you can find your own.

There Goes the Neighborhood

People choose the neighborhoods they live in for many different reasons. The choice can be based on whether the home buyer wants a rural, urban, or suburban setting. He might want a neighborhood with lots of kids for his kids to play with. Or he might choose a particular neighborhood because it's near his work, his family, or his favorite shopping mall. Some people choose neighborhoods close to those in which they grew up. Or they move to a new town and look for a neighborhood that's similar to the one in which they grew up. Other people choose to live far away from neighborhoods, seeking space and solitude.

Regardless of why you choose the neighborhood you do, be sure to check it out thoroughly before buying a home there. If you visit a home in a particular neighborhood during the day, be sure you go back at night to see what's going on. A nice, quiet neighborhood in the day can turn into a noisy place if 15 teenagers gather on the corner with their CD players every night. Noises you might never notice in the daytime can be annoyingly loud at night. Is there a train track near the neighborhood? If so, how many trains will pass through while you're trying to catch some Zs?

Early morning is another good time to visit. What's the traffic like? If you're near a school, consider bus traffic. Do trucks use your street as a thoroughfare?

Talk to some of the neighbors and try to get the lowdown on the neighborhood. Just remember, some people will tell you anything you want to know, and others won't tell you anything. You might have to ask around a little bit before you find somebody willing to talk.

Money Pit

Always ask the person who's selling his home why he's moving. If he gives you a reason, but you suspect there's something he's not telling you, press a little bit harder for a more honest answer. There could be a problem you're not hearing about.

Don't Forget to Check Out the Schools

I know. You don't have any kids. Maybe you're not even married. The locations and qualities of the surrounding schools are of little concern to you. For now. A lot can change in three or four years, and life often moves quickly and without much advance notice. The schools may be insignificant to you now, but they'll probably become important a bit further down the road. Your real estate agent should be able to get you information concerning particular schools and districts, and you should factor this information into your decision. In addition to coming in handy if you happen to have some kids, being in a good school district makes your house easier to sell when you decide it's time to move on.

Pier One, Here We Come

An important financial consideration when you're thinking about moving is what you're going to need to buy once you've purchased the home. Make sure you think about this before you decide to buy, or you could be in for a big shock later. If you absolutely can't stand the wallpaper in the living room, you'll have to factor in the cost of redoing the room or having somebody else redo it. Are you going to need new rugs? What about furniture? If you're moving from a small apartment to a fairly large house, you're apt to have some empty rooms.

Be sure to find out what stays in the house. Appliances like stoves and refrigerators (known as attached appliances) are often required to be included in the sale. Curtains, drapes, and custom-made furniture that fit in a particular spot are usually extras.

Attempt to negotiate to retain as many items from the seller as possible. This will enable you to replace the items as you can afford to, not immediately.

You've just committed to spending a huge amount of money for the next 15 or 30 years, and now you realize you need furniture for three empty rooms! What's a new homeowner to do? Consider these tips:

Money Pit

Many people are very emotional when it comes to home buying, and don't sufficiently consider the practical matters. We know someone who fell in love with a home, bought it, and moved in, only to discover the windows were really old and extremely difficult to open and close. She spent a fortune on replacement windows, and her finances suffered because of it for years. Be sure you know what you're getting and what you'll need to buy before signing the sales agreement.

➤ Accept that you can't buy everything you want as soon as you move in. Make do with what you have, borrow furniture from a family member or friend, or make bookshelves out of stackable crates or cinder blocks and boards.

➤ Check out the second-hand shop for some bargains. But don't go overboard. You can end up spending a ton of money on stuff you don't plan to keep.

➤ Adopt a minimalist philosophy and a less-is-more mindset. Remind yourself that your rooms look a lot bigger with no furniture in them, and you get a lot more of the morning sunlight if you don't have curtains hanging in front of your windows.

➤ Be patient. Not rushing to buy everything at once gives you a chance to get a feeling for the house. That will make it easier for you to decide where to put the things you eventually will get.

The Least You Need to Know

➤ Not everyone is cut out to be a homeowner.

➤ If you want to buy a house, you'll need to figure out how much you'll be able to pay.

➤ The amount of money you put down will affect your mortgage payment and is a key factor in how expensive a home you'll be able to consider.

➤ It's very important to get a real estate agent you trust professionally, as well as one you like and can work with effectively.

➤ When you start looking for house, remain open-minded concerning the type of structure and the location.

➤ You need to consider after-moving costs, such as the cost of furniture and home repairs, when you think about buying a house.

Chapter 22

We'd Like to Borrow Some Money, Please

In This Chapter

➤ Understanding the concept of a mortgage

➤ Finding out about different types of mortgages

➤ Determining which mortgage makes sense for you

➤ Where to get a mortgage

➤ Bettering your chances of getting the mortgage approved

➤ Defining settlement

Buying a home is an exciting proposition. You have to find a house you love in an area that's right for you. You have to make sure there's enough closet space and decide whether you'd rather have the place with the deck or the screened-in porch. You can get completely immersed in the great house hunt, spending hours and hours driving around in your car, poking around potential homes, and debating the pros and cons of what you've seen.

Owning a home is the American dream, right? The home you buy will be your very own. You can paint the walls whatever color you'd like, invite your friends over for parties, and plan to raise a family there. Of course, you have to pay for your piece of the dream, and it's probably the biggest chunk of change you'll ever put down for anything.

Just What Exactly Is a Mortgage?

The cost of homes varies tremendously, depending on where you live or want to live. Even within a 25-mile radius, location can have a great effect on the cost of homes. The cost varies even more from region to region, across the country. In Nashua, New Hampshire, rated number one in *Money* magazine's 1997 best-places-to-live-in-America survey, the average cost of a four-bedroom house was $125,000. A four-bedroom house in a desirable area outside of New York City, however, could cost four or five times that much.

Pocket Change

Remember that the three most important words in real estate are location, location, and location.

Regardless of whether we pay $80,000 or $220,000 for a house, the great majority of us cannot plunk down the entire amount at one time. So we do the next best thing. We borrow. No, we don't go to Uncle Marvin and ask him for a big, fat loan. (You could if you have an Uncle Marvin who has a lot of money to spare, but most of us don't have Uncle Marvins who will graciously offer to loan us thousands and thousands of dollars.) We do something a little different; we get mortgages.

A *mortgage* is a loan that you get from a bank or other lender. You borrow the difference between the cost of the house and the money you have for a down payment and agree to pay it back over a specified period of time and at a specified rate of interest. On one hand, mortgages are great, because most of us couldn't buy houses without them. On the other hand, they can be financially crippling if not managed properly.

In this chapter, we'll look at various topics associated with mortgages. It's really important to understand what's involved with mortgages so that you can get the one that's best for you, and make sure you'll be able to handle it, financially. When you borrow money for your house, the mortgage lender has a big piece of collateral—your home. The lender holds a lien on your home, just in case you default on, or don't pay, your mortgage. If you don't pay, the lender can take your house. This collateral usually means the interest rate you pay for the mortgage is lower than other loans.

Show Me the Money

A **mortgage** is a loan for the cost of your home, minus the down payment.

Because you're going to be stuck with your mortgage for a long time, usually between 15 and 30 years, it's important to understand the different kinds of available mortgages and to get the one that makes the most sense for you. Because you're paying back such a large amount of money over a long period, the interest rate you get is extremely important. A couple of percentage points makes a huge difference when you're talking about $125,000 paid back over 30 years.

A common, and serious, mistake among home buyers is getting a house that's more expensive than they can afford. Although most people want a nice house that friends and families will admire, some people take home buying to the extreme. They'll borrow as much money as they possibly can get, buy the biggest, fanciest house they can, and end up sitting in it for the next 10 years because they have no money to do anything else. This situation is commonly called being "house poor," and it means that you've committed too much of your total income to paying back your mortgage.

When you decide on the house you want, consider how much you'll owe and whether you'll have to make any lifestyle changes to make the payment. Maybe you're used to spending your weekend days on the golf course and Saturday nights checking out the hottest new restaurants in town. You have to consider those expenses when you go to get a mortgage. Are you willing to make concessions? If you're going for a huge house, you'll probably need a huge mortgage that will consume all of your income. If you want a house, you have to be willing to give up some of the things you were able to afford before the mortgage.

And, don't forget that there are other costs associated with a mortgage. You pay much more than just the price of the house. You'll have to consider fees for inspections, legal fees, points, and the like. All these have to be factored in when you're figuring out what you can afford.

Maybe you've always dreamed of owning a perfectly restored 18th-century, New England farmhouse with lots of land, and maybe you'll be perfectly happy to spend every bit of your income on the mortgage for that house. But if you want the house, and you want to buy and keep horses in the barn, continue to take two expensive vacations each year, have dinner a couple of times a week in trendy restaurants, and hire somebody to make custom curtains for every window in the house, you'd better take a close look at your income versus your expenses. Now that you've had your frugality lecture, let's get back to mortgages.

Money Pit

First-time homeowners frequently get themselves into trouble by buying a house that's too expensive for their incomes and lifestyles. Many first-time buyers try to get their dream house immediately, instead of getting a starter home and waiting until their incomes can support the dream house.

Getting the Mortgage That's Best for You

The two most common types of mortgages are fixed-rate and adjustable-rate. There are some other kinds that we'll mention briefly, but fixed-rate and adjustable-rate are the big two.

Fixed-Rate Mortgages

Fixed-rate mortgages are the most common kind of mortgages, sort of the industry standard, and they're the easiest to understand. You agree to pay a certain amount of interest on your mortgage for as long as you have it. If you pay 8 percent interest the first month, you'll pay 8 percent interest the last month, too. The rate doesn't change and neither does your monthly payment. You'll receive a schedule of payments, and you'll know exactly how much you'll pay each month. So if you like to know exactly how to plan your long-term budget, you'll probably like fixed-rate mortgages. It removes the guesswork.

Interest rates change on a mortgage, or any loan, because of the general economic environment, usually dependent on inflation. Interest rates are controlled by the Federal Reserve through interest rates that this federal agency charges to banks. If the Fed charges banks high interest, your mortgage rate will be high; if rates are low, a mortgage you take out should have a low rate.

Show Me the Money

A **fixed-rate mortgage** is one where the interest rate remains constant over the life of the loan. An **adjustable-rate mortgage** is one where the interest rate normally stays the same for a specified amount of time, after which it may fluctuate.

A problem with fixed-rate mortgages, though, is that if the interest rates drop dramatically, you're still stuck paying the higher rate. You can *refinance* your mortgage to take advantage of low rates, but this process requires time and involves significant expense for things such as appraisals, title insurance, points, and the like. These fees can easily add up to $2,000 or $3,000. When you refinance your mortgage, you're basically trading it in for a new one. Still, there are reasons why more people have fixed-rate mortgages than any other kind. They're easy to keep track of, and you can count on a specific payment you'll make each month. Let's have a look at how the other kinds compare.

Show Me the Money

Refinancing your mortgage is trading in your old mortgage for a new one. People refinance to get better interest rates and thus lower their monthly payment and/or shorten the term of the loan, or to change their mortgage from one type to another.

Adjustable-Rate Mortgages

Adjustable-rate mortgages (ARMs) are different from fixed-rate mortgages because the interest rate doesn't stay the same for the entire term of the loan. Because of that, your monthly mortgage payment varies. Home buyers generally are attracted to ARMs because they offer initial savings. You often can get an ARM without paying *points*, which are the fees (actually prepaid interest) you pay your mortgage lender to cover the cost of completing the mortgage application. (We'll talk more about points a little later on in this chapter.) Also, the beginning interest rate of an ARM, also known as a variable-rate mortgage, is normally lower than the rate for a fixed-rate mortgage.

You generally agree to pay a fixed interest rate for a certain amount of time, after which your rate and monthly payment may start to fluctuate. The interest rates for ARMs are tied into various indexes, which determine how they'll rise or fall. The indexes used for the interest adjustment are based on the current interest rate scenario evident at the time the ARM rate is adjusted. Whatever index is used will be specified by the lender. Most ARMS also include annual caps, so your interest rate can't keep increasing forever. You could, however, end up paying hundreds of dollars more on your monthly payment down the road than you do initially if the interest rates rise dramatically. On the other hand, if interest rates stay low, an ARM can be a good deal.

The following are two of the more common types of available ARMs:

➤ A 7/1 ARM has an initial rate that's locked in for seven years. The rate can change every year after that.

➤ In a 3/3 ARM, the initial rate is locked in for three years, then the rate can be adjusted every three years. It can be raised 2 percent at a time, with a 6 percent increase cap for the life of the loan.

Fortunately for the buyer, most ARMS offer caps that protect against really huge increases in payments. There are different kinds of caps:

➤ A lifetime cap limits how much the interest rate can rise over the life of the loan.

➤ A periodic rate cap limits how much your payments can rise at one time.

➤ A payment cap limits the amount that your payment can rise over the life of the loan.

The initial savings of an adjustable-rate mortgage over a fixed-rate mortgage can be tempting. Don't get sucked into an adjustable-rate deal, however, unless you fully understand how it works and are willing to take the risks.

Show Me the Money

Points are prepaid interest you pay to your mortgage lender to cover the cost of completing the mortgage application and to make him some extra money. One point is one percent of your total mortgage. Points are paid when the mortgage deal is closed.

Which Is Better: Fixed–Rate or Adjustable?

If you're trying to decide between a fixed-rate or adjustable-rate mortgage, it's good to get all the information you can about each. After you have a pretty good understanding of the differences between the two types of mortgages, ask yourself these questions:

➤ How long do you plan to live in the home you're buying?

➤ How often does the ARM adjust and when is the adjustment made?

➤ How high could your monthly payments get if interest rates were to rise?

Pocket Change

More than three-quarters of people who get mortgages choose fixed-rate mortgages.

If you're only going to live in the house for a few years, an ARM might make more sense than a fixed-rate mortgage. Remember, the initial interest rate usually is lower with an ARM, and you might be able to avoid paying points. If you're only going to live in the house for three years, and your interest rate can't be adjusted within that time, you may be able to get a good deal with an ARM.

After the initial, fixed period, during which time the interest rate on an ARM can't change, most ARMs adjust every year on the anniversary of the date you closed on the mortgage. A 3/3 ARM means you'd have the initial payment for three years, after which it can be adjusted every three years. You're normally notified of your new rate about 45 days before it takes effect.

Suppose you have an ARM with a cap that allows your interest rate to jump 2 percent a year, with a lifetime cap of 6 percent. If you have a $100,000 mortgage and started with an interest rate of 5.75 percent, your monthly payments could jump more than $400 by the time your lifetime cap kicks in. Quite a hammering, isn't it? In that case, and that's a worst-case scenario, you'd be better off having a fixed-rate mortgage. Economists and financial experts who study these things say that if you can get a good fixed rate, you're probably better off with it, even if you don't plan to stay in the house too long.

The chart below shows you different monthly payments for a 15-year versus a 30-year mortgage and the differences in the total interest paid.

Monthly Payment on $75,000 Mortgage— Varying Interest Rates

7%			
15-year	20-year	25-year	30-year
$674.13	$581.48	$530.09	$498.98
9%			
15-year	20-year	25-year	30-year
$760.70	$674.80	$629.40	$603.47
12%			
15-year	20-year	25-year	30-year
$900.13	$880.87	$789.92	$771.46

The following chart shows the different monthly mortgage payments and the differences in total income paid for mortgages at different interest rates. Quite a difference!

Sample Adjustable Rate Mortgage Payment Differential

2% adjustment, permitted 4 times (6% maximum increase in rate)		
5% rate	$402.62/month	$4,831.44/year
7% rate	$498.98/month	$5,987.76/year
9% rate	$603.47/month	$7,241.64/year
11% rate	$714.25/month	$8,570.91/year

Before you choose a fixed-rate or adjustable-rate mortgage, you need to determine how comfortable you are with risk. If you choose an ARM, and your interest rate zooms up, will you be able to afford the higher payments? Do you have an emergency fund you could borrow from if you had trouble? Are you likely to be incurring additional expenses soon? Do you need to buy a new car, or are you planning on starting a family? Are you sure your income will continue rising, or is it possible that it will decrease?

These are all questions you'll have to think about and answer before making a decision. An ARM can pay off, but it's a gamble. Sometimes there's a lot to be said for something that's safe and dependable, like a fixed-rate mortgage.

Dollars and Sense

Before assuming an adjustable-rate mortgage, figure out what the highest possible, worst-case scenario payment could be. If you don't think you could swing it, go for a fixed-rate mortgage.

Other Types of Mortgages

Remember we mentioned earlier in the chapter that fixed-rate and adjustable-rate mortgages aren't the only games in town? Here's a look at some of the other types of available mortgages:

➤ **Hybrid mortgage.** As the name implies, this type of mortgage is a mixture of fixed-rate and adjustable-rate models. There's a two-step mortgage, for instance, that adjusts either up or down, one time. The adjustment is made at either five or seven years, and that's it. After that, the interest rate remains the same for the rest of the mortgage period. The rate can jump no more than six percentage points, but there's no limit on how much lower that rate can be.

Pocket Change

While researching mortgages, you're likely to hear the terms **Fannie Mae** and **Freddie Mac**. These aren't mortgage lenders from Arkansas; they're publicly chartered corporations that buy mortgage loans from lenders. This ensures that mortgage money is available at all times, everywhere across the country.

➤ **Balloon mortgage.** Another type of hybrid mortgage is a balloon mortgage. With this type of mortgage, you make payments with lower-than-normal interest rates for a while, and then you're expected to pay off the principal balance of the loan all at once! You normally have between 3 and 10 years before your lump-sum payment is due. This type of mortgage isn't a good idea unless you're absolutely sure you'll have money available to pay off the balance. If you default on the mortgage the lender could take your house. Balloon payments are often seen with owner financing to help people purchase a home who wouldn't easily obtain a mortgage, or on investment property. Homeowners use them when rates are high, hoping they'll be able to lock in a lower rate when the balloon is due.

➤ **Jumbo mortgage.** This type of mortgage doesn't apply to the great majority of us. A jumbo mortgage, as the name implies, is one that exceeds the limits set by Fannie Mae and Freddie Mac. The 1998 limit was $227,150. You can see why a mortgage bigger than that would be called jumbo! Jumbo mortgages usually have higher interest rates than smaller mortgages.

➤ **Assumable mortgage.** This is when the buyer of a home takes over the mortgage from the seller. It can be advantageous if the owner got the mortgage at a terrific interest rate, and the rates have increased significantly. An assumable mortgage might make the house easier to sell, which would help out a seller who was having trouble unloading a house. If an assumable mortgage is available, carefully review the mortgage with your attorney to verify exactly what you have assumed.

➤ **Seller financing.** The seller of the home provides financing to the buyer, and the buyer pays back the seller instead of a mortgage lender. Again, the legal implications of this type of financing should be checked out thoroughly by both the buyer (for example, can the seller ask for repayment of the full mortgage on demand) and the seller.

➤ **Biweekly mortgage.** We'll get into more detail about this kind of mortgage in our next chapter, so for now we'll just tell you that the monthly payment is split into two, and you pay half of it every two weeks. This shortens the length of the loan dramatically. We'll tell you how in the next chapter.

As you can see, there's a lot to think about when choosing a type of mortgage. Try to get as much information as you can, and then make an intelligent, informed decision. But wait! There are other things to consider before choosing one.

Thirty-Year Versus Fifteen-Year Mortgages

Mortgages can be paid back over varying amounts of time, depending on the terms you agree on. The two most common payment periods are 30 years and 15 years. A 30-year mortgage has the advantage of lower monthly payments, because your loan is spread out over a longer period of time. However, you end up paying thousands of dollars more in interest on a longer-term mortgage.

With a 15-year mortgage, you have a higher payment each month, but you can usually get an interest rate that's one-quarter to one-half of a percent lower than on a 30-year mortgage. Paying off the loan at a lower interest rate and in half the time results in big savings, as the following chart shows:

Total Interest Paid over Life of Mortgage

7% Loan	
15-year Mortgage Loan	$46,350
30-year Mortgage Loan	$104,632
9% Loan	
20-year Mortgage Loan	$86,951
30-year Mortgage Loan	$142,249

As you can see, your interest savings are tremendous. Something to be considered though is how paying off a mortgage affects your taxes. The interest you pay on your mortgage is 100 percent tax-deductible, which reduces your after-tax cost. With a 30-year mortgage, more of your monthly payment is for interest, and you have a larger deduction than with a 15-year mortgage.

Some people choose 30-year mortgages even though they could afford the higher monthly payments of a 15-year mortgage, because they'd rather take the difference and invest it. They figure that in a good market, it pays off to invest rather than shorten the length of your loan and decrease your interest.

So what will it be? A 30-year fixed-rate mortgage? A 15-year adjustable? Before you decide, there's one more thing to consider: points.

Points

We've told you that points are fees (or actually prepaid interest) that amount to one percent of your loan. The tricky thing is that lenders charge different numbers of points on different mortgages. Usually, the lower the interest rate is, the more points you'll be charged and vice versa. If you want to lower your monthly payment, you probably will pay more points to do so.

Because points are prepaid interest, the more interest you pay initially means you pay less throughout the term of the mortgage via a lower interest rate. An example of this is a 6.7% mortgage with 3 points: If you don't want to pay the points, you can obtain a 7.45% mortgage, with no points. You pay the interest one way or the other. Which scenario is best for you depends on how much cash you have available to pay points. Ask your lender how the points affect your total loan interest payment, and then decide what is best for you.

You can either pay the points up front, at settlement, or you can finance them as part of your loan. For instance, if your mortgage is for $100,000, each point is worth $1,000. If your lender charges you 3 points, and you finance them, you'd have to increase your mortgage to $103,000—or, pay no points but pay a higher interest rate. Sound confusing? Just remember to compare the total interest to be repaid. This is the bottom line for you. When you choose a mortgage, you usually can lock in your interest rate by paying a commitment fee equal to 1 point at the time of application.

Alternative Types of Mortgages

There are some government programs available to help people who don't have a lot of money for down payments and closing costs. Most, although not all, of these programs are aimed at first-time buyers. These programs are intended to provide affordable housing for middle- or low-income families, who may not qualify for other types of mortgages. There are several of these programs available.

Federal Housing Administration Loans

The name of this type of loan is confusing, because the Federal Housing Administration (FHA) doesn't actually lend the money. Private lenders make the loans, and the government guarantees them and pays off the loans in full if the borrower defaults.

Typically, a buyer can't get as large a mortgage if it's administered by the FHA as he could otherwise, but an FHA loan requires a low down payment and offers a lower interest rate than a standard mortgage. FHA mortgages can be for 15, 20, 25, or 30 years.

Veteran's Administration Loans

Available to those who have served or are currently serving in the U.S. military, Veteran's Administration (VA) loans also are guaranteed by the U.S. government. VA loans, which usually carry lower interest rates than other mortgages, require no down payment and are available both as fixed-rate or adjustable-rate mortgages. The fixed-rate mortgages can be for either a 15- or 30-year term, and the adjustable-rate mortgage is for 30 years.

Community Home Buyer's Program

This program is offered in partnership with Fannie Mae, a publicly chartered corporation that buys mortgage loans from lenders. The Community Home Buyer's Program (CHBP) requires only a 5% down payment, and 2% of that can be a gift from family or friends. Money that's considered a gift doesn't show up on a credit report, and doesn't count as debt that you owe. People seeking CHBP loans are required to attend educational programs regarding personal finances and issues regarding home ownership.

Fannie Neighbors

Also in partnership with Fannie Mae, a Fannie Neighbors loan requires that the property being purchased is located in an area designated for low- to middle-income housing. Fannie Neighbors loans, which are fixed-rate loans, require lower down payments than conventional mortgages, and less cash for closing costs.

While these types of loans come with restrictions concerning the amount of income a borrower may have, the geographic area in which the borrower want to buy a home, the length of the loan, and so forth, they are good alternatives for people who don't qualify for standard mortgages.

Where to Go to Get Your Mortgage

Once you decide what kind of mortgage you want, and the length of your loan, you'll need to find a lender. Mortgages, like most products, vary in cost, making it necessary to shop around to find the best value. Getting a mortgage that carries an interest rate of just half a percent less than another rate will save you thousands of dollars over the life of your loan.

Lots of places offer mortgages. Although the number and variety means there's lots of competition—and that competition often results in lower rates for you—it can make finding the right lender a bit of a chore. But you can do it.

You can get an idea of the mortgages available by checking out your Sunday newspaper's real estate section. It should include rates from various banks and other types of lenders. If your paper doesn't list mortgage rates, just get the paper from any good-sized town. Don't assume, though, that the rates listed are the only ones available or the best ones.

Large banks are able to advertise their rates, but that doesn't mean they're the best ones around. Check out the smaller banks in your area, too. They might have lower rates than the big boys. And don't forget about mortgage bankers, who do only mortgages. Stay away from slick salesmen, who fast-talk you into thinking their deals are the best, when they're not even close.

Some people prefer to get their mortgage with a local company or bank. This is fine, as long as you don't end up paying higher rates. There's an advantage of using a local company when it comes to making payments because you can hand-deliver them and know that they're credited to you for that very day. If you have to send your payment 3,000 miles across the country, you have no control over when your payment is credited for, and that can subject you to late fees.

Dollars and Sense

The Internet has some cool sites that make it easy to get the lowest up-to-date interest rates. Here are a few to get you started:

Mortgage Rates in Your State at **www.interest.com/rates**

LoanWeb at **www.loanweb.com**

HSH Associates at **www.hsh.com**

Lenders also charge other fees, charged up front and supplemental to the mortgage amount, in addition to the actual mortgage, so be sure you find out what they are and how much they add up to. Fees for things like appraisals, copies of your credit report, and loan applications and processing can add up to thousands of dollars that you'll need to pay up front. Consider that information when choosing your lender.

If you think you can't get the best mortgage on your own, you can hire a mortgage broker to do it for you. You have to pay for his services, but if you just don't have time to shop around, or you feel intimidated by it all, it might be worth your while to have a broker. If you apply for a mortgage and are turned down, then you should call a broker. It's his job to match you with a lender, and if he's worth his salt, he'll do just that.

Getting Your Mortgage Approved Faster

After you've located a lender and decided on the type of mortgage you want, you have to fill out an application and then wait patiently while the lender takes his good old time deciding whether to approve your loan. You'll probably meet with a mortgage officer, who will help you with the application.

To speed up the mortgage process, take the following items to your appointment. Having this information ready will save time and speed up your application:

➤ Your W-2 forms from the previous year.

➤ Documents showing two years of residence and employment history.

➤ A current paycheck to prove your salary.

➤ Your employer's name, address, and telephone number.

➤ Any financial statements for your personal assets, and proof of income if you are self-employed.

➤ Tax returns from the last three years.

➤ Lists of all your assets, including loans and deposit account numbers. Also, take the last monthly statement available on each account.

Hopefully, you've followed our advice from earlier chapters and reduced your credit card and other debt before applying for a mortgage. You also should have checked your credit report. Looking at your credit report before a mortgage lender does can eliminate any nasty surprises the report might contain that you don't know about. Credit reports are notorious for containing mistakes, or it could be something that happened, but that you've forgotten about.

If you suspect you're on shaky ground for getting your mortgage approved, try to come up with some more money for a down payment. This will greatly improve your chances and will make your mortgage payments less, as well.

What Happens at Settlement?

After your mortgage has been approved, you've found the house of your dreams, and the seller has agreed to the sale, you're in business. The only thing standing between you and moving into your new dream house is settlement. But what is this mysterious thing, and what goes on there?

Settlement is the final closing of the sale of your home. It's when the bank (the lender) pays the seller your mortgage funds. You'll drink coffee, sign about a million papers, wait around while people make copies, and then sign some more papers. In addition to taking up your time, settlement will cost you money. Costs for things such as a one-percent transfer tax, notarization fees, a check to make sure your taxes are paid, a check to see whether your house is in a flood plain, and a fee to prepare the deed will be tallied up and presented to you during settlement.

The number of complaints from homeowners who say they were slapped with fees at settlement that they were never told about is on the increase. When you make an offer on a house, the real estate agent is obligated to give you a good-faith estimate of the money you'll need at settlement. Be sure you ask, and ask your real estate agent to be as specific about what fees to expect as possible. Try to enjoy

Dollars and Sense

Most lenders will give you a copy of your credit report if you ask. They'll probably charge you for the copy, but they'll do it. You can get a free copy of your credit report from TRW, one of the large credit agencies. Call TRW at 800-682-7654.

Show Me the Money

The final closing on your house purchase is called a **settlement**.

Money Pit

Beware of hidden fees that can affect your settlement. Tacking on extra fees at settlement has become so common that federal housing and finance officials are pressing for legislation to stop them. The Federal Reserve Board of Governors and the Department of Housing and Urban Development presented a joint report to Congress in July 1998, urging reforms in this area.

your settlement. Unless there are special circumstances, your house will be yours to move into immediately afterwards. Settlement, which takes about an hour, might be the last chance you'll have to sit down for a while!

The Least You Need to Know

➤ A mortgage is a loan for the cost of the house, minus your down payment.

➤ There are various types of mortgages, but the two most popular are the fixed-rate and adjustable-rate mortgages.

➤ Most people get mortgages that they agree to pay back over 15 or 30 years.

➤ It pays to shop around when looking for a mortgage lender because rates can vary greatly.

➤ You can improve your chances of getting your mortgage approved and speed up the process by doing some simple preparations.

➤ You should be aware of settlement costs and on the lookout for any extra fees.

Chapter 23

Paying It Off, Little by Little

In This Chapter

➤ Understanding the benefits and drawbacks of paying off your mortgage early

➤ Where your mortgage money goes

➤ Missing a payment or two

➤ The importance of private mortgage insurance (PMI)

➤ Putting money in an escrow account

You're in your new house and loving every minute of it. Well, maybe not every minute. The fire in your oven on Thanksgiving Day was something you'd like to forget about, as was that night the pipes froze and burst. Then there was that major fight the two of you had while you were painting the living room and the can of paint that tipped over onto the rug. Not to mention the time he decided to weed the garden and pulled out every last marigold you'd planted a few days before.

Yeah, there have been a few rough spots, but having your own house sure beats renting that apartment with the faucet that continued to drip, regardless of how many times you called the super in to fix it. Even paying the mortgage doesn't seem so bad because you know you're paying for something of value.

Even though it seems as though the newest mortgage bill is in the mailbox the day after you paid the last one, you've been doing fine with the payments. It's been no problem keeping up with them. In fact, you're thinking you might like to speed things along a little bit and make an extra payment or two. You also heard somebody at work talking about a biweekly mortgage payment. They were raving about it, saying it reduces your total mortgage payment. You've been wondering whether it might be a good idea to convert your mortgage to a biweekly.

This chapter examines the issues related to paying mortgages. You'll learn about making extra payments on your mortgage and exactly what parts of your mortgage your payments are applied to throughout the life of your loan. We'll also see what happens if, for some reason, you can't make a mortgage payment or are late with a payment. We'll also have a look at the pros and cons of escrow accounts.

How Quickly Should You Pay Your Mortgage?

Mortgage payment periods vary. Some people pay off their debt over 15 years; others take 30 years. There's no right way or wrong way to pay a mortgage; you just have to decide what makes the most sense for you.

Pocket Change

The two most common mortgages are 15-year and 30-year mortgages. Less common, but still out there, are 20-year or 25-year mortgages.

One thing that most financial experts agree on though is that, if you can, paying off your mortgage early makes sense. If you make extra payments, you'll reduce what you'll pay over the life of the loan and increase the *equity* in your home all that much sooner. Not everyone agrees, mind you. Some experts would tell you it's better to take the extra money, find yourself a good investment with potential for big returns, and go for it. That's the way to go, they say, especially if you'll get a tax break, as with a retirement account. Decide what is right for you, invest or prepay. Calculate the total return of both scenarios, and then, *do it!*

If you do decide you want to pay extra on the mortgage, there are several ways you can do it. You can pay a little bit extra every month, or you can make periodic lump sum payments. Most financial experts agree that if you're going to prepay your mortgage, it's better to do it sooner, rather than later. For instance, instead of making a lump-sum payment once a year, make smaller monthly payments. Why? Because the sooner you pay off your mortgage, the more interest you save, and the more equity you have.

Show Me the Money

Equity is the net value of your house. It's the market value, less the balance of your mortgage. If your house is valued at $100,000, and you have an $80,000 mortgage, you have equity of $20,000 in your home.

Home equity is important for several reasons. It's *collateral* you can use for a car or other loan. If you ever want to get a home equity line of credit, this line will be based on the amount of *equity* you've built up in your home. The equity in your home also serves to give you a larger down payment if you decide to move up to a larger home.

If you save the extra money every month and pay it in a lump sum at the end of the year, you won't cut your interest as much because you're not lowering your mortgage as quickly. If you make a lump-sum payment every five years, you'd have even less impact. That's not to say that if you can't pay extra every month, you shouldn't pay. It's just that the sooner you pay, the more you'll save.

When you first get your mortgage, the lender will give you an *amortization schedule*. The schedule will show the amount of your mortgage month by month based on regular payments, with no prepayments. If you pay exactly what is required each month, you'll stay on the schedule. You pay interest on your mortgage, which is calculated each month on the remaining balance of the loan. Every time you pay extra on your principal, you're reducing the amount of your loan and the amount of interest you'll have to pay.

Once you start paying off your mortgage, you'll make the payments according to the amortization schedule your lender will provide. The following is an example of an amortization schedule:

Show Me the Money

Collateral is the assets pledged as security for a loan. It's something that the lender holds as assurance of payment.

Amortization Schedule

Mortgage Amount	Interest Rate	Monthly Payment	
$63,812.99	7.875%	$607.01	

Payment Number	Interest Payment	Principal Payment	Principal Balance
2	$418.77	$188.24	$63,624.75
3	417.54	189.47	63,435.28
4	416.29	190.72	63,244.56
5	415.04	191.97	63,052.59
6	412.51	194.50	62,859.36
7	412.51	194.50	62,664.86
50	349.34	257.67	52,975.29
51	347.65	259.36	52,715.93
52	345.95	261.06	52,454.87
53	344.24	262.77	52,192.10
54	342.51	264.50	51,927.60
96	258.88	348.13	39,100.90

continues

continued

Payment Number	Interest Payment	Principal Payment	Principal Balance
97	256.60	350.41	38,750.49
98	254.30	352.71	38,397.78
99	251.99	355.02	38,042.76
100	249.66	357.35	27,685.41
143	133.59	473.42	19,882.40
144	130.48	476.53	19,405.87
145	127.35	479.66	18,926.21
146	124.20	482.81	18,443.40
147	121.03	485.98	17,957.42
177	15.67	591.34	1,796.64
178	11.79	595.22	1,201.42
179	7.88	599.13	602.29
180	3.95	602.29	

Extra payments on your mortgage don't have to be regular, and they don't have to be for the same amount each time. If you have some extra money at the end of the month, add it to your mortgage payment. It doesn't have to be anything formal or planned in advance. But you do need to make sure the lender realizes that the extra money is a prepayment on your principal, not extra money to be put into an escrow account for taxes (more on escrow later in this chapter).

Show Me the Money

An **amortization schedule** is the schedule of repayments you're required to make to your lender over a specified period of time.

How Much Extra Do I Have to Pay?

You don't have to pay a great deal extra to make a difference in paying off your mortgage. Adding just $25 a month to a $100,000, 30-year, fixed-rate mortgage at 8 percent will save you $23,337 in interest before taxes over the life of the loan. If you can swing $100 extra a month, you'll save $62,456.

You can see that it makes sense to pay extra. So how can you do it? Review Chapter 10 for tips on saving money, and tack the savings onto your mortgage payment. You can easily spend $25 a week on extras. If you cut down and apply the saved money to your mortgage, you'd see a big difference in the long run.

Here are a few suggestions for making extra mortgage payments:

➤ Use your bonus. If you get a year-end bonus, turn it into an extra payment on your mortgage. It's money that you wouldn't have had anyway, so, theoretically, you won't miss it. Be sure to include a note designating the extra money as "partial prepayment of mortgage."

➤ Save your change. Get everybody in the house to throw their change into a jar or bowl. At the end of each month, get it to the bank and write a check for the amount you saved.

➤ Designate one day of the week as mortgage day. Make a sandwich to take with you to work, then put the money you would have used to buy lunch that day in a jar. Write a check at the end of the month for the amount that you saved. If there are two of you in the house, you'll double your savings if you both participate. If you can't give up a lunch, sacrifice a cup of coffee or your afternoon soda and pack of crackers from the vending machine.

➤ Enjoy your new house by eating at home instead of going to a restaurant. You can apply the money you save to an extra payment and spend a relaxing evening in the house that you worked so hard to get.

➤ Round your mortgage payment up to the next $25. For example, if your monthly payment is $783, shell out an extra $17 and pay $800 every month. If you pay $912 per month, make a payment of $925. It's not a lot of extra money, but you'll be surprised at how it eats into your principal.

Dollars and Sense

When you make prepayments, enclose a note with your mortgage payment asking the lending company to apply the extra money to your mortgage principal. Many places aren't set up for prepayments, and don't know what to do with the money if you don't specify. Remember to include a note each time you make an extra payment.

Money Pit

Some mortgages include prepayment penalties that could force you to pay 2 or 3 percent of your total loan if you pay it off early. Be sure to ask whether your mortgage includes this. It's something that might just slip by and could end up costing you thousands of dollars.

What About Biweekly Payments?

Ask about biweekly mortgages, and you're practically guaranteed to start an argument or two. Some people swear by them, saying it's the only way you can be assured of getting ahead on your mortgage. Others say they're a just a scam by lending companies to generate extra fees.

Nearly all biweekly mortgages are set up through banks, savings and loans, or credit unions. That's because these types of institutions have access to your accounts and can make automatic withdrawals from them. Mortgage companies normally can't make these withdrawals, so they're unable to offer biweekly mortgages.

Pocket Change

For some people, the primary benefit of a biweekly mortgage is that it's deducted automatically, saving them the task of sending the payment to the lender. Another benefit is having to accumulate smaller payments per month instead of one large payment.

Let's have a look at how biweekly mortgages work. Instead of paying 12 large monthly installments each year, you pay half of your monthly payment every 14 days. It's not as painful as it sounds because the money is deducted automatically from your checking or savings account. Because you pay every 14 days, you end up making 26 payments a year instead of 24.

By making biweekly payments, you can pay off a 30-year mortgage in a little less than 23 years and a 15-year mortgage in less than 14 years. That's the good stuff on biweekly mortgages. The downside is that not all lenders offer this option, so if you're sold on it, it could limit from whom you can get your mortgage.

The following table shows the savings in interest paid and when the mortgage term is decreased. It sure is interesting to see how paying extra cuts down the interest paid over the term of the loan.

Biweekly vs. Standard Mortgage Payment Comparison

$100,000 loan @ 6%

Term	Mortgage Payment	Interest Paid	Interest Saved	Shortened by
15 year (180 months)	$843.86	$51,895		
15 year biweekly	$421.93	$45,144	$6,751	1.33 years
30 year (360 months)	$599.55	$115,838		
30 year biweekly	$299.78	$91,260	$24,578	6.83 years

Critics of the biweekly mortgage say it's of little benefit to the consumer, but of great benefit to the lender. There's often a fee to switch your payment plan over to the biweekly system, and it can be quite hefty. A fee between $250 and $400 is not unusual. There also can be a transaction fee of $3 or $4 for every payment you make, in addition to the one-time charge.

Critics say these fees are rip-offs, pure and simple. They blast the lending institutions for charging customers the extra fees, even though the lender saves money from automating data entry and not having to send you monthly envelopes. You should be able to find financial institutions that provide biweekly mortgages but don't charge a fee. High fees defeat the purpose of prepaying your mortgage, so just say no to lenders who charge them.

Be wary of critics of the biweekly payment plans. Is the information they provide conflicted by their not being able to offer biweekly plans? Comparison shop at several financial institutions before you choose the payment format that is best for you.

Critics also say that telling people that paying biweekly reduces the interest payments over the loan is confusing. It makes consumers believe they're getting a better interest rate on their mortgage, when the interest rate doesn't change. In the end, they say, you'll do just as well by making one extra payment a year on your own, without the benefit of the bank's biweekly mortgage plan.

That sounds good, but we all have a lot of places we could spend our money. What happens if it's time to make your extra payment, but you've just surprised your wife with plane tickets to Italy to celebrate your fifth wedding anniversary? If you don't think you have the discipline to put aside the extra money for the payment, it probably makes more sense for you to add some extra money to your payment each month.

Money Pit

Multiply a $4 transaction fee by 26 payments, and you'll find you're paying $104 a year for the privilege of having a biweekly payment. If you save that money instead of spending it on fees, you could apply it to your mortgage!

Put Your Money Where Your Mortgage Is

Your mortgage payment has four main components:

1. Principal, which is the amount you borrow from the lending institution

2. Interest, which is the fee you pay the lender to borrow money

3. Tax, which is the money you pay to your city or county, based on the value of your property

4. Insurance, which is the amount you pay for homeowner's insurance (which is required by most lenders)

Tax and insurance costs may or may not be included in your mortgage bill, depending on your lender. Be sure you know ahead of time if those expenses are figured into your mortgage or if you'll need to pay for them on your own. If these costs are part of your mortgage payment, they're held in an escrow account (for more info on escrow accounts, read the section "Putting Money in an Escrow Account").

During the first year of a typical 30-year mortgage, you pay more than 10 times more in interest than you do on the principal of your loan. It can be frustrating to think about. You faithfully make your mortgage payments, month after month after month. You think you're making great progress, and then you discover that after paying for several years, you've barely dented the principal.

Although the bulk of your mortgage payment is applied to interest during the first few years, eventually your payments kick in and start reducing your principal. Less and less of each payment goes toward the interest, and you start to build up equity (value) in your home. By the time you get about two-thirds through your mortgage payments, about the same amount will be going to principal and interest. The amount of principal you're paying will increase each month until your mortgage is paid off.

This is why it gets increasingly difficult to make extra payments on your mortgage. It's easy to throw in a couple extra months of principal payments when you first start paying off the mortgage, because you're hardly paying anything toward the principal. But as your principal payments get higher, it gets increasingly difficult to come up with the money for extra payments. So, rather than make an entire payment, pay what you can. Every little bit helps.

By the time you've made your mortgage payment for 30 years, it's likely that you will have paid double the cost of your original loan. Pretty amazing, isn't it? It's good to know where your mortgage payment goes, but don't dwell on it. There's no point in making yourself crazy.

What If I Can't Make a Payment?

Gasp! The mortgage payment is due, and you don't have the money to pay it! Will the bank take your house? Put you in jail? Send big, nasty-looking creditors over to beat it out of you? Harass you with sarcastic phone calls? What will you do?

Relax. Probably none of these things will happen. Okay, you might get a phone call, but you won't lose your house for being late or missing one payment. Granted, missing a mortgage payment is serious business, and it's not at all good for your credit rating, but it's not the end of the world.

If you know you can't make this month's payment, call the lender. It looks better for you to take action, instead of waiting around until the lender calls you. Your lender will know that you're concerned about repayment and are on top of the situation.

Tell the lender why you can't make the payment: You lost your job, your son's medical bills are outrageous, or whatever the reason is. Just tell the truth. Then work together to come up with a reasonable plan to begin paying again. Make whatever payment you can to show that you're acting in good faith. It's important that you be up-front with your lender. Don't say you'll be able to catch up on your payments the following month if you're not going to be able to. If you've had a financial catastrophe or you've just gotten in over your head, make sure you tell the lender what's going on.

Be honest with yourself, too. Will the situation get better, or will you eventually need to sell your house? These are all things that will have to be considered as you work with the lender. Remember that honesty's the best policy.

Late Penalties

If you're payment is late, you'll probably be hit with a penalty. The amount of the penalty is set up by the mortgage company or bank and is zapped on you whether your payment is one day late or 30. If paying late gets to be a habit, you can be sure it will show up on your credit report, which is not a good thing! Late fees are considered a deduction for income tax purposes, but that's not enough reason to pay them. Do everything you can to pay your mortgage bill on time.

A potential problem with making your mortgage payment is one of postal service. You might think you mailed your payment in plenty of time for it to get that post office box in Georgia by the due date. The problem is that you're at the mercy of the U.S. Postal Service, as well as the mortgage company's payment processing speed.

We have no problem with the postal service, but, as they say, stuff happens. Your payment could be held up for a day or two along the way, and guess what? You're late! Or somebody at the mortgage company may decide to take a half-day's vacation to go shopping, leaving your payment sitting on her desk, unprocessed. If you're close to the payment due date for your mortgage, and your check isn't in the mail, send the payment by overnight, two-day, or priority mail. It will cost extra, but not as much as a late penalty.

Money Pit

Another down side to being late with your mortgage payment is that it makes the next payment seem like it's due within days of the previous one. If you're two weeks late with your August payment, that September bill is going to be coming in before you know it.

If the lender charges you a late fee in error, call the lender immediately. Tell the lender when you mailed the check. Often, the lender will refund the fee, but don't ask too often. A once-sympathetic lender can turn nasty when pressed too hard.

Mortgage Insurance

Your lender didn't just fall off of the cabbage truck. Lending companies are well aware that people miss mortgage payments. There have been many, many instances in which people have gotten a payment or two behind and stop paying at all. They *default* on their mortgages.

That's why you'll hear from your lender if you miss just one payment. People who have been in the lending business for any amount of time know that once you fall behind on your payments, it's easy for a snowball effect to begin. When that happens, a little problem easily becomes a big problem.

Because many people do default on their mortgages, lenders have to protect themselves with something called private mortgage insurance. Purchasing *private mortgage insurance* (PMI) protects the lender against any default on the loan. It usually is required by the lender if you have less than 20 percent of the cost of the home for a down payment. PMI charges normally amount to about one-half of one percent of the loan.

So, if you put down 10% on a $100,000 house, your mortgage will be for $90,000. The lender multiplies the amount of the mortgage by 0.05% and come us with $450. That's the annual cost of your PMI, which breaks down to $37.50 a month.

If you do default on your mortgage, look out. It takes years for your credit rating to recover from something like that. Go ahead, default on your mortgage, and then just try getting a car loan. You'd better pump up the old bike tires.

Your lender will cash in on the private mortgage insurance policy you've been paying for, along with the rest of your mortgage payment, and be on his merry way. You, meanwhile, will have lost your home and ruined your credit. In case you didn't know, if you don't pay your mortgage, you are forced to sell your home. The bank doesn't let you stay in it just because you put that pretty wallpaper in the bedroom.

If you are forced to sell the home, and it's sold for less than the remaining mortgage owed to the lender, your mortgage insurance will cover the difference. You will lose your down payment, though. You are responsible for all fees incurred by the lender concerning paying off the mortgage. If the home is sold for more than

Show Me the Money

To **default** on your mortgage is to not repay the debt as agreed to in the terms of the mortgage. It is a failure to live up to the agreement.

Show Me the Money

Private mortgage insurance (PMI) is insurance that protects the lender against a default on his loan.

what is due the lender, you get the difference back. Hopefully, the amount you get back will be more than you put down on the house originally.

Most people who can't make their mortgage payments try to sell their homes themselves, rather than foreclosing and/or going through a sheriff's sale. There are hefty fees for *foreclosures*, which are when lenders take back properties that have been defaulted, and most people are pretty mortified to have their names listed among those with properties up for public auction at a *sheriff's sale*. If you see trouble down the road with keeping up with your mortgage payment, make a plan.

Putting Money in an Escrow Account

Most lenders, but not all, require you to put money into an *escrow account* to cover taxes and insurance if you owe more than 80 percent of the value of your home. That means, if you don't have at least a 20 percent down payment and your lender requires an escrow account, you'll have no choice in this matter. Some lending institutions require that you have an escrow account regardless of how much you have for a down payment.

When you reach the point where you've paid at least 20 percent of the value of the home, you can decide whether to continue paying the tax and insurance money and having it go into escrow or to pay the taxes yourself. Many people prefer to have that money put into escrow, knowing it will be available when the tax or insurance bill comes due. It's a comfort to a lot of people to not have to worry about putting money aside for those bills. Others, though, want to keep control of their money and use it any way they want until the payments are due.

Dollars and Sense

Keep track of your payments on the principal of your mortgage. When you reach 80 percent equity, which means you've paid for 20 percent of the cost of your home, notify your lender. In most cases, you'll no longer be required to carry PMI. Tax changes in 1998 now require the PMI to automatically be dropped when your mortgage amount drops to 78 percent (or your equity is 22%) of the original price of the house or the original appraisal, whichever is lower. Once your mortgage is paid off, you may qualify to get some of your PMI payments back. Contact the U.S. Department of Housing and Urban Development at 202-708-1422 for more information.

Show Me the Money

A **foreclosure** is legal action by the lender to take back the property on which the loan has been defaulted. The lender can resell it privately, or offer it for public auction at a sheriff's sale. A **sheriff's sale** is for the purpose of recouping debts on the property—or it can also be done for delinquent taxes or water bills, even if the mortgage is up to date.

Show Me the Money

An **escrow account** is an account set up for a particular purpose. The money put into an escrow account is to be used only for the designated purpose, such as paying for insurance or taxes.

Pocket Change

If you go the escrow route and forego the interest you could make on your money, just consider it a service charge you have to pay the bank for keeping track of your payments.

Rather than paying your homeowner's insurance and your taxes in one or two payments a year, your expected annual payments are anticipated and paid in $1/12$ the increments each month. It's nice—your payments are there when the bills are due. When you escrow, you, as the homeowner, are responsible to send your tax bills to the lender for payment. Your homeowner's insurance company should bill the lender directly; however, it is wise to verify that the payment has been made.

If you feel strongly about not having to put money in an escrow account, you can hunt around until you find a lender that doesn't require it. Or you can start with an escrow account, and then pay your own insurance and taxes after you've got more than 20 percent of the cost of your home paid off. Remember that you'll have to request that the escrow account be closed and that you pay the bills on your own. The lender doesn't have to notify you when you've reached the 20 percent mark.

Shock occurs the first time you receive notification that your mortgage payment is increasing. How come? You have a fixed rate mortgage, right? Well, your mortgage didn't increase, the escrow payment did. Either the homeowner's insurance or the real estate taxes increased, thus the lender needs more from you each month to cover the cost. Escrow accounts should be reviewed by the lender annually, so you don't get too far behind with the funds in your account.

The Least You Need to Know

➤ If you decide you want to repay your mortgage ahead of schedule, there are several ways you can do it.

➤ Biweekly mortgages are highly regarded by some and scoffed at by others.

➤ Your initial mortgage payments go almost entirely toward paying interest, but eventually they shift over to paying the principal.

➤ Being late or missing a mortgage payment is likely to result in a penalty, and it can damage your credit rating.

➤ Many lenders require you put money in an escrow account to pay for insurance and taxes on your home.

How Owning a Home Affects Your Taxes

In This Chapter

➤ Understanding how owning a home can reduce your taxes

➤ Knowing what deductions you can claim

➤ Weighing the tax advantages and disadvantages

Owning your own home, or at least *living* in the home that you one day will own (15 or 30 years from now), gives you a lot of advantages. It also carries with it some inherent disadvantages.

Advantages of having your own home include things such as home equity and the freedom to paint the dining room walls fuchsia if you so choose. You get a sense of pride that can come from being a homeowner and even better, you get some really good tax breaks.

Disadvantages include things such as the certainty that repair and replacement of parts will be necessary. The wood around the windows rots, and the contractor discovers that water has been seeping into your walls. Paint peels, and brick walls buckle. Ants crawl in and over your kitchen counters, and lightning strikes a tree in the backyard. There are also some pretty hefty taxes you'll have to pay now that you're a homeowner.

If you noticed that the common theme among the advantages and disadvantages was taxes, consider yourself astute. Owning a house gives you significant tax advantages, but it also means you have to pay property taxes, which can be quite high. To make things a little more confusing, although you have to pay property taxes, you can deduct the full amount. Being able to deduct the taxes isn't as good as not having to pay them in the first place, but it sure makes it a little easier to bear.

Pocket Change

If you refinance your mortgage, the points you pay can be deducted from your taxes over the life of the loan, but you don't get a one-time deduction for the entire expense.

Tax Benefits of Owning a Home

When you buy a house, Uncle Sam gives you a little housewarming gift (he's real generous with the gifts, isn't he?). You get to deduct two of the biggest owning-a-home expenses from your federal income tax:

1. The interest on your mortgage

2. Your property taxes

There are other, one-time deductions, such as the points you pay at closing, but interest and property taxes are the biggies.

These deductions are great news for homeowners. When paying the mortgage bill every month starts to seem like more than you can bear, remember that, come April, you'll be happily filling out Schedule A, which is a part of your federal income tax return (see Chapter 14). If you itemize deductions, the interest and taxes paid on your loan lowers your tax liability.

Deductions, Deductions

If you remember from Chapter 14, tax deductions can be itemized and subtracted from your adjusted gross income (commonly known as AGI), if they're greater than the standard deduction allowed by Uncle Sam. The deductions and personal exemptions are subtracted from your income before you figure out how much tax you have to pay on it. If your total income is $45,000, but you have $7,500 in deductions and two exemptions (totaling $8,500), you'll pay tax on only $29,000.

When you become a homeowner, you get the privilege of taking some pretty hefty deductions. If you haven't itemized your deductions before buying the house, make sure you find out all the deductions you're entitled to before you pay this year's taxes. Mortgage interest and property taxes are both expensive, and they can take quite a large chunk out of your income when you total them up for tax purposes. That's good news for your wallet on April 15th. If you haven't compared your itemized deductions to your standard deduction before buying the house, make sure you do it before you pay this year's taxes.

Take a look at lines 10-14 on the Schedule A on the next page. This will give you an idea of where the deductions are used. Also, if line 28 is greater than your standard deduction, you'll save money at tax time.

SCHEDULES A&B	**Schedule A—Itemized Deductions**	OMB No. 1545-0074
(Form 1040)	(Schedule B is on back)	19**98**
Department of the Treasury Internal Revenue Service (99)	➤ **Attach to Form 1040.** ➤ **See Instructions for Schedules A and B (Form 1040).**	Attachment Sequence No. **07**

Name(s) shown on Form 1040   Your social security number

Medical and Dental Expenses		**Caution:** *Do not include expenses reimbursed or paid by others.*		
	1	Medical and dental expenses (see page A-1)	**1**	
	2	Enter amount from Form 1040, line 34 . ⎣ **2** ⎦		
	3	Multiply line 2 above by 7.5% (.075)	**3**	
	4	Subtract line 3 from line 1. If line 3 is more than line 1, enter -0-		**4**
Taxes You Paid (See page A-2.)	5	State and local income taxes	**5**	
	6	Real estate taxes (see page A-2)	**6**	
	7	Personal property taxes	**7**	
	8	Other taxes. List type and amount ➤	**8**	
	9	Add lines 5 through 8		**9**
Interest You Paid (See page A-2.) **Note:** Personal interest is not deductible.	10	Home mortgage interest and points reported to you on Form 1098	**10**	
	11	Home mortgage interest not reported to you on Form 1098. If paid to the person from whom you bought the home, see page A-3 and show that person's name, identifying no., and address ➤	**11**	
	12	Points not reported to you on Form 1098. See page A-3 for special rules	**12**	
	13	Investment interest. Attach Form 4952 if required. (See page A-3.)	**13**	
	14	Add lines 10 through 13		**14**
Gifts to Charity If you made a gift and got a benefit for it, see page A-3.	15	Gifts by cash or check. If you made any gift of $250 or more, see page A-3	**15**	
	16	Other than by cash or check. If any gift of $250 or more, see page A-3. You **MUST** attach Form 8283 if over $500	**16**	
	17	Carryover from prior year	**17**	
	18	Add lines 15 through 17		**18**
Casualty and Theft Losses	19	Casualty or theft loss(es). Attach Form 4684. (See page A-4.)		**19**
Job Expenses and Most Other Miscellaneous Deductions (See page A-5 for expenses to deduct here.)	20	Unreimbursed employee expenses–job travel, union dues, job education, etc. You **MUST** attach Form 2106 or 2106-EZ if required. (See page A-4.) ➤	**20**	
	21	Tax preparation fees	**21**	
	22	Other expenses–investment, safe deposit box, etc. List type and amount ➤	**22**	
	23	Add lines 20 through 22	**23**	
	24	Enter amount from Form 1040, line 34 . ⎣ **24** ⎦		
	25	Multiply line 24 above by 2% (.02)	**25**	
	26	Subtract line 25 from line 23. If line 25 is more than line 23, enter -0-		**26**
Other Miscellaneous Deductions	27	Other–from list on page A-5. List type and amount ➤		**27**
Total Itemized Deductions	28	Is Form 1040, line 34, over $124,500 (over $62,250 if married filing separately)? **NO.** Your deduction is not limited. Add the amounts in the far right column for lines 4 through 27. Also, enter on Form 1040, line 36, the **larger** of this amount or your standard deduction. **YES.** Your deduction may be limited. See page A-5 for the amount to enter. ⎫⎬⎭ ➤		**28**

For Paperwork Reduction Act Notice, see Form 1040 instructions.   Cat. No. 11330X   Schedule A (Form 1040) 1998

Interest and taxes are the biggest mortgage-related deductions, but there are others. You also can deduct the points you pay at settlement, but you can only get this deduction in the year that you first get the mortgage.

Dollars and Sense

To get a quick idea of how much you'll save on taxes as a home-owner, add up the amounts of your property taxes and your mortgage interest if you itemize, and multiply that amount by your marginal federal tax rate. It's not an exact formula, but it will give you a good idea of the savings you can expect.

As you learned in Chapter 22, points are a fee (really prepaid interest) that the lender often charges at the time you get your mortgage. You can be charged one, two, or even three points, which are calculated by taking one percent of the loan. Three points on a $100,000 loan is $3,000, and that can hurt.

Points usually are the responsibility of the buyer, but a seller that really wants to sell can sometimes be convinced to assume responsibility for paying for some, or all, of the cost of the points. If you can convince the seller to pay the points, you win in two ways. One, you don't have to pay the points. Two, you can still deduct them from your income tax. If you and the seller split the points, you still get to deduct the total amount.

Be aware that, if you buy a home late in the year, you won't see too much tax advantage the first year. People often buy homes in September or October and are convinced they'll get great tax breaks when it comes time to file. But remember that the standard deduction for a married couple filing jointly is $7,100. You can't itemize things such as your mortgage interest and property taxes until your deductions add up to more than the standard deduction. So if you buy your home in October, you might not have enough time to build up deductions that will total more than $7,100.

If you don't take the deduction for points the same year you buy the house, you lose that deduction. So if your itemized deductions didn't reach more than $7,100, you'd get no tax advantage from the points, and the government gets you again.

Show Me the Money

Capital expenses are those currently non-deductible expenses that can be deducted against your profit. This is considered part of the cost basis of your house, and it's used to lower any capital gain liability when you sell your house at a profit.

To take full advantage of the deductions offered to homeowners, plan ahead and buy your house early in the year. This way, you'll be assured of getting the tax advantages you're entitled to. An additional way to increase your mortgage interest deduction is to pay your January bill in December. This extra payment can help increase your tax deduction.

Consider this: It's February. You've just borrowed $100,000 with three points. You pay $500 a month in interest for the rest of the year, plus the points. Your interest payments for the year would total $5,000, and your points payment would be $3,000. You're over the standard deduction, and you can itemize. But if you bought the house in November, you wouldn't have enough interest payments to bring your total over $7,100, and your potential tax savings would be lost. This isn't to say that if you see the house of your dreams for sale in October, you shouldn't buy it because you won't get the tax advantage that year. Deductions are only a byproduct of owning a home.

In addition to deducting mortgage interest and points, you can deduct some of the property taxes and other expenses that are finalized at settlement. Some of the expenses you pay at settlement can be deducted from your income tax, and some of the other expenses are considered *capital expenses* when you sell your home. Capital expenses are expenses used toward the "basis" of your property which are considered part of the cost.

Let's have a look at the following tax deduction chart. The chart displays the different rates and standard deductions permitted if you don't itemize your deductions.

1998 Tax Guide

Income Tax–1998 Income Tax Rates
(For Returns Due in April 1999)

Single Taxpayer Rates

Over	But Not Over	Flat Amount	+%	Of Excess Over
0	$25,350	0	15%	0
$25,350	$61,400	$3,803	28%	$25,350
$61,400	$128,100	$13,897	31%	$61,400
$128,100	$278,450	$34,574	36%	$128,100
$278,450	—	$88,700	39.6%	$278,450

Married Filing Jointly Rates & Surviving Spouse

Over	But Not Over	Flat Amount	+%	Of Excess Over
0	$42,350	0	15%	0
$42,350	$102,300	$6,353	28%	$42,350
$102,300	$155,950	$23,139	31%	$102,300
$155,950	$278,450	$39,770	36%	$155,950
$278,450	—	$83,870	39.6%	$278,450

Head of Household Rates

Over	But Not Over	Flat Amount	+%	Of Excess Over
0	$33,950	0	15%	0
$33,950	$87,700	$5,093	28%	$33,950
$87,700	$142,000	$20,143	31%	$85,350
$142,000	$278,450	$36,976	36%	$142,000
$278,450	—	$86,098	39.6%	$278,450

Married Filing Separately Rates

Over	But Not Over	Flat Amount	+%	Of Excess Over
0	$21,175	0	15%	0
$21,175	$51,150	$3,176	28%	$21,175
$51,150	$77,975	$11,569	31%	$51,150
$77,975	$139,225	$19,885	36%	$77,975
$139,225	—	$41,935	39.6%	$139,225

1998 Standard Deduction Amounts

	1998 Standard Deduction
Single	$4,250
Married, filing jointly	$7,100
Married, filing separately	$3,550
Head of household	$6,250
Surviving Spouse	$7,100

1998 Phaseout of Personal Exemption
Personal Exemption in 1998–$2,700

Filing Status	Threshold Phaseout Amount	Completed Phaseout After
Single	$124,500	$247,000
Married, filing jointly	$186,800	$309,300
Married, filing separately	$93,400	$154,650
Head of household	$155,650	$278,150

Show Me the Money

Capital gains are the profits for the sale of an investment or asset. Tax on this gain is usually due the year the asset is sold.

Pocket Change

The 1997 Taxpayer Relief Act was great news to persons under age 55 who wanted to sell their homes and buy smaller ones. Before this act, people who owned their homes for many years often had to pay high capital gains taxes at sale time.

Show Me the Money

A **capital gains exclusion** is an exclusion to the practice of taxing capital gains. It applies to those who sell their homes who are within parameters set by the government: up to a $500,000 sum if married, $250,000 if single.

Capital Gains Exclusion

You've just moved into your house, so this section on capital gains might be a little premature. This information will be helpful someday, though. A capital gain occurs when you sell your home at a profit. Say you bought it for $100,000, keep it for a while, and then sell it for $200,000. You've made a $100,000 profit or capital gain. Most profits, such as those on many investments, are taxed for capital gains purposes. A portion of the capital gains from selling your home, however, is not.

Capital gains used to be bad news for taxpayers, who saw a big bite taken out of the money they made on the sale of a house. Fortunately, the Taxpayer Relief Act of 1997 made big changes in the capital gains taxes you pay on the sale of your house. The 1997 law says you can take a $500,000 exclusion on your income tax if you're married and filing jointly or a $250,000 exclusion if you're single.

Before the 1977 changes to the tax law, you were required to move up to a bigger or more expensive home or pay capital gains on a portion of your profit until you reached age 55. The only way to avoid capital gains taxes was to keep your house until you turned 55, even if your kids had left and you no longer needed, or wanted, a big home.

You can file for the *capital gains exclusion* every two years at any age, as long as you've used the property as your principal residence for at least two of the last five years. If you only own your house for one year, you can take a partial (50 percent) exemption. If you have to move because of unexpected or uncontrollable reasons, such as a job transfer or health reasons, you get to take the total exemption. It won't be pro-rated, even if you haven't lived in the house for two years.

Don't rush out and sell your house now that we told you about the $500,000 exemption. It sounds like a huge amount to be sure, but you'd be surprised at how quickly costs add up. Always save any receipts associated with fixing up or improving your house.

This is smart in case you need them for an insurance claim. Saving the receipts also gives you a record of capital improvements for the calculation of any gain for your state income tax return. Note that although the IRS allows a $500,000 exclusion for capital gains on a house sale, your state's allowable exclusion may be considerably less.

You Wanna Play House? You Gotta Pay Taxes

As we mentioned in the beginning of the chapter, it's not all good news concerning taxes and owning a home. There's this pesky thing known as *property tax*, and it can be a real strain on the old pocketbook.

It varies, but your property taxes usually run about one and a half percent of the value of your property. Because paying property taxes can be prohibitive, many lenders require that home-owners pay money into escrow accounts to cover the cost of the taxes when they come due. See Chapter 23 for more information about escrow.

In most areas, you pay local property taxes (also known as your school tax), county taxes, and sometimes some oddball municipal taxes, too. A municipality is a zoned area, such as a city or township, that has an incorporated government. Taxes can vary, depending on the quirks, wishes, and wealth of the municipal boards that impose them. The majority of property tax you'll pay will go toward funding your local school district. A portion goes to the borough or township in which you live, and some goes to your county. You normally pay your taxes to a local tax collector, who distributes them to the proper places.

You can be assessed for your taxes once a year, twice a year, or even more often. Property taxes have gotten so high in some areas that officials are allowing residents to pay their taxes quarterly in order to relieve the burden of huge lump sums.

Pocket Change

The principal residence capital gains exclusion was especially good news for taxpayers, who had long complained about paying the tax or waiting until they were 55 to sell their homes. After all, no allowances were made (and still aren't) on tax returns for capital losses when selling a home. So if you made money on the sale of your home, you were expected to pay taxes. If you lost money—tough break, buddy.

Show Me the Money

Property taxes are taxes levied by the municipality and/or school district within which you live. They're based on the value of your property.

Pocket Change

Many municipalities and school districts are trying to save money by collecting their own taxes, rather than paying a tax collector to do it.

The really annoying thing about property taxes is that the municipality imposing them can raise them by reassessing your home. Every now and then, municipal governments rampage and declare a major property reassessment. When that happens, look out. The municipality, at this point, has probably reached its upper allowable tax limit and is looking for a way to make more revenue. If it can't up your tax rate, it can reassess your home.

If you think the assessment on your home is too high, you can challenge it. You'll need to know the assessments of the other homes in your neighborhood, and your appeal might be denied. But if your property taxes seem out of line with those that others in your neighborhood are paying, it might be worth a fight. If you get an appeal, make sure you're prepared. Know the number of rooms in your house and how your home compares to others with lower assessments.

Obviously, there are expenses other than taxes involved with owning a home, and you can expect to pay various taxes in addition to your property tax. You might be charged additional taxes for street lights, water hydrants, trash collection, sewage, water, and the like. Unfortunately, these taxes are not tax-deductible.

This means you have to be careful when breaking down your expenses for your tax return. The bank might pay $1,000 to your municipality for your taxes, but only $850 of the $1,000 is deductible on your taxes. It's a good idea to keep copies of all your tax bills to use at income tax time.

Home Equity Loans and Lines of Credit

Again, this information might be a little premature because you haven't been in your house very long. But there's another neat tax advantage that comes with home owner-ship, and it's called a *home equity loan*. If you get one of these handy little (or big) loans, you're allowed to write off 100 percent of the interest charges up to $100,000.

You've probably seen the ads for home equity loans. They normally show a tanned and fit couple frolicking on the beach during their dream vacation or an all-American-looking family smiling in front of their gorgeous new van. Sometimes they show a blushing bride-to-be wearing an engagement ring with a diamond the size of a Volkswagen or a kid grinning ear to ear as he opens the best Christmas present of his life.

Show Me the Money

A home equity loan is a loan that's taken against the equity you've built up on your home.

Home equity loans and home equity lines of credit can be very convenient. In fact, they can be lifesavers if you have unexpected expenses or expenses you just can't cover. These types of loans are taken, as the name implies, against the equity you've built up in your home. Your equity is used as collateral on the loan. Always remember, though, that there's a big risk associated with home equity loans. If you default on the loan, you lose your home.

There are several types of home equity loans. The first type is a line of credit. This means you're given approval from the lender to borrow up to a specified amount of money against the equity in your home. You don't get the money in a lump sum, but it's there for you to borrow, if you need it. This kind of loan can be extremely useful in the event of an emergency or unexpected expense. You don't have to pay interest on the money until you use it, so if you don't use it, it costs you nothing. The interest rate on this type of loan is variable—that is, it fluctuates with the current interest rates.

The other kind of home equity loan is a fixed-rate loan. Your equity is calculated, and you borrow money against it. You repay the loan on a fixed schedule at a fixed rate of interest. You can always pay more on the loan than is required, but don't not pay the full required amount. This is a loan, not a line of credit.

There usually aren't as many fees associated with a line of credit as with a mortgage, but be assured, there are some. You'll probably have to pay a mortgage application fee, an appraisal fee, a fee for a credit report, and possibly processing fees. You won't have to pay points, however. If you're in line for a home equity loan, go to the first meeting prepared as you would be if you were applying for a mortgage (see Chapter 22). The application and processing time will be shortened considerably if you're well-prepared.

Home equity loans make sense in many cases. For instance, if you want to borrow $20,000 for a new Honda, you can take a car loan. Back in the good old days (before the tax law revamping in 1986), you could have even deducted your car loan. Not now. If you get a home equity loan, however, and use it to pay for the car, you can deduct the interest and save yourself some money. But we can't stress how important it is to understand the risks of home equity loans.

Especially with a home equity line of credit, use caution. It's like having a huge credit card to use whenever you want. The problem is, if you don't control the spending, it's your house that's on the line. Can you imagine having to go home and tell your spouse you're going to lose the house because you didn't know when to stop dipping into the line of credit? You'd be sleeping on the couch forever!

Money Pit

Lenders have been getting fee happy lately when it comes to home equity loans. If your lender tries to tell you that you have to pay points, however, tell him to take a hike, and go elsewhere.

Weighing the Tax Advantages Against the Disadvantages

Hopefully, you're not too discouraged about the taxes you have to pay as a home-owner. Try to concentrate, instead, on the tax advantages. At least the big-ticket items are tax-deductible. Consider that when you were renting, you were still paying taxes.

Your landlord, nice guy that he was, wasn't picking up all the slack for property taxes. Those taxes were reflected in your rent costs, but you couldn't deduct any of it. At least when you own a home, you have some leverage when April 15 rolls around.

Remember that owning a home is not all about taxes. It's not even all about money, although there sure is a lot of that involved. If your home is just a business venture, you're missing out on a lot of what a home can and should be.

The Least You Need to Know

➤ One of the advantages of owning a home is the deductions you get to claim on your federal taxes.

➤ The interest on your mortgage and your property taxes are often two of your biggest deductions.

➤ Property taxes can be prohibitive, but it's possible to challenge the amount you're paying.

➤ You can use home equity loans to your tax advantage, but be careful with them. The stakes are high.

➤ Generally speaking, it's a good idea to own a home, not only for tax purposes, but for less-tangible reasons, such as comfort, security, and pride.

Chapter 25

Homeowner's Insurance

In This Chapter

➤ Yes, you really do need homeowner's insurance

➤ Insuring your home

➤ Insuring your stuff

➤ Covering damage to other people and their property

➤ Protecting yourself against natural disasters

➤ Shopping around for a homeowner's policy

Did you ever wake up in the middle night, and, unable to go back to sleep, stare at the ceiling and start thinking about the strangest things? Some people claim that they're struck with inspired ideas in those wee hours. It's our opinion, however, that lying awake at night with your head filled with thoughts usually leads to nothing but trouble.

Those nocturnal thoughts usually don't start out to be too bad. Maybe you think about something that happened during the previous day or something that's coming up the next afternoon. You roll those thoughts around for a while, and then, before you know it, those little ghosts start whispering. They keep pestering you, getting louder and louder, and pretty soon your head is filled with thoughts of fires, terrible storms, accidents, and other catastrophes.

The harder you try to get rid of them, the more firmly entrenched these thoughts become. At that point, the best thing to do is to get up, find your insurance policies, and read over them to make sure they're up-to-date and have all the coverage you need. Then, you say a prayer, drink your chamomile tea, and try to go back to sleep.

If you believe in conspiracy theories, you might think that insurance salespeople somehow get these thoughts to infiltrate your slumber. They want you to look at those policies and come to the conclusion that you're terribly underinsured, call them up the next day, and double all your coverages. Those who aren't into conspiracies might blame it on stress, too much work, or the Chinese takeout they had for dinner. No matter what triggers the thoughts that wreck your rest, you can feel a little more secure if you know you have insurance to protect yourself, your loved ones, and your property against at least most of the terrible things that might possibly happen.

Getting and maintaining good insurance policies that will protect your home and its contents takes some planning and follow-through, but the peace of mind it will provide is well worth the trouble. We discussed homeowner's insurance briefly in Chapter 15, but if you own a home, homeowner's insurance is too important to just skim over. In this chapter, we'll have a look at how much insurance you need and the types of coverage you should have. Then we'll figure out some of the best places to buy insurance. First, let's look at why homeowner's insurance is so important.

Nobody Should Be Without Homeowner's Insurance

Your home is probably the biggest investment you'll ever make, and unlike a mutual fund, it involves much more than your money. Your home is where you live, and it's a part of who you are. It's where you should feel safe and able to escape from the world. It's the place that holds the people and things that are most important to you and where you can put aside pretenses and impressions and just be yourself.

If your mutual fund takes a nose-dive, you lose money. If your house burns down, however, you lose much, much more. To protect your home, you buy *homeowner's insurance*. But how much should you have? What kind? What should you do about deductibles? Exactly what will it cover?

Those are some of the questions we'll look at in this chapter. But, first, let's get one thing straight. People sometimes ask whether homeowner's insurance is necessary. The answer to that question is a firm and resounding "yes!" For one thing, most lenders make you get insurance before they'll give you a mortgage, but that's not the best reason to have it.

The best reason to have it is that if your house burned to the ground, destroying everything in it, you'd have no recourse to get anything back unless you have insurance. So unless you're willing to walk out of your house with only the clothes you're wearing, close the door behind you, and never go back, get out your policy and make sure your insurance is sufficient.

Briefly, most insurance companies offer six basic types of homeowner's policies. They're known in the industry as HO-1 through HO-6, and they cover a variety of different *perils* or potential dangers. Some of the perils covered under the six basic policies are fire, damage caused by falling objects, an explosion in your heater or air conditioner, riots, vandalism, and hurricanes. (For a list of the 11 basic perils, see Chapter 15.) There are also expanded versions of these policies, such as HO-3000, and they're all based on various coverages that different people need.

The perils covered under any of the six policies might vary from insurer to insurer and state to state. For instance, in Pennsylvania, damage to your home from wind is covered under your normal policy. But in Texas, which is considered a high-risk tornado area, wind damage is not covered under the normal policy; you need additional coverage.

In addition, not all insurers offer every type of policy. That's why it's so important to know exactly what your policy covers and doesn't cover. Be sure to ask your agent to explain the entire policy, and don't be afraid to ask questions.

Show Me the Money

Homeowner's insurance covers your home and its contents against perils. **Perils** are the insurance industry's word for every bad thing that could possibly happen. Homeowner's insurance includes **personal property coverage** for the contents of your home and **liability insurance** for damage you do to other people and other people's property.

How Much Homeowner's Insurance Do You Need?

Homeowner's insurance is designed to repair or replace your primary residence if it's somehow damaged or destroyed. Coverage usually is based on the sale price of the home when purchased, but remember that the sale price includes the value of the land. If you've got an old farmhouse on a gorgeous piece of property with a creek running through it and a view of the horse farm across the valley, the price of your property might have been based as much on the value of the land as on your home. If that's the case, you might not need homeowner's insurance that's as high as the sale price of your home. If your entire property is valued at, say, $175,000, but your house is valued only at $85,000, you don't need homeowner's insurance based on the entire value.

The part of your homeowner's insurance that covers your house (the structure, that is) is called *dwelling coverage*. Dwelling coverage isn't based on how much you paid for your house or how much money you borrowed to buy it. It's based on how much it would cost you to rebuild your house if it were completely destroyed.

The cost to rebuild is normally based on the square footage of your home, the type of home you have, and when it was built. If you have an older home with lots of details, such as a wooden staircase, stained glass above the doors, or ornate plaster work, your insurer is likely to tell you that sort of detail could not be matched if your house had to be replaced. You can expect to pay more for your homeowner's insurance if you have a lot of "extras" in your home, such as garbage disposals, ceiling fans, spas, French doors, fireplaces, and so forth.

Show Me the Money

The part of your homeowner's insurance that covers the structure in which you live is called **dwelling coverage**. If that structure is damaged, and your policy has a **guaranteed replacement cost provision**, the insurance company will pay for the rebuilding, even if it ends up costing more than your limits.

Money Pit

We can't stress enough how important it is for you to closely examine your insurance policies and know exactly what coverages you have and don't have. It can be financially devastating to assume you're covered for something, only to find out after a catastrophe that you're not.

Look for a Guaranteed Replacement Provision

If your home costs more to rebuild than the limits of your insurance policy, what will you do? Pay the extra yourself, or leave your home unfinished? Some insurance policies pay off your mortgage if your home is destroyed, but don't pay to rebuild the home. Or they'll pay you the amount of your policy coverage, but not the replacement amount for your home. Guess you could always pitch a tent on that lot you own.

If you have a *guaranteed replacement provision*, you won't have to pay for construction, leave your home unfinished, or pitch that tent; the insurance company will pay for the rebuilding, even if it ends up costing more than your limits. Most insurers will give you a certain amount more than your policy's limit. For example, if it costs $150,000 to rebuild your home, and your policy limit is $100,000, your insurer might give you 25 percent over your limit. That means you'd get an extra $25,000, but you'd still be $25,000 short of the actual construction costs.

To make sure that your replacement cost provision will truly cover the full replacement cost, you must have the amount of insurance that you need. If your home is valued at $100,000, and your policy's limit is $50,000, you're underinsured. What you want in your coverage is a policy that guarantees the cost of construction, regardless of whether it costs $100,000, $150,000, or $200,000.

As if the replacement cost provision isn't already complicated enough, another thing to think about is inflation. If inflation, which relates to the increase in value of your house, rises 3 percent a year for 10 years, you'll have a 30 percent increase on the value of your home. This is great news if you're planning to sell, but it can be dangerous as far as your insurance is concerned. While the value of your home is increasing, your insurance is losing ground. All of a sudden, you don't have enough coverage because your home has gotten more expensive.

To solve this problem, insurance companies offer *inflation riders*, additions to your policy that keep your coverage on par with the value of your home. The downside of this handy-dandy rider, though, is that (big surprise) it increases the cost of your coverage. If the value of your home should happen to decrease, you'll be paying for more coverage than you need. If you are attentive to your insurance, you can buy an inflation rider only when you need it because the value of your home is increasing.

Show Me the Money

A **rider** on an insurance policy is extra coverage added to your basic policy. An **inflation rider** is a rider specifically designated to cover increased costs due to inflation (increased cost of living).

There's a lot to think about regarding replacement cost provisions, but they're definitely worth paying extra for. You should have a replacement cost provision to cover your personal property, as well. Be aware, however, that the definition of guaranteed replacement cost varies from insurer to insurer. Be sure to clarify your guaranteed replacement cost coverage with your insurer.

Personal Property Coverage

It's amazing how much stuff we accumulate. Walk around your house some time and take a good look at everything in it. Chances are your rooms are filled with chairs and tables, sofas, lamps, television sets, computers, stereo systems, and cabinets. Then there's the important stuff like your photographs, stamp collection, guitar, family jewelry, and your great-grandmother's diaries from the beginning of the century.

You can't be certain that nothing will ever happen to these things. If it does, know that some of them will be irreplaceable. Remember though, as hard as it is to lose things you care about, that they're still only things. If there is a fire or other catastrophe, consider yourself very lucky if you and your family manage to escape unharmed.

Some things you will be able to replace. You can go out and buy furniture, clothing, kitchenware, and most of the other things you use every day. What you need to make sure of is that your insurance policy will adequately cover the cost of these things.

Dollars and Sense

Cleaning out some of your stuff and donating it to a charity such as Goodwill Industries can be beneficial in several ways. It will help when tax time comes around (charitable contributions are tax-deductible if you itemize deductions), it will reduce the total value of your property and make your insurance cost less, and it will relieve some clutter in your home. So which closet will you clean out first?

The best kind of personal property coverage includes *replacement cost guarantees*, which means you'll be reimbursed for what it costs to replace the damaged, stolen, or destroyed items at today's prices. Without replacement cost guarantees, your insurance company will give you about half of what you paid five years ago for that sofa you liked so much. You won't be able to begin to get anything comparable. If you do have the replacement cost guarantee, your insurer will pay you today's price for the sofa, and you'll be able to go out and find one that's similar to what you had, only newer.

The amount of personal property coverage insurance companies provide is usually based on the amount of your dwelling coverage. Your personal property should be insured for 50 percent to 75 percent of your dwelling coverage. The premium for replacement cost insurance increases the cost of your personal property insurance by about 13 percent a year, but it's worth it.

Show Me the Money

The best kind of personal property coverage includes **replacement cost guarantees**, which means you'll be reimbursed for the covered items at today's prices.

Exactly What Should You Insure?

You should insure all the property you would need to replace if it were destroyed or stolen. Your furniture, dishes, electronic equipment, washer and dryer, and all the other things in your home that you need should be covered by insurance.

Be aware that some policies limit your coverage for certain items if they are damaged or stolen. You may have to purchase special riders to cover these things. The list varies from insurer to insurer, but some items to ask about include the following:

➤ Computers and other electronic equipment

➤ Silverware

➤ Firearms

➤ Jewelry

➤ Coin collections, gold, or silver

Pocket Change

Most insurance companies require that you replace the item that's been damaged or stolen. Your insurer won't hand over a check for $400 for you to buy a new TV, for instance, and let you use the money instead to upgrade your computer. You have to come up with some proof (a sales receipt) that you did, indeed, purchase a TV.

Make Sure You Know What You Have

We're going to ask you to do something that might make you uncomfortable. No, you don't have to recite any silly chants or anything like that. We simply want you to think about something: If your house burned down today while you were at work, and it, and everything in it, was completely destroyed, how would you prove to your insurance company what you lost? Would you even be able to identify everything that you lost?

What about that silver tray you got for a wedding gift and just haven't had the opportunity to use? Or that antique brooch your aunt gave you when you graduated from college that's been sitting in your dresser drawer? Or the VCR that you stashed in the downstairs closet because you and your husband each had one in your apartments when you were single, and you just didn't need it after you got married and moved in together? Would it even occur to you to inform the insurance company of these things, or would you think about them six months down the road, long after your claim had been completed and settled?

What you need to do is document the property that you have. The best way to do it is to take photographs or videotapes of your stuff, write a brief description of each thing, and estimate each thing's value. You also should keep receipts for major purchases. Sounds like a lot of work, doesn't it? Most people will never do this because they think it's too much trouble. But if you need to file a claim to recover the value of personal property, you'll be very, very glad that you made the effort to document your possessions.

You don't need to document every single item in your home. The wine bottle you've been using as a candle holder isn't worth a mention, nor is the consumable stuff such as food. But be sure think about things that may be little-used, but valuable. They're easy to overlook.

Keep in mind that personal property insurance doesn't cover only items that are inside your house. It also covers property in your possession that might be damaged or stolen while you're traveling and the stereo in your daughter's college dorm room.

Dollars and Sense

After you've inventoried and documented your personal property, be sure you store the documentation somewhere out of your home or in a secure, fire-proof box or safe. It will do you no good to go to all the trouble of documenting your possessions if the documentation is destroyed along with your property.

Liability Insurance

The other big part of homeowner's insurance protects you from liability (that means lawsuits) for accidental damage. This coverage applies in the event that the following occurs:

➤ Someone is injured in your house or on your property

➤ Someone is injured by you or a family member, anywhere

➤ Someone else's property is damaged or destroyed by you or a member of your family

➤ Someone claims you've slandered them

How much liability coverage should you have? That's a tricky question. You should have at least enough to cover your financial assets; it's preferable to have enough to cover them twice. If you have all kinds of cash, you might have to purchase an umbrella liability policy or personal catastrophic policy to cover your many assets. These types of policies give you additional liability insurance, which is added to the coverage you already have. They're usually sold in one million dollar increments, which might sound excessive. Remember, though, many people are sued for more than that. If you have a swimming pool, a pit bull, one of those big trampolines that are the cause of so many accidents, or anything else that could cause trouble above and beyond the norm, you probably should carry extra liability coverage. Personal umbrella coverage is available at very reasonable prices, and if you're sued, you'll be glad that you have it. Some umbrella (PCAT—personal catastrophic casualty) policies will not provide extra coverage for automobile accidents. Find a company that does. If you feel you need an umbrella policy, you'll certainly need the coverage if you are sued in a car accident.

Pocket Change

Liability insurance covers only unintentional incidents. Intentional incidents are more likely to get you to the police station than to your insurance company.

Money Pit

Insurers say that there's always a big jump in applicants for flood or earthquake insurance after a flood or earthquake has hit an area. Typically, though, many homeowners will cancel their policies or not renew them if another disaster doesn't occur in the following few years. Once you have the insurance, you should do yourself a favor and keep up the policy!

Insuring Against Natural Disasters

You can't pick up a newspaper or turn on the news without reading about one natural disaster or another, yet we never think it will happen to us. We know that floods, tornadoes, and earthquakes occur all the time, but we still don't believe they'll happen to us. That's why many people, even those who live in areas that are prone to certain types of natural disasters, don't bother to insure themselves against them.

A typical homeowner's policy will protect you from damage caused by fire or rioting, but it won't help you out if your home is flooded or your foundation cracks during an earthquake. You have to buy extra coverage for those things if you live in an area considered to be at high risk for them.

We Don't Have Earthquakes Here!

We live in the Reading/Lancaster area of Pennsylvania, and we didn't think we ever had earthquakes either until one Sunday afternoon in the mid-1980s when the newsroom of the Reading Eagle/Times shook and rumbled. Even the cynical, nothing-surprises-me news staff was impressed to silence. We knew immediately that it was an earthquake, even though none of us had ever felt one before.

There was some minor property damage from that quake, and there have been a couple more since then. The point being: Don't be too sure you won't feel the ground shaking some day wherever it is you're living. Earthquakes and floods are not considered (thank goodness) standard perils, so they're not covered by a standard policy. If you live in an area prone to floods, earthquakes, hurricanes, or other natural disasters, check to see exactly what coverage you have and talk to your agent about what you may need to get.

Flood insurance is available through the National Flood Insurance Program for communities that have adopted and enforced flood plain management ordinances. This federally subsidized program is administered by the Federal Insurance Administration, which is part of the Federal Emergency Management Agency. You can call the National Flood Insurance Program at 800-638-6620.

Many homeowners in Florida had a rude, collective awakening in 1992 when Hurricane Andrew slammed into the coast of that state, flooding and otherwise damaging or destroying 135,000 homes. It turned out that some homeowners had coverage through their insurance companies that predated guaranteed replacement cost. After the hurricane had come and gone, they found out their policies left them in a huge lurch and unable to rebuild their homes.

Pocket Change

If you don't live in a flood plain, you can't buy flood insurance.

Dollars and Sense

If you live in a flood plain, but your community hasn't adopted a flood plain management ordinance, lobby your local officials to do so. You can't be eligible for federally subsidized flood insurance if they don't.

The Government Will Take Care of Us

Uncle Sam is getting tired of bailing out (no pun intended) people who live in flood plains but don't have flood insurance. There are moves underway to get more people to buy flood insurance, so the government won't have to keep putting out federal relief funds. You can't always count on federal funds in the event of a flood or other natural disaster, though. Less than 50 percent of flood sites are declared federal disaster areas, a designation necessary in order for them to be eligible for federal funds.

Even if you can get federal disaster relief funds, most of them are low-interest loans, not giveaways. Flood insurance program people say the interest you'd have to pay back on your federal loans would cost more than the approximately $300 yearly fee for

Pocket Change

During the terrible flooding along the Mississippi River in 1994, the federal government shelled out $6 billion in disaster relief funds. That comes out to about $24 for every person in the country!

flood insurance. And, they note, if you receive federal funds, you have to buy flood insurance afterwards to be eligible for any more funding. To be sure, $300 (or whatever) is a lot of money, but a flood can effectively wipe out your home and everything you own along with it.

As much as we like to think we can control our environment, every now and then Mother Nature shows us she's still the boss. If you're not sure what your coverages are, check with your insurance company as soon as possible. You never know when an unexpected earthquake is going to rumble through your area.

The Best Places to Buy Homeowner's Insurance

Shop around when you're looking for homeowner's insurance because coverages and costs vary for different properties. Find a good agent who will be able to tell you exactly what coverage you need for your circumstances and will help you with claims. These companies have good reputations for claims handling and customer service:

➤ Prudential

➤ GEICO

➤ Nationwide Mutual

➤ Allstate

➤ Erie Insurance

➤ Liberty Mutual

You can call a local agent who sells these brands, or you can find the company's 800 number in the phone book and call for information.

Don't forget to ask if you qualify for any special discounts. Insurers look kindly on your extra protective measures, such as home security systems, dead-bolt locks, fire extinguishers, and smoke detectors. If you have these things, or others, you may qualify for a discount. In any event, it can't hurt to ask!

Here are some other ways you might be able to save a few bucks on your homeowner's insurance:

➤ Compare the rates of several companies. You can call the companies or ask your agent for quotes from various large companies. Just make sure the rates you're getting are for the same coverages. Don't try to compare apples and oranges (or kiwis with pineapples).

➤ Learn about how raising your deductible can lower your rate. Figure out how much you can afford to pay for a deductible in the event of a claim, and compare that amount to how much you'll save on your premium. If you can afford a $1,000 deductible, you might be able to save between 10 and 15 percent on your policy.

➤ If you buy your car insurance and homeowner's insurance from the same company, insist on a discount. If you don't get it, take your business elsewhere. Remember, there's strong competition among insurers.

➤ You might get a discount for paying annually instead of monthly or quarterly. Getting your payment all at once means less work for your insurer.

The most important thing to take from this chapter is that it is vitally important for you to be very familiar with your insurance policy. Next time you wake up at night and can't sleep for all the thoughts whirling around in your head, pull out your policy and have a good, long look. Wait until morning, though, to call your agent or company with questions.

The Least You Need to Know

➤ All homeowners need homeowner's insurance.

➤ Dwelling coverage is the insurance you have on your home.

➤ Personal property coverage is the insurance you have on the things in your home.

➤ Make sure you have guaranteed replacement cost insurance; it's worth the extra cost.

➤ Liability insurance protects you from lawsuits if something bad happens to someone while on your property or if you or a family member accidentally injures someone else.

➤ Natural disasters happen. You should be insured against them.

➤ Shop around and check out the available discounts to save money when buying homeowner's insurance.

Additional Resources

Now that you're into personal finance, here are some other books you might want to check out. The ones that contain the most information for fledgling financial wizards are listed first. The books get more complicated as you move down the list. Run on over to your favorite bookstore or hop on the Internet to order a couple of these books. Better still, go to your local library and borrow the book. Borrowing instead of buying is a great way to save money!

Everything You Need to Know About Money and Investing: A Financial Expert Answers the 1001 Most Frequently Asked Questions by Sarah Young Fisher and Carol Turkington

The Complete Idiot's Guide to Managing Your Money by Robert K. Heady and Christy Heady

The Complete Idiot's Guide to 401(k) Plans by Wayne G. Bogosian

The Complete Idiot's Guide to Making Money on Wall Street by Christy Heady

The Complete Idiot's Guide to Getting Rich by Larry Waschka

The Complete Idiot's Guide to Doing Your Income Taxes by Gail A. Perry and Paul Craig Roberts

1001 Ways to Cut Your Expenses by Jonathan P. Pond

Keys to Investing in Common Stocks (Barron's Business Keys) by Barbara Apostolou and Nicholas G. Apostolou

The Consumer Reports Money Book: How to Get It, Save It, and Spend It Wisely (3rd edition) by Janet Bamford, Jeff Blyskal, Emily Card, Aileen Jacobson, and Greg Daugherty

Building Your Nest Egg With Your 401(k): A Guide to Help You Achieve Retirement Security by Lynn Brenner

The First Book of Investing: The Absolute Beginner's Guide to Building Wealth Safely by Samuel Case

Dictionary of Finance and Investment Terms by John Downes and Jordan Elliot Goodman

The Motley Fool Investment Workbook by David Gardner and Tom Gardner

The Truth About Money: Because Money Doesn't Come with Instructions by Ric Edelman

Investing from Scratch: A Handbook for the Young Investor by James Lowell

The Wall Street Journal Guide to Understanding Personal Finance by Kenneth M. Morris and Alan M. Siegel

10 Steps to Financial Success: A Beginner's Guide to Saving and Investing by W. Patrick Naylor

The 9 Steps to Financial Freedom by Suze Orman

The Green Magazine Guide to Personal Finance: A No B.S. Book for Your Twenties and Thirties by Ken Kurson

10 Minute Guide to the Stock Market by Diane Vujovich

Making the Most of Your Money by Jane Bryant Quinn

How to Buy Stocks by Louis Engel

Beating the Paycheck to Paycheck Blues by John Ventura

The following books cover more advanced and complicated topics regarding personal finance, especially investing. Don't rule them out, though. You have a good basic understanding of personal finance, and these books may serve to greatly expand that knowledge:

Capital Ideas: The Improbable Origins of Modern Wall Street by Peter Bernstein

Bogle on Mutual Funds by John C. Bogle

Big Profits from Small Stocks: How to Grow Your Investment Portfolio by Investing in Small Cap Companies by Samuel Case

The Sophisticated Investor by Burton Crane

Buying Stocks Without a Broker by Charles B. Carlson

New Guide to Finding the Next Superstock by Frank Cappiello

Mutual Fund Superstars by William Donoghue

The Motley Fool Investment Guide: How the Fool Beats Wall Street's Wise Men and How You Can Too by David Gardner and Tom Gardner

You Have More Than You Think: The Motley Fool Guide to Investing What You Have by David Gardner and Tom Gardner

How to Retire Rich: Time-Tested Strategies to Beat the Market and Retire in Style by James O'Shaughnesy

The Mortgage Book (Consumer Report books) by John R. Dorfman

The Common Sense Mortgage by Peter G. Miller

The Banker's Secret by Marc Eisenson

Challenge Your Taxes: Homeowner's Guide to Reducing Your Property Taxes by James E. A. Lumley

The following Web sites might interest you as well. Please remember that we don't endorse these sites. The authors of the sites are responsible for their content.

American Express: http://www.americanexpress.com/401k

American Stock Exchange: http://www.amex.com

Bloomberg News: http://www.bloomberg.com/bbn/index.html

Current Budget: http://www.efmoody.com/planning/budget.html

Family Money: http://www.familymoney.com

FinanCenter: Budgeting Center: http://www.financenter.com/budget.htm

Household Budget Management: http://www.netxpress.com/users/hadap/budget.html

Internet Finance Resources: http://www.lib.Isu.edu/bus/finance/html

Investorama: http://www.investorama.com

John Hancock: http://www.jhancock.com

Meta-Site: Consumer World: http://www.consumerworld.org/pages/money.htm

Morningstar, Inc.: http://www.morningstar.net

National Association of Investors Corporation: http://www.better-investing.org

NASD Regulation: http:///www.nasdr.com

North American Securities Administrators: http://www.nasaa.org

S&P Equity Investor Service: http://www.stockinfo.standardpoor.com

Securities and Exchange Commission: http://www.sec.gov

The Motley Fool: The Fribble, A Foolish Budget, by George Runkle: http://www.fool.com/Fribble/1998/Fribble980409.htm

The Syndicate: http://www.moneypages.com/syndicate

USA Today Money: http://www.usatoday.com/money/mfront.htm

Wall Street Research Net: http://www.wsrn.com/

Yahoo! Finance: http://www.quote.yahoo.com

Your Household Budget: http://www.merrill-lynch.ml.com/investor/budgetprintform.html

The following financial publications contain all kinds of information you might find useful. Check them out at your local newsstand or access them at the Web sites listed here:

Barron's: http://www.barrons.com

Business Week Online*:* http://www.businessweek.com

The Economist: http://www.economist.com

Money Online: http://www.money.com

The New York Times: http://www.nytimes.com

Reuters News and Quotes: http://www.reuters.com/news

Wall Street Journal: http://www.wsj.com

Show Me the Money Glossary

adjusted gross income (AGI) Your gross income, less certain allowed business-related deductions. These deductions include alimony payments, contributions to a Keogh retirement plan, and, in some cases, contributions to an IRA.

adjuster An individual who inspects damage as reported on an insurance claim and determines a settlement amount for the claim.

aggressive growth fund A type of mutual fund that has a primary investment objective of seeking capital gains. It is understood that the potential for above-average returns in such an investment is countered by above-average risks.

amortization Reducing the principal of a loan by making regular payments.

amortization schedule A schedule of regular payments with which to repay a loan. The schedule indicates to the borrower the amount of each payment that is principal, that which is interest, and the remaining balance of the loan.

annual dividend A share of a company's net profits that are distributed by the company to a class of its stockholders each year. The dividend is paid in a fixed amount for each share of stock held. Although most companies make quarterly payments in cash, dividends also may be made in other forms of property, such as stock. Dividends must be approved by the company's directors before each payment is made.

annual fee The amount a cardholder pays to a credit card company for the right to hold a particular credit card.

annuity A stream of equal payments, as to a retiree, that occur at predetermined intervals (for example, monthly or annually). The payments may continue for a fixed period or for a contingent period, such as the recipient's lifetime. Annuities are most often associated with insurance companies and retirement programs.

adjustable-rate mortgage A mortgage set up with an interest rate that can change at specific intervals, as determined under the initial contract.

arbitration The hearing and determination of a dispute between parties by a third party.

asset allocation The process of determining the assignment of investment funds to broad categories of assets. For example, an individual allocates funds to bonds and equities, with the proportions based on financial objectives and risk tolerance. An investment manager may allocate clients' funds to common stocks representing various industries.

baby boomer A common term used to define individuals born between 1946 and 1964.

balanced mutual fund A mutual fund whose primary objective is to buy a combination of stocks and bonds. These middle-of-the-road funds balance their portfolios to achieve both moderate income and moderate capital growth. These funds tend to be less volatile than stocks-only funds. Balanced funds tend, on average, to be invested as 45 percent bonds and 55 percent stocks.

bear market An extended period of general price decline in the stock market as a whole.

beneficiary The person who is named to receive the proceeds from an investment vehicle, trust, or contract. A beneficiary can be an individual, a company, or an organization.

beta A mathematical measure of the risk on a portfolio or a given stock compared with rates of return on the market as a whole. A beta of less than one is less volatile than the general market. A beta above one is more volatile than the market.

blue-chip investment A high-quality investment involving a lower-than-average risk. Blue-chip investment is generally used to refer to securities of companies having a long history of sustained earnings and dividend payments.

bond A debt instrument. The issuer promises to pay the investor a specified amount of interest for a period of time and to repay the principal at maturity.

bond fund A mutual fund that invests in bonds and passes current income to its shareholders, with capital gains as a secondary objective. Some bond funds purchase long-term securities providing a relatively high current yield but varying substantially in price with changes in interest rates. Other funds choose short-term securities having lower yields but fluctuating little in value.

broker A person who earns a commission or fee for acting as an agent in making contracts or sales.

budget A schedule of income and expenses commonly broken into monthly intervals and typically covering a one-year period.

bull market An extended period of generally rising prices in the market as a whole.

capital expenses Expenses spent to improve property.

capital gain Profits from the sale of an investment or asset. Tax on this gain is usually due when the asset is sold.

capital gains exclusion An exclusion to the practice of taxing capital gains that applies to the sale of real estate.

capitalization The sum of a corporation's long-term debt, stock, and retained earnings—also called invested capital.

capitalized cost In leasing, the cost a leasing company pays for a vehicle.

cash-value life insurance In this insurance, part of the premium is used to provide death benefits, and the remainder is available to earn interest. Cash-value life insurance is a protection plan and a savings plan that charges significantly higher premiums than term insurance.

certificates of deposit (CD) A receipt for a deposit of funds in a financial institution that permits the holder to receive interest plus the deposit at maturity.

certified financial planner (CFP) A professional financial planner who has completed a series of correspondence courses and passed a 10-hour examination in subject areas such as insurance, securities, and taxes. The designation is awarded by the College for Financial Planning in Denver, Colorado.

certified public accountant An accountant who has met certain state requirements as to age, education, experience, residence, and accounting knowledge. Accountants must pass an extensive series of examinations before becoming CPAs.

chartered financial consultant (ChFC) A professional financial planner who has completed a series of 10 courses and examinations in subject areas such as economics, insurance, real estate, and tax shelters. The designation is awarded by American College of Bryn Mawr, Pennsylvania.

churning and burning To trade securities very actively in a brokerage account in order to increase brokerage commissions rather than customer profits. Brokers may be tempted to churn accounts because their income is directly related to the volume of trading undertaken by the customers. Churning is illegal and unethical.

collateral Assets pledged as security for a loan. If a borrower defaults on the terms of a loan, the collateral may be sold, with the proceeds used to satisfy any remaining obligations. High-quality collateral reduces risk to the lender and results in a lower rate of interest on the loan.

commercial bank Financial institutions, either chartered by the federal or state governments, that take deposits, loan money, and provide other services to individuals or corporations.

common stock Shares of ownership of a company; a class of capital stock that has no preference to dividends or any distribution of assets.

compound interest Interest paid on interest from previous periods in addition to principal. Essentially, compounding involves adding interest to principal and any previous interest in order to calculate interest in the next period. Compound interest may be figured daily, monthly, quarterly, semi-annually, or annually.

consumer price index (CPI) A measure of the relative cost of living compared with a base year (currently 1967). The CPI can be a misleading indicator of inflationary impact on a given person because it is constructed according to the spending patterns of an urban family of four. Used as a measure of inflation.

co-payment The amount the insured is responsible to pay at each time of service under a health insurance contract.

corporate bond A bond issued by a corporation as opposed to a bond issued by the U.S. Treasury or a municipality.

credit history The record of an individual's past events that pertain to credit previously given or applied for.

creditor A person or agency to whom money is owed under the terms of an agreement, promise, or law.

credit union A nonprofit, cooperative financial institution providing credit to its members who share a common bond. Credit unions often pay slightly higher rates of interest on passbook-type savings accounts and charge lower rates on consumer loans.

customer service representative (CSR) A front-line bank employee who opens checking and savings accounts, certificates of deposit, and so forth. They know the products their financial institutions provide.

cyclical stock Common stock of a firm whose earnings are heavily influenced by cyclical changes in general economic activity. As investors anticipate changes in profits, cyclical stocks often reach their high and low levels before the respective highs and lows in the economy.

debit card A plastic card used for purchasing goods and services or obtaining cash advances in which payment is made from existing funds in a bank account.

deductible The amount the insured must pay before an insurance company pays a claim.

deduction An expenditure permitted to be used in order to reduce an individual's income tax liability.

default Failure to live up to the terms of a contract or to meet financial obligations. Generally, the term is used to indicate the inability of a borrower to pay interest or principal on a debt when it is due.

defensive stock A stock that tends to resist general stock market declines and whose price will remain stable or even prosper when economic activity is tapering.

defined benefit plan A qualified retirement plan that specifies the benefits received rather than contributions into the plan, usually expressed as a percentage of pre-retirement compensation and number of years of service. The responsibility for the benefit is on the company, not the employee.

defined contribution plan A qualified retirement plan that specifies the annual contribution to the plan, usually expressed as a percentage of the employee's salary. Contributions can be made by the employer, the employee, or both.

disability The lack of competent power, strength, or physical or mental ability; incapability.

disability insurance Insurance intended to cover loss of income due to a disability.

discretionary expenses Expenses that are incurred for nonessentials; money spent as a person chooses.

disposition charges Expenses charged to leasee for selling the vehicle or property leased at the end of the lease.

diversification The acquisition of a group of assets in which returns on the assets are not directly related over time. Proper investment diversification, requiring a sufficient number of different assets, is intended to minimize risk associated with investing.

dividend A share of a company's net profits distributed by the company to a class of its stockholders. The dividend is paid in a fixed amount for each share of stock held. Dividends are usually fixed in preferred stock; dividends from common stock vary as the company's performance shifts.

dividend reinvestment plan (DRIP) Stockholders may automatically reinvest dividend payments in additional shares of the company's stock. Instead of receiving the normal dividend checks, participating stockholders will receive quarterly notification of shares purchased and shares held in their accounts. Dividend reinvestment is normally an inexpensive way of purchasing additional shares of stock because the fees are low or are completely absorbed by the company. In addition, some companies offer stock at a discount from the existing market price. Normally, these dividends are fully taxable even though no cash is received by the stockholder.

dollar cost averaging Investment of an equal amount of money at regular intervals, usually each month. This process results in the purchase of extra shares during market downturns and fewer shares during market upturns. Dollar cost averaging is based on the belief that the market or a particular stock will rise in price over the long term and that it is not worthwhile (or even possible) to identify intermediate highs and lows.

Dow Jones Industrial Average (DJIA) One of the measures of the stock market that includes averages for utilities, industrial, and transportation stocks, as well as the composite averages. See *index*.

down payment Funds the purchaser puts down when property is sold. Remaining funds for purchase are borrowed.

dwelling coverage The part of your homeowner's insurance that covers the structure in which you live.

dwelling insurance See *renter's insurance.*

earned income Salary, wages, and self-employment income derived as compensation for services rendered. Unearned income includes the return you receive from your investments.

emerging growth fund The common stock of a relatively young firm operating in an industry with very good growth prospects. Although this kind of stock offers unusually large returns, it is very risky because the expected growth may not occur, or the firm may be swamped by the competition.

emerging market stock The term which broadly categorizes countries in the midst of developing their financial market and financial economic infrastructures.

equity The value of your ownership in property or securities. The equity in your home is the difference between the current market value of the home and the money you still owe on the mortgage. Equities are used interchangeably with stocks.

enrolled agent A designation given by the IRS showing that a tax preparer has adequately passed required testing.

escrow The holding of assets (for example, securities, cash) by a third party, which delivers the assets to the grantee or promisee on the fulfillment of some condition. Some parts of mortgage payments are held in escrow to cover expenses like taxes and insurance.

Fannie Mae A security issued by the Federal National Mortgage Association (FNMA) that is backed by insured and conventional mortgages. Monthly returns to holders of Fannie Maes consist of interest and principal payments made by homeowners on their mortgages.

fair market value The price at which a buyer and a seller willingly consummate a trade; the prevailing price of a security or property.

Federal Home Loan Mortgage Corporation (FHLMC) A government organization established in 1970 to create a secondary market in conventional mortgages. The FHLMC purchases mortgages from federally insured financial institutions and resells them in the form of mortgage-backed, pass-through certificates. All income on securities issued by the FHLMC is subject to federal, state, and local taxation.

Federal National Mortgage Association (FNMA) A privately owned profit-seeking corporation that adds liquidity to the mortgage market by purchasing loans from lenders. It finances the purchases by issuing its own bonds or by selling mortgages it already owns to financial institutions.

finance charges Interest expenses incurred from lending or leasing.

financial advisor A professional who guides individuals to arrange and coordinate their financial affairs.

financial consultant Someone who provides an overview of financial information and options, in order for you to choose products and services from which you will benefit.

financial planner A person who counsels individuals and corporations with respect to evaluating financial status, identifying goals, and determining ways in which the goals can be met.

financial planning The process of defining and setting goals to achieve financial security.

fixed-income assets Assets that produce income, such as certificates of deposit, fixed annuities, and most bonds.

fixed-interest rate loan A loan that has a set rate throughout the period of the loan. Payments are usually set at a specified, equal payment throughout the loan.

fixed-rate mortgage A mortgage in which the annual interest charged does not vary throughout the period of the loan.

foreclosure When a lender claims a property on which the loan has been defaulted.

401(k) plan A retirement plan into which you can contribute a portion of your current salary (usually before taxes). Contributions can grow tax-deferred until they are withdrawn upon retirement.

Freddie Mac A security issued by the Federal Home Loan Mortgage Corporation that is secured by pools of conventional home mortgages. Holders of Freddie Macs receive a share of the interest and principal payments made by the homeowners.

front-end load See *load fund*.

gap insurance Insurance purchased to pay the difference between the value your auto insurance will pay if a leased vehicle is stolen or totaled and the amount required to terminate the lease.

Generation Xers (Gen Xers) The name given to the 46 million Americans between the ages of 19 and 30.

global fund A mutual fund that includes at least 25 percent foreign securities in its portfolio. The value of the fund depends on the health of foreign economies and exchange rate movements. A global fund permits an investor to diversify internationally.

Government National Mortgage Association (GNMA) A government-owned corporation that acquires, packages, and resells mortgages and mortgage purchase commitments in the form of mortgage-backed securities.

government obligations A debt that is backed by the full taxing power of the U.S. government. Direct obligations include Treasury bills, Treasury bonds, and U.S. savings bonds. These investments are generally considered to be of the very highest quality.

government securities Bonds, bills, or notes sold by the federal government to raise money.

gross income All income except as specifically exempted by the Internal Revenue Code.

group insurance Insurance offered only to members as a group, such as employees, often for only as long as they remain members of the group.

growth fund An investment company whose major objective is long-term capital growth. Growth funds offer substantial potential gains over time but vary significantly in price, depending on general economic conditions.

growth stock The stock of a firm that is expected to have above-average increases in revenues and earnings. These firms normally retain most earnings for reinvestment and therefore pay small dividends. The stocks, often selling at relatively high price-earnings ratios, are subject to wide swings in price. Object of investment is capital appreciation and long-term capital growth.

guaranteed replacement cost provision An insurance provision that promises to pay the total cost to replace property upon loss or damage.

health maintenance organization (HMO) The oldest form of managed care, an HMO is a health insurance plan that requires you to use specified providers. The plan usually has no deductibles, though it may have co-payments. These plans are strongly supportive of preventative medicine.

high-yield/junk bond A high-risk, high-yield debt security issued by corporations or municipalities that are of lower quality. Junk bonds have a greater risk of default than higher-rated bonds. These securities are most appropriate for risk-oriented investors. They usually pay a higher interest rate than higher-rated bonds.

home equity loan A loan in which property is used as collateral. Usually a second mortgage on a property.

homeowner's insurance Insurance obtained by a property owner to protect the property and contents. It also provides liability coverage for accidents that occur on the property.

hybrid funds A mutual fund that has characteristics of several types of securities. An example would be a convertible bond, which is a bond that has a conversion feature that permits the investor to convert the security into a specified number of shares of common stock of the company.

ILYA (incompletely launched young adults) The acronym for the group of 65 million people between the ages of 18 and 34 who still live with their parents.

income fund An investment company, the main objective of which is to achieve current income for its owners. Thus, it tends to select securities such as bonds, preferred stocks, and common stocks that pay relatively high current returns.

income stocks A stock with a relatively high dividend yield. The stock's issuer is typically a firm having stable earnings and dividends and operating in a mature industry. The price of an income stock is heavily influenced by changes in interest rates.

index The measurement of the current price behavior of a representative group of stocks in relation to a base value set at an earlier point in time. The best-known indexes are the Dow Jones Industrial Average and Standard & Poor's 500 index.

index fund A mutual fund that keeps a portfolio of securities designed to match the performance of the market as a whole. The market is represented by an index such as the Standard & Poor's 500. An index fund has low administrative expenses; it appeals to investors who believe it is difficult or impossible for investment managers to beat the market.

individual retirement account (IRA) A retirement savings plan in which you can contribute up to $2,000 per year. Funds can grow tax-deferred until they are withdrawn at retirement. Contributions may or may not be tax-deductible depending on income level and participation in other retirement plans.

inflation A general increase in the price level of goods and services.

inflation rider Additional insurance coverage that is purchased to provide that the underlying policy coverage increases with inflation.

initial public offering (IPO) A company's first sale of stock to the public. Securities offered in an IPO are often, but not always, those of young, small companies seeking outside equity capital and a public market for their stock. Investors purchasing stock in IPOs generally assume very large risks for the possibility of large gains.

insurance A mechanism that permits individuals to reduce risk by sharing in the losses associated with the occurrence of uncertain events.

interest The cost for the use of borrowed money.

interest-sensitive stock A stock that tends to move in the opposite direction of interest rates. Interest-sensitive stocks include nearly all preferred stocks and the common stocks of industries, such as electric utilities and savings and loans. A common stock may be interest-sensitive because its dividend is relatively fixed (as with an electric utility) or because the firm raises a large portion of its funds through borrowing (as with a savings and loan).

international fund A mutual fund that invests only outside of the country in which it is located.

investment The process of purchasing securities or property for which stability of value and level of expected returns are somewhat predictable.

investment return The return achieved on an investment, including current income and any change in value during an investor's holding period; also known as total return.

itemized deductions An expenditure permitted to be used to reduce an individual's income-tax liability.

Keogh A federally approved retirement program that permits self-employed people to set money aside for savings up to $30,000 (or up to 25 percent of their income). All contributions and income earned by the account are tax-deferred until withdrawals are made during retirement.

large cap stock Stocks in companies with over $10 billion in capitalization—the largest companies.

lease A contract under which someone obtains the use of an object, such as a vehicle or property for a specified time, and for a specified amount of money.

lending instrument A debt instrument; companies borrow money from investors and agree to pay a stated rate of interest over a specified period of time, at the end of which the original sum will be returned.

liquidity The ability to quickly convert assets into cash without significant loss.

load fund A mutual fund with shares sold at a price including a sales charge (typically 4 percent to 9.3 percent of the net amount invested). Thus, load funds are sold at a price exceeding net asset value, but they are redeemed at net asset value.

marginal tax rate The percentage of extra income received that must be paid in taxes or the proportional amount of taxes paid on a given income or the given dollar value of an asset. If the tax is calculated on the basis of total income, it is the average tax rate. If the tax is calculated only on extra units of income, the rate is the marginal tax rate.

market value The prevailing market price of a security or property; an indication of how the market as a whole has assessed the security's or the property's worth.

maturity The termination of the period that an obligation has to run bond; mortgages have a date of maturity, when they are due to be repaid in full.

mid-cap stock Stocks in companies with $1 billion to $10 billion capitalization.

misrepresentation To represent a financial product incorrectly, improperly, or falsely.

money manager A person who is paid a fee to supervise the investment decisions of others. The term is usually used for management of individual portfolios as compared to institutional funds (see *portfolio manager*).

money market fund A mutual fund that sells shares of ownership and uses the proceeds to purchase short-term, high-quality securities such as treasury bills, negotiable certificates of deposit, and commercial paper. Income earned by shareholders is received in the form of additional shares of stock in the fund (normally priced at $1 each). Although no fees are generally charged to purchase or redeem shares in a money market fund, an annual management charge is levied by the fund's advisors. This investment pays a return that varies with short-term interest rates. It is relatively liquid and safe, but yields and features vary.

mortgage A conditional conveyance of property to a creditor as security for the repayment of money.

mortgage life insurance Term insurance that will pay the outstanding balance on the insured's home loan should he or she die.

municipal bond The debt issue of a city, county, state, or other political entity. Interest paid by most municipal bonds is exempt from federal income taxes and often from state and local taxes. Municipal bonds with tax-exempt interest appeal mainly to investors with significant amounts of other taxable income.

municipal bond fund A mutual fund that invests in tax-exempt securities and passes through tax-free current income to its shareholders. Some municipal bond funds purchase long-term securities providing a relatively high current yield, but varying substantially in price with changes in interest rates. Other funds choose short-term securities having lower yields but fluctuating little in value.

mutual fund An open-end investment company that invests its shareholders' money in a diversified group of securities of other corporations. Mutual funds are usually diversified and professionally managed.

net income The income you have after you've paid taxes and any and all other liabilities, expenses, or charges against it.

net worth The amount of wealth calculated by taking the total value of assets owned and subtracting all liabilities.

no-load fund A mutual fund sold without a sales charge. No-load funds sell directly to customers at net asset value with no intermediate salesperson charging a fee.

non-discretionary expenses Expenses, such as mortgage payments and utility bills, that an individual must pay.

non-routine expenses Budgeted expenses, such as a furnace repair or unexpected medical expenses, that are not regular or customary.

non-taxable income Income specifically exempted from taxation. On federal income tax returns, interest from most municipal bonds, life insurance proceeds, gifts, and inheritances are generally non-taxable income.

non-variable expenses Expenses that remain constant in amount from month to month, such as rent, a mortgage payment, fees for a class or club, car payments, and so forth. You pay the same cost each month for these expenses.

odd lot Less than 100 shares of stock.

pension plan An employer-sponsored retirement plan in which a retiree receives a fixed periodic payment made in consideration of past services, injury or loss sustained, merit or poverty, and so on.

personal finance Every aspect of one's life that deals with money.

points Prepaid interest paid as a fee to a mortgage lender to cover the cost of applying for the loan. One point is one percent of the loan's value.

portfolio A group of investments assembled to meet an investment goal.

portfolio manager A person who is paid a fee to supervise the investment decisions of others. The term is normally used in reference to the managers of large institutions such as bank trust departments, pension funds, insurance companies, and mutual funds.

preferred provider organization (PPO) Health insurance coverage that rewards you for using providers from a specific list of care providers. The difference between an HMO and a PPO is that a PPO will pay for services of a nonspecified provider, but an HMO usually will not pay for such services.

preferred stock A security that shows ownership in a corporation and gives the holder a claim prior to the claim of common stockholders on earnings and also generally on assets in the event of liquidation. Most preferred stock issues pay a fixed dividend set at the time of issuance, stated in a dollar amount or as a percentage of par value. Because no maturity date is stipulated, these securities are priced on dividend yield and trade much like long-term corporate bonds. As a general rule, preferred stock has limited appeal for individual investors.

premium The amount paid, in one sum or periodically, for a contract of insurance.

prenuptial agreement A written agreement by a couple to be married in which financial matters, including rights following divorce or the death of one spouse, are detailed.

price/earnings ratio (P/E ratio) A common stock analysis statistic in which the current price of a stock is divided by the current (or sometimes the projected) earnings per share of the issuing firm.

principal The capital sum, as distinguished from interest or profit.

private mortgage insurance (PMI) Insurance required by mortgage lenders for persons borrowing more than 80 percent of the value of a property. This insurance guarantees the lender repayment of the entire loan value in case of default.

property taxes Taxes assessed on real estate. Most common are municipal and school taxes. Also called real estate tax.

prospectus A formal written document relating to a new securities offering that delineates the proposed business plan or the data relevant to an existing business plan. Investors need this information to make educated decisions about whether to purchase the security. The prospectus includes financial data, a summary of the firm's business history, a list of its officers, a description of its operations, and a mention of any pending litigation. A prospectus is an abridged version of the firm's registration statement, filed with the Securities and Exchange Commission.

public transportation Transportation other than one's personal vehicle, including buses, trains, subways. It's the most efficient way to transport the greatest number of people in a largely populated area.

qualified retirement plan A plan sponsored by an employer and designed to meet retirement needs.

rate The amount charged to borrow money.

refinancing Reapplying for a new mortgage, usually to receive a lower interest rate. Refinancing is done for consolidation or additional funding.

renter's insurance Similar to homeowner's insurance, it provides insurance protection for a resident's personal property, along with liability coverage.

replacement cost guarantee A provision of homeowner's insurance that guarantees that the full cost of rebuilding, replacing, or repairing a home is covered in the policy. It also applies to replacing personal property within the house.

residual value The value of a vehicle when it comes off a lease; the value you need to pay to acquire the vehicle.

rider An addition or amendment to a document.

risk The chance that the value or return on an investment will differ from its expected value. Business risk, financial risk, purchasing power risk, interest rate risk, market risk, default risk, and foreign currency risk are all types of risk associated with investments.

Roth IRA New in 1998, an individual retirement account in which the funds placed into the account are non-deductible. If held more than five years, all funds withdrawn are received tax-free.

round lot The standard unit of trading in a particular type of security. For stocks, a round lot is 100 shares or a multiple thereof, although a few inactive issues trade in units of 10 shares.

routine expenses Expenses that occur on a regular basis, such as food costs, dental checkups, church contributions, etc. These expenses may vary in amount, but they occur on a regular basis.

sector fund Securities or other assets that share a common interest. Sector funds permit an investor to concentrate on a specific investment segment and yet diversify investments among various issuers. Sector funds entail more risk, but offer greater potential returns than funds that diversify their portfolios.

secured credit card A credit card for a person without credit or with poor credit. The account limit on the card is guaranteed by funds held by the bank in an interest-bearing account. Usually, after 18 months, the funds in the bank account can be returned to the cardholder.

securities Investments that represent evidence of debt, ownership of a business, or the legal right to acquire or sell an ownership interest in a business.

security deposit Amount required by a landlord to cover expenses at lease termination if property is damaged by the tenant. The deposit, if held for more than two years, should be returned to the tenant with interest added if there is no damage.

settlement The settling of property and title on an individual or individuals; the transaction when you finally purchase the property.

shareholder A person who owns shares in a corporation.

sheriff's sale When a foreclosed property is sold at public auction in order for the lender to recoup his losses.

simple interest Interest paid on an initial investment only. Simple interest is calculated by multiplying the principal times the annual rate of interest times the number of years involved.

simplified employee pension plan (SEP) A special type of joint Keogh-individual retirement account, permitting contributions from employees and employers. The SEP was developed to give small businesses a retirement plan that is easier to establish and administer than an ordinary pension plan.

SEP-IRA A retirement plan for the self-employed that permits contributions up to $25,000 per year. Similar to an IRA except that the contribution limits are higher.

small-cap stock Companies which have less than $1 billion capitalization.

speculation Taking above-average risks to achieve above-average returns, generally during a relatively short period of time. Speculation involves buying something on the basis of its potential selling price rather than on the basis of its actual value.

standard deduction The minimum deduction from income allowed a taxpayer for calculating taxable income. Individuals with few itemized deductions use the standard deduction instead of itemizing deductions.

stock Shares of ownership in a company. These shares include common stock of various classes and any preferred stock outstanding.

stock fund A mutual fund that limits its investments to shares of common stock. Common stock funds vary in risk, from relatively low to quite high, depending on the types of stocks in which the funds invest.

stock market The organized securities exchanges for stock and bond transactions. Major exchanges are the New York Stock Exchange, the American Stock Exchange, and the National Association of Securities Dealers Automated Quotation System (NASDAQ).

sublet Leasing an apartment from the current tenant rather than from the landlord.

taxable income Income that is subject to taxation; adjusted income minus standard or itemized deductions and exemptions.

tax attorney A lawyer who has earned a master's degree in taxation (LLM).

tax-deductible An expense that can be used to offset gross income when calculating your taxable gross income.

tax-deferred Income that is earned but neither received nor taxed until a later date, when the funds are withdrawn or mature. Tax-deferred assets include those within an IRA, 401(k) plan, 403 (b) plan, tax-deferred annuity, tax-deferred life insurance, EE savings bonds, and others.

tax preparer An individual who prepares a tax return according to the law.

term insurance Life insurance in which the insurance company pays a specified sum if the insured dies during the coverage period. Term insurance includes no savings, cash values, borrowing power, or benefits at retirement. On the basis of cost, it is the least expensive insurance available, although policy prices can vary significantly among firms.

thrift A financial institution that derives its funds primarily from consumer savings accounts set up to provide personal mortgages. The term originally referred to those institutions offering mainly passbook savings accounts. The word thrift often refers to savings and loan associations, but it also can mean credit unions and mutual savings banks.

total return Dividend or interest income plus any capital gain, generally considered a better measure of an investment's return than dividends or interest alone.

treasury bond Longer-term (over 10 years), interest-bearing debt of the U.S. Treasury, available through a bank or brokerage firm or directly from the Federal Reserve. Treasury bonds are quoted and traded in 32nds of a point.

treasury note Intermediate-term (1 to 10 years), interest-bearing debt of the U.S. Treasury. Treasury bonds are quoted and traded in 32nds of a point.

treasury stock Shares of a firm's stock that have been issued and then repurchased. Treasury stock is not considered in paying dividends, voting, or calculating earnings per share. It may be eventually retired or reissued.

trust A form of property ownership in which legal title to the property is held by someone (trustee) for the benefit of someone else (the beneficiary).

trustee A person or corporation appointed to administer or execute a trust for the beneficiaries.

value stock A stock in which the price is considered below normal using valuation measures common to the market.

variable expenses Expenses that are changeable, alterable.

variable interest rate Interest, either paid or received (depending on whether you are borrowing or investing funds), that changes periodically, depending on the initial contract.

vested To pass into possession. Usually this means working long enough in a company for an employee to have the right to the employer's contributions into the retirement plan.

vesting schedules A schedule predetermined by an employer (within governmental guidelines) in which employees vest in the company's retirement plan.

warranty A statement of promise or assurance in connection with a contract or purchase.

yield The percentage return on an investment; also known as return. The dividends or interest paid by a company as a percentage of the current price.

Index

Rule of 72, 165
savings accounts, 166
short-term gains, 241
speculating, 238
stocks, 248-254, 249-252
   IPOs (initial public
      offerings), 251
   odd lots, 251
   purchasing, 243-244
   risk, 259
   round lots, 251
   shares, 250
tax-free, 170
taxation, 239-242
timetable, 239
total return, 249
type, selecting, 166
types of investors,
   236-239
Web sites, 245
IPOs (initial public offerings),
  251
IRAs, 226-227, 236
   contributions, 223
      restrictions, 225
   early withdrawal
      penalties, 232
   planning, 222-225
   see also retirement plans
IRS (Internal Revenue Service),
  Web site, 189
itemized deductions,
  181-186

J-K

jobs
   benefits, 90
   retirement plans, 222-225
      annuities, 230-231
      IRAs, 226-227
      keoghs, 229-230
      Roth IRAs, 227-228
      SEP-IRAs, 229
   salary, 84-89
   searching, 86-89, 89-91

expenses, deducting, 182
experience, 90
JobSmart (Web site), 86
jumbo mortgages, 300
Jump Start Coalition for Personal
  Financial Liberty, 7
keoghs, 229-230

L

large cap stocks, 250
late fees
   credit cards, 50-52
   mortgages, 314-317
   see also early withdrawal
      penalties
learning personal finance, 5-8
   fundamentals, 7-8
   getting started, 12-13
leasing
   apartments, 56-57,
     159-161
      up-front-costs, 57-58
   automobiles, 73-78
      comparing to buying,
       71-77
      information resources, 75
legal disputes, arbitration, 275
legislation
   COBRA (Consolidated
     Omnibus Budget
     Reconciliation of
     1985), 195
   Fair Credit Reporting
     Act, 144
   Federal Credit Union
     Act, 35
   National Banking Act, 34
lending investments,
  252-258
liability insurance, 337-338
liberal arts graduates, as
  employees, 86
life insurance
   cash value insurance, 202-203
   coverage, expanding, 195

HMOs (health maintenance
  organizations), 196
  purchasing, 202-203
  term life, 194, 202
lifestyles
  personal finance, 3-5,
   98-99
     managing, 5-8
  ILYA (Incompletely Launched
   Young Adults), 17
  living alone, 16-18
  living with parents, 16
  married couples
   financial considerations,
    214-215
   prenuptial agreements,
    215-216
  singles, financial
   considerations, 210-211
  unmarried couples, financial
   considerations, 212-214
lifetime caps (ARMs), 297
limitations
  car insurance, 197-203
  contributions
   annuities, 231
   retirement plans, 225
  credit card use, 45-46
  income, Roth IRAs, 228
  insurance deductibles, 204
limited partnerships, 11
line of credit (home
  equity loan), 329
load funds, 167
loans
  401(k) funds, 174
  applying for, 139, 144
  car loans
   financing, 71-72
   payments, 77-78
   residual value, 73
  home equity, 328-329
  mortgages, 294-295
   affordability, 282-285
   amortization schedules,
    309-310
   approval process, 304-305